DATE DUE			

East of Chosin

EAST OF Chosin

Entrapment and Breakout
in Korea, 1950

by Roy E. Appleman, Lt. Col., AUS, Ret.

Texas A&M University Press
College Station

The paper used in this book meets the minimum requirements of
the American National Standard for Permanence of Paper for
Printed Library Materials, Z39, 48-1984. Binding materials have
been chosen for durability.

Library of Congress Cataloging-in-Publication Data

Appleman, Roy Edgar.
    East of Chosin.

    Bibliography: p.
    Includes index.
    1. Korean War, 1950–1953 – Campaigns – Korea (North) –
Changjin Reservoir. 2. United States. Army. Regimental
Combat Team, 31st. 3. Korean War, 1950–1953 – Regimental
histories – United States. 4. Changjin Reservoir Region
(Korea) – History. I. Title.
DS918.2.C35A66 1987   951.9′042   86-22184
ISBN 0-89096-283-9

Contents

Illustrations

vii

Maps

Preface

The men of the United States Army who fell on the east side of Chosin (Changjin) Reservoir in the winter of 1950 have no white-marble markers at their final resting places as do thousands of others memorialized in Arlington National Cemetery, in other national cemeteries, and in other lands. They have no markers of any kind—only the fragile link of memory that endures from generation to generation in the recollection of their countrymen who know our nation's history. To preserve this link of memory, there must be recorded a history of the events.

This book tells the neglected story of American soldiers from the US Army's 7th Infantry Division who fought on the east side of Chosin Reservoir in the Korean War. It concerns an Army force of about 3,000 men, of near-regimental size, hastily assembled to protect the east flank of the 1st Marine Division at Chosin. They fought a battle that lasted four days and five nights in late November and early December, 1950. The place was a 10-mile stretch of frozen, snow-covered dirt road on the east side of Chosin Reservoir, the adjacent bleak hills and ridges that rose precipitously from the water's edge, and the frozen marshy inlet valleys that drained westward from the eastern mountains through these ridges to the reservoir.

Chosin Reservoir fills an irregular trough of the Changjin River valley at an elevation of 3,870 feet in the mountainous plateau south of Manchuria. The weather in winter is Siberian, with night temperatures that reach −35° F. In winter darkness comes early to this land, in late November and early December at about 4:30 P.M. Daybreak comes late, at 7:30 to 8:00 A.M.

The Army's battle story at Chosin contains as many "if's" as Kipling's poem. Its hallmarks were misery, soul-crushing cold, privation, exhaustion, heroism, sacrifice, leadership of high merit at times, but, finally, unit and individual disaster. For many it was a lonely death in a distant land. It would be hard to find a more nearly hopeless or more tragic story in American military history. Lieutenant Colonel Don C. Faith, Jr., the final commander of the force, received the Congressional Medal of Honor, Posthumously.

The background of *East of Chosin*, like a dramatic overture setting the theme for stage action, was Gen. Douglas MacArthur's plan to drive the Communist forces beyond the Yalu River, unify the peninsula, and end the Korean War. He set in motion a last major offensive to accomplish this on November 24, 1950, in the Eighth Army zone of operations, in the west of Korea, and on November 27 in the X Corps zone of operations, in northeast Korea.

Then a mass of soldiers out of China, dressed in quilted, padded uniforms, wearing fur caps, and laden with grenades and automatic burp guns, suddenly appeared before the unsuspecting soldiers in the darkness of night. That was the beginning.

When I began to research what happened east of Chosin, I had in mind only a chapter in a book on the X Corps operations in northeast Korea in the fall and winter of 1950 – the X Corps's part in MacArthur's effort to end the war. But in the records in the National Archives, at the Federal Records Center, in Suitland, Maryland, I found no operational journals, no unit histories of those who fought east of Chosin. There was a 7th Infantry Division Special Report on Chosin Reservoir, undated but signed by Maj. Gen. Claude B. Ferenbaugh, who had assumed command of the division on January 26, 1951. The report had been prepared by unnamed persons some months after the events related and was fragmentary and unreliable. There was one other document, a 7th Division Action Report, which was nearly barren regarding the units east of Chosin. But attached to this report were a few memorandums and affidavits by Army survivors at Chosin who had reached Hagaru-ri, at the south end of the reservoir, written there a day or two after their escape. The most important of these documents was a four-page typed report by Maj. Robert E. Jones giving a summary of what he knew, addressed to the G-3 Section (operations section) of the 7th Infantry Division, represented at Hagaru-ri by Maj. William R. Lynch, Jr., and a one-page report by Capt. Robert E. Drake covering his 31st Tank Company.

The records of X Corps gave the corps orders affecting the Chosin Reservoir operations, but no details of what happened. The 1st Marine Division records are complete, or nearly so, but their G-3 Journal and Message files contain only limited information on Army action.

Three published works touched on the Army units at Chosin. Lynn Montross and Nicholas A. Canzona's *The Chosin Campaign*, vol. 3 in *U.S. Marine Operations in Korea, 1950–1953* (4 vols., 1962), the Marine Corps's official history of its part in the Korean War, covers very well the action of the 1st Marine Division at Chosin but touches only briefly on Army units there. Capt. Russell A. Gugeler, in his *Combat Actions in Korea* (1954), published by the Association of the US Army, gives a partial account of some aspects of the Army action based on limited interviews with some survivors and examination of available records. Andrew Geer's *The New Breed: The Story of the U.S. Marines in Korea* (New York: Harper and Row, 1952) contains details based on personal interviews.

It became apparent that the information needed to relate the events east of Chosin in any coherent and comprehensible form could come only from survivors, if a substantial number of them could be found, 25 years after the event. One man's recollections must be compared with other men's recall, and use of all preserved contemporary notes would be necessary to find consensus where possible and to establish a weight of evidence on alleged or questionable facts. From the start I ruled out the use of hearsay evidence.

Gradually I became engulfed by the mystery of the Chosin Reservoir tragedy. I put aside most other work on the Korean War in which I was engaged. The survivor of Chosin who helped me get started was Col. Wesley J. Curtis, then S-3 (operations section of battalions and regiments) of the 1st Battalion, 32nd Infantry, now retired from the Army. Additional survivors were found, and their number increased over passing months; only two of them refused to share their knowledge. I could not have foreseen when I began this work that it would continue for seven years.

That I have been able to write this story is due to those survivors of events east of Chosin whom I finally found and who gave their help gladly. A few of them had made notes in Japanese hospitals while they were recuperating from wounds, recording events and episodes while memory was fresh. In several instances these notes were compiled into narratives, which must now be considered contemporary documentary sources. Among the personal narratives are those of then Majors Curtis, Crosby P. Miller, and Hugh W. Robbins and Capt. Edward P. Stamford.

For information on the role of higher headquarters in the action east of Chosin, I had the help of the late Lt. Gen. Edward M. Almond, X Corps commander in northeast Korea in 1950, and Lt. Col. William J. McCaffrey, Almond's trusted deputy chief of staff (now Lt. Gen., USA, ret.).

The ranks of the officers and men are those they held at the time of action. An effort has been made to give the full name and rank of each the first time used. Afterward I often use only the last name to avoid a tedious repetition and overuse of military terminology. Occasionally I have been unable to establish the full name of a person. There were no rosters in the official records of the units in action with which to check full names or establish correct spelling.

Most of the persons mentioned as sources or quoted in the narrative read the manuscript and concurred in, disagreed with, or amended passages that involved their statements of facts or views to ensure that their information and opinions were correctly stated.

In these pages are many quotations from the survivors of Chosin. I thought it important to let these men tell significant parts of what they remembered in their own way, and not in a rewrite that I might attempt. What I have quoted is just as they wrote it to me or as they expressed it in early notes or narratives. When I felt that identification of a place or of a person or clarification of an ambiguity was necessary in a quotation, I supplied such information in brackets.

The place-names used in the book are those found on the early maps issued to the troops when they moved to the Chosin Reservoir area in November, 1950. The names they became familiar with and used in their notes, reports, and statements to me were the names used in the official military records of the day and are the names on the first maps issued to them. These were copies of older Japanese maps, which used 1916 topographical data. Where possible I have added the modern place-name in parentheses after the first mention.

There were no sketch maps of perimeters, situations, military movements, or terrain overlays in the records. I have prepared all the maps in this book after an exhaustive study of 1:50,000-scale military maps of the area involved, correlated with the terrain features and actions described in the narrative.

Most of the ground-level photographs were taken at the inlet perimeter. The first prints I saw were small snapshots provided to me by Col. Ray O. Embree and Lt. Col. Ivan H. Long, all apparently taken by the same unidentified photographer. Three small snapshots were provided to me by Colonel Miller, now retired, the photographer also unidentified. Long received his snapshots while he was in a hospital in Japan recuperating from wounds. Colonel Embree, who was in the same hospital, does not remember how he obtained the snapshots, but probably in the same way Long received his. None of these unique photographs of the area east of Chosin have been previously published. The prints were rephotographed and enlarged for use in this book.

All the oblique aerial views of Chosin Reservoir and the terrain on its east side were taken by the US Army Signal Corps, apparently just before the reservoir froze over in most places, and therefore they do not show the ice and snow that covered the reservoir during the battle period at the end of November and in early December. Taken together, they show clearly the terrain features and defense perimeter areas and the course of the road and the narrow-gauge railroad through the combat area. Only one of these pictures has been published before, that of the northern end of the reservoir, which was outside the combat area.

In writing military history, one would like to approximate the standards Julius Caesar established in his *Commentaries*, in which he recorded his military campaigns between 58 and 50 B.C. His Roman contemporary Marcus Tullius Cicero in 46 B.C. described the *Commentaries* as "bare, straight and handsome, stripped of rhetorical ornament like an athlete of his clothes. . . . There is nothing in a history more attractive than clean and lucid brevity." Marguerite Yourcenar, in her *Memoirs of Hadrian*, expressed a precept which I applaud and have striven to approximate: "Keep one's own shadow out of the picture; leave the mirror clean of the mist of one's own breath."

One must be modest, and indeed humble, in assessing his own work and be forever critical of it, remembering that "he who seeks for truth, or at least for accuracy, is frequently the one best able to perceive . . . that truth is not absolute or pure." One must do the best one can, then do it over again, and improve parts bit by bit, even if ever so slightly.

In this work on the events east of Chosin I believe a substantial segment of our history that was on the verge of being lost forever has been salvaged in a credible way.

My wife, Irene, who was as interested as I in getting the story told, served throughout as a discriminating reader and critic to help me as I tried to write it.

If I were to dedicate this work to anyone, it would have to be to those who survived and helped with their recollections and documents, because all these taken together made the book possible, and, finally, to their one-time comrades—American soldiers—unnamed, for the most part, who left their mortal remains in that far corner of the world for eternity.

East of Chosin

The War in Korea, November, 1950

This is the story of a near-regimental combat team of approximately 3,000 soldiers of the United States Army's 7th Infantry Division and the events on the east side of Chosin (Changjin) Reservoir, in northeast Korea, in late November and early December, 1950. It took place during five nights and four days of subzero Manchuria-type weather, snow, and bitter winds. There is no other story of the Korean War to compare with it. The complete story has never before been told.

Before the narrative can unfold, it is necessary to frame the picture—to provide the background for what came to pass. At the time of the Chosin campaign, the Korean War was five months old, dating from the attack on South Korea by the North Koreans on June 25, 1950. After the victorious Inchon Landing by United Nations forces, the recapture of Seoul, the crossing of the 38th parallel, and subsequent rapid advance toward the Yalu River and the Manchurian border, the North Korean Army had disintegrated and largely disappeared from the scene as a fighting force.

In late October, however, a new enemy, the "Chinese Volunteer Forces," suddenly appeared below the border in the northwestern part of Korea. In surprise attacks they routed or destroyed two South Korean infantry divisions and an American regiment of Gen. Walton H. Walker's Eighth Army. Following quickly on these successes, Chinese in unknown numbers pushed the American Eighth Army back to the Chongchon River, 70 air miles south of the border. Then the Chinese phantom force suddenly melted back northward into the hills.

While this Chinese force in the west checked the Eighth Army's approach to the Yalu River and the border, another, smaller force of Chinese

"Volunteers" approached Hamhung and Hungnam, on the east coast, where the X Corps had landed to deploy troops for the occupation of northeast Korea. The Chinese came down the road from the Chosin Reservoir, 45 air miles and 70 road miles from Hungnam. Moving northward on the same road at the same time was the 26th Regiment of the ROK (Republic of Korea) 3rd Division. On October 25, about 30 miles inland from Hamhung, it captured a prisoner, the first Chinese soldier captured in the X Corps area in northeast Korea.

On October 28 a heavy battle broke out between the ROK 26th Regiment and an enemy force in the vicinity of Sudong. The next day the ROK troops captured 16 Chinese soldiers, who identified themselves as members of a mortar platoon of the 370th Regiment of the 124th Division, 42nd Army, XIII Army Group, Fourth Field Army. They said that three divisions —the 124th, the 125th, and the 126th—were in position behind them on the north toward the Chosin Reservoir.

On October 30, Maj. Gen. Edward M. Almond, commanding general of X Corps, went to the ROK I Corps prisoner compound and questioned the prisoners through an interpreter. All 16 were former members of Chiang Kai-shek's Chinese Nationalist Army, which had surrendered to the Communist forces near Peking the year before. This meant that there were more than "Volunteer" Chinese in Korea. Almond immediately discussed with his principal staff officers the information obtained from the interrogation of the Chinese soldiers and then sent a personal radio message to Gen. Douglas MacArthur in his Far East Command Headquarters in Tokyo. The Far East Command took the news in stride and showed no great surprise or concern. Their attack plan would go on.[1]

But Almond's message to MacArthur did cause a high-level delegation from the Far East Command to fly to Wonsan, in northeast Korea, then the X Corps Headquarters. MacArthur's delegation consisted of Maj. Gens. Doyle O. Hickey, acting chief of staff; Charles A. Willoughby, G-2; and George L. Eberle, G-4; and Brig. Gen. Edwin K. Wright, G-3. They came for a firsthand estimate of the degree of Chinese intervention. In an earlier discussion with Willoughby, Maj. Gen. Clark L. Ruffner, Almond's chief of staff, had spoken with concern about the great number of Chinese Communist Forces (CCF) divisions identified in the Eighth Army and X Corps zones of operations. Willoughby had answered that there might be only elements of that many divisions.

Now in the Wonsan conference General Hickey asked Willoughby substantially the following question: "If, as General Almond states, Chinese forces have intervened, how many Chinese troops do you estimate are now in Korea?" Willoughby said again that only volunteers had entered Korea and that probably only a battalion of volunteers of each division identified was actually in Korea.

Almond then asked what had happened when the Chinese destroyed the 8th Cavalry Regiment of Eighth Army in the west. Willoughby replied that the regiment had failed to put out adequate security and had been overrun in a small, violent surprise attack and been scattered in the following hours of darkness.[2]

After the capture of the 16 Chinese prisoners it took the 7th Marine Regiment, which relieved the ROK 26th Regiment on November 2, five days and five nights of fighting to drive the Chinese 124th Division from the lowlands to Funchilin Pass, all but destroying the CCF force, whose survivors moved north over the pass to Hagaru-ri.

The 1st Marine Division cautiously followed them, its advance elements arriving at Hagaru-ri on November 14. Temperatures during that first day and night on the plateau reached $-8°$ F, accompanied by winds of 30 to 35 miles an hour, producing a wind-chill factor of nearly $-60°$ F.

General MacArthur, speculating on the situation from his office in the Dai-Ichi Building in Tokyo, decided that the Chinese would not dare cross the Yalu in force but that if they did his air force would destroy them. He also decided that the time had come to resume the march to the border and end the war. A big offensive, coordinated from Tokyo, would start for Eighth Army in the west on November 24; for X Corps the offensive would begin three days later. By Christmas, General MacArthur hoped, a secured border could be turned over to the South Korean government, and some of the American troops could be home, the war ended. Apparently disregarded were the disasters inflicted by the Chinese in the Eighth Army zone north of the Chongchon River in late October and early November and the simultaneous heavy fighting with the CCF 124th Division on the road from Hamhung to Hagaru-ri in the X Corps zone.

The principal inland road running north from the Wonsan-Hamhung coastal plain led to the Koto-ri Plateau and 12 miles farther reached the town of Hagaru-ri, near the southern end of the Chosin Reservoir. This axis of advance toward the Yalu and the border was to be the principal X Corps

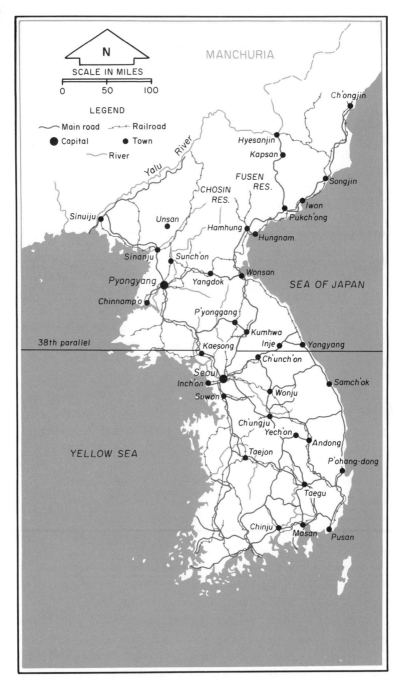

MAP 1. The peninsula of Korea, which extends from the border of
China (along the Yalu River) into the Yellow Sea.

route of attack, and the 1st Marine Division was assigned to follow it north-ward from the coast. On November 11, Almond moved his X Corps Command Post (CP) from Wonsan to Hamhung.

The mission of X Corps in eastern Korea had initially been to attack west from the Wonsan area to help Eighth Army capture Pyongyang, the capital of North Korea. MacArthur changed these instructions on October 17 when the Eighth Army's accelerating approach to Pyongyang made it reasonably certain that it would not need X Corps's help in capturing the city. In this situation MacArthur alerted General Almond on October 17 that if Eighth Army captured Pyongyang on its own, which it did on October 19–20, then the X Corps would attack north instead of west. On October 24, MacArthur made this a formal order: X Corps was to attack north in the eastern part of Korea. For this purpose the place to concentrate forces was the Hungnam-Hamhung area, not Wonsan.

Thus the matter stood for three weeks. On November 16 the Far East Command took much of the vagueness out of its last order to X Corps "to attack north in the eastern part of Korea." Now it made an important change in the corps's missions. It was instructed to develop a plan to orient its main attack to the border by advancing west from Changjin, 35 miles north of the Chosin Reservoir. At Changjin it was to turn west and cut the Manpojin–Kanggje–Huichon road, which ran south from the Yalu River into the Eighth Army zone. This maneuver would have X Corps aid Eighth Army by attacking into the rear of the Chinese forces facing the Eighth Army.[3]

On November 17 the X Corps staff had a plan ready for Almond's review. It called for the 1st Marine Division, upon reaching Changjin, to turn west toward Kanggje. Almond rejected the plan because it extended the main supply road too far north; it would be better, he thought, for the 1st Marine Division to turn west at Hagaru-ri, move to Yudam-ni, and from there advance on Kanggje. Almond's plan thus departed from the Far East Command's suggestion that the 1st Marine Division advance by way of Changjin. In his review of the plan Almond also added another important change to the Far East Command's suggestions of November 16. He wanted a regimental-size force, to be provided by the US 7th Infantry Division, to go north on the east side of the reservoir to Changjin and free the 5th Marine Regiment on that side of the reservoir so that it could join the main force of the 1st Marine Division on the west side of the reservoir at Yudam-ni. This would concentrate the whole of the 1st Marine Division for the push west to Kanggje and would give the mission of protecting the right or east flank of this attack to another force—a new regimental task force from the 7th Infantry Division. Now, for the first time, the 7th Division was brought into the Chosin Reservoir campaign plan.

Meanwhile, on October 29 the US 7th Infantry Division had begun landing over the beaches of Iwon, 150 miles up the coast north of Wonsan. Its first regiment ashore, the 17th, began carrying out the advance of the division, which was to attack north to the Yalu. The 17th Regiment headed for Hyesanjin by the road that ran through Pukchong and Pungsan. Its axis of advance was about 60 air miles east of that of the 1st Marine Division on the road to Hagaru-ri and Yudam-ni. Neither could assist the other. Almond now had about 84,000 men in his command. Later, after the arrival of the US 3rd Infantry Division, X Corps would have 100,000 men. The 31st Infantry landed after the 17th, and the last of the three regiments of the 7th Division, the 32nd Infantry, went ashore on November 4 and moved to a bivouac northeast of Hamhung. Maj. Gen. David G. Barr, of the 7th Division, was moving the entire division north to the border in the Hyesanjin and Singpaljin areas while General Almond and his X Corps staff were working on the plan to implement General MacArthur's last order.

On November 21, Almond's staff had a new, revised plan ready, labeled "Operation Plan No. 8, Draft 2." It satisfied Almond's earlier objections. Almond sent it at once to Tokyo for review by the Far East Command. On November 24, General MacArthur directed Almond to implement it, making only one minor change that moved the boundary between Eighth Army and X Corps farther west and south in the 1st Marine Division zone. Upon receiving approval of his plan, Almond issued a warning order that evening, and the next day, November 25, he issued Operational Order No. 7, which stated that X Corps would attack on the morning of November 27 with the purpose of severing the Chinese line of communication at Mupyong-ni and destroying the enemy from there north to the Yalu River border and eastward to the mouth of the Tumen River, at the Soviet border.[4]

The two X Corps subordinate commanders most involved were Maj. Gen. Oliver P. Smith, 1st Marine Division, and General Barr, US 7th Infantry Division. Since their attack dates were set for November 27, this gave them only two days to get their troops in position for jump-off. The 1st Marine Division was already in motion for the Chosin Reservoir, but most of the 7th Division was more than 100 miles away, at or near the Yalu River, and the last of its regiments, the 32nd, was not yet there. For General Barr it was nothing less than a chaotic scramble to try to assemble a regimental

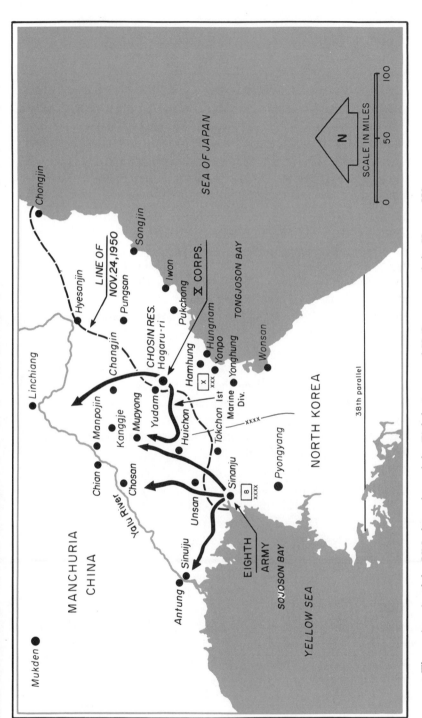

MAP 2.　The main axis of the UN planned attack by Eighth Army and X Corps to end the Korean War.

combat team and get it to the Chosin Reservoir by the morning of November 27.

Lieutenant Colonel Raymond L. Murray, a young, strapping 6-foot, 4-inch Marine commanding the 5th Marine Regiment, had already made an enviable record in Korea. Orders reached him on November 17 to concentrate his regiment on the east side of the reservoir, seize a village called Sinhung-ni on the Pungnyuri-gang Inlet about 8 miles north of Hagaru-ri, and be prepared to go farther. On November 23, Lt. Col. Robert D. Taplett's 3rd Battalion led the advance down the east side of the reservoir. Taplett found a good defensive position about 4 road miles north of the Pungnyuri-gang Inlet and the village of Sinhung-ni, where hills and a saddle between them straddled the dirt road. His battalion dug in there. By November 25 the other two battalions of the 5th Marines were behind the 3rd Battalion on the east side of the reservoir. That was the situation there when the corps operation order mandated their move to the west side of the reservoir to join the 7th Marines at Yudam-ni. But the 5th Marines could not leave the east side of the reservoir until they were replaced by a 7th Division regiment.

The corps order called for this regiment to be on the east side of the reservoir by noon on November 26. That was a tall order, easy to issue but almost impossible to execute, given the distant and scattered deployment of the 7th Division units. The 7th Division had to use its troops nearest the reservoir. General Barr's effort to assemble a regimental combat team quickly was entirely ad hoc. This force, later referred to generally as the 31st RCT, commanded by Col. Allan D. MacLean, included the 31st Infantry Regimental Headquarters and Headquarters Company; the regiment's 2nd and 3rd battalions; the 1st Battalion, 32nd Infantry; the 31st Tank Company; the 57th Field Artillery Battalion, normally in support of the 31st Infantry, together with D Battery, 15th Antiaircraft Artillery Automatic Weapons Battalion (AAA AW), Self-Propelled (SP), attached, as the main combat elements. The 1st Battalion, 32nd Infantry, had been chosen as the third infantry battalion of the combat team because it happened to be closest to the reservoir. It was the first unit of the 7th Division RCT to arrive there.

On November 24, 1950, General MacArthur stood triumphant over the doubters and the critics of his policy. On that day he flew to northwest Korea to see Eighth Army launch its attack from the Chongchon River toward the border. All went well during the first day of the advance and appeared to be going well on the second day, when General Almond issued his order to X Corps to join in the attack from the Chosin Reservoir on the 27th.

Not all members of Almond's staff were complacent about the impending attack from the reservoir. Col. Edward H. Forney, of the Marine Corps, on liaison duty with the X Corps as an amphibious-movement expert, was a quiet, thoughtful, outstandingly competent military man. He opposed what he considered a rash action that would endanger the 1st Marine Division. Lt. Col. William J. McCaffrey, deputy chief of staff, X Corps, a long-time confidant of and trusted adviser to General Almond, was also uneasy about the projected attack. Others in X Corps questioned the pending operation. McCaffrey expressed this view and the climate of thought at the time:

> We were all trying to get General Almond to exercise some caution in attack-ing over the mountains from Yudam-ni. All the Marines were concerned that they would be cut off, but General Almond was not about to protest an order from General MacArthur. After all, everyone had said Inchon wouldn't work and this was a replay of that series of disagreements between the Navy, Marines, and CINCFE [Commander in Chief, Far East]. Forney argued that the Marine Division was on loan from the Joint Chiefs as US strategic reserve for the Pacific. If it was used up the JCS [Joint Chiefs of Staff] should first be notified that there was a serious chance of this happening.[5]

Commenting on Almond's ready acquiescence to MacArthur's orders in this phase of the Korean War, Gen. Matthew B. Ridgway wrote: "One must keep in mind Almond's relation to MacArthur, whose Chief of Staff he still was, on paper; MacArthur's brilliance of concept and perseverance in carrying through his plan of wide envelopment at INCHON, deserving of the highest praise; and his world-wide fame, which made it extremely diffi-cult for a subordinate to question his judgment. Recognition of these facts would indicate that only if MacArthur's decisions were, in Almond's judg-ment, likely to sacrifice his Corps, would he have felt justified in openly protesting."[6]

Army Troops Assemble at Chosin Reservoir

On November 4 the 32nd Infantry had been the last regiment of the 7th Infantry Division to disembark over the beaches at Iwon. It moved southwest along the coastal road through Hamhung and there turned north. Just south of Oro-ri it turned northeast up the valley of the Songchon-gang on a road leading toward Fusen Reservoir. It went into bivouac near the crossroads village of Kujang-ni, approximately 25 road miles northeast from its junction with the Hamhung–Hagaru-ri road to Chosin Reservoir. The latter road was the only entrance to Chosin Reservoir and similarly the only exit from it.

When units of the 31st RCT began their hurried movement toward the Chosin Reservoir, they had to pass through the heavy supply traffic of the 1st Marine Division. The roads were among the poorest and most precarious of any used in the war by American motorized forces. No American troops before or since have fought in as harsh or hostile an environment.

The road distance from the coast at Hamhung to Hagaru-ri was 60 miles. After reaching the plateau, roughly 4,000 feet high, on which the Chosin Reservoir lay, the road meandered 25 miles from the escarpment through Hagaru-ri northward to what will be called the forward perimeter, the most northerly position held by the 1st Marine Division and later by the 1st Battalion, 32nd Infantry, on the east side of the reservoir.

The Songchon River rises in the mountains east of the Chosin and Fusen reservoirs and flows southwest into the Sea of Japan. The city of Hamhung lies in its delta; Hungnam, the largest port of northeast Korea, is on the north side of the river mouth. A western tributary of the Songchon, the Hungnim, flows south to join the Songchon at Oro-ri, 8 miles north of

Hamhung and 16 miles inland from Hungnam. A narrow-gauge railroad, 2½ feet wide, and a dirt-gravel road ran inland along the east bank of the Songchon from Hungnam through Hamhung to Oro-ri, where they crossed the stream to the west side and then followed the Hungnim River upstream northwest toward the 4,000- to 4,500-foot plateau.

From Oro-ri the road continued on flat or semiflat ground with gentle curves through low hills, following closely the narrowing channel of the Hungnim River and a tributary through Majon-dong (sometimes referred to as Santong) to the village of Chinhung-ni. Thus far the road was relatively level but with many turns and twists along the channel of the narrowing stream. From Chinhung-ni the road went northward to the top of the Koto-ri Plateau by a cliff-hanging, twisting, narrow alignment that climbed 2,500 feet in 8 miles. This stretch was called Funchilin Pass. On top of the plateau, 2 miles beyond its edge, was the village of Koto-ri. There the Changjin River came in from the west and bent sharply north to empty its waters into the Chosin Reservoir. The narrow-gauge railroad and the vehicular road followed the valley of the Changjin River from Koto-ri to Hagaru-ri. There was a stretch of about 1½ miles of marshland between Hagaru-ri and the waters of the reservoir.

In 1950 the Hungnam–Hagaru-ri road was two way as far as Chinhung-ni. There it degenerated into a narrow, one-way trail that climbed Funchilin Pass to the Koto-ri Plateau. From there on to Hagaru-ri the road was of varying width, but never more than a narrow two-way dirt-gravel track, and seldom straight or semistraight for more than short distances.

At Samgo Station, at the foot of Funchilin Pass, 500 yards north of Chinhung-ni, the narrow-gauge railroad became a cableway for the climb up the escarpment. The steep incline of the cableway began at the village of Pohu-jang, about a mile beyond Samgo Station, and went straight up the eastern side of the pass to the top of the plateau southeast of Koto-ri. On the top the cableway ended, and the railroad track resumed. It followed north down the valley of the Changjin River, parallel to the dirt and gravel road, to Hagaru-ri. From there it continued down the east side of the reservoir, following the shoreline north to the Pungnyuri-gang River. The railroad turned east there to follow the Pungnyuri-gang upstream.

Early maps showed a small village called Sinhung-ni about a mile east of the reservoir, on the inlet where the vehicular road crossed to the north side of the Pungnyuri-gang. Sinhung-ni is named in contemporary military reports and shown on military situation map overlays. In 1950, Sinhung-ni,

View of Hagaru-ri, at the south end of Chosin Reservoir (upper left), looking northeast. East Hill, on the east side of the remains of Hagaru-ri, shows at top right. The 1st Marine Division had a defense perimeter around the destroyed town. US Marine Corps photograph A 5679.

like Hudong-ni some miles to the south, had largely ceased to exist, but a few scattered huts still stood on the south bank of the Pungnyuri-gang Inlet and eastward.

The 1916 data maps issued to the troops showed the narrow-gauge railroad ending at the western base of Hill 1221, about 2½ miles north of Hudong-ni. In fact, by 1950 it had been built almost to the Fusen Reservoir, following the drainage of the Pungnyuri-gang upstream to a divide that separated that drainage from another, which fed into the Fusen Reservoir. There the track ended, apparently awaiting the construction of an incline, or a tunnel, to carry it on to the Fusen Reservoir.[1]

Once troops had been ordered to the Chosin Reservoir area, X Corps assigned the 73rd Engineer Battalion to improve and maintain the main supply road (MSR) from Hamhung to Chinhung-ni; the 185th Engineer

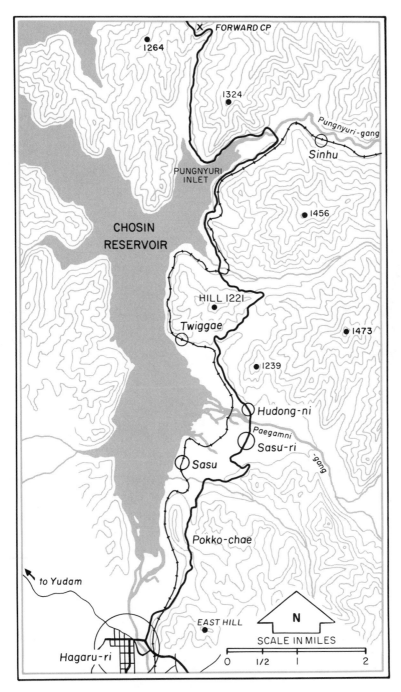

MAP 3. The Chosin Reservoir scene of action.

Typical terrain in northeast Korea: a narrow dirt road, rice paddies between road and stream, and precipitous mountains rising on either side. Shown here is an American tank-infantry team, interspersed with AAA AW weapons, advancing into enemy-held territory, February, 1951. Photograph courtesy of Maj. James R. McClymont.

Battalion had a similar responsibility for the road from Chinhung-ni to Hagaru-ri.[2]

Lieutenant Colonel Edward L. Rowny, the X Corps engineer, was responsible for the work on the MSR from Hamhung to Chosin Reservoir. The most difficult part of the route was Funchilin Pass. A few months after the Chosin operation Rowny summarized what was done:

> The pass was a V-cut in the side of the hill from the coastal plain to the plateau, a climb of 4,000 feet from approximately 500 feet to 4,500 elevation. The road was blocked by snow on only one occasion for a duration of approximately 12 hours. Sand piles were stockpiled, snow stakes placed, plows procured, culverts constructed in order to prevent icing of road, narrow places widened, bridges strengthened and, in some cases, new bridges

Section of the road climbing Funchilin Pass from Chinhung-ni to Koto-ri, a cliff on one side, a chasm on the other, 1950. Photograph courtesy of Brig. Gen. Edward A. Craig, US Marine Corps.

built. Construction of C-47 strips at Division HQ locations was a standard practice within X Corps, to provide against any type of interruption of the MSR by weather, combat action, land slides, etc. It was also to assist in command, evacuation and resupply. Approximately 15 miles of MSR were widened from one-way to two-way. By-passes were constructed around 20 bridges or defiles in order to make unlikely the blocking of traffic by bridges or defiles being blown by the enemy.[3]

When the 31st RCT arrived at the reservoir, it found that only one bridge north of Hagaru-ri had been destroyed. It was a modern span across the Paegamni-gang, a tributary to the reservoir from the east about 5 road miles above Hagaru-ri and just south of Hudong-ni. American planes had bombed the bridge. The Paegamni-gang at that point was a shallow stream during low water. The stream divided into two or more channels at the highway crossing, flowing through a mile-wide low, marshlike valley to the reservoir.

The village of Sasu-ri lay in this low ground on the south side of the main stream of the Paegamni-gang at the bridge site. The 1st Marine Division sent A Company, 1st Engineers, to Sasu, a sawmill town, to get timbers to rebuild the bridge on the MSR. As a temporary measure the Marine engineers built a good bypass on the west side (downstream) of the blown bridge.[4] It was used by all troops and traffic during the Chosin operation. Major Crosby P. Miller remembered the road well:

> While moving up to the new position, I took particular notice of the terrain. The single road running north along the east side of the reservoir was dirt and barely wide enough for two trucks to pass. The ground sloped up steeply from the reservoir and was deeply cut by many stream lines leading to the lake level. The road twisted up and down over these cross-compartments, usually running around the widest inlets but crossing the narrow streams by narrow wooden bridges. The one modern concrete bridge at Sasu-ri (5475) on the entire stretch of road from Hagaru-ri to the battalion position had been blown. However, this stream was fordable by vehicles just below the bridge site. A narrow gauge railroad ran along the edge of the reservoir, at times running parallel to the road and then leaving the road in favor of more level terrain on the shoreline. The railroad crossed streams on its own unfloored wooden trestle. The reservoir itself was frozen over to a sufficient thickness of ice to support foot troops. I have been told since that the temperature was approximately twenty-seven degrees below zero. This was further aggravated by a piercing wind which never ceased.[5]

On November 20, General Barr had begun moving the 32nd RCT from the Kujang-ni area to an assembly area nearly 200 road miles to the northeast, behind the 17th Regiment, which was then approaching Hyesanjin and the Yalu River border. At the end of November 21 the 1st Battalion was all alone in "Happy Valley," as the troops called their pleasant bivouac area near Kujang-ni. The battalion was to follow the rest of the regiment to the Yalu as soon as a unit from the 3rd Infantry Division arrived to relieve it in place.

Meanwhile, 2nd Lt. Robert C. Kingston, a platoon leader of K Company, 32nd Regiment, led the regimental advance on Singpaljin, on the Yalu, west of Hyesanjin. Kingston arrived there on November 28 but barely had time to look at the Yalu River before he was ordered to turn back to Hungnam. Thus the 7th Infantry Division reached the Yalu in two places in November, 1950, the only American troops ever to reach the Yalu River and the Korean border.

The 7th Division, with a minor exception, had met no Chinese soldiers, only scattered and retreating North Koreans. The exception occurred
when the 3rd Battalion, 31st Infantry, encountered some reconnaissance
units of the Chinese 376th Regiment of the 126th Division near the Fusen
Reservoir between November 8 and 16. After brief exchanges of fire and
skirmishing, the Chinese units departed, having learned that the power plant
at the Fusen Reservoir had never been completed.[6]

Back at "Happy Valley," anticipating that a relief force would arrive on
the morning of November 23, Lt. Col. Don C. Faith, Jr., commander of
the 1st Battalion, sent Maj. Robert E. Jones, the 1st Battalion S-1 and adjutant, with a quartering party to the battalion's designated new assembly
area near Pukchong, the 7th Division's rear CP. During the day the 3rd Division relief battalion arrived.

By dawn of the 24th the 1st Battalion, of more than 1,000 men—715
Americans and 300 Koreans attached to the US Army (KATUSA)—left
"Happy Valley" at Kujang-ni for their day-long 160-mile road trip to Pukchong.[7] Earlier that morning Faith had gone ahead to get his orders from
the regimental commander at Pukchong. He had instructed his executive
officer, Major Miller, to bring the battalion along behind him.

About 9:00 A.M. the 1st Battalion approached the northern outskirts of
Hamhung, where it was met by a 7th Division liaison officer from X Corps,
who told Major Miller to halt the battalion and report to the G-3, X Corps
Headquarters, for instructions. The liaison officer was supposed to have
stopped the battalion commander also, but Faith had already passed through
Hamhung. Faith, now out of communication with his battalion, continued
on to Pukchong, where he learned of the change in plans.

After stopping the 1st Battalion in the outskirts of Hamhung, Miller
reported to X Corps Headquarters, where he met Generals Almond and
Barr. Barr informed Miller that he was to take the battalion north to the
area of the 1st Marine Division and to proceed down the east side of the
Chosin Reservoir as far as possible. He told Miller that the 1st Battalion
was now attached to the 1st Marine Division.[8]

While Miller received his new orders at the X Corps CP, Maj. Wesley J. Curtis, the battalion S-3, assembled the battalion in a schoolyard close
to the road. Men in the battalion cheered a radio news broadcast from the
Far East Command that Eighth Army that morning had launched its offensive to end the war and that it expected some divisions to be back in Japan
by Christmas.

When Miller rejoined him, Curtis learned that the 1st Battalion was to relieve the 5th Marine Regiment on the east side of Chosin Reservoir and wait there for the arrival of other 7th Division units.

At 11:30 A.M. on November 24, Curtis started north with guides to locate a battalion assembly area for the night. Miller would follow with the battalion in half an hour. Curtis reached the village of Chinhung-ni, at the foot of Funchilin Pass, where the road started its climb to the Koto-ri Plateau. There he found a suitable assembly area. During the evening orders were issued that the battalion movement would continue at 6:30 A.M.[9]

Lieutenant Colonel Faith, in the meantime, had driven all the way to Pukchong, and only upon arrival there did he learn that his battalion had been ordered to the Chosin Reservoir. He started back immediately on the lonely road. Half an hour after midnight he arrived at Chinhung-ni and there rejoined his battalion. The night was intensely cold and was noisy from the heavy traffic on the MSR. The troops slept poorly.

With Faith's arrival the three principal officers of the battalion were together again. All had had experience in World War II. Faith had commanded the battalion for more than a year, ever since the 7th Division had been reorganized in Japan. From Virginia, he had enlisted in the army on June 25, 1941. Eight months later, on February 26, 1942, he was commissioned a second lieutenant of infantry from the Fort Benning Officer Candidate School (OCS). During World War II he served as aide to General Ridgway for more than three years, advancing to lieutenant colonel. After several assignments in the Pacific and in the United States at the end of the war, he served on General Barr's joint military advisory group in China.

In 1949, Faith was ordered to Japan to command the 1st Squadron of the 12th Cavalry Regiment, 1st Cavalry Division. When the 32nd Infantry was organized in Japan, the 1st Squadron became a nucleus of the new regiment, and Barr, now commanding the 7th Infantry Division, named Faith commander of the 32nd's 1st Battalion. On November 24, 1950, Faith, 32 years old, was one day away from Chosin Reservoir, but except for the limited experience in the Inchon Landing in September he had never commanded any kind of military organization in combat.

Faith was of athletic build, 6 feet tall, and he wore a crew cut on his black hair. His eyes and complexion were dark, reflecting partial Spanish heritage. He was friendly, forceful, and charismatic to his enlisted men and officers alike.[10]

Major Crosby P. Miller, the battalion executive officer, graduated from

Lt. Col. Don C. Faith, Jr., talking over his SCR 300 radio in the summer of 1950 during battalion maneuvers in Japan before going to Korea. Photograph courtesy of Col. Wesley J. Curtis.

the Virginia Military Institute, at Lexington, Virginia, in the class of 1940 with a degree in civil engineering. From his ROTC training he obtained a commission as second lieutenant on May 31, 1940 and entered the Army. He served in World War II in Europe as armor officer, tank platoon leader, commander of several different tank companies, and adjutant, S-3, and S-2 for a tank battalion. After the war, in July, 1946, Miller received a commission as first lieutenant in the Regular Army. Immediately after completing the advance course at the Armor School in 1950, he was ordered to the Far East Command. There he was assigned to the 7th Infantry Division, which in turn reassigned him to its 32nd Regiment, and from there he went to its 1st Battalion. Miller was one of hundreds of armor officers who, in Korea, were assigned to infantry vacancies. After Inchon and Seoul, Lieutenant Colonel Faith felt assured that Miller could function as an infantry officer, and he let him don the crossed rifles as his insignia.[11]

Major Wesley J. Curtis, the battalion S-3, or operations officer, enlisted in I Company, 17th Infantry, in 1938, when he was 20 years old. While he was in that company, he received an appointment as a cadet to West Point. Graduating in the class of January, 1943, Curtis was commissioned an infantry second lieutenant. He was sent to the Pacific Theater and served as an infantry officer for 34 months in the noted "Wolfhound Regiment," the 27th Infantry of the 25th Division. In that period Curtis moved successively through platoon leader, company executive officer, company commander, and regimental S-4. He had just completed the 9-month Infantry School course on battalion tactics at Fort Benning in June, 1950, when he was sent to Japan for assignment in Korea. He ended up in the 7th Infantry Division and was sent to the 1st Battalion, 32nd Infantry. Curtis was 32 years old, the same age as Faith. He was of medium height, modest, a student of military affairs, and a steady soldier.[12]

On the morning of November 25 the traffic officer at the regulating point would not allow the 1st Battalion to proceed at once up Funchilin Pass because traffic in some places was one way. He did agree, however, to let a small party start at once, and Faith, Curtis, the operations sergeant, and the sergeant major left Chinhung-ni at 6:00 A.M. in two vehicles. Miller was to bring the battalion up the pass as soon as traffic conditions would allow. He started half an hour later.

On top of the plateau at Koto-ri, Faith and his party found the road covered with snow and ice. Directional signs began to appear pointing the way to various 1st Marine Division units. Upon reaching Hagaru-ri, 1½ miles south of the reservoir, Faith's party took the right-hand road and entered the 5th Marine Regiment's zone of responsibility.[13]

About 9:00 A.M., a mile north of Hagaru-ri, Faith met Lt. Col. Raymond L. Murray coming south. Murray told him that his Marine CP was with one of his battalions on the south side of the Pungnyuri-gang, a large inlet stream emptying into the reservoir 8 miles north of Hagaru-ri, and that his lead 3rd Battalion was in a perimeter defense position about 4 miles beyond his CP. Murray assigned an assembly area for Faith's battalion 2 miles south of his own CP. It was on low but dry ground around the village of Twiggae and the lower, southern slope of Hill 1221, immediately north of Twiggae. Part of Murray's 5th Marines had occupied the area and had established defensive positions, bunkers and foxholes, on the hill, facing

Capt. Robert F. Haynes (*left*) and Maj. (later Col.) Wesley J. Curtis in Japan in August or September, 1950, before the Inchon Landing. Photograph courtesy of Colonel Curtis.

north. These positions commanded the road below to the north, east, and southeast. Murray instructed Faith to occupy this position with at least defensive outposts.

Murray added that the 1st Battalion had not been attached to the 5th Marines but that he would take control of it in case of an enemy attack. He explained that he had not yet received definite orders for his anticipated movement to the west side of the reservoir but expected to receive them the next morning. He then continued on his way for a reconnaissance of the position he expected to occupy at Yudam-ni.[14]

Meanwhile, Miller led the battalion up the twisting and sometimes narrow road of Funchilin Pass. The trucks jolted over the bumpy, frozen, mostly snow-covered road. The mountainsides were almost bare of vegetation; some low spots resembled arctic tundra. If the men, most of them with their heads wrapped in wool scarves under their helmets, glanced northward as they passed through Hagaru-ri and started down the east side of the reservoir, they saw distant mountains standing ever higher over an almost trackless waste, sentinels for one of Korea's most inaccessible areas. It reached into the Yangnim Range, where peaks rose to 8,000 feet.

The battalion closed in to its assembly area at Hill 1221 about 3:00 P.M. The CP was established in a Korean hut on the lower slope of the hill. From it there was a clear view westward to the Chosin Reservoir, a mile away. The battalion established a partly closed perimeter, occupying the high ground on both sides of the road. Major Curtis and others described this position as the strongest they saw on the east side of the reservoir.[15] The weather was cold and threatened more snow, which already covered the ground.

Second Lieutenant James O. Mortrude and his 3rd Platoon of C Company relieved a Marine squad still manning a ridgeline position on Hill 1221. Mortrude put his platoon in the foxholes the Marines had vacated and organized his position for night security. He wanted maximum troop rest, but two men in each squad area were to remain awake at all times. Mortrude gave himself the 2:00 A.M. "witching-hour" shift.[16]

That evening Faith, Curtis, Major Powell (the S-2), and Capt. Erwin B. Bigger (commanding D Company, heavy weapons) met Lieutenant Colonel Murray at the latter's CP at the inlet near Sinhung-ni. Murray told them that during the day Lieutenant Colonel Taplett, commanding the 3rd Battalion, 5th Marines, had sent a platoon-size reconnaissance patrol, including two tanks, from his forward perimeter down the road toward Kalchon-ni,

MAP 4. Movement of the 31st RCT to Chosin Reservoir, November 24–27, 1950.

a village near the dam at the lower end of the reservoir. It had encountered and scattered a few small groups of Chinese soldiers, killing five and capturing one, and had destroyed an abandoned 75-mm gun. The patrol, finding no evidence of large-scale enemy activity, had turned back just short of the northern tip of the reservoir. Taplett had made a helicopter reconnaissance over the same area and farther north but had observed no sign of significant enemy activity. Little was known of the enemy situation or of enemy plans for future operations.[17]

After the meeting with Murray, Faith and his staff drove north 4 miles to Taplett's 3rd Battalion at its hill perimeter astride the road. There they made a partial inspection of the Marine position.

The night of November 25–26 passed quietly on the east side of the reservoir, and Sunday dawned cold and clear. At officers' breakfast mess that morning Lieutenant Mortrude created a small disturbance by reporting to Capt. Dale L. Seever, his C Company commander, on night-security laxness. As Mortrude tells it:

> Awakened 0200. Weather very cold with fresh snow falling. Checked platoon area and found only one man awake. Awakened Platoon Sergeant and required him to organize walking security patrols in each squad area for remainder of night. Visited adjacent platoon areas and found same situation of "no challenge" and only one or two people awake along entire company front. Returned to my platoon area and found guard up and functioning as desired. Got into sleeping bag at 0400 hours and slept remainder of night.
>
> Awakened after daylight . . . to find weather somewhat moderated with some sunshine. Conducted brief investigation of night security failure, censured and counseled NCOS, and imposed latrine excavation duty on key enlisted offenders (those failing to awaken reliefs).
>
> Company call to hot breakfast. Platoon Sergeant organized mess call. When I reached mess tent all other officers clustered around extra burner. Informed Company Commander of disciplinary action being taken in my platoon and reasons therefore [sic]. Commander assented but another platoon leader precipitated a confrontation with me by remarking on the absence of any such problem in his platoon. Captain Seever eventually restored order and discussed night security after I had adamantly expressed my opinion of our past night's vulnerability.[18]

Mortrude was born in Seattle, Washington, on February 19, 1922. He had three years of enlisted service in the infantry in World War II in North Africa, the Middle East, and Europe. At the University of Washington he

Lt. (later Lt. Col.) James O. Mortrude about November, 1950. Photograph courtesy of Colonel Mortrude.

received an ROTC commission as a second lieutenant, and later, at the end of 1949, he entered the Infantry School at Fort Benning, Georgia, completing the course on June 16, 1950. In early August he arrived in Japan, where he was assigned as a platoon leader in C Company, 1st Battalion, 32nd Infantry, 7th Infantry Division. In the fighting for Seoul he won the Distinguished Service Cross for leadership and heroism. Twenty-eight years old at Chosin, Mortrude by his experience as an enlisted man and his demonstrated judgment and leadership under fire was one of the most valuable platoon leaders in the battalion.[19]

Another platoon leader, 2nd Lt. James G. Campbell, of D Company, also has recollections of that first day at the reservoir and the bitter cold of Funchilin Pass. D Company (Weapons Company) set up its tents at the southeast base of Hill 1221. His machine-gun platoon dug a few hasty foxholes, which did not constitute a defense position. Campbell, like Mortrude, had received his first commission as ROTC second lieutenant when he graduated from the University of California. He had entered the Regular Army on October 15, 1949. Seasoned senior officers of the battalion judged him to be one of its best platoon leaders.[20]

The 1st Battalion was in poor shape for a winter campaign in a cold climate. Most of the men, however, had received shoepacs, long underwear, pile liners, and parka shells. Lieutenant Colonel Faith did not like shoepacs and favored wearing combat boots with rubber overshoes. Many followed his example. This practice later reduced the incidence of frostbite and frozen feet in the battalion. But the battalion was short of winter gloves and many other items needed for cold weather. Vehicles lacked tire chains and tarpaulin covers. Each company had only a kitchen fly for tentage.

Brigadier General Henry I. Hodes, assistant 7th Division commander, arrived at the battalion CP at Hill 1221 about half an hour before noon on November 26. Many officers and men of the division considered him its driving force. In World War II, Hodes had commanded the 112th Infantry Regiment in Europe. General Barr had sent Hodes to the reservoir as his agent in directing the operations of Col. Allan D. MacLean's 31st RCT after it had assembled.

Hodes brought much news to Faith. He said that the 3rd Battalion, 31st Infantry, and the 57th Field Artillery Battalion, less its C Battery (attached to the 2nd Battalion, 31st Infantry), were on their way to join his battalion. He said that Colonel MacLean, commander of the 31st Infantry Regiment, and his staff; the 31st Intelligence and Reconnaissance (I&R) Platoon; a medi-

Col. (formerly Lt.) James G. Campbell about 1978. Photograph courtesy of Colonel Campbell.

cal detachment; and a communications detachment would arrive soon. Upon his arrival MacLean would assume command of the composite force. This meant, in effect, that the 1st Battalion, 32nd Infantry, would no longer be attached to the 1st Marine Division. That became a reality the next day when the battalion relieved the 3rd Battalion, 5th Marines, in its forward position. Hodes added that the 31st Tank Company had started on its way from Hungnam but that because of road conditions and traffic congestion the time of its arrival was uncertain.

While eating lunch with Faith and his staff, Hodes told the group that the situation at Eighth Army front was unclear. In this conversation Faith told Hodes that if the Marine Division could give him a tank platoon and some artillery support he could attack north before the arrival of other 7th Division elements. Hodes disapproved this suggestion, left the 1st Battalion about 1:00 P.M., and went back southward on the road to Hudong-ni.[21]

Faith, Curtis, Powell, and all company commanders and platoon leaders drove north the 6 miles to Taplett's 3rd Marine Battalion perimeter. There they made a detailed reconnaissance of the forward position, learning that several Marine foot patrols sent out during the day had made no enemy contacts. Faith and his party returned to their own CP at dark.

At the 1st Battalion CP at Hill 1221 the assistant intelligence officer had interrogated many Korean civilians trudging south past him on the road. They had revealed that there were Chinese soldiers in the vicinity who had said that they intended to recapture the reservoir area within three to five days. These stories were largely discounted because there had been no enemy activity. Major Powell, the S-2, meanwhile, had gathered information from the Marines that they had encountered only rearguard Chinese actions since arriving at the reservoir and that their patrols had seen Chinese patrols only at long range.

A few hours after Faith returned from his reconnaissance of the Marine position, Lieutenant Colonel Murray sent a jeep messenger to him with a copy of his 5th Marines regimental order issued that day, November 26. It directed the 5th Marines to move from the east side of the reservoir to the west side early the next morning to join the 7th Marine Regiment at Yudam-ni. This order meant that at some time during the next day the 1st Battalion, 32nd Infantry, would be the only American troops east of Chosin until other units of the 7th Division arrived.

During this changeover Faith had no orders on what his mission would be—presumably he was to stay where he was. He telephoned and asked for instructions, but Murray said that he had no information or instructions and suggested that he proceed no farther north without orders from the 7th Division.[22]

About an hour later Col. Allan D. MacLean, commander of the 31st Infantry RCT, arrived at Faith's CP. With him were Lt. Col. Berry K. Anderson, his S-3, and two or three other staff officers. Colonel MacLean told Faith that he intended to attack north just as soon as his task force had closed on the area. He said that the 3rd Battalion, 31st Infantry, would arrive the next day. He also told Faith that his own battalion was now attached to the 31st Infantry Regiment. Faith asked permission to move to the forward Marine position the next morning after the Marines had vacated it. MacLean approved the request.[23]

Faith, in making this proposal, did not follow the Marines' caution in assembling regimental strength before moving farther into the unknown. His proposal for the battalion and regimental approval of it on the evening of November 26 were probably the first important mistake and command failure affecting the fate of the 31st RCT at Chosin.

The tempo of events began to pick up. An hour and a half after MacLean's arrival Lt. Col. Ray O. Embree, commanding officer of the 57th Field Artillery Battalion, arrived. He confirmed that his battalion was on the road and should arrive before dark the next day.

MacLean went to establish his CP in a schoolhouse about a mile south of Hill 1221.[24] The schoolhouse, in good condition, stood on the site of a former village called Hudong-ni. There was no village there now—only a number of foundations outlining former structures. The name Hudong-ni in orders, dispatches, communications, and the subsequently compiled Army and Marine reports concerning the action east of Chosin derives from the copy of the old Japanese map the troops carried, but in 1950 it referred to the schoolhouse on the north side of the Paegamni-gang, opposite the village of Sasu-ri, on the south side of the same stream.[25]

With MacLean now present, Faith could feel some relief from the pressure of being the senior troop commander on the east side of the reservoir. The Chosin mission had also come to MacLean as a surprise. He first learned of it in a telephone conversation with General Barr on the evening of November 24. MacLean had been in command of the 31st Regiment only about two months, succeeding to the command during the fight for Seoul, after the Inchon Landing. During the summer he had been a senior staff officer in the G-3 Section of Eighth Army. Before that he had been commander

Col. Allan D. MacLean (*left*) and Lt. Col. Don C. Faith, Jr., Japan, spring, 1950. Photograph courtesy of Col. Erwin B. Bigger.

Lt. Col. Faith and his principal staff officers, 1st Battalion, 32nd Infantry, Japan, early 1950. *Front row:* Capt. (later Col.) Robert E. Jones; Lt. Col. Don C. Faith, Jr.; Capt. Banyon Patterson. *Back row:* Capt. Erwin B. Bigger, Capt. Ed Scullion, Capt. Wayne E. Powell, Captain Warren. Photograph courtesy of Colonel Jones.

of the 32nd Infantry for about a year during its organization in Japan. Accordingly, he was well acquainted with Faith and with all the officers of the 1st Battalion, 32nd Infantry, who were with it at the time.

MacLean was born in Delaware in 1907. He graduated from the United States Military Academy in the class of 1930 and was commissioned in the infantry. In World War II he served in the European Theater. MacLean was aggressive by nature. His officers and men in the 31st Infantry had discovered in the action near the Fusen Reservoir in October that he liked to be up front when action threatened or was in progress. This big, robust man was 43 years old when he arrived at Chosin Reservoir.

On November 24, when MacLean first learned of the Chosin Reservoir mission, most of his regiment was assembled near the east side of Fusen

Officers of the 1st Battalion, 32nd Infantry, 7th Division, June, 1950 (several of this group did not go to Korea). *First row:* Capt. Erwin B. Bigger; Capt. Ed Scullion; Lt. Col. Don C. Faith, Jr.; Maj. J. O. Donahue; Capt. (later Col.) Robert E. Jones; Capt. Banyon Patterson; Captain Warren. *Second row:* Capt. Dale L. Seever, Lt. Harvey Hott, Lieutenant Jackson, Capt. Wayne E. Powell, Lt. Jack Tevis, Lt. James Houghton, Lt. Hugh May, Lt. Carlos Ortenzi. *Third row:* Lieutenant Hoddinott; Lieutenant Maher; Lt. Robert D. Wilson; Lt. Henry M. Moore; Lt. Everett F. Smalley, Jr. (top of head showing); Lt. Dixie Neighbors; Lt. E. E. Fitzgerald. *Fourth row:* Officer behind Lt. Dixie Neighbors unidentified. Photograph courtesy of Col. Robert E. Jones.

Reservoir and out of contact with enemy forces. He informed the regiment that it was to prepare for immediate movement to the Chosin Reservoir and ordered a quartering party to be assembled at once and sent on in advance. Major Hugh W. Robbins, the 31st Infantry adjutant, assembled the party on the morning of November 25 and started over snow-covered trails for Pukchong, the 7th Division Rear CP, where he met MacLean. Robbins and his party stayed at Pukchong overnight. MacLean; Lieutenant Colonel Anderson, his S-3; and Maj. Carl G. Witte, his S-2, went on ahead toward

Hagaru-ri. Lieutenant Colonel George E. Deshon, the 31st Infantry executive officer, stayed behind with the Regimental Rear at the Iwon beaches
and never had an opportunity to join the 31st RCT at Chosin.

On November 26 Robbins led his party to Hamhung, where he left
guides for the 3rd Battalion, 31st Infantry, which was following him. He
then continued north toward the reservoir, reaching the Marine traffic-control
checkpoint at Chinhung-ni by 9:30 that night. Robbins was able to reach
MacLean at the reservoir by telephone, and the latter arranged with the
1st Marine Division to clear with traffic control authority for Robbins to
continue on up Funchilin Pass that night. MacLean told Robbins that his
CP was in a schoolhouse at Hudong-ni. Robbins and his party arrived there
after midnight.[26]

At 8:00 A.M. the next morning, MacLean, Anderson, Witte, Robbins,
and McNally, the 31st Infantry communications officer, drove from Hudong-
ni to Faith's CP. MacLean and his officers, accompanied by Faith, drove on
to the positions the 5th Marines were vacating. MacLean made a reconnaissance of the position, noting the bodies of two Chinese soldiers who
had been killed in front of a Marine outpost two nights earlier.

MacLean then told Robbins to select a site for a small forward 31st
RCT CP south of Faith's forward battalion position. He also said that when
the 3rd Battalion, 31st Infantry, arrived it would take up a position about
two miles south of his forward CP on the south side of the Pungnyuri-
gang Inlet of the reservoir. Robbins then sent Lieutenant McNally back
to the Hudong-ni schoolhouse to bring up the quartering party of about
35 men he had left there. Robbins, meanwhile, selected a site for MacLean's
forward CP on the east side of the road, not far from the reservoir.[27]

McNally returned from Hudong-ni with his group about 2:00 P.M.
They began digging in the frozen ground to establish the CP. Robbins had
already put 15 Korean refugees to work on a foundation for an operations
tent and had collected pieces of equipment left behind by the Marines. By
dark tents had been erected, and the CP was ready to operate.

Before leaving to drive south on the MSR after his reconnaissance of
the forward battalion position, MacLean had told Robbins that he intended
to stay that night at the Hudong-ni schoolhouse but would be at the forward CP the next morning. Later in the night Robbins learned that Mac-
Lean had changed his mind and had returned to his recently established
forward CP during the night. He had then gone on to Faith's CP.

On his way south to Hudong-ni, MacLean received a report that a Chinese force of several hundred soldiers was in a village east of the inlet. During the afternoon he ordered 1st Lt. Richard B. Coke, Jr., commanding the 31st I & R Platoon, to patrol up the valley of the Pungnyuri-gang northeastward toward the Fusen Reservoir to check on the report. They started up the narrow dirt road that followed the Pungnyuri-gang northeastward toward Fusen in jeeps mounting machine guns.

No I&R report ever reached MacLean. Coke's platoon seemed simply to vanish. In response to an inquiry to Col. Carl G. Witte, then major, the 31st RCT S-2 at Hudong-ni, Witte wrote to me: "We were all concerned by the time 24 hours had gone by and we had not heard from Coke. I asked Ray Embree to see what he could do with Arty Liaison AC. We also jerry-rigged a 1/4 wave antenna. We also went back to X Corps via Field phone on the basis that Coke may have gone to the west and contacted the right flank of Eighth Army. Nothing worked and by this time we were all well occupied. I heard rumors that some of the I&R had returned but even with a concerted effort I never met any of them."[28]

In March or April, 1951, while Colonel McCaffrey commanded the 31st Infantry in central Korea as a part of Eighth Army, a glimmer of information about the fate of the I&R platoon came to light. His S-2 section frequently monitored Chinese English-language broadcasts. Some of these broadcasts released names of American POWs in China. McCaffrey recalled that on one or more of these broadcasts his S-2 section picked up the names of two members of the missing I&R platoon and that he wrote letters to next of kin after advising the Department of the Army.[29]

All day on the 27th long columns of Lt. Col. William R. Reilly's 3rd Battalion, 31st Infantry, climbed from Hamhung northward toward the Chosin Reservoir. Behind them came Lieutenant Colonel Embree's 57th Field Artillery Battalion (minus C Battery). The 3rd Battalion arrived on the east side of the reservoir in the afternoon, closing there before dark. Reilly and MacLean stopped the battalion on the south side of the Pungnyuri-gang Inlet in a limited bivouac area, where it prepared to spend the night. The bivouac area was a poor defensive position, in low ground surrounded on three sides by ridges and high ground. On the fourth — north — side the inlet bordered it.

A Battery, 57th Field Artillery Battalion, began arriving at the reservoir about 11:00 A.M. The remainder of the artillery closed there during the afternoon. During the morning of the 27th, MacLean and Embree reconnoitered the area to locate the artillery when it arrived. They decided to place A and B firing batteries, with the battalion fire-direction center, at the inlet along with the 3rd Battalion, 31st Infantry. The 57th Field Artillery HQ and Headquarters Battery would not go to the inlet but were to stop in a cove on the eastern side of the MSR about one road mile south of the inlet perimeter or bivouac, on the south side of Hill 1456, which intervened between the two positions.[30]

On November 26, D Battery, 15th AAA AW SP (minus the 2nd Platoon), was attached to the 57th. Captain James R. McClymont commanded the battery. When he came to the 57th Headquarters area in the cove half a mile south of the inlet, he pulled his battery off the road to join it at dusk. McClymont was not well acquainted with the 57th Field Artillery personnel. A Marine major, one of the last of the 5th Marines to leave the area east of the reservoir, was packing his things. In a brief exchange with McClymont the Marine officer said that he had sent out patrols for a distance of 10 miles, and none had seen any signs of the enemy.[31]

McClymont's platoon of antiaircraft weapons was of the utmost importance to Colonel MacLean's forces east of Chosin. The platoon had eight weapons carriers: four M19 (dual-40) full-track gun carriages, each mounting two 40-mm Bofors antiaircraft guns, and four M16 (quad-50) half-tracks, each mounting four .50-caliber machine guns, heavy barrels, M-2. On both the M19s and the M16s the guns were mounted on revolving turrets. The M19 fired a bursting shell, and on automatic resembled in killing and maiming power 240 fragmentation grenades dropping every minute on an enemy. The M19 40-mm shell was also good for hard-hitting flat trajectory fire at specific enemy emplacements or weapons up to a distance of 2 or 3 miles. An M16, quad-50, could fire its four machine guns on automatic at the rate of 1,800 rounds a minute. It could sweep a front like a scythe cutting grain.

When McClymont arrived at Chosin, each vehicle pulled a fully loaded trailer packed with ammunition, C rations, gasoline, and bedrolls. The trailers carried two basic loads of ammunition that he had had the foresight to obtain, instead of the usual one.

McClymont set up his own CP a short distance from Embree's. For protection he placed an M19 close to the road in front of the artillery CP, another just south of the first one, and an M16 south of the second M19. A few hundred feet east of his own CP, McClymont positioned another M16. In the center of the cove he emplaced his 1st Platoon CP and an M19 and an M16 nearby. At the southern edge of the cove he placed his two remaining weapons carriers, the M16 close to the road.

Accompanying the 3rd Battalion, 31st Infantry, to Chosin on the 27th was Capt. George Cody's 31st Heavy Mortar (4.2-inch) Company, less one platoon that was attached to the 2nd Battalion, 31st Infantry, which Mac-Lean expected to arrive at any time. Cody emplaced his heavy mortars in the flat marshland about halfway between the inlet and the 3rd Battalion on the south and Faith's 1st Battalion forward position on the north. The mortar position was west of the MSR and nearly opposite MacLean's forward CP. From its position the 31st Heavy Mortar Company could deliver supporting fire for both infantry battalions. Faith had with him one platoon of the 32nd Infantry's Heavy Mortar Company. When Cody arrived, Faith had Lt. Robert Reynolds take the platoon of heavy mortars to join him. The latter then had the equivalent of a full company of 12 heavy mortars, 4 to a platoon.

During the afternoon A and B batteries (each with four 105-mm howitzers) of the 57th Field Artillery Battalion emplaced on the south side of the inlet where the ground flared into semiflat land just short of the bridge and causeway that crossed the Pungnyuri-gang. A Battery emplaced farther east and closer to the bridge than B Battery, which was behind, or west, of it. Captain Harold L. Hodge commanded A Battery; Capt. Theodore C. Goss commanded B Battery.

First Lieutenant Thomas J. Patton, a member of A Battery, said that on arrival at the inlet the artillery occupied its positions without difficulty and that "perimeter defenses were set up with men in foxholes." He continued: "The Battery CP was set up in a log hut on the left side of the battery position – Gun Sections were dug into the rear of the pieces in covered over shelters – Wire communications were laid and radio communications were made with Battalion – the Battery Mess was set up in a log hut in the forward position some 30 yards inside the perimeter defense line."[32]

Reilly placed two rifle companies of his 3rd Battalion on a ridge about 900 yards east of his CP. This spur ridge ran northward from Hill 1456, south of the bivouac area, descending to the south bank of the Pungnyuri-gang about half a mile east of the bridge. This long finger ridge controlled a view of all the low ground lying westward along the southern side of the inlet, where the artillery and the 3rd Battalion had bivouacked for the night. Reilly placed Capt. Robert J. Kitz's K Company on the lower part of the ridge and Capt. Albert Marr's I Company above K Company on the upper extension of the ridge. Captain Earle H. Jordan, Jr.'s M Company was to the west, behind I Company. These three companies constituted the eastern defense of the perimeter. Captain William Etchemendy's L Company appears to have been bivouacked in the vicinity of the artillery, but its initial location on the 27th has not been determined.

Captain Jordan emplaced the 81-mm mortars of the Weapons (M) Company in a dry wash just east of his CP and between it and I Company. Companies K and I each had a section of machine guns and a section of 75-mm recoilless rifles attached to it from M Company. Jordan says that it was dark before he had his mortars emplaced and local security established on the evening of November 27.[33]

It appears from what is known about the troop dispositions of the 3rd Battalion and the 57th Field Artillery on the night of November 27 that there was a defensive line only on the east; on the north there was the frozen inlet; on the west and south there was no organized line—only scattered foxholes; and in between were the foxholes of the artillerymen near their howitzers and the parked trucks and other vehicles of the troops north of the artillery pieces just off the road.

Registrations of mortar defensive fires for both the 1st and the 3rd battalions, at both the forward position and at the inlet, were not completed until about 8:30 P.M., well after dark. These were normal precautions. No one expected an enemy attack that night; no enemy were known to be in the vicinity.

The 31st Tank Company was expected to join MacLean's infantry and artillery forces at the reservoir and to be a powerful part of the combat team in the projected attack northward. In the X Corps movement from the Inchon-Seoul area to northeast Korea, the 7th Division had moved overland to Pusan and there loaded on ships for the sea voyage up the coast to Iwon. The tank company was not with its regiment on the overland journey to Pusan. Instead, it loaded on an LST at Inchon and had a three-week sea trip around the tip of Korea and northward up the east coast of the peninsula to Hungnam.

The company, commanded by Capt. Robert E. Drake, arrived at Hungnam, long overdue, at full strength in authorized tanks. It had four platoons of five M 4A4 tanks each, all armed with 76-mm guns. There were two additional tanks in the command section armed with 105-mm howitzers, making a total of 22 tanks. In Korea seldom did a tank company operate as a unit; usually it was employed in platoons or sections. But at Chosin, Drake's company was employed as a unit.

In unloading from the LST at Hungnam, the tanks submerged in salt water and needed immediate maintenance. Drake assembled them in an apple orchard on the outskirts of the port city, provided the necessary maintenance, and then had a fine Thanksgiving Day dinner, which included pies made from the orchard's apples. That day he received instructions to proceed at once to Chosin Reservoir to join the 31st RCT.

Drake obtained a black-and-white Japanese map based on 1916 data, which the Army had hastily reproduced for the Chosin operation. The next day, November 27, he led the tank company out of its bivouac area and started for Chosin.[34]

In the afternoon, after a tiring climb from the coastal plain to the Koto-ri Plateau, the tankers arrived at the reservoir. Drake stopped the tank company at Hudong-ni for a rest and refueling. Colonel MacLean had already established his rear CP there, together with an ammunition and petroleum dump. When Drake pulled off the road into the Hudong-ni schoolhouse area, the last combat unit of MacLean's RCT to reach Chosin had arrived. The 2nd Battalion, 31st Infantry, with C Battery, 57th Field Artillery Battalion, never made it.

Drake instructed his men to make a full maintenance check of the tanks while he went on a search for the regimental commander. Members of MacLean's staff told Drake that he was somewhere forward. Drake, with his Korean interpreter, started down the road northward. After some miles he came to what he later remembered as a CP, probably that of Reilly's 3rd Battalion, 31st Infantry. MacLean was not there. At this stop, however, Drake learned that MacLean had sent the 31st I&R Platoon to check a report of enemy troops in a village to the northeast. Drake drove on as far as Faith's CP at the forward position. MacLean was not there, but Faith told him that the regimental plan called for an attack the next morning to Kalchon-ni, at the north end of the reservoir. He advised Drake not to try to bring his tanks up during the night but to wait until the next morning.[35]

It is one of the curious mishaps of the campaign that Drake never saw MacLean at the reservoir. On the way back to Hudong-ni he did not find him. Drake arrived there sometime after MacLean had left the schoolhouse to return to his own forward CP. The two officers passed each other somewhere between the 31st rear at Hudong-ni and Faith's forward position.

One can speculate on what MacLean's orders might have been that night if the two had met, and whether Drake would have moved his tanks forward to either of the infantry battalions. The tanks probably could have made it to the inlet if they had moved on by evening. It is probable that neither Hodes nor MacLean had any definite plan for the tank company or felt any urgency that evening for it to join the infantry forward at once. Both of these officers conferred at the Hudong-ni schoolhouse after the tanks had arrived there and could have left orders for Drake. Indeed, Hodes was at Hudong-ni all night.

As it was, upon his return to Hudong-ni, Drake made arrangements for local security for the night, planning to move forward in the morning. He did not know that Hodes was in the area until the next morning.

The same evening Maj. William R. Lynch, Jr., of the 7th Infantry Division G-3 Section, arrived at Hudong-ni. The time of his arrival and what he observed that night are significant relative to the situation of the 31st RCT. Lynch had been with the 17th Regiment in its advance toward Hyesanjin but had been recalled to the division CP at Pungsan. There Colonel Paddock, the Division G-3, told Lynch that General Hodes was going to fly to Hamhung to the X Corps CP to check on a rumor that the corps planned to move the 31st Infantry to join the 1st Marine Division. He instructed Lynch to take Sergeants Cox and Hammer of the G-3 Section and drive at once to Hamhung, where they were to join Hodes as his G-3 assistants.

Lynch and the two sergeants left Pukchong, the division rear CP, on the morning of November 26 and made the long, cold, desolate journey to Hamhung. They arrived late that evening. Lynch reported to X Corps G-3 Section, where he learned for the first time about the Chosin Reservoir operation and that General Hodes had already hurried to the area to check on unit deployments. Lynch and the two sergeants planned to leave the next morning to join Hodes at the reservoir.

At the X Corps morning briefing, when Lt. Col. William W. Quinn, the G-2, discussed the intelligence situation along the X Corps front, he made only passing reference to the presence of some Chinese in the 1st Marine Division sector and seemed to attach no importance to it. After the briefing Lynch and the two sergeants got on the road and headed for the reservoir. They found that they had cut in just behind the tail of the 31st Tank Company, also on its way to Chosin. They traveled all day behind the tank company and eventually reached and passed Hagaru-ri. Some miles north of the shattered village Lynch remembers Sergeant Cox pulling off "the ice-covered, narrow road and crossing two branches of the Paegamni-gang. Cox drove the jeep through hub-deep water. He stopped momentarily to keep backwash from the vehicle ahead from drowning out our jeep."

Immediately upon his arrival at Hudong-ni about 5:30 P.M., Lynch entered the schoolhouse. There he found Hodes in conversation with MacLean. Subsequently he heard MacLean instruct Lt. Col. Berry Anderson, his S-3, to bring forward the rest of the regimental headquarters staff still at the schoolhouse the next morning. Colonel MacLean left about half an hour later, stating that he was going north to his forward units. Thus it appears that MacLean left Hudong-ni about 6:00 P.M., during darkness. Hodes and Lynch remained at the schoolhouse overnight.[36]

The Hudong-ni schoolhouse and the 31st rear CP stood at the southwestern base of a large hill mass, Hill 1472 – Kobong or Nopun-Bong, some early maps called it. Drake had been there three nights and three days and knew the area well. He said that below the schoolhouse the ground sloped south toward the low marsh area at the Paegamni-gang, affording an expanse of about 25 to 30 acres that could be used for an assembly area, ammunition and petroleum products dumps, a tentage area, and a tank park. The road ran on the west side of the schoolhouse area. Beyond the road the Chosin Reservoir was in view about a mile away.

After Lynch's arrival at Hudong-ni, only Service Battery of the 57th Field Artillery (FA) Battalion, which had lagged behind the rest of the artillery, reached Hudong-ni. It settled down for the night about a mile south of Hudong-ni. The next morning it joined the 31st rear CP at the schoolhouse.[37]

Thus, on the evening of November 27 elements of the 31st RCT were scattered along the road from Hagaru-ri northward on the east side of the reservoir in seven different locations in a distance of 10 miles, beginning on the south at a point 4 miles north of Hagaru-ri and extending northward to the forward perimeter of the 1st Battalion, 32nd Infantry, 14 miles north of Hagaru-ri. Beginning with the most forward 1st Battalion position and moving south, the seven positions in succession were:

1. 1st Battalion, 32nd Infantry
2. 31st Infantry Advance CP
3. 31st Heavy Mortar Company
4. 3rd Battalion, 31st Infantry, and A and B Batteries, 57th Field Artillery Battalion
5. HQ and HQ Battery, 57th Field Artillery Battalion, and D Battery (minus one platoon), 15th AAA AW Battalion

6. 31st Infantry Rear CP and 31st Tank Company

7. Service Battery, 57th Field Artillery Battalion

Those units of MacLean's 31st RCT that had arrived east of Chosin by the evening of November 27 were far from concentrated. MacLean did not even know where the 2nd Battalion, 31st Infantry, was.[38]

The Army Occupies the Marines' Forward Position

While the 31st Infantry and the 57th Field Artillery were climbing to the reservoir on November 27, the 5th Marines completed their move from the east side of Chosin Reservoir to Yudam-ni, on the west side. Faith could not move his battalion to the Marines' forward position east of Chosin until they had cleared on the road past Hill 1221, where the battalion was located.[1]

It should have been clear to Faith and his staff that Lt. Col. Robert D. Taplett's 3rd Marine Battalion would start its movement from the forward perimeter at first light. That is what it did; it never had any intention of waiting until Faith's battalion arrived to relieve it. Later complaints by the 7th Infantry Division that this was not done were unjustified. By the evening of November 27 the only Marines left on the east side of the reservoir were A Company, 1st Marine Engineer Combat Battalion, at Hill 1203 and the sawmill town of Sasu just north of it, about two miles north of Hagaru-ri.[2]

All morning on Monday, November 27, Marines raised a haze of dust on the road past the 1st Battalion, 32nd Infantry. Faith's men learned from the Marines moving south past Hill 1221 that a few small enemy patrols had probed their positions during the night. In one instance a Chinese soldier had pulled a Marine from his foxhole and disarmed and beaten him.[3]

It was early afternoon when Faith started his battalion, mounted in vehicles, north to occupy Taplett's vacated positions. The battalion occupied the same positions; there was no compelling reason to make changes. The Marine defense line was well situated, with several bunkers constructed and foxholes dug. Being considerably fewer in number than the Marines, how-

44

An aerial view looking north over the lower (north) end of Chosin Reservoir. Near the bottom of the picture the road leading south to the A Company, 32nd Infantry, position can be seen. The Changjin River can be seen near the center of the picture, extending from the dam (and Kalchon-ni) at the edge of the reservoir to the northeast (upper right). The photograph was taken at a point directly above the position occupied by the 1st Battalion, 32nd Infantry, on November 27, 1950. This and other aerial shots appearing in this book were taken on November 1, 1950, before ice had formed at the reservoir, except at the shallow edges of tributaries. By November 24 the reservoir had frozen solid enough to hold the weight of a man and generally appeared to be frozen over. US Army photograph SC 363268.

ever, the 1st Battalion did not occupy all the positions, particularly those on the right, or southern, flank. This did not concern the battalion; it expected to be there only one night. After settling into their positions, the battalion began registration of defensive fire. The mortar registrations were completed about 8:30 P.M., after dark.

Col. (Maj. at Chosin) Crosby P. Miller, in February, 1966. Photograph courtesy of Colonel Miller.

In his narrative, Major Miller, the battalion executive officer, included a description of the position occupied during the afternoon of the 27th:

> When I reached the new CP (5384) [Miller had not accompanied Faith when he and his party reconnoitered it earlier], I found the battalion position to be on high ground which stretched around in a huge horseshoe, the open end of which was generally southwest of the Bn CP. In order to cover this ground, the battalion was extended beyond its capabilities, but the one road leading north was adequately covered. Able Company on the north and west (left) end of the horseshoe was well disposed to block the road. Charley Company extended east from the right flank of Able Company, along the northern side of the horseshoe to its bend. Baker Company closed off the bend and back along the southern leg to the road [B Company did not extend to the road]. Dog Company [Heavy Weapons], HQ Company, and the Battalion HQ were in a deep ravine immediately behind Able and Charley Companies. An ammunition dump also was located in the ravine. This ravine was crowded. The battalion was thinly spread, but the position had excellent control of the ground and the key road to the north.[4]

To expand on Miller's description of the position, one can confirm that Faith's CP was in a Korean house just northeast of the road where it bent around a finger ridge on the south side of the deep ravine that ran down from the high ground to the east. Captain Erwin B. Bigger's D Company CP and his 81-mm mortars were across the road west of Faith's CP. After bending around the nose of ground just south of Faith's and Bigger's CP positions, the road turned sharply to the right. It climbed almost due north about half a mile to the front-line position of A Company, which held a commanding position west of the road at the point where it passed through a saddle. It then dropped north down the side of a ridgeline to a draw that met the reservoir.

Across the road at the saddle, on ground higher than that of the right flank of A Company, C Company went into position. There was a physical gap between the two companies at the road, but both commanded it from their elevation and had visual control of the road north. Lieutenant Mortrude's 3rd Platoon held the left flank of C Company near the road and opposite A Company. He describes how his platoon established its position: "Detrucked on road behind ridgeline pass to our front. Proceeded to occupy Marine prepared forward slope positions to right of road through pass. Tied in by fire with Co. A CP group on lower ground across road. Heavy ma-

An aerial view, photographed November 1, 1950, looking north across the frozen Pungnyuri-gang Inlet (bottom center), where the 3rd Battalion, 31st Infantry, and the two A and B Battery 105-mm howitzers of the 57th FA Battalion went into bivouac perimeter on November 27, 1950. The road and the narrow-gauge railroad can be seen on the south (right) side of the inlet. The vehicular road crosses the inlet at a bridge and causeway at the east end of the inlet, and the road then runs west along the north side of the inlet and turns north around a large hill mass (Hill 1324) to the 1st Battalion, 32nd Infantry, position (Hill 1316). At the left center the road can be seen crossing the shallow saddle pass in the 1st Battalion position. Hill 1475 is to the upper right, covered with snow. Near the bottom center is Hill 1250, and in the lower right is Hill 1456. US Army photograph SC 363264.

chine guns on my right flank. Located my own platoon CP in excellently prepared, former Marine bunker with overhead cover and good view to front, flanks, and rear."[5] Telephone communication was established between Mortrude's CP and battalion just as darkness came. The temperature began to drop sharply. Mortrude allowed his men to build squad warming fires in pits on the rear slope behind the front lines. But both Captain Seever, C Company commander, and battalion headquarters telephoned to tell him to extinguish the fires.

Mortrude subsequently walked along the platoon line at intervals to see that security was in effect and that his men were not allowing their feet to freeze. He found that the Korean augmentation troops (KATUSA) were in their usual "ostrich" posture. Mortrude pulled some of the men from their holes and ordered them to walk with him until their circulation was restored. When he returned to his platoon CP, he examined his weapon and had difficulty loading and unloading it. There was icing of the bolt, which made operation sluggish or ineffective, interfering with automatic and semi-automatic fire. Icing proved to be a major problem throughout the operation.

The battalion front line was about 2 miles long, with C Company holding the longest company sector from a point east of the road along the ridge-line that ran uphill northwest to southeast toward the summit of Hill 1470, the boundary with B Company. B Company's line turned at a right angle down another spur ridge that ran southwest toward the road. There is some difference of opinion among survivors about just where the right flank of B Company's line ended, but certainly it did not extend to the road by way of Hill 1324. I believe that B Company did not extend its line down the desirable spur ridge leading to Hill 1324 because of a lack of men for such a defense line. Instead it came down a lower spur ridge from the high ground at its left flank some distance north and northwest of Hill 1324. Even so, it did not reach the road. The shore of the reservoir lay about 1½ miles west of the battalion CP.

The weakest place on the perimeter was at its highest ground, at the boundary of C and B companies, where a spur ridge from a still higher peak eastward provided a good approach downhill to it.[6]

At Chosin a Marine battalion had about 30 percent greater strength than an Army infantry battalion, thus making the position far more manageable for the Marines than for Faith's Army battalion.

The Enemy at Chosin:
What Was Known —
The Unknown

In the three weeks before the 31st RCT hurriedly assembled on the east side of Chosin Reservoir, it had become known throughout X Corps that the Chinese 42nd Army with three divisions, the 124th, 125th, and 126th, had crossed from Manchuria into North Korea and was in the Chosin Reservoir area. This army was an element of the XIII Army Group from Lin Piao's famous Fourth Field Army. Its mission in October and the first half of November, 1950, had been to provide left-flank security for the Chinese XIII Army Group, which had attacked Eighth Army north of the Chongchon River.

As related earlier, the ROK 23rd Regiment and the 7th Marine Regiment had encountered the CCF 124th Division in the vicinity of Sudong, on the road from the reservoir to the coast at Hungnam, and in hard fighting had driven it back north to the foot of Funchilin Pass. From there the remnants of the Chinese division had withdrawn to Hagaru-ri.

At the same time the 126th Division had moved eastward toward the Fusen Reservoir, apparently to discover the degree of hydro development there. One of its regiments had had several minor skirmishes with the 3rd Battalion, 31st Infantry, on the east side of the reservoir. The Chinese regiment had withdrawn without offering major battle. There appears to have been no American contact with the 125th Division. Knowledge of Chinese contact presence in the Chosin area itself came when the 1st Marine Division and, later, the 31st RCT climbed to the reservoir. There the Marines had minor contact with a few members of the 125th Division and some unidentified Chinese. Knowledge, therefore, was limited to the presence of the three divisions of the Chinese 42nd Army, only two of them now considered to be combat-effective. The Marines believed that there was some evidence that the 42nd Army might have withdrawn from the Chosin area or was in the act of doing so.

On November 22 patrols from the 1st Marine Division made contact with a new Chinese formation in skirmishes west of Hagaru-ri. The formation was identified as the Chinese 89th Division, but its small contact forces showed no inclination to fight. These events led to an optimistic view in X Corps.

A significant incident occurred on November 26. About 4:00 P.M. two miles southwest of Yudam-ni three Chinese soldiers carrying leaflets came up to a patrol of the 7th Marines and surrendered to it. Five days earlier, November 21, they had deserted from the Chinese 60th Division, 20th Army, Third Field Army. They said that other divisions in the 20th Army were the 58th and the 59th. They had crossed the Yalu River with their division at Manpojin on November 11 and had reached Yudam-ni on November 20– 21. The 20th Army's mission, they said, was to cut the Marines' MSR southeast of Yudam-ni after two American regiments had passed their own position west of the town. Their attack was to be launched only at night. The order of march of the 20th Army to preassigned positions after it reached Yudam-ni was the 60th, the 59th, and the 58th divisions. Already, then, according to their story, three new Chinese divisions were in position south and east of Yudam-ni waiting to cut off the 1st Marine Division. Korean civilians told Marine interrogators of recent Chinese troop movements after dark that tended to corroborate this story.[1] With soldiers from the 89th Division already identified, this information indicated that four divisions from the CCF 20th Army were now in the reservoir area. This startling information was transmitted to X Corps on the afternoon of the 26th, but there is no evidence that it was given to the army units on the east side of Chosin.

One of the curious things throughout the Chosin Reservoir operations was the lack of communication between the 1st Marine Division and the Army's 31st RCT. Their radios did not net on the same channels, and neither could communicate with the other. An exception was the ability of Capt. Edward P. Stamford, the forward air controller (FAC) with Faith's battalion, to communicate with the Air Control Center at Hagaru-ri through relay by Corsair fighter pilots overhead. Through them he could inform the Control Center at Hagaru-ri of the need for Marine fighter planes for close ground support.

On this Sunday, November 26, when X Corps received news that three new Chinese divisions were already below Yudam-ni, General Almond at X Corps also had disturbing news from the Eighth Army front to the west. He passed it on to Maj. Gen. Oliver Smith at the 1st Marine Division Headquarters. Large Chinese formations had hit hard the right, or east, flank of Eighth Army during the night of November 25–26, routing the ROK II Corps. Unfortunately, none of this information reached the 31st RCT that day or the next.

In contrast to the assumptions and optimistic complacency that characterized the X Corps command in general, what was the reality?

The few small groups of enemy the 5th Marines had seen on the east side of the reservoir before the arrival there of much of the 31st RCT (–) were in fact the advance scouting parties of the Chinese 80th Division of the CCF 27th Army, IX Army Group, Third Field Army. Eight Chinese divisions of the IX Army Group had crossed into Korea and were hidden at various points around and below the reservoir. Another four divisions were held in reserve at the Yalu River in the vicinity of Linchiang. Aerial reconnaissance had discovered neither the crossing of these divisions nor their movements at night to the reservoir area, where they went into preplanned positions to await the arrival of X Corps troops. The Chinese meant to spring the trap when the Marines had concentrated at Yudam-ni and had begun their push west toward Mupyong-ni. The areas west and south of Yudam-ni and eastward toward Hagaru-ri were the focal points of Chinese concentration. One or more divisions were to move down the east side of the reservoir and attack Hagaru-ri from that side.[2]

In the People's Liberation Army the Third Field Army was considered second only to Lin Piao's Fourth Field Army in combat efficiency. The 20th and 27th armies of the IX Army Group were among its most noted for mobility. Most of their equipment was of Japanese origin, but much was American, obtained when the Nationalist divisions of Chiang Kai-shek surrendered to the Communists at the end of the Chinese Civil War in 1949.

General Sung Shih-lun commanded the IX Army Group. Born in 1910, Sung was about 40 years old in 1950 when his troops confronted the 1st Marine Division and the 31st RCT at Chosin. He had commanded troops in battle since he was 17 years old. In the Long March from Kiangsi Province to Yenan in 1934–35 he had commanded a regiment. In 1949, after the final defeat of the Nationalist forces in the Chinese Civil War, Sung became garrison commander of the Shanghai-Wusung area. Quick-tempered, he was nevertheless considered a good tactician and a master of guerrilla warfare. His bravery in battle was unquestioned—he had been tested many times. On occasion he had served as commander of the Third Field Army.

Much of Sung's IX Army Group entered Korea from Manchuria between November 15 and 20. Counted in his strength were former Nationalist divisions which brought their American weapons with them, with the Thompson submachine gun prominent. When Sung entered Korea, the 42nd Army left the Chosin area and moved toward Tokchon to join its parent organization, the XIII Army Group of the Fourth Field Army, which was then massing against the US Eighth Army. Sung then took over responsibility for the Chosin Reservoir area. He had a double mission: provide east-flank protection to the larger XIII Army Group in the west that was to attack Eighth Army and, more important, destroy the 1st Marine Division and any other troops then assembling in the Chosin area.[3]

Nearly all these Chinese soldiers came from the Chinese province of Shantung and were farmers or sons of farmers. Shantung lies on the west side of the Yellow Sea on the Chinese coast, opposite the southern tip of Korea and Kyushu. The climate there is relatively mild, like that of Illinois in the United States, and these soldiers were not inured to the harsh winters of northern Korea, as were many of the XIII Army Group soldiers, who were natives of Manchuria.

In the fighting at Chosin Reservoir the combat effectiveness of the 27th Army was easily the best. It attacked the 1st Marine Division at Yudam-ni on the west side of the reservoir and the 31st RCT on the east side of the reservoir in the initial surprise attacks on the night of November 27. The 20th Army was next in combat effectiveness. It cut the American MSR at numerous places south of Yudam-ni and Hagaru-ri and fought most of the battles along that road south to the coast. The 26th Army was the least effective, most of its participation being near Koto-ri.

General Lui Fe, commanding the CCF 20th Army, led the vanguard into Korea. The 20th Army began leaving Shantung Province by rail on November 6, 1950 and closed into Chian, Manchuria, by November 10. It crossed the pontoon bridge over the Yalu River, moved the 6 miles northeast to Manpojin, and there entrained for the next leg of the journey. The trains moved only at night, remaining hidden in tunnels during the daytime. The railroad ran 40 miles southeast of Manpojin at Kanggje, an important road-

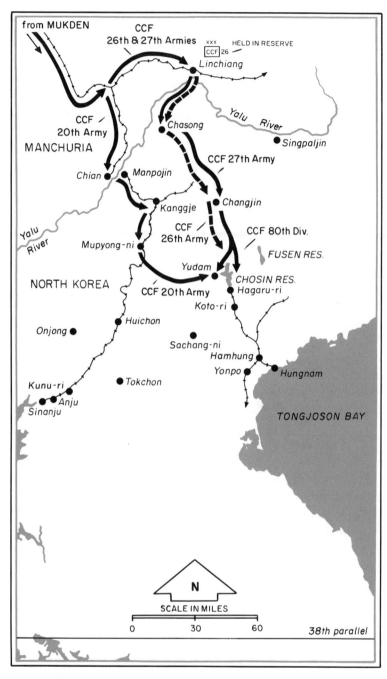

MAP 5. Chinese Communist forces movement to Chosin Reservoir, November 15–20, 1950.

junction center, and from there another 28 miles southwest to Mupyong-ni. There the 20th Army left the rail lines and marched along the narrow, twisting dirt road that led eastward 55 miles to Yudam-ni, on the western side of Chosin Reservoir. It closed there between November 13 and 15, five days after crossing the Yalu, and relieved the 42nd Army of responsibility for the Chosin area. Except for a few small groups, the 20th Army remained effectively concealed until November 27.

The 26th Army left Tenghsien, Shantung Province, by train beginning on November 1, and by November 5 it had closed on Linchiang, Manchuria. Sung held it there in IX Army Group reserve until about the end of November. When it became apparent that the 20th and 27th armies were not going to defeat the X Corps troops and destroy them in the reservoir area, he belatedly started the 26th Army south. Two divisions arrived in the Chosin area in time to join efforts to cut off the 1st Marine Division and 7th Division troops before they reached the Hungnam Perimeter at the coast.[4]

The 27th Army was directly involved with the 31st RCT in the battles on the east side of Chosin Reservoir. This army was capable of long, sustained marches and had distinguished itself in China in attacks against fortified places. It had behind it a long string of battles in the Chinese Civil War, including the battle for Shanghai.

On October 25, 1950, the 80th Division and the rest of the 27th Army began a rail movement to Linchiang on the Yalu River. It arrived there on November 1. The 79th and 80th divisions immediately crossed the river and headed for the Chosin Reservoir. The 27th Army was to make the frontal attack on the X Corps troops. In its plan of attack on the 1st Marine Division at the reservoir the 27th Army was to divide its forces in a pincer movement that would close at Hagaru-ri. Its 79th Division was to move down the west side of the reservoir and attack Yudam-ni. The 80th Division was to move down the east side of the reservoir and simultaneously attack Hagaru-ri from that side.

It appears that the CCF 80th Division conducted most if not all of the operations against the 31st RCT east of Chosin. It is not certain that the entire division was engaged in these actions, nor is it certain that other enemy formations were not engaged there.[5]

The movements and locations of the 81st and 90th divisions of the 27th Army during the Chosin battles remain something of a mystery. They were somewhere in the vicinity of the reservoir, apparently at first being held in reserve. There are no recorded battle contacts with them until after the X Corps troops at Chosin had withdrawn into the Hungnam Perimeter. It is possible, however, that elements of these divisions took part in the battles on East Hill at Hagaru-ri in early December and were not identified. The 79th and 80th divisions were the most effective of all Chinese units engaged.[6]

On the afternoon of November 27, after the 5th Marines had started their attack west from Yudam-ni, a large Marine patrol met a company-size Chinese force and fought a skirmish with it north of Yudam-ni. Papers taken from one of the enemy dead identified the group as part of the CCF 79th Division.[7] Thus during the 27th this crack division was moving into place just north of Yudam-ni. The US Army troops on the east side of the reservoir seem never to have identified the 80th Division as being in their vicinity. Further, the 31st RCT never identified this enemy division during the battles there. It took some Chinese prisoners but apparently had neither the time nor the facilities for extensive interrogation of them. Surviving records of the 31st RCT or personal recollections of participants do not identify the enemy units encountered there—only that they were Chinese.

When the 2nd Battalion, 5th Marines, headed west on the dirt road toward Mupyong-ni on the morning of November 27, it did not get far. Chinese hidden in the hills manned previously dug positions on the high ground flanking the road and with the use of numerous physical roadblocks all but halted the battalion in its tracks. By the end of the day the 5th Marines had advanced only two miles. They went into a defensive position astride the road and on surrounding hills late in the afternoon, not knowing what the night would bring. The 31st RCT had not yet concentrated on the east side of the reservoir and was unable to start its attack that day. It expected to do so the next morning.

The First Night—
November 27–28

Unlucky in many things, the 1st Battalion, 32nd Infantry, had good fortune during the evening of November 27 in the return of Maj. Robert E. Jones, its adjutant. He had left the battalion bivouac at "Happy Valley" on the morning of November 23 with an advance party to establish an assembly area for the battalion in the 7th Division area in the Pungsan or Pukchong areas for future operations near the Yalu River. Jones had reached the 17th Infantry area near the Yalu before he learned that the battalion's mission had been changed and that he had to hurry back.

Early in the morning of November 27, Jones left the 7th Division's rear CP at Pukchong in a 2½-ton truck loaded with a two weeks' accumulation of mail and some early Christmas packages, heading for Chosin. He reached Hudong-ni and in a brief stop there found General Hodes and Colonel MacLean conversing in the schoolhouse. Jones asked for the location of the 1st Battalion and then continued on his way, stopping briefly at the 31st Heavy Mortar position.[1]

About 8:30 P.M., soon after Jones's arrival at the CP, a liaison officer from Colonel MacLean's forward CP brought an operations order directing the battalion to attack at dawn toward Kalchon-ni. At 9:30 P.M., Faith gave his company commanders orders concerning the battalion advance the next morning.[2]

Jones was an "old-timer" in the battalion and the regiment. He had been with both since the early days of the 32nd Regiment's reorganization and had come to it from the 11th Airborne Division when the latter returned to the United States from Japan in 1949. Most of the time he had commanded C Company in the battalion.

Capt. (later Col.) Robert E. Jones in Japan, 1950. Photograph courtesy of Colonel Jones.

A native of Poyner, Texas, Jones graduated from New Mexico State College in May, 1939, and received an ROTC commission as second lieutenant of infantry. He entered active duty in the army on August 21, 1940. He began airborne training at Fort Benning in 1942, graduating from its Parachute School in May. A little more than a year later he was in the European Theater as a member of the 502nd Parachute Regiment of the 101st Airborne Division. He jumped with his division in September, 1944, at Arnhem, Holland, in that ill-fated operation. Injured, he was evacuated to the United States.

In May, 1948, Jones was sent to Japan as S-3, 3rd Battalion, 511th Parachute Infantry, 11th Airborne Division. When the division returned to Fort Campbell, Kentucky, in March, 1949, Jones stayed behind and became commanding officer of C Company, 32nd Infantry. In the battle for Seoul, following the Inchon Landing in September, 1950, when his company was driving the enemy from a key hill, a .30-caliber machine-gun bullet hit him over the heart. What might have been a fatal wound was converted to a minor one when the slug hit the steel button on his left breast pocket and then passed through a 50-page notebook and a 20-page company roster before a rib stopped it.[3] In October, 1950, Jones was promoted to major, and Faith at once made him his adjutant and S-1. Jones was 32 years old at Chosin.

Running through the story of the 31st RCT at Chosin is the dark thread of the KATUSA. These were young men who were picked up on the streets of South Korean cities and towns by President Syngman Rhee's impressment agents and without any military training turned over by the thousands to US Army authorities to fill depleted ranks of American units. This practice was at its peak in the summer of 1950 when the North Koreans seemed on the verge of breaking through the Naktong Perimeter in the south of the peninsula. The 7th Division had been "cannibalized" of infantry junior officers, noncommissioned officers, and experienced riflemen to fill the ranks of the three American divisions fighting in Korea. In a sense the 7th Division was a hollow shell in Japan when the Inchon Landing was being planned. It was essential to bring the division up to some level of strength. In addition to replacements coming from the United States, the 7th Infantry Division received in Japan approximately 8,600 KATUSA, more than any other American division. They were distributed to every unit.

At that time the 1st Battalion, 32nd Infantry, at Camp McNair received 500 KATUSA. By the time the battalion reached Chosin Reservoir, the number was down to about 300. Each of its three rifle companies had 45

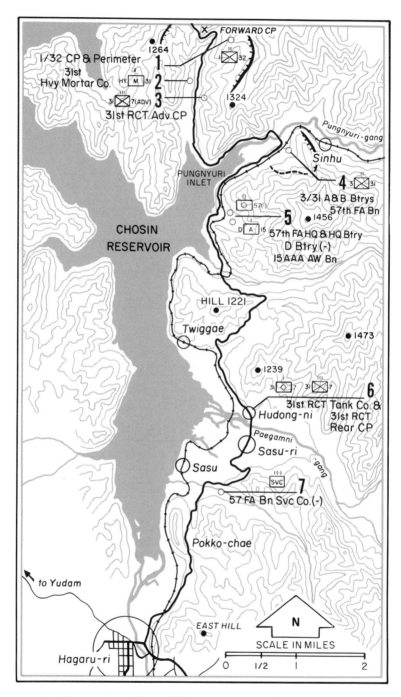

MAP 6. The seven positions of the 31st RCT on the evening of November 27, 1950.

to 50 assigned South Koreans, or ROKs, as they were generally called. They constituted about one-fourth of a company's numerical strength. The American squad leaders could rarely communicate satisfactorily with their ROK soldiers. In the action east of Chosin they were frequently a handicap to the Americans rather than a help. Later in the war, when the South Koreans were properly trained and supported, they proved to be good soldiers. That was not the case at the Chosin Reservoir. This unsatisfactory situation must be kept in mind constantly in evaluating the problems Americans had in meeting the daily and nightly demands on all their energies and courage.

In contrast to the Army units at Chosin, the overstrength 1st Marine Division, fighting under similar conditions at Chosin, had almost no KATUSA, and the few they had served as interpreters. On November 24, 1950, the 1st Marine Division had an assigned strength of 25,323 men, with only 110 attached South Korean interpreters, for a total strength of 25,433 men. At the same time the 7th Division had a strength of 16,001 men, including 6,794 assigned South Koreans, more than a third of its foxhole strength.[4]

Late in the afternoon of November 27, Lieutenant Colonel Faith ordered Capt. Edward P. Stamford, USMC, the forward air controller with the battalion, to move his Tactical Air Control Party (TACP) to A Company's position so that he would be in a position to run air support, if needed, for the battalion attack in the morning. A Company held the left flank of the battalion perimeter on the high ground of Hill 1316 and west of the road where it passed through a saddle between Hill 1316 and east of the road higher ground climbing eastward. Stamford's stay overnight with A Company on the evening of the 27th imposed on him duties no one expected. He had been attached to the 1st Battalion, 32nd Infantry, together with his Marine TACP of four enlisted men, just as the battalion was loading out in Japan for the Inchon Landing. At that time the Navy had lent him to the Army battalion as a forward air controller for the landing operation. He served with the battalion during the battle for Seoul and remained attached to it when the division moved to northeast Korea.

Stamford was one of the many Marine enlisted pilots who received commissions in World War II. Stamford received his in September, 1943, and the next month he went to the South Pacific, serving first as a second lieutenant in antisubmarine search. Later he was a dive-bomber pilot in the Solomon Islands, Green Island, and other South Pacific combat areas. In 1944 he returned to the United States, where he attended the 13-week course at the Marine Air–Infantry School at Quantico, Virginia. This training

Capt. (later Maj.) Edward P. Stamford, US Marine Corps, Fort Lewis, Washington, late September, 1949. Stamford was forward air controller with the 1st Battalion, 32nd Infantry, and Task Force Faith at Chosin Reservoir in 1950. Photograph courtesy of Major Stamford.

course was important for Stamford in his later duties as a forward controller. It greatly increased his competence in that role because it gave him an understanding of infantry tactics and problems, and he was better able to act as liaison between the fighter and bomber pilots overhead and the infantry on the ground. He was the communication link between the two. This training also qualified him for performance as an infantryman.

In 1950, Stamford was in Japan helping develop the Air Naval Gunfire Liaison Company (Anglico) teams that were to direct naval gunfire in support of ground troops making a landing and establishing a beachhead. The Marine Corps was the first of the services to develop this technique, but the Army wanted the same capability. That summer in Japan, Stamford's Forward Air Controller Anglico Team trained nine teams from the Fifth Air Force for use by the 7th Infantry Division battalions in the Inchon Landing. Each such team had one officer and three enlisted men. Two of the enlisted men were radio operators; the third was a technician. The TACP equipment was mounted on a jeep, but comparable equipment could be placed on a pack board and carried on foot. In the loading out of the 7th Infantry Division in Japan, Stamford's party was attached by chance to the 1st Battalion, 32nd Infantry. He met the battalion commander for the first time when he boarded the transport. It should be noted that Stamford's TACP with the battalion consisted of four men: one officer (himself—now a captain) and three enlisted men.

Stamford was powerfully built, about 5 feet, 10 inches tall, compact, with a barrel-shaped chest, heavily muscled legs and arms, and big hands. He was an experienced, practical, cool operator at all times. He knew his business. There was never any question that he would do his duty as a soldier.[5]

Two months after the Chosin Reservoir action Stamford wrote of the situation he found at A Company when he joined it on the evening of November 27:

> Able Company's CP was protected by company headquarters personnel and the platoons were from the left in the order of 1st, 3rd, and 2nd. The 2nd was bent back to the rear on a spur. I was given two bunkers for myself and my 4 men. Captain Ed Scullion, Able Company commander, ordered me to use the bunker between the CP and the right flank of the 1st Platoon. I was given an SCR 300 [infantry company radio] to be in contact with him. I moved into the bunker with 2 of my men and put the other 2 in the bunker about 50 yards to the rear and bedded down for the night, keeping a radio watch. The end of the bunker to the north [the one Stamford occupied]

Members of Captain Stamford's TACP with the 1st Battalion, 32nd Infantry, and Task Force Faith. *From left:* Cpl. Myron J. Smith, Pfc. Wendell P. Shaffer, and Pfc. Billy E. Johnson, all US Marines. Photograph courtesy of Major Stamford.

had a soldier on watch and the south end was covered with a poncho to
keep the snow out.[6]

Behind Stamford's bunker and slightly east of it Scullion had his company command bunker. It was behind the crest (south) of Hill 1316, near
the center of the A Company line. At the right of Stamford's bunker the
3rd Platoon held the center of the company line in an arc around the military crest of Hill 1316. A spur ridge dropped southeast from this hill, angling
into the road at the saddle. The 2nd Platoon held this spur ridge and had
observation of the road approaching from the north. Neither A Company
nor C Company, opposite A Company on the east side of the saddle, had
a block on the road.

The 1st Platoon of A Company formed the western flank of the 1st Battalion. Beyond it westward to the reservoir the continuing steep slope of
Hill 1316 was unoccupied.

Beginning at the 1,200-meter contour line elevation behind the front line
at Hill 1316, a deep draw ran almost due south. The A Company 60-mm
mortars were placed in this draw. A Company's position was in the shape
of an uneven triangle, its western side longer than its eastern side, and the
northern apex a rounded arc at the crest of Hill 1316. There was no physical
contact between A and C companies where the road ran through the saddle
between them.

Shortly before 11:00 P.M. men at the battalion CP heard scattered rifle
fire in the A Company position. At first this did not cause any great concern
for it was common for ROK soldiers attached to the battalion to fire at
imaginary enemies after dark, and sometimes their ruckus developed into
what sounded like a fire fight before it could be stopped.

Actually, however, Chinese soldiers had appeared. The first group spotted in front of the A Company perimeter carried shovels. One of the Chinese soldiers was captured; the others scattered. Enemy patrols probed the
company front for the next hour. Then, just after midnight, after their reconnaissance was apparently completed, the Chinese struck. This was part
of a coordinated attack that had begun several hours earlier against the 1st
Marine Division at Yudam-ni, on the west side of the reservoir.

The Chinese came from the north, marching straight up the road against
A Company. Either at the saddle or just south of it they veered to their
right, west of the road, and immediately either penetrated or moved around
the right flank of the 2nd Platoon on the spur ridge that paralleled the road

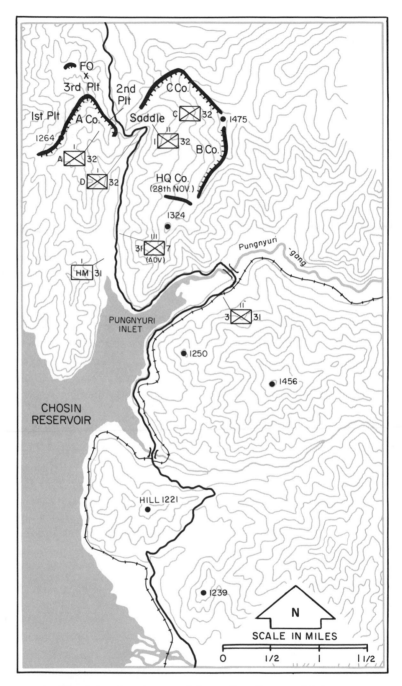

MAP 7. The forward perimeter of the 1st Battalion, 32nd Infantry, on the night of November 27–28, 1950.

at that point. This put the Chinese behind the company CP, in the vicinity of the draw where 60-mm mortars were positioned.

This first enemy attack accomplished two things. Some of the Chinese turned back in a hairpin movement against the center of A Company from its rear. That put them in the area of the CP and behind the 3rd Platoon on the high ground of Hill 1316, in the center of the company line, before anyone knew of their presence. Other Chinese turned sharply south after the penetration and went for the mortars in the draw. Sergeant James J. Freund of the mortar squad said later that the Chinese marched up the hill and quickly penetrated A Company to the mortar position behind the front line. The mortarmen, surprised, gave way and abandoned their weapons.[7]

Just behind the left center of the company line Stamford awoke sometime after midnight to the sound of shots and heard Scullion shouting. Before he could get up, he heard voices chattering outside his bunker. The poncho at the back end was pulled aside, and Stamford saw a fur-rimmed face in the moonlight. He fired at it from a sitting position, but the Chinese soldier had already dropped a grenade inside the bunker, which blew up on the sleeping bag between Stamford's feet. Fragments wounded one of the two men with him, but he was untouched. Stamford fired more rounds through the poncho. Enemy rifle fire then hit the bunker, some shots coming down from the top through cracks in the log roof. He and his two men moved from the bunker into the escape slit trench at the back end and remained hidden there for a few minutes. One of A Company's machine guns now opened up and swept a spray of bullets across the top of the bunker, clearing it of Chinese soldiers. Stamford climbed out of the slit trench.

He at once began assembling the scattered men in his vicinity into a defense. Scullion, whose shouts had helped awaken him, lay dead nearby, shot down only a few yards from his CP bunker when he hurried out to learn what was happening. Stamford gathered enough men to hold the ground immediately around the command bunker. He then moved off to the 1st Platoon position on the left to learn the situation there. He found that Lt. Raymond C. Dentchfield, the platoon leader, had been wounded. Stamford asked for 1st Lt. Cecil Smith, the company executive officer, and was told that he was directing the troops near the CP.

First Lieutenant Carlos J. Ortenzi, A Company mortar officer, came up to Stamford and informed him that as the next senior man he would have to take the company. Stamford sent one of his Marine TACP helpers to obtain reports on the situation of the other platoons and placed Smith in charge of the 1st Platoon. Stamford soon had reports that the enemy had thus far hit A Company only in the vicinity of the 3rd Platoon, the company CP, and had overrun the mortars.

He moved two squads of the 1st Platoon from the left to the right flank to strengthen the 2nd Platoon there. He left Corporal Smith of his TACP with the one remaining squad at the 1st Platoon line to act as a getaway man to warn him in case the enemy attacked there. He then set about searching out and destroying enemy in the CP area. He accomplished this without much trouble, and with his defense now organized, he repulsed other attempts to overrun the company position.

After the initial penetration, enemy pressure developed frontally on the 3rd Platoon in the center of the line, but this was repulsed. Near dawn the Chinese discovered that the 1st Platoon had shifted most of its men to the right flank, and they began a buildup on the left for an attack there. Stamford learned of this in time to move the two squads of the 1st Platoon and a machine-gun section back to their original positions and repelled attacks there, which never gained much strength.[8]

Meanwhile, Lieutenant Ortenzi had rallied his mortarmen behind the line and counterattacked the Chinese at their overrun mortar position. In protracted fighting behind the line Ortenzi and his men inflicted heavy casualties on them and halted further penetration. Their stout defense behind the center of the line prevented Chinese penetration southward to the battalion CP, Captain Bigger's D Company CP, the 81-mm mortars, and possibly farther to Captain Cody's heavy mortars, which were wholly outside and south of the 1st Battalion perimeter.

Stamford could see from his place near the center of the company line that the Chinese had penetrated about 200 yards behind the front line and had overrun the 60-mm mortars and that a fire fight was in progress behind him. Both telephone lines and radio communications were out between A Company and the battalion CP. Stamford learned later that two wire teams had been lost when Captain Bigger tried to reestablish communication between his 81-mm mortars and the rifle company, a distance of only 600 yards. Without communication the mortars could not give A Company supporting fires. They were, however, able to fire support for both C and B companies during the night.

With the position reestablished, Stamford gave orders to the company to hold precisely where it was because if the Chinese broke through they could enlarge the penetration south up the road to the battalion CP and reach the 81-mm mortars. He had to reduce the company's rate of fire because it was expending too much ammunition – a common fault – and he feared that it would run short before daylight. Stamford also strengthened his position by setting up two machine guns to cover a shallow draw the enemy was using to gain a new entrance to the perimeter. A 57-mm recoilless rifle fired on an enemy assembly area and did much to prevent the Chinese from mounting a successful attack from that point.

In discussions with me, Stamford expressed strong views about how the Chinese accomplished their initial surprise penetration of A Company. He believed that they infiltrated through the line because of the men's lack of alertness. He believed that the Chinese caught the soldiers dozing in their foxholes and simply bypassed or overran some positions before they were discovered. Stamford heard no shooting in front of his own position before the Chinese overran his bunker, which was slightly behind the right flank of the 1st Platoon. The enemy had reached Scullion's CP before there was any general alarm. The lack of alertness in the outposts and in the front line was, Stamford said, "one fault that was common to all the units I came in contact with. It was a continual gripe of all officers even while we were in the Seoul area. They'd check their lines and were scared to walk through them because they knew the men were asleep. If they kicked them to wake them up, they were scared of being shot, though many of them did on their rounds of the lines arouse at least one man in each [two- or three-man] foxhole. They threatened the men, . . . and still they dozed in their holes when they should have been watchful."[9]

In his overnight impromptu command of A Company, Stamford had performed like a veteran infantry officer. After daylight Major Miller, the battalion executive officer, came up to A Company and relieved Stamford, placing Lieutenant Smith in command. Stamford was needed as the FAC at battalion headquarters.

Telling of his night's experience, Stamford had some comments about the men of A Company. He said that there was a lot of difficulty keeping the ROK soldiers on the line. Most of them had no stomach for facing the enemy. He added, "The company was easy to handle because the officers and men respected the position I had and did an excellent job in carrying out my orders." He thought that the company's casualties were light considering the number of enemy who came against it.[10]

Meanwhile, at the battalion CP the Chinese surprise attack had started off on an incongruous note. When the first scattered shots were heard in the A Company area, Faith called for Captain Bigger of D Company to come to his CP at once. Faith said to him, "Do you suppose those ROKs are firing at each other again?" Faith had had no word yet of a CCF attack. But he added, "I have had a garbled report that something has happened to Ed Scullion — that maybe he has been killed." Faith then turned to Capt. Robert F. Haynes, the battalion assistant S-3, and said to him, "You had better go up there to A Company and see what the situation is." Bigger quickly offered to go with Haynes, saying, "I know the troop situation up there, and I want to check on my heavy weapons with the company."[11]

Bigger and Haynes started up the road toward A Company. Neither they nor those back at the battalion CP were yet thinking of a CCF attack. Moving around at night near the front line was a common concern of officers in the battalion, for their own men or the South Koreans might mistakenly fire on them.

As Bigger and Haynes climbed the hill and approached A Company, they were suddenly challenged by a dark figure dressed in a parka, lying on the road and facing away from them. They did not understand the challenge, but this would not be uncommon if it came from a South Korean. It sounded to Bigger like "Eeeya, eeya." Thinking that the prone figure was a South Korean, they replied with the countersign. The figure began to turn, and Bigger told him that they were American soldiers, but the figure began to raise a rifle. Bigger alerted Haynes, and they dived for the ditch as the unknown person fired. Bigger heard the wind go out of Haynes and heard him groan as he fell into the ditch.

Bigger moved to his side to learn how badly he was wounded. As he reached him, he saw that the man who had fired the shot was coming toward him. He tried to work the bolt of his carbine, but it was frozen. He got to his feet to escape, but before he could move, two grenades exploded near him, one partly deafening him. Fortunately, they were weak concussion grenades and did no other damage. Bigger now saw three other Chinese on the road embankment coming toward him. He dashed into the brush alongside the road and escaped to the battalion CP, where he reported the incident.[12] This encounter occurred near the 60-mm mortar position which the Chinese had just overrun.

After Bigger's report to Faith there was no longer any doubt that Chinese troops were behind A Company's front. A mess sergeant named Casey overheard Bigger reporting to Faith. A little later, entirely on his own initiative, he gathered together a few men from the headquarters area and started up the road to rescue Haynes. More confusion resulted when members of Casey's party returned to the CP and reported that Casey had been killed, that Chinese were on the road, and that they had been unable to reach Haynes.

Bigger confirms that a mess sergeant, apparently Casey, did go up the road in an effort to reach Haynes but that he was not killed because he talked with him the next day, and the sergeant told him that they had not been able to bring Haynes into the CP until after daylight. Haynes was then barely alive. He had been shot through the stomach and also had bayonet wounds. Captain Raymond Vaudreaux, battalion S-4, a former candidate for priesthood in the Roman Catholic church, performed last rites for Haynes in the CP just before he died from his wounds and exposure.[13]

Comprehension of what was happening seemed to come slowly to Faith's CP on the night of November 27–28. The report that the Chinese were behind A Company's front line and the encounter of Bigger and Haynes with some of them on the road did not bring them to an understanding of the situation. Bigger commented: "After I returned to the Bn CP we were still trying to piece together what was happening. As I remember, Col. Faith was still planning an attack of sorts the next morning. We couldn't understand why we could not get the artillery support we needed—we had not yet, as far as I know—been informed that the 31st was under attack. One minute we were planning an attack—the next, we were fighting for our lives in a situation where we knew little of what had hit us."[14]

When enemy action started in A Company's position, 1st Lt. Hugh R. May, the battalion transportation officer in Headquarters Company, was in the ravine below the road, about 100 yards from the battalion CP. He reported to Faith, who asked him to stand by. A little later Faith instructed him to check CP security. He and 1st Lt. Henry Moore, the Pioneer and Ammunition (P&A) Platoon, Headquarters Company, established internal security and placed machine guns on both sides of the road, one gun controlling the road north, and other south. After doing this, they and their men helped drive out the Chinese who had penetrated down the road behind A Company.[15] May remained in command of internal security until late in the afternoon of November 28.

While the attack against A Company was in progress, the enemy attacks spread to the rest of the battalion line. One of the first of these tried to penetrate between A and C companies by driving straight up the road between them with a tank and a self-propelled gun. Both the tank and the

First Lt. Raymond Vaudreaux, in Pusan, October, 1950. Photograph courtesy of Maj. Edward P. Stamford.

gun were of North Korean origin, having come northward from the coast, and now were pressed into use by the Chinese. It is the only instance known to me of the use of an enemy tank in the Chosin operation.

These two formidable weapons clanked up the road from the north about 2:00 A.M. on November 28. C Company, on the east side of the pass, had the best view of the road, since it was cut into the ridge slope on the west side of the drainage it followed. Corporal James H. Godfrey, of D Company, had a 75-mm recoilless rifle, and his squad was on a high point east of the pass and had a commanding view of the road from the north. From this vantage point, when he judged the distance right, Godfrey opened fire on the enemy vehicles, destroying them both.

Immediately a force of about 100 Chinese soldiers, who had crawled unseen to within 50 yards of the 75-mm recoilless rifle, rushed from cover and tried to overrun the American squad. Godfrey at once turned the gun on them, killing and wounding many and scattering the others. The survivors fell back in disorder. This successful action was of tremendous value to A Company and helped it reform its lines and hold the left end of the battalion perimeter that night.

Later in the night Godfrey destroyed an enemy mortar with his recoilless rifle and with its firepower helped repel five more enemy attacks on the left side of C Company's line. Captain Bigger, Godfrey's Weapons Company commander, said of him: "He could do more with the 75 RR than anyone I have ever seen. He loved the weapon. Corp. Godfrey actually deserved the CMH. No telling how many Chinese he accounted for."[16]

Another officer of the Heavy Weapons Company made a trip to the same part of C Company's line that night to check on a section of machine guns from his platoon attached to C Company. Lieutenant Campbell, platoon leader of the Heavy Machine Gun Platoon of D Company, went up to Mortrude's 3rd Platoon position on the east side of the pass. He described the position of the heavy weapons there in dominating the road and related approaches from the north: ". . . from a platoon leader's viewpoint, I can still see the position of the forward foxholes on the north side of the military crest positioned logically where you could both look and fire down the noses and draws that were the approaches to the company's defensive position (also the approach down the ridgeline from the east was the most dangerous to us and quite apparently the most advantageous to the CCF.)"[17]

Other parts of the C Company line east of the pass were not defended as successfully against the Chinese. A strong enemy assault hit the middle

First Lt. (later Maj.) Hugh R. May, spring, 1952. Photograph courtesy of
Major May.

of C Company's line. Another 75-mm recoilless rifle and its crew positioned there did not repeat Godfrey's success. The crew fired one shot, disclosing its location, and an assault team of Chinese immediately overran it and dragged the weapon away.

On C Company's right flank Chinese drove away the right-hand squad and seized the highest ground of the perimeter at the boundary of C and B companies. This key point was never regained; the Chinese held it against every counterattack and mortar barrage and several subsequent air strikes. But the Chinese were never able to exploit this success. Nearby, Cpl. Robert L. Armentrout, gunner of a heavy machine gun from D Company attached to C Company for the night, held a position almost by himself. A group of Chinese started up a steep slope toward his gun. He could not depress it enough to bring its fire trajectory on them, but he was strong enough to pick up the gun, hold it in his arms, and fire it directly into the Chinese. He decimated them with this fire. Captain Bigger said that Armentrout was "another of those soldiers that are a credit to the United States Army."[18]

The greatest damage to the battalion perimeter during the night came at its center when the enemy captured the high ground at C Company's east boundary. Captain Dale L. Seever's C Company CP, set up in a Korean hut, came under mortar fire, and he had to displace to a sheltered spot just behind the line. His weapons platoon likewise had to displace to a defiladed position nearby. From there Seever directed his defense, though he had already suffered leg wounds. "Captain Seever," said Col. Wesley J. Curtis, "was the quiet one. He never protested an order or instruction." Seever had been the battalion S-2 earlier, but in the battle for Seoul in September, Faith had become dissatisfied with the officer who had succeeded Jones in command of it, and he moved Seever to command the company.

Bigger's 81-mm mortars continued to give good support to the C Company front, but there was no artillery from the howitzers emplaced at the inlet. Wire communication between the 1st Battalion and the artillery was cut at the beginning of the enemy attack. It was only when radio communication was established about 1:00 A.M. on November 28 that Faith learned that the 57th Field Artillery and the 3rd Battalion, 31st Infantry, were also under heavy attack. The artillerymen were having a desperate time trying to defend their guns; it was out of the question for them to provide support for the 1st Battalion.

Captain Cody's 4.2-inch heavy-mortar fire, which at first had been reli-

able for C and B companies, had begun to miss the mark because the mortars' baseplates were breaking through the marsh crust and shifting. Cody
hurriedly moved the mortars to firmer ground and was able to resume good
support for both battalion perimeters.[19]

Before the fighting began, Colonel MacLean arrived at Faith's forward
perimeter with his driver. When he learned later that the 57th Field Artillery at the inlet was under attack, he was surprised.

A crisis in B Company, which held the perimeter southeast of the battalion CP, came late in the night, about 4:30 A.M. By then the high ground
at the boundary of C and B companies had been lost, and the Chinese occupied it in strength. Lieutenant Kemper, of B Company, was killed during the fighting there, and the situation turned bad so quickly that Captain
Turner ordered 1st Sgt. Richard S. Luna to rouse everyone in B Company,
including Headquarters personnel, and send them forward to the line, holding behind "only a handful" of cooks and command post personnel. Luna
did as ordered. He sat at the company CP with his "handful" until noon.[20]

Before dawn the weather turned colder, and it began to snow. The attack tapered off with daylight. The night battle had been loud and bloody.
Chinese horns and bugles had sounded frequently.

After sunup on the 28th relief came as four Marine Corsairs roared in.
This was just what Stamford and his TACP wanted. He directed them in
a napalm attack on a ridge 300 yards from A Company where a body of
Chinese soldiers had taken cover and also instructed the pilots to hit the
reverse slope of the ridge where the Chinese had set up mortars and were
lobbing shells into the 1st Battalion positions. When the aircraft struck the
ridge, many Chinese ran into the open to escape the napalm. American
machine-gun and small-arms fire cut them down. The Corsairs followed up
their napalm drops with 5-inch rocket and 20-mm strafing fire. This early-
morning air attack eased the situation for the ground troops at that part
of the perimeter.

In Jim Mortrude's 3rd Platoon, C Company position, daylight revealed
a grotesque sight. In his foxhole at the left end of the platoon position, a
ROK soldier sat minus his head. His weapon and ammunition were gone.
The evidence indicated that a Chinese soldier had crawled close to the hole
while the ROK apparently slept or dozed at the beginning of the attack,
shoved a pole charge against his head, and set it off.[21]

A count on the morning of November 28, after daylight and the conclusion of A Company's counterattacks, revealed that A Company had lost

8 men killed, including Captain Scullion, the company commander, and had 20 wounded, including Lieutenant Dentchfield, the 1st Platoon commander. The number of killed and wounded in the rest of the battalion in the night battle is not recorded, but by afternoon about 100 men had passed through the battalion aid station. Casualties were considered heavy. About noon Sergeant Luna went to the Battalion CP from B Company and saw the casualties. Many of the dead had been carried in frozen stiff.

The Night of November 27–28: Inlet Perimeter

It is clear that from the time the Chinese began their attack against the 3rd Battalion, 31st Infantry, and the 57th Field Artillery at the inlet perimeter it was coordinated with the attack against Faith's forward perimeter. The Chinese attack against the inlet came from the east. As it happened, this was the only direction from which the inlet bivouac had any defense. But the Chinese had no trouble penetrating the eastern defenses, such as they were, and very quickly they overran the infantry line. They reached the 3rd Battalion CP and overran it and continued on into the artillery position of A Battery and the truck parking area. The attack at the inlet was far more successful than that at Faith's position—it all but overran the entire inlet position the first night.

No contemporary overlay or sketch of the inlet position and the troop dispositions there for the first night, November 27–28, was ever made. The few verbal descriptions are partial and to a degree speculative. But from some specific information, especially that from Lt. Col. Earle H. Jordan, Jr., then captain and commander of M (Heavy Weapons) Company, 3rd Battalion, and from a contemporary affidavit of Capt. Robert J. Kitz, commanding officer of K Company, we know the general disposition of troop units on the east side of the battalion position. And we know where the two artillery firing batteries of the artillery were located.

I have never been able to locate L Company, the third rifle company of the battalion, though it was heavily engaged during the night within the bivouac area. The company was either near the bridge and causeway across the inlet or farther west, near the artillery batteries. Little or nothing is known of the part the 3rd Battalion CP played in the action during the night, except that it was quickly overrun and almost everyone was either killed or wounded.

Like everyone else, Lieutenant Colonel Reilly, the 3rd Battalion com-

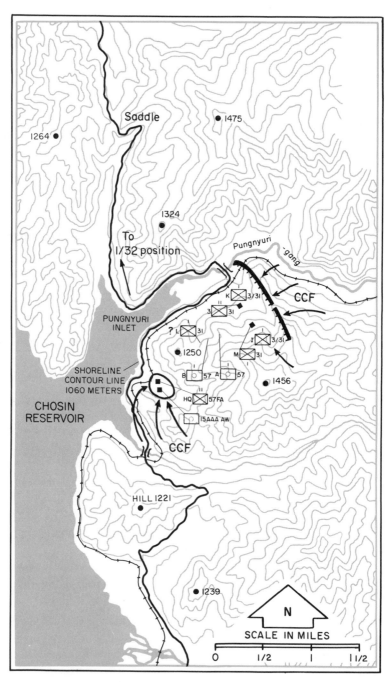

MAP 8. The positions of the 3rd Battalion, 31st Infantry, on the night of November 27–28, 1950.

mander, did not expect an enemy attack. His CP was only a few hundred feet south of the bridge and causeway and perhaps 500 yards west of K Company on the front line eastward. South of Kitz's K Company and higher on the spur ridge, Capt. Albert Marr's I Company held the front line in front of Captain Jordan's M Company. Except for the possibility that Capt. William Etchemendy's L Company may have been on the north of, or possibly behind, K Company near the bridge and causeway, there were no other defensive positions for the inlet bivouac that first night except the individual foxholes of the artillerymen near their howitzers—all of them about 1,000 yards west of the infantry line of K and I companies and the Weapons Company behind I Company. Jordan says that everyone called Captain Marr "Pop" because he seemed rather old for a rifle-company commander. But Pop handled his company that night as well as or better than any other rifle-company commander.

On his way back that evening from Hudong-ni to his own advance CP, and from there on to Faith's forward CP, Colonel MacLean stopped briefly to see Reilly at the inlet. It was then about 8:00 P.M., and no sign of the enemy had yet appeared. Reilly proposed to MacLean that he and his 3rd Battalion move out the next morning, pass through Faith's 1st Battalion, and attack north. MacLean disapproved this proposal and told Reilly to remain in place. This incident shows Reilly's estimate of the situation only hours before he was left for dead in his CP.

At 10:00 P.M., Captain Kitz received a flash alert from the battalion CP to alert K Company and double his guards. Captain Jordan says that he received no alert. It is not known whether the alert extended beyond K Company, nor is it known on what information the alert to K Company was made. The only outpost known to have existed beyond the rifle-company line east of the bivouac was a small roadblock up the valley of the Pungnyuri-gang from the bridge and causeway. After the early alert everything remained quiet for some hours.

The Chinese attack began about 1:00 A.M. on November 28 against the K Company line, coming from the east. Kitz in his company CP first heard small-arms fire at his front line. At first it was light, but it gradually built up in volume. The K Company roadblock force farther east up the valley of the Pungnyuri-gang reported that it heard firing between it and the K Company line. Thus far it had not been disturbed—enemy forces apparently bypassed it purposely. By 1:30 A.M., the Chinese attack had built up to one of heavy pressure against both K and I companies on their ridgeline at the east side of the inlet perimeter. Within another half hour the Chinese were closing in on the K Company CP. At this point the ROK troops assigned to K Company broke and ran for the rear. Kitz intercepted and stopped them. But the Chinese had already broken through one platoon of K Company, and the entire company line quickly disintegrated.[22]

As this fight rapidly approached the area of the inlet bivouac, A Battery, the artillery closest to the infantry, began direct fire against the enemy, and some of its shells began dropping in the K Company area. Kitz was able to have the howitzer fire lifted, but the Chinese had taken advantage of the developing chaos to press their close-in attack. Kitz had to abandon his position.

Sergeant First Class John C. Sweatman, an assistant mess sergeant of K Company, has left an interesting comment about the enemy breakthrough that night:

> The first night our kitchen got burnt up. We were overrun by the Chinese about 0130, . . . so I grabbed my carbine and ammunition and went into an open field. In that field there were about 16 trucks. About four (4) of them were loaded with ammunition. We used the trucks as a shield and started shooting back at the Chinese. About that time I heard Capt. Kitz calling that anyone that ran would be shot. About that time a bullet landed about 3 inches over my head. I went up the road about 50 yards and went to a railroad track. I found a wounded man and took his M-1. I had 6 bandoliers of ammunition and I went up on the railroad track so I could see better and started shooting as *the Chinese came over the bridge* [italics added]. That lasted until about 0800. Then the Chinese took off up into the mountains again. I then went around to see how many cooks I had left under me. I found all but one. I never could find him. I don't know whether he was killed or captured.[23]

Sweatman's statement is important for it shows clearly that some Chinese entered the inlet perimeter over the bridge and causeway, indeed a logical approach. But I have seen no other evidence to indicate that the Chinese used that approach. Such an approach would place the Chinese well behind the infantry line on the spur ridge over 500 yards east and bring them directly into the area of the trucks, the 3rd Battalion CP, and the battalion communication center and near the howitzers of A Battery. A dirt road down the valley of the Pungynuri-gang ran directly to the bridge from the east, hugging the mountainside on the north.

Captain Kitz had to hurry to get his K Company CP out of the path of the Chinese onslaught. He led it hurriedly west about 1,000 yards to the rear, to the A Battery howitzer position. Some of his frontline troops followed him, closely pursued by Chinese. When this happened, Lieutenant Colonel Reilly's 3rd Battalion CP was fully exposed. Indeed, it may have been exposed to enemy attack even earlier, if many enemy soldiers crossing the bridge and causeway reached it. We do not know which enemy forces, those that crossed the bridge or those that broke through K Company, reached the battalion CP first. Little is known about what part, if any, the battalion command staff played in the developing battle. It appears that they were surprised in their hut and overrun before they had a chance to take part in the battle.

Also, it is not clear just what happened in I Company, up the slope on the spur ridge above K Company. The Chinese broke through there, overran one of the company's platoons, and then penetrated to the 81-mm mortars in the dry wash between the ridge and M Company's CP. Private First Class Lewis D. Shannon, 1st Platoon messenger for I Company, stated that "as soon as enemy contact was learned I was told to tell our platoon leader to hold at all costs. Our company did not give any ground that I know of." Captain Marr may have been able to hold part of the original I Company line at its upper end.

The artillerymen were not spared long. Everyone in front of them except M Company had folded within an hour of the first enemy attack. First Lieutenant Thomas J. Patton, of A Battery, 57th Field Artillery Battalion, has left a good firsthand account of how the night battle erupted in the artillery positions:

> The night was quiet and blackout restrictions were followed. At approximately 0230 hours 28 November 1950, I was awakened by personnel of the Firing Battery Headquarters who said that we were attacked by Chinese Communists. About 0245 hours, Lt. Sickafoose, forward observer, K Company, 31st Infantry Regiment, came running into the CP and said the infantry was withdrawing to our rear. Capt. Harold L. Lodge, Battery Commander "A" Battery, made a round of all the gun sections and perimeter defense telling them to fight as long as they possibly could.
>
> Within 3 to 5 minutes, our CP received several bursts of machine gun fire forcing us out of the CP on the right side near the BC jeep and the radio ¾ ton truck. There was a great deal of confusion in the area with a lot of yelling in foreign tongue which was impossible to tell from our Koreans who were with A Battery. A mortar or hand grenade exploded near two five gallon cans of gasoline setting the CP on fire. The CP group withdrew

some 20 yards to the rear where foxholes had been dug by some of the A Battery ROKs. It was still impossible to tell our men from the CCFs until several CCFs ran up to where the CP was burning and started warming themselves by the fire. Capt. Hodge killed one and the others were shot by some of the members of the gun sections. Part of the battery started withdrawing past us toward Battery B. We then fell back entering Battery B's perimeter about 0325 hours where our men joined into the B Battery perimeter. There was heavy firing for a period of 30 to 45 minutes which then died down to intermittent firing the rest of the night.

When daylight came we found sections of L and K Companies were mixed in with Battery A and B personnel. Captain Kitz organized a force to retake Battery A's guns with Captain Hodge leading the remainder of A Battery. . . . When the battery was retaken our howitzers were turned upon the fleeing CCFs. We then discovered that approximately 30 men from Battery A had remained in their foxholes and continued fighting even though they were completely overrun.[24]

After the Chinese were driven out of the A Battery position after dawn, the battery mess was used for a temporary aid station, and the kitchen was moved outside the building. About one-third of the men of A Battery were casualties. Four cooks who had remained inside the mess hall during the fight saw Chinese march off one American and 15 ROK prisoners. Private First Class Shannon, of I Company, said that Captain Marr helped drive the Chinese away from the overrun battery position in the counterattack there in the morning. He said that enemy dead lay all about the guns and that a few artillerymen were still fighting from their foxholes. He said that in this counterattack "to my knowledge there were thirty or so prisoners taken."

It appears that nearly all the survivors at the inlet except M Company retreated to the B Battery artillery perimeter and found there a good defensive position in which they all joined to fight off the Chinese in the hours before dawn. There were infantrymen from all three rifle companies, L, K, and I, as well as the A Battery artillerymen. There is some indication that, strange as it may seem, the I Company CP was adjacent to B Battery and that one platoon was there when men from all points of the perimeter came running to it as a place of last refuge. Throughout the night battle, however, many men were cut off in different places and continued their resistance isolated from the main center that developed around B Battery.[25]

In the fighting around A Battery, Sgt. Stanford O. Corners, a member of the medical detachment with the battery, performed valiantly. Under small-arms and mortar fire, he succeeded in getting wounded to an aid station set up in a house and subsequently loading them into a truck when A Battery position was being overrun, then moving them to a position of safety in the rear, where he continued to help with the wounded.[26]

In the rapid onslaught of the Chinese that carried them to B Battery position, the last defensive perimeter in their path in the main inlet bivouac area, the Chinese overran the 3rd Battalion, 31st Infantry CP. What happened there was not known to the rest of the battalion until after dawn. The enemy held it from about 3:00 A.M. until just after daybreak. It was generally assumed that Lieutenant Colonel Reilly and most of his battalion staff had been killed or captured.

Shortly after daybreak 1st Lt. Henry (Hank) Traywick, the 3rd Battalion motor officer, organized a counterattack party to drive enemy soldiers away from the 3rd Battalion CP and communication section. Under heavy machine-gun and small-arms covering fire Traywick reached the two houses, drove away the last of the Chinese soldiers, and entered the CP. To their surprise Traywick and his men found Reilly unconscious but alive when they entered the battered, bullet-riddled, and grenaded shack. Apparently the Chinese had thought Reilly dead. They had stripped him and others there of all weapons and anything else they considered of value. The bodies of several of his staff were strewn around inside the small structure. Traywick and his group took Reilly to the battalion aid station, where he recovered consciousness.[27]

Mrs. Reilly learned of the Chinese attack on the 3rd Battalion's CP in a letter from her husband. He told her that when the CCF suddenly arrived at the CP he and several of his staff were inside. Reilly said that he sat facing a window with gun in hand. Chinese soldiers tried to climb through the window, and he shot several as they made the attempt. While the fight at the CP was going on, Captain Adams, the battalion S-4, who was inside the house, received a chest wound through the lungs. He died during the day. Reilly noticed that Lieutenant Anderson, the battalion assistant S-3, appeared frustrated that he could not get his pistol out of its holster. Reilly went over to him in the semidarkness to see what was wrong. He found that Anderson's right arm had been blown off by a grenade and that Anderson seemed not to know that his arm was missing. Reilly took the pistol from its holster and placed it in Anderson's remaining hand. Anderson died during the night. Reilly himself was knocked unconscious by a grenade burst near his head. Altogether he had four wounds—a .50-caliber bullet wound through the right leg, a bullet through the toes of one foot, a splattering of mortar fragments on his upper legs and hands, and the hand-grenade concussion over the right eye that had knocked him unconscious.[28]

During the CCF attack on the 3rd Battalion CP and the artillery batteries, First Lieutenant Johnson, the Fifth Air Force forward air controller attached to the battalion, was killed and his equipment damaged.[29] This was a serious loss because now the battalion had no means of directing air strikes against the enemy. The Corsairs would be left to their own devices in trying to help the beleaguered troops. Another serious loss during the night was the regimental surgeon, who was killed while working on a critically wounded man in a blackout tent.

The only forward unit of the 3rd Battalion, 31st Infantry, to hold its CP during the night battle was Capt. Earle Jordan's M Company. During the evening the weapons company had been ordered, over Jordan's protest, to send its 75-mm recoilless rifle and machine-gun platoons to K and I companies on the line. Each of these companies, therefore, had a section of 75-mm recoilless rifles and a section of machine guns from the weapons company at the time of the enemy attack. All these weapons were temporarily lost to the enemy in the night battle. Jordan had with him only his headquarters personnel. His mortar platoon with its 81-mm mortars was just in front of his CP in a broad, shallow wash, about 200 yards south of Reilly's 3rd Battalion CP in a thatched mud house standing in a courtyard. Darkness had fallen before he completed emplacement of his mortars and established local security.

Jordan's first knowledge of trouble came between 1:30 and 2:00 A.M., when he awakened to the sound of small-arms fire in his mortar position. He hurriedly arose and alerted all personnel at the CP. He then went outside and saw that enemy soldiers were overrunning his mortar position and that small-arms fire, coming from the east and south, was hitting around his CP. Chinese soldiers were already in the draw around the mortars. Jordan shouted to his mortarmen to fall back to the CP hut and courtyard. There he organized his defense, which held all night against repeated close-in Chinese attacks. Most of the men in Jordan's group were either killed or wounded during the night, but the less critically wounded continued to fight in the desperate battle. Jordan said, "When it was light enough to see I went around to check the damage, and counted over 60 dead enemy soldiers within yards of our position, nearly all armed with American sub-machine guns, 45 cal. [Thompson submachine guns] and American ammunition."[30]

Jordan was wounded during the night battle but did not relax his control of the defense. An enemy hand grenade exploded a few feet from him, and fragments cut several flesh wounds on both legs, and the blast of the explosion severely wrenched his back. In addition, he had frostbite in both feet.[31] Jordan described how the first night's fight seemed to him at his position; no doubt it was much the same elsewhere. He wrote: "The first night it seemed to me to be just a continuing battle at very close range, sometimes hand to hand, grenades used in large numbers by the Chinese, until dawn, when the remaining enemy withdrew. There was little room where one might assemble a group for counterattack as such. It would seem to me to be more clearly stated as a close range fight for individual positions."[32] When daylight came, Jordan walked over to the communications hut, where he encountered Lieutenant Traywick. The latter told him he had just driven off the last of the Chinese soldiers. The battle was over for a while.

It is interesting to note that Jordan's M Company, which had an outstanding record in the Chosin Reservoir fighting, had its full complement of KATUSA. Moreover, at Camp Crawford in Japan during the previous summer, when stringent measures had been taken to bring the 7th Infantry Division up to strength for the Inchon Landing, Jordan had received an unusual group of replacements. About 70 percent of the American troops sent to Jordan at that time came on "early release from the 8th Army Stockade"— bad actors all, from the Army standpoint. Under Jordan's leadership these men became good soldiers, and they were better fighting men at Chosin than the average—they killed their share of Chinese. Jordan's record speaks for itself, and those who knew him spoke words of praise that fully reinforce his record as a soldier. He was a large man, a native of Auburn, Maine, born in 1917. He was a veteran of World War II: he had been commissioned a second lieutenant in infantry upon graduating from the Infantry School at Fort Benning, Georgia, in 1942. Most of his service was in the 143rd Infantry Regiment, 36th Division, which engaged in some of the hardest battles of the Italian campaign.

It is clear that the Chinese almost overran the 3rd Battalion, 31st Infantry, and the two batteries of the 57th Artillery Battalion in their initial attack at the inlet on the night of November 27–28. No count of American and ROK casualties at the inlet perimeter during the night's battle was ever recorded. Nor was there ever any knowledge of the number of enemy casualties, but they were heavy. So far as can be determined, the enemy attack came entirely from the east, down the valley of the Pungnyuri-gang and the hill mass just south of it at the head of the inlet. Chinese troops apparently had not had time to deploy on the slopes of Hill 1456, south of the American bivouac area, or west of it. If they had been there, as they were on subsequent nights, the 3rd Battalion and the artillerymen at the inlet would have been effectively surrounded and might have been destroyed.

The CCF 80th Division's plans for the night of November 27–28 did not include action against the Hudong-ni perimeter, possibly because of the presence there of the 31st Tank Company. In any event, all was quiet there during the night. But there was action only a mile or two north although those at Hudong-ni were unaware of it at the time.

An hour or two after Captain Drake returned to Hudong-ni from his trip up the road searching for Colonel MacLean, the 31st Medical Company arrived at Hudong-ni. It was a unit of the 31st Infantry that was to join MacLean's Headquarters group at the reservoir. Drake talked with the medical company's captain, informing him how the men of the 31st Infantry that had already arrived had been dispersed and what he had seen on his recent trip up the road. The medical company's commander was eager to continue on at least as far as the inlet and join the 3rd Battalion there for the night. Drake tried to persuade the officer not to continue but to remain at Hudong-ni that night and go forward with the tank company the next morning. The commander decided, however, to continue on, and after midnight he and his company pulled out and disappeared up the road.[33]

Sometime later in the night, the exact time unknown, the first sergeant of the medical company reappeared at Drake's CP. He was in an excited and disheveled condition. He said that a Chinese force had ambushed the company a mile or two up the road and that he had escaped by crawling back in the road ditches. He did not know much about what had happened. He was the only member of the medical company whom Drake saw after the ambush, but three or four others got back to Hudong-ni, according to Maj. Carl G. Witte, the regimental S-2. None of them knew how many might have broken through the ambush and reached the 3rd Battalion at the inlet. It appeared that the Chinese had killed an unknown number and had destroyed several vehicles on Hill 1221, the first hill north of Hudong-ni.

It was there, indeed, that the ambush had taken place, as was verified after daylight. American dead and several destroyed medical-company vehicles cluttered the road about 400 to 500 yards south of the hairpin turn in the saddle, where the road bent sharply toward the reservoir to the west in continuing generally northward toward the inlet.

The ambush and roadblock on Hill 1221 were typical Chinese tactics. In attack the Chinese usually made one or more frontal assaults and sent a sizable force around a flank to cut the main exit road behind those they were attacking frontally. They were adept at picking ridgelines or hills close to the road, overlooking the point where they put in their fire and road-blocks. The latter were nearly always defended. So, while the CCF 80th Division was attacking the forward perimeter and the inlet frontally it was also putting in its roadblock behind them, cutting off their escape. Later events showed that the Chinese had at least a battalion of troops at the site and held the roadblock throughout the entire period of action east of Chosin. This Chinese-defended roadblock was a dominant factor in the ultimate fate of the 31st RCT.

By the early hours of November 28 the Hudong-ni CP was receiving garbled messages reporting enemy action at both the forward perimeter and the inlet. But there was never any clear understanding there of what was taking place. Communications soon deteriorated to the point of being virtually nonexistent.

Soon after the first messages of enemy action at the 31st RCT perimeters north of Hudong-ni came in, Major Lynch tried by the regimental SCR 193 radio to reach Colonel Paddock, the 7th Infantry Division G-3 at Pungsan Headquarters, 60 air miles northeast. To Lynch's surprise General Barr, the division commander, answered the call. Barr told Lynch that he wanted to talk with General Hodes, who proceeded to outline the situation as he knew it and asked Barr to arrange for air support the next day. He also said that the 2nd Battalion, 31st Infantry, had not arrived and was badly needed. Radio communication was broken off before the end of the conversation and could not be reestablished. This was the only time the 31st RCT, on the east side of Chosin Reservoir, had direct communication with its division CP.[34]

Lynch's importance at Chosin came from his association with General Hodes as the latter's G-3 aide. He never got farther north than Hudong-ni, but there and later at Hagaru-ri he was the one person who knew most about Hodes's efforts to obtain help to extricate the 31st RCT from enemy entrapment.[35] Major Lynch had long experience in the Army. Born in Madisonville, Texas, in 1917, he enlisted at age sixteen in the 143rd Infantry, 36th Division, Texas National Guard, at Huntsville, Texas. By 1939 he had earned a second lieutenant's commission. When the 36th Division was mobilized in November, 1940, he commanded one of its rifle companies. He served with the 143rd Regiment throughout the war, participating in some of the hardest-fought battles in Italy, southern France, and the Vosges Mountains of northern France: Salerno, San Pietro, Rapido River, Cassino, Anzio, and the Colmar Pocket. In August, 1950, Lynch, now a major in the Regular Army, was one of 35 "extra" majors sent to Japan for duty with the 7th Infantry Division. He was assigned to the Division G-3 section.

There is no indication that Hodes was in communication with Colonel MacLean after the latter left Hudong-ni in the evening of November 27. MacLean had planned to stay at Hudong-ni overnight, but he changed his mind during his conversation with Hodes and started back north to join his forward units. We know that when Lieutenant McNally, the communications officer at MacLean's forward CP, shook Maj. Hugh W. Robbins awake at 1:00 A.M. on November 28 and told him that there was enemy action north and south of them, he also told Robbins that MacLean had returned from Hudong-ni but had gone on north to Faith's CP.[36]

Major Curtis remembers an incident at Faith's CP late that evening which indicates that MacLean had arrived well before the beginning of enemy action. First Lieutenant Rollin W. Skilton, 31st Infantry liaison officer with the 1st Marine Division at Hagaru-ri, arrived at Faith's CP to deliver to him a copy of the 1st Marine Division's operations order. After delivering the document, Skilton drove off into the night back to Hagaru-ri.[37] He arrived there safely, ahead of the Chinese who established the fire block at Hill 1221.

So, when the enemy attacked that night, the two senior officers east of Chosin were at opposite ends of the 31st RCT positions and out of touch with each other. MacLean was at Faith's forward perimeter; Hodes was at the 31st rear CP at Hudong-ni.

During the night of November 27–28, the Chinese made one more major attack, their third, but it came late, just before dawn. It must have been an afterthought, and it probably grew out of their establishment of the roadblock at Hill 1221 and the ambush of the medical company.

In their small valley, a covelike area at the western base of Hill 1456 and immediately east of the MSR, half a mile from the mouth of the Pungnyuri-gang Inlet, Lt. Col. Ray Embree and his Headquarters of the 57th Field Artillery Battalion and Captain McClymont with his D Battery (−), 15th AAA AW SP Battalion, spent the night quietly, not knowing that a mile north of them a furious battle was being fought, involving their two artillery batteries.

McClymont had arrived at this bivouac area, where the 57th Field Artillery Headquarters group had already established itself, just before dark. He placed his four full-track M19s, with their powerful dual-40-mm guns, and his four half-track M16s, with their quad-50s, in defensive positions to protect the 57th Artillery Headquarters and his own CP near it and to command the road just west of the bivouac area. He set up his 1st Platoon CP in the south-central part of the little valley. There was no infantry in the bivouac area. McClymont was able to get wire strung between his CP and his 1st Platoon, field telephones established each place, and wire and phones to each of his M19s and M16s. In the evening the mess tent was raised, and all members of his battery had a hot meal.[38]

The 30-year-old captain who controlled this array of firepower had been born in a small town in the state of Washington in 1920. Like many others who had a rural or semirural background, he knew how to shoot like a marksman long before entering the armed services. In 1940, McClymont joined the National Guard as a member of the 200th Coast Artillery Regiment. He finished a special course in fire control at Fortress Monroe, Virginia, and then served with his regiment in the Aleutian Islands. From there he went as an officer candidate to the Antiaircraft Artillery (AAA) School at Camp Davis, North Carolina, and was commissioned a second lieutenant on August 26, 1943. He volunteered for overseas duty. McClymont stayed in the Army at the end of World War II, served in the occupation of South Korea from 1947 to 1949, and was then assigned to Japan. He commanded D Battery, 15th Antiaircraft Automatic Weapons Battalion, Self Propelled (15th AAA AW Battalion, SP), when it was assigned to the 7th Infantry Division. He was attached to the 57th Field Artillery Battalion near the end of November, 1950. The next day he was on his way to Chosin Reservoir and the first combat experience of his life.[39]

The night of November 27–28 was quiet in the little valley alongside Chosin Reservoir, and McClymont and those with him heard no sound of battle to the north of them, nor did they know anything of the ambush of the medical company just to the south of them.

A change came suddenly. Shortly before dawn on November 28 enemy soldiers appeared. The first sign was mortar fire that dropped around the 57th Artillery Headquarters and McClymont's AAA CP. McClymont rang the field phone for his 1st Platoon. Warrant Officer Roscoe M. Calcote answered, saying that they were under small-arms and mortar fire. McCly-

A view to the northeast from the A Battery, 57th FA Battalion position, inlet perimeter, which the Chinese overran on the night of November 27–28, 1950. American dead are in the foreground. The photograph was taken on the morning of November 28, 1950, by an unknown photographer. Photograph courtesy of Col. Ray O. Embree.

mont ran to Sfc. Robert Denham's M19 near his CP tent, and climbed on its back. Small-arms fire was now whistling about, and the mortar fire had increased in volume. McClymont relates what happened:

> I raised my field glasses. The M19 crew were at their posts. I looked through the field glasses and with their light gathering ability, I could see movement on the side of a hill alongside of the road leading back to Hagaru-ri. I focused the glasses and I could see that there was a column of soldiers marching in formation along the road, heading directly towards our position—they were about 200 yards from my CP and were closing on us. They would soon be on top of my 1st Platoon CP. Just then some sort of illumination shell or mortar round went off and we could see the column clearly. Dressed in dark winter clothes, quilted coats, with flapped caps, they were moving toward us. I ordered the M19 commander to load his

Capt. (later Maj.) James R. McClymont in Korea, early 1951. Photograph
courtesy of Major McClymont.

twin 40 mms and to open fire. The twin 40s crumped simultaneously, and the tracers leaped out. Immediately, the high explosive shells burst in the column of men, and I ordered fire at full automatic. In only seconds there was no movement from the column.

I felt someone grab my ankle. One of my cooks was standing on the ground. I leaned over and he said I was wanted on the field telephone. I jumped down and went to the phone in the CP tent. "This is Major Tolly [S-3] of the 57th [Field Artillery Battalion]," I was told, "those are friendly troops out there, cease fire!"

My heart sank. I had just erased a whole column of men.[40]

McClymont had indeed erased a whole column of men—but they were Chinese, as he had thought. However, after taking the telephone call, McClymont ran back to the M19 and told Sergeant Denham to cease fire. Quiet now prevailed, with only an occasional mortar round dropping in the bivouac area. The quiet was suddenly broken by a large volume of noise and weapons fire at the 1st Platoon CP. McClymont phoned the CP but got no answer.

Daylight was beginning to give visibility, and McClymont could see that the hut where his 1st Platoon CP was set up was on fire. He took three men, left Lieutenant Ballard in charge of the CP, and moved south along the edge of the road. He planned to make sure that the road was secure and then turn east to his 1st Platoon CP.

As McClymont's small group moved down the road, they approached a sandbagged outpost which either the 5th Marines or the 57th Field Artillery had established. They were about 35 to 40 yards from the post when they were fired on from it. McClymont's carbine would not fire; its mechanism was sluggish from the intense cold. He dropped it and picked up a submachine gun lying on the road. It fired once, and then the clip froze. McClymont then got an M-1 rifle from a nearby soldier and led his three men toward the enemy-held hole. Again they were fired on. The four of them hit the dirt. McClymont shouted back to his CP for someone to bring him a bazooka. A 3.5 bazooka with one round of ammunition was soon delivered to him. He fired it at the sandbags but missed low. He asked for another round of ammunition, got it, and again missed. This time the round went too high and demolished a 57th Field Artillery jeep parked just beyond the sandbagged hole.

Disgusted, McClymont asked for a grenade. One of the men handed him one. He crawled to a point near the sandbags, pulled the pin, and lobbed

Capt. (later Maj.) James R. McClymont and a group of enlisted men of D Battery, 15th AAA AW Battalion, Korea, ca. February, 1951. Pfc. Robert M. Slater is third from left in the front row; Sgt. Grantford R. Brown is on the far left, back row; Captain McClymont is second from left, back row. Photograph courtesy of Major McClymont.

the grenade into the foxhole. It exploded, and McClymont was getting to his feet when a Chinese inside the foxhole pushed a machine gun over the edge of the sandbags and let loose with about 20 rounds.

McClymont sent one of his men to move around the foxhole to a higher point where he could look down into it while he himself climbed the road embankment and reached a point where he could see into the foxhole. Both of them then fired into it. All was quiet from within the hole. McClymont and the other man started toward it. Suddenly a grenade sailed out and exploded with a dull, weak pop. The two of them ran to the edge of the sandbags, and, holding their weapons as high as possible and pointing them down so that their fire would enter the hole, they cut loose. Nothing moved inside the hole. McClymont put his helmet on the end of the M-1 and moved

An M19 full-track (dual-40), Korea, February, 1951. Two 40-mm Bofors anti-aircraft guns are mounted in a revolving turret. This M19 is exactly like those in D Battery, 15th AAA AW Battalion, at Chosin. Photograph courtesy of Maj. James R. McClymont.

it over the edge of the sandbags. Nothing happened. Then McClymont and his companion carefully peered over the top. Five Chinese soldiers were dead inside—one of them torn apart when he apparently threw himself on the grenade McClymont had thrown into the hole.

McClymont decided that he needed more men before he started for his 1st Platoon CP. He shouted back for more men. About 10 men came up, a few of them from the 57th Field Artillery Headquarters. He led his reinforced group down the road toward Hagaru-ri to the spot where his M19 40-mm fire had earlier stopped the enemy column. Scattered along about 150 feet of the road lay the bodies of the Chinese, about 80 of them. As McClymont reached the clusters of bodies, four or five who had played dead jumped to their feet and ran for the road bend to the south. They did not make it. The wholesale destruction of this marching column of men showed how deadly the 40-mm shell was against massed men at close range. McClymont could see places where a shell had hit one man and also brought down three or four others nearby. Chinese equipment and weapons lay all around.

Most of the Chinese had been armed with American-made Thompson submachine guns. As an accessory each soldier who carried the Thompson wore a canvas apron strapped to his chest. The apron had slots to hold a 20-round straight clip for the gun. There were different models of the Thompson on the ground, one with pistol grips front and back and later models with a rear pistol grip and a forearm in front. Some used the 50-round drum, but most of them used the 10- or 20-round clip. McClymont tried several of the Thompsons and finally picked one of the later models using a 10- or 20-round .45-caliber clip. He also took one of the canvas apron vests. He carried this weapon and its ammunition apron through the rest of his time in Korea. He set his newfound weapon on single fire (it also had full automatic setting). In examining the Thompsons that lay on the road, McClymont observed that they had little oil on them; that was one reason they seldom failed to fire for the Chinese in cold weather —there was no fluid to freeze in the subzero temperature. (It is interesting that in World War II the German soldiers who fought on the Eastern Front in the Soviet Union in wintertime used no oil on their weapons; they had found that if they were oiled they froze up and would not function; instead they used a fine, dry powder or no lubricant at all.)

Finding the road secure at least as far as the bend where it curved eastward around high ground at the south side of the little valley, McClymont centered his attention on getting to his 1st Platoon CP. It was about 300 yards to the east, near the south side of the valley. McClymont took the point, with his 13 or 14 men fanned out behind him. They advanced cautiously. Before moving 50 yards, McClymont was fired on. He could not see an enemy. Still advancing, he broke into a weaving, dodging run. Then he saw a Chinese soldier in a clump of grass. McClymont fired one shot from his Thompson. The bullet hit the Chinese soldier in the head and killed him.

Two other Chinese, unseen until now, stood up with their hands in the air. McClymont motioned them to come toward him, and one of his men took their grenades and ammunition pouches.

From a greater distance another Chinese stood up and fired at McClymont's group and then started running toward the 1st Platoon CP. Mc-

An M16 half-track (quad-50), Korea, February, 1951. Four .50-caliber machine guns are mounted in a revolving turret. Photograph courtesy of Maj. James R. McClymont.

Clymont fired on him at about 75 yards, but he kept running up the old Korean ox trail. Wearing tennis shoes, he was making good speed. Again McClymont fired and missed him. Then, as the Chinese soldier neared the crest of a small rise, McClymont took more careful aim. This time as the Thompson fired the Chinese threw up his arms and fell to the ground.

McClymont's group continued their careful advance toward the 1st Platoon CP. A little distance from it they came to one of their half-track M16 quad-50s. No one was there. The quad-50 was inoperable. From the half-track McClymont could see the CP hut. It was still burning; there was no movement around it.

A sudden burst of heavy small-arms fire hit around the quad-50. It came from the high ground on the south side of the valley. Everyone took cover; McClymont rolled under the quad-50 trailer. A group of Chinese soldiers at the foot of the ridge got to their feet and began climbing the hillside away from the valley. McClymont and his men took them under fire. It did little damage, and it was only when one of the full-track M19s on the north side of the valley near the artillery CP opened up on the Chinese climbing the open hillside that they began falling. Not many made it over the crest.

Thinking that the area was now clear of Chinese, McClymont started to leave the cover of the trailer. Again Chinese bullets hit the frozen ground around him. He rolled back under the trailer. Then one of his men yelled to him to get out, that the trailer was on fire. One glance upward and McClymont confirmed the fact. He got free of the trailer and took a running dive for a fold of snow-covered ground about 20 feet away. One of the 5-gallon gasoline cans in the trailer went up in flames, and soon the .50-caliber ammunition in the trailer was exploding.

The enemy fire that had set the trailer ablaze died down as McClymont's group approached the 1st Platoon CP, and all enemy action had stopped by the time they arrived there. McClymont found Maj. Max Morris, the 57th Field Artillery Battalion executive officer, dead in the yard of the hut. Apparently he had cut directly across the valley from the artillery CP and was heading toward the 1st Platoon CP when the action there broke out, while McClymont and his group went up the road. Inside the hut Warrant Officer Calcote lay dead, face down. His right hand had been mangled by a grenade burst. McClymont learned later from survivors of the 1st Platoon CP that when the Chinese closed on the CP and began throwing hand grenades inside the hut, Calcote threw several of them back. Then one exploded in his hand. But small-arms fire killed him. Lieutenant Chapman, the 1st Platoon leader, was found alive. The first sergeant of D Battery had left McClymont's CP to go to the 1st Platoon after McClymont had started down the road and was killed halfway there. Altogether at the 1st Platoon CP and in the vicinity McClymont found two officers and four enlisted men killed and one officer and six enlisted men alive.[41]

Of the 1st Platoon's four full-track M19s and 4 half-track M16s the Chinese had knocked out the M19 near the 1st Platoon's CP. The nearby M16 would not operate because of the frigid air and battery failure. Enemy small-arms fire had shot up two 2½-ton trucks.

This Chinese attack had come from the south. The column that had come along the road was destroyed by the M19, as described, only 200 yards from the 57th Field Artillery Headquarters CP. A second force had come over the trail that crossed the southwestern spur of Hill 1456 and entered the little valley on its south side near its middle. It was the latter force that had caused most of the damage and casualties.

It is not known how many artillerymen were killed or wounded in the attack other than those in McClymont's battery. The Chinese never reached the 57th Field Artillery Headquarters CP, according to Embree, but it was under enemy mortar and small-arms fire during the early-morning fight, and this caused some casualties. Small-arms fire wounded Embree in the upper legs early in the engagement. With Embree wounded and Major Morris killed, the ranking officer left in the 57th Artillery was Major Robert J. Tolly, the battalion S-3.

It seems probable that if McClymont's M19s and M16s had not been in the bivouac area with the 57th Artillery Headquarters, the Chinese attacking from the *south* might have overrun the position and continued on the half mile to the Pungnyuri-gang inlet. There it could have taken B Battery in the rear just at the time it was serving as the rallying point for nearly all the remaining 3rd Battalion, 31st Infantry, and A and B batteries of artillerymen. That might have been enough to complete the overrunning and destruction of the inlet position.

The Chinese who came from the south, from the direction of Hagaruri, wore the usual brown-green field uniforms, and can be assumed to have belonged to a different battalion, and probably a different regiment, from the one that had made the attack on the inlet. Logic and circumstantial evidence, based largely on the direction from which the attack came, indicate that these enemy soldiers were from the force that had established the roadblock and fire block on Hill 1221, just south of them. This force may have started north after the ambush of the medical company to make contact with their units attacking the inlet perimeter, without knowing of the Artillery Headquarters and AAA AW bivouac in the little valley cove along the road just short of the Inlet.

After assessing the damage in the bivouac area, McClymont pulled what was movable of his weapons and equipment to his CP and then went to the 57th Field Artillery CP for orders. He learned that they were all to prepare at once for movement to the 3rd Battalion, 31st Infantry, perimeter at the inlet.[42]

The Next Day—
November 28

Colonel MacLean had left Faith's forward position about dawn on November 28 and returned on the road to his own advance CP. He told his staff that he thought the 1st Battalion, 32nd Infantry, had come through the night in pretty good shape. He apparently knew little about the situation at the inlet position—only about the heavy fighting there during the night. Certainly he knew nothing of the Chinese attack just before dawn on the 57th Field Artillery Headquarters and the AAA Platoon just south of the inlet. His view of the general situation at daylight on November 28 was reasonably optimistic. He expected his 2nd Battalion, 31st Infantry, to arrive during the day, and he felt that with this reinforcement and the tank company at Hudong-ni he could gain control of the situation.

About noon Faith's CP reestablished telephone communication with MacLean's advance CP and learned that he intended to move his CP group to the inlet position with the artillery and the 3rd Battalion, 31st Infantry. That did not happen, however; only part of the group went to the inlet, and most of MacLean's advance CP joined the 1st Battalion at its forward position. There is some confusion about what happened in the intended move. Intelligence Sergeant Ivan H. Long, who was with MacLean, said that MacLean ordered him to lead a group of men south to the inlet and infiltrate them across to the 3rd Battalion. He said that he did this but that they came under enemy small-arms fire when they tried to cross the inlet in twos and threes and that some of them did not make it. It appears that this difficulty prompted MacLean to decide to take most of his group to join Faith. The move to his forward position under Major Robbins, the

A view, looking southwest toward Hill 1250, from within the western end of the inlet perimeter, showing foxholes and some automatic-weapons positions. Chosin Reservoir is on the west, where a depression in the terrain marks the mouth of the Pungnyuri-gang inlet. The photographer is unknown. Photograph courtesy of Col. Ray O. Embree.

S-1, was completed about 3:00 P.M. that afternoon. Robbins reported to Faith that he had brought in 10 vehicles and 35 men.[1]

At Faith's position the first part of the morning was devoted largely to reestablishing the original lines with the help of air strikes and bringing in the dead and wounded. Enemy activity, though greatly reduced, did not entirely cease, but, except at the boundary of C and B companies on the high ground on the east, it was not important.

Ammunition was redistributed. In this connection luck intervened. About 9:00 A.M. a noncommissioned officer, probably from the Ammunition and Pioneer (A&P) Platoon of Headquarters Company, arrived at the forward position with a resupply of ammunition. The A&P party had been on the road to Chosin during all of the 27th but did not reach the troop positions there

A view looking northwest from the west end of the inlet perimeter, November 28, 1950. The road on the north side of the inlet turns north around the nose of the long ridgeline (Hill 1324) near the left side of the picture. The photographer is unknown. Photograph courtesy of Col. Ray O. Embree.

before dark. Continuing on, they passed Hill 1221 before the CCF established their roadblock and were able to reach MacLean's advance CP and the Heavy Mortar Company position, where they stopped for the night.

During the night and early in the morning of the 28th the 1st Battalion had taken a few prisoners. The S-2 interrogated them and learned that a large Chinese force had surrounded the Marines and the 31st Infantry on both sides of the reservoir and that the enemy attack would be resumed everywhere that night.[2]

At one sector in the 1st Battalion perimeter the fight continued after daylight and throughout most of the day, despite the best efforts of Marine air strikes. This was in the key terrain in the center, at the boundary of B and C companies. Reinforcements arrived from headquarters to try to recapture a commanding knoll the Chinese had seized during the night.

The view southeast from B Battery position, where a successful stand was made during the Chinese attack on the night of November 27–28, 1950. Note the M19 full-track (dual-40) at the left center. This and other weapons arrived at the inlet perimeter in the afternoon of November 28, just before the photograph was taken by an unknown person. Photograph courtesy of Lt. Col. Ivan H. Long.

Lieutenant Henry M. Moore's A&P Platoon bore the brunt of the fight during the day. Moore was wounded in the legs by shrapnel but refused evacuation. This young officer made an enviable reputation during the Chosin battles and was admired by everyone. The contest for the knoll went on despite repeated air strikes. Master Sergeant Russavage, the battalion sergeant major, joined the fight, leading a charge with his pistol. He fell in enemy territory, and his body could not be recovered when his group was driven back.

In this continuing fight Captain Stamford called in Marine Corsair strikes on the hill, but C Company counterattacks failed to retake the dominant knoll. The CCF had brought up heavy machine guns, which they zeroed

Lt. Col. Ivan H. Long (ca. 1965), who was intelligence sergeant at Chosin.
Photograph courtesy of Lieutenant Colonel Long.

in on the crest of the knoll, and when C Company counterattacked, the Chinese pulled back and let the machine guns rake the crest, forcing the Americans to pull back.

The nature of the air support should be explained. Stamford called the strikes from the 1st Battalion CP area. Company commanders and platoon leaders at the point of enemy contact telephoned Faith or Stamford where they wanted the strikes. Stamford in turn sent the information to the pilots, who then made the strikes. Sometimes a platoon leader arranged for a ground marking or a signal to guide the pilots. Stamford thought that this method of directing air strikes was ineffective because pilots did not receive enough information to make accurate hits. He believed that he as forward air controller should be up front to see the situation and give the pilots specific instructions for accurate strikes. But Faith would not let him go forward, keeping him at the battalion CP.

On the right of this critical fight in C Company the enemy was also pressing B Company, which had a hard time holding its position. The right flank of B Company bent around to the rear of the battalion CP, and there the CCF attacked hard on the south side. Faith organized most of Headquarters Company as an infantry force and put it into the line there. Stamford gave the heaviest air support during the day to C and Headquarters companies.[3]

The situation at the boundary of B and C companies led to a readjustment of some troops from C Company's left flank to buttress its right flank. About midmorning Lieutenant Sherrard, executive officer of C Company, came to Mortrude's platoon position at the left flank just above the road at the pass and told him he was to move his platoon to a position on the company's right flank and from there to counterattack to regain lost ground. Mortrude was induced to save time and avoid carrying unnecessary weight by leaving behind his platoon's bedrolls; Sherrard assured him that they would be brought to his new position. He never saw them again, and in the nights that followed, he and his men suffered considerably from their loss. Mortrude described his platoon's move to the counterattack area:

> Proceeded generally east up the ridge line through abandoned positions without resistance or casualties. Observed some of our "C" Company dead who had apparently been killed in their sleeping bags during the Chinese attacks the night before.
>
> By midafternoon, we encountered a series of enemy occupied knolls. By the use of the very close (50 to 100 yards) air support of US Marine Corsair

aircraft, coordinated by telephone communications down to the Battalion Air Controller at the base of the ridge and spotted by our white phosphorus hand grenades, we were able to take the first couple of knolls without a fire fight. Our air support so close we could frequently look down into the cockpit of the aircraft and wave to the pilots. The Air Controller would tell me by telephone that the pilot was on "station" and ready for a run, I would throw my WP grenade as far out in front as possible, and the Aircraft would strike just beyond it.

Later in the afternoon, we were stopped just short of the crest of a larger knoll and a bisecting ridge line [the B and C companies' boundary] by heavy enemy fire which could not be suppressed by our friendly air support. An unsuccessful diversionary attack by my Platoon Sergeant with one squad around the right (south) flank confirmed the enemy was well dug in [in] a reverse slope defense. At this point, after sniper fire killed one man of the Company Headquarters just as they reached our location, I was ordered to pull back and defend the right flank of the previous knoll. Enemy fire ceased on our withdrawal and we established our new defensive positions for the night without incident. Miraculously, and because of our excellent air support, my platoon had suffered no casualties during the afternoon counterattacks.[4]

During the afternoon personnel of the 1st Battalion observed on the eastern skyline long columns of Chinese troops marching past them, going south. Some of the troops were mounted on Mongolian ponies. The columns were out of range of 1st Battalion fire. Colonel MacLean received reports from the inlet that men there also saw the Chinese troops bypassing them in the mountains on the east. Major Miller, commenting on this disturbing sight, gave some idea of the volume of the enemy movement: "We watched Chinese troops by-pass us to the east the entire rest of the day." Captain Bigger learned later that air strikes killed "hundreds of these Mongolian ponies," and presumably many CCF soldiers as well, east of the 1st Battalion and the other Americans troops east of Chosin on November 28.[5]

One good report spread throughout the forward perimeter as evening fell. Captain Stamford recorded it: "About sundown the Able Company observed [artillery forward observer] about 300 to 400 enemy troops moving down the road with a tank and couple of self-propelled guns. By using an SCR 300 to talk to the observer I was able to direct 4 F4Us and 4 RAAF F-51s on them with devastating results. It took about 20 minutes to knock out this group as a fighting force."[6] South African pilots flew the F-51s. The tank and the self-propelled guns were North Korean.

When dusk began to settle over the 1st Battalion battleground, Faith called off the attacks against the enemy-held high ground at the right flank of C Company and concentrated his efforts on trying to consolidate his defense for the night. Headquarters Company was already on the line at its southwestern end, at the rear of his CP, and now he sent all available personnel — clerks, cooks, drivers, and others — to various units on the perimeter to strengthen them for another night of battle. At the end of daylight about 100 casualties had passed through the 1st Battalion aid station.[7]

General Almond Visits the Forward Position

On November 28, Maj. Gen. Edward M. Almond, the X Corps commander, visited the 7th Division's forward element, the 1st Battalion, 32nd Infantry, at its battle-scarred perimeter, as he had the day before when he went to the 1st Marine Division position on the west side of the reservoir at Yudam-ni. He had driven from Hamhung to Yudam-ni by jeep on the 27th partly to observe the deplorable condition of road traffic, which he ordered improved. He came back down the tortuous mountain road from Yudam-ni in bitter cold, just ahead of the multiple Chinese roadblocks that were being established that night all the way from Yudam-ni to Chinhung-ni, at the foot of Funchilin Pass. The only traffic that got through after that was a large convoy of empty 2½-ton supply trucks that had just finished unloading Marine supplies at the Yudam-ni forward positions.

On the morning of the 28th, General Almond, with his 26-year-old junior aide, 1st Lt. Alexander M. Haig, Jr., flew from Hamhung to Hagaru-ri in an L-17 plane. There he conferred with Maj. Gen. Oliver P. Smith, the 1st Marine Division commander, who had just arrived to establish his CP. He then arranged for a helicopter landing near Faith's CP to meet Faith and MacLean.[8]

In his conversation with these two officers Almond learned that neither of them knew any more about the situation than he did. Almond thought that the previous night's battle had been fought against elements of three Chinese divisions, the 124th, the 125th, and the 126th. These troops, as explained earlier, had been in the Chosin Reservoir area for more than a month.

During these discussions Almond thought that Faith seemed on edge and resentful of the situation. He had suffered heavily in the surprise Chinese attack of the previous night when he had lost several men killed and others wounded. And he had also lost the highest ground of his perimeter to the enemy. Almond told Faith that he should try to get possession of the high ground to the east before nightfall. Part of this high ground was the area that C Company had lost the night before and during the morning.

MacLean told Almond that he planned to establish his CP just south of Faith's position; he thought that his task force could hold on, that he could get his CP completed and functioning. Almond agreed and added that he thought that the combat force could advance northward when the 2nd Battalion, 31st Infantry, arrived. It is not clear whether at this meeting Almond or MacLean knew much about the condition of Lieutenant Colonel Reilly's 3rd Battalion, 31st Infantry, and the artillery at the inlet, 4 road miles south. Also, in this meeting Almond seems not to have known that the 2nd Battalion, 31st Infantry, had met serious delays on the road, making it almost certain that it would be unable to join MacLean's force at Chosin.

Before he left for Hagaru-ri, General Almond remarked to Faith that he had three Silver Stars he wanted to award, one to him and the others to persons Faith should select. Faith saw Lt. Everett F. Smalley, a C Company platoon leader, who had been wounded in the night's battle, sitting nearby and asked him to come over to receive one of the decorations. George A. Stanley, a Headquarters Company mess sergeant, chanced to be passing the group. He had performed well in the battle for the high ground the Chinese had captured during the night, and Faith stopped him and asked him to become the third recipient. Almond had awarded three Silver Stars to members of the 7th Marine Regiment at Yudam-ni the day before, and this ceremony was intended to be even-handed treatment of the Army units at Chosin. Major Curtis came up as the ceremony ended and saw Haig make an entry in his notebook to have official orders issued to confirm the awards.

Later there was considerable comment in the 7th Division that, after General Almond left to return to Hagaru-ri, Lieutenant Colonel Faith and Lieutenant Smalley ripped their Silver Stars off their jackets and threw them into the snow. Curtis, Bigger, Jones, and 1st Lt. Hugh R. May have confirmed to me that they were present at the ceremony and that Faith did throw away his Silver Star. Jones recalled that Smalley took his Silver Star off his jacket and put it in his pocket. May was standing close to Almond and Faith when Almond awarded the medals. He wrote:

When Lt. Col. Faith was presented the Silver Star I was about 4 to 5 feet from him. Col. Faith did protest to Gen. Almond that there were others more deserving of the decoration but the General would not hear of this and pinned the Star to Col. Faith's jacket.

During this time Gen. Almond told Col. Faith not to worry as the Chinese we saw were only the stragglers fleeing north. After Gen. Almond departed Col. Faith ripped off the Silver Star and threw it on the ground at the same time muttering "What a damned (something)" but as his voice was lowered I could not be sure what he said.[9]

General Almond was the only officer of the 7th Infantry Division, the 1st Marine Division, or the X Corps to visit the forward infantry battalion on the east side of the reservoir after the Chinese launched their surprise attack. The only other visit to the 31st RCT at Chosin was made by Maj. Gen. David G. Barr, who went to the inlet perimeter on November 30 and conferred briefly and privately with Faith. No general officer in Korea went to front troop positions more often than did Almond, frequently at considerable risk to himself. He tried to inform himself about frontline situations and to encourage the troops in their efforts.

On the west side of Chosin Reservoir the situation was no better than on the east. Lieutenant Colonel Raymond L. Murray's 5th Marines had been stopped by Chinese forces with almost no gain in the first day of their attack west. And overnight, November 27–28, at the same time that MacLean's army troops were hit hard, massed Chinese assault troops had given the 5th and 7th Marines at Yudam-ni a night they would not forget.

General Almond's nature would have prevented him from questioning General MacArthur's standing order to attack toward the Yalu, even if the American forces involved had suffered initial setbacks. One should note that in the conference Colonel MacLean said that he thought he could still attack to the north if his third infantry battalion, the 2nd Battalion, 31st Infantry, joined his RCT, as he expected it to do.

From Hagaru-ri, Almond flew back to his CP at Hamhung. He soon continued on to the 7th Division CP near Hungnam, where he conferred with General Barr in midafternoon. There he received an order from General MacArthur to fly at once to Tokyo for a conference that night because of the crisis in Eighth Army in the west. General Walker, the Eighth Army commander, received the same call.[10]

Drake's Tank Attack toward the Inlet

Unknown to either of the infantry battalions or to the artillery battalion at the inlet and the forward position, Captain Drake's 31st Tank Company moved out of Hudong-ni's 31st Rear CP area on the morning of November 28 to break through the Chinese roadblock on Hill 1221 and link up with them. The night before, Drake had learned from the first sergeant of the ambushed medical company that there was a strong enemy roadblock on the road over Hill 1221, about two miles north of Hudong-ni, and that he would have to overcome it before he could move on to make a junction with the infantry and the artillery of the 31st RCT. Drake did not have any precise information, however, of the enemy strength he expected to meet at Hill 1221.

Drake did not know that General Hodes had spent the night at the Hudong-ni schoolhouse 31st Rear CP. During the night Hodes had decided that in the morning he would have Drake's tanks attack north to join the infantry and that he would accompany the tanks. Hodes and Drake conferred on the matter the next morning; Hodes made no change in plans.

After all had breakfasted, Drake assembled three platoons of five tanks each with one of his command tanks mounting a 105-mm howitzer and having communications with regimental netting. This made a total of 16 tanks at his line of departure, which he marked on his map as ¼ mile north of Hudong-ni. Drake pulled his jeep second in line behind the command tank. Hodes and the first sergeant of the medical company rode with him. Drake left his 4th Platoon of tanks and the second command tank with Lt. Hensen at Hudong-ni to defend the 31st Infantry Rear CP and the regimental dumps there.[11]

Major Lynch watched the tank column form and then start up the road. Lynch's observation of Drake at Hudong-ni and later in the Marine defense perimeter at Hagaru-ri (where on the night of November 30 Drake's tanks slaughtered CCF attacking down East Hill in an effort to overrun the northeast arc of the Hagaru-ri perimeter) caused him to characterize Drake as an outstanding tank commander.

Born in California in 1923, Drake graduated from West Point in the class of 1944 and was commissioned an infantry-armor officer. He was assigned to the 9th Tank Battalion, 20th Armored Division, and received his field training under Maj. Gen. Orlando Ward, who took the division to Europe in World War II. He served with the 9th Tank Battalion of the 20th Armored Division in Europe in 1944–45, and in Japan during 1949–50 he commanded A Company, 77th Tank Battalion, up to the outbreak of the Korean War. His tank company was in action following the Inchon Landing

Capt. (later Col.) Robert E. Drake (*right*) talking with Maj. Gen. Edward M. Almond, X Corps commander (*left*), and Maj. Gen. David G. Barr (*center*), commander, 7th Infantry Division, Hungnam, Korea, December, 1950. Photograph courtesy of Colonel Drake.

from Suwon north to the Han River and the capture of Seoul. Drake was 27 years old at Chosin.

Brigadier General Henry Irving Hodes, 7th Division assistant commander, who now rode beside Drake, was born in the District of Columbia on March 19, 1899. Like Drake, he was a West Point graduate, class of 1920. Hodes was now 51 years old. He had been commissioned from West Point as an infantry officer but later transferred to cavalry. In World War II he had served in the War Department General Staff from 1942 to 1944 and had then commanded the 112th Infantry Regiment, 28th Division, in Europe. He was known as a taciturn officer. When he rode north with Drake on the morning of November 28, he let Drake exercise complete command of the tank attack, assuming the role of an officer who merely sought transportation to the forward infantry battalions.[12]

Maj. Gen. Henry I. Hodes, deputy chief of staff, Eighth Army, at Munsan-ni on his return from the first meeting of the armistice conference at Kaesong, Korea, July 10, 1951. Hodes was assistant division commander, 7th Division, at Chosin Reservoir, November–December, 1950. US Army photograph SC 372286.

From the line of departure the command tank led off northward with Drake and his passengers next in line. The three tank platoons followed without any infantry. About half a mile north the road seemed headed straight into Hill 1221, which rose about 400 feet above the low ground at Twiggae. There a tributary rising in the high mountain mass of Hill 1456 on the northeast emptied into the reservoir. The road thus far had been level, or nearly so, and ran near the edge of the reservoir. It crossed a small bridge and came to the edge of Twiggae, where it turned sharply northeast, angling up the lower slope of Hill 1221 toward a saddle about a mile away. There it made a hairpin turn and started northwest down the opposite (north) face to another inlet valley, where it met the reservoir.

Near Twiggae the stretch of road leading up to the saddle of Hill 1221, where the enemy had ambushed the medical company the night before, came into full view. At this turn the medical sergeant asked Drake to stop the jeep so that he could point out places where the Chinese had been the night before when they ambushed the medical company. While he was speaking and pointing to various places, a single shot from a sniper hit him in the head. Blood spurted over the map the three had been examining. The sergeant died immediately. Hodes took cover, and Drake ran to his command tank. It was about 10:00 A.M. on November 28.[13]

When Drake reached his command tank, he divided his force into three platoons. One platoon started up the road along the south slope of Hill 1221, a second attacked the south face of Hill 1221 north and west of the road, and Drake held the third platoon as a reserve at first behind his command tank. After the engagement was joined, however, Drake sent the third platoon east of the road along the right-hand edge of the flat ground at the lower edge of Hill 1473 (Ko-bong) in an effort to give flank support to the tanks on the road.

When the lead tanks advancing on the road neared some knocked-out vehicles of the medical company, the precise site of the ambush was revealed—about 400 to 500 yards south of the saddle at the east end of Hill 1221. There enemy bazooka teams and supporting riflemen attacked the two lead tanks, scored hits with American-built 3.5-inch rocket launchers, and knocked them out. One of the tanks blocked the road; the other slid off toward one side. Under covering fire the crew members escaped, some wounded.

Meanwhile, the tanks that tried to cross the low ground east of the road found the ground soft in spots. Chinese soldiers rushed down to the tanks,

The view toward the northeast from near the middle of the inlet perimeter, showing the area the Chinese overran on the night of November 27–28. The photograph was taken on November 28. Several American dead, in sleeping bags, are in the foreground. The vehicular road runs along the south side of the inlet just out of sight beyond the narrow-gauge railroad, which is visible. The photographer is unknown. Photograph courtesy of Col. Ray O. Embree.

scrambled up their sides, and tried to lift the heavy engine compartment doors, intending to drop grenades inside. Drake's command tank from the lower part of the road swept the tops of these tanks with machine-gun fire and tried for tree bursts of 105-mm howitzer shells above the Chinese. Other tanks of the platoon directed machine-gun fire across the tops of the forward tanks and quickly swept the Chinese soldiers away. Two of the tanks, however, became mired down for a while, and it was a struggle to free them.

The tanks on the slope of Hill 1221, west of the road, were having a difficult time. They could not negotiate the slippery, frozen slope. One went out of control over a steep incline, and another threw a track. The third

The view from within the eastern part of the inlet perimeter on the morning of November 28, showing American litter parties gathering American dead in the area overrun by Chinese during the previous night. Two Chinese dead (in white uniforms) can be seen in the foreground. The photographer is unknown. Photograph courtesy of Col. Crosby P. Miller.

platoon, which had tried to skirt the marshland on the east, or south of the road, finally extricated itself and returned to Hudong-ni earlier than the others.

General Hodes watched the progress of the tank attack and saw that it would not succeed. Drake and Hodes discussed the situation, knowing the attack was failing. Drake said that if he could get some infantry support he would try again the next day to get to the top of Hill 1221 and dislodge the CCF. Drake also said that he wanted air strikes to help his attack. Hodes promised to do what he could, got into Drake's jeep, and drove back to Hudong-ni. Drake continued his efforts for some time after Hodes left but called off the attack in the afternoon. He reported his personnel casualties as two officers and 10 enlisted men. He had lost four tanks.

Hodes arrived back at Hudong-ni about noon. He seemed intent on going to Hagaru-ri, the only place where help might be sought. While he was considering the situation at Hudong-ni, he told Lieutenant Hensen of the tank company to make a reconnaissance from there to the area northeast of the road to find a route in that direction to bring the tanks around the Chinese roadblock at Hill 1221 and get them to the inlet.[14]

Hodes then told Anderson, Witte, and Lynch that he was going to Hagaru-ri to get help.[15] He planned to go in a jeep. There was discussion among the 31st RCT officers about whether the road might be closed. Hodes did not seem disturbed by the prospect. But that morning the 31st Rear CP had picked up a message over its SCR 193 radio that Hodes's van had stalled in Funchilin Pass, below Koto-ri, and had been pushed over the cliff to clear the road. Other messages indicated that the 2nd Battalion, 31st Infantry, probably would not arrive and that enemy action had stopped traffic over the pass to Koto-ri. The enemy might likewise have cut the road between Hudong-ni and Hagaru-ri, but there was no information on that point. By this time the 31st Rear CP at Hudong-ni had lost communication with the inlet and forward positions, and none of this news went forward to the infantry and the artillery, only a few miles away. Lynch recalled that the night before, the 27th, Colonel MacLean had discussed with Hodes his concern that he had had no word from Lieutenant Coke's I&R Platoon, which he had sent east on reconnaissance.

In the discussion about the danger in setting out alone for Hagaru-ri in a jeep, someone had a persuasive thought. It was suggested that it would be better for Hodes to go in a tank since it would provide better protection for the trip and had radio facilities as well. This changed Hodes's mind, and he said that he would go in one of the tanks. He left Hudong-ni just after noon and soon arrived at Hagaru-ri, only 5 miles south, without incident. Hodes never returned to Hudong-ni.[16]

In the afternoon Lieutenant Hensen began reconnoitering for a route around the Chinese roadblock. He took two tanks and started up a trail that ran northeast from behind the schoolhouse along the sloping ground of the hillside. The trail was only wide enough for one tank at a time. On this trail enemy fire hit the lead tank on its right track and stopped it. Lieutenant Hensen sighted the enemy gunner who had fired the round and had his tank gunner fire on him with a round of white phosphorus. This shot destroyed the enemy position. A member of Hensen's tank crew, Sgt. Jimmy P. Howle, tells what happened next:

We all got out of the tank. Lt. Hensen wanted some volunteers to go on to the top of this saddle to try and reconnoiter a new route to your [Capt. Drake's] position. When we reached the top of this saddle, we could see you at a distance. We became engaged in a fire-fight with some Chinese. They wanted to surrender. Lt. Hensen said that we would take them prisoner. They were in a group, and as we walked toward them they spread apart, and a man with a machine gun opened fire on us. I saw where the bullets striking Lt. Hensen in the front. . . . The bullets were pushing in his stomach and I could see his jacket pushing out in the back. I and Kim ran for cover of the trees nearby. We used up all our ammunition while trying to get back to our disabled tank and the other guys. I reported what had happened, and had it radioed to the CP. I then went inside the tank and re-plenished my ammunition, also some hand grenades. I asked if there were any volunteers to go with me and retrieve Lt. Hensen's body. No one would go. I started out alone. I didn't go far when I observed two Chinese down the hill to my right. I opened fire on them, neutralized them. When I looked to my left I saw the Chinese that had wanted [to] surrender just standing above me. I opened fire upon him. I think I emptied the clip into him. Then I saw many Chinese in the trees. I think that is when I realized just how crazy I was. That is when my nerves went berserk. I ran as fast as

A panoramic view, looking over the eastern end of the inlet perimeter, photographed on November 28, 1950, by an unknown photographer. The valley of the Pungnyuri-gang lies at the left along the base of the mountains. CCF sniper fire came from the ridge at the far right. Photograph courtesy of Col. Ray O. Embree.

I could back to the safety of the tanks. 1st Sgt Keck and your [Drake's] executive officer (I don't recall his name) had just arrived. They were forming a group to go and retrieve Lt. Hensen. I wanted to lead them to where Lt. Hensen was. Your exec. ordered me to the CP, telling me that I was in no condition to go anywhere. I told 1st Sgt Keck about the Chinese that I had emptied the clip into. He informed me later that he had shot him about three more rounds to make sure that he was dead. The exec told the jeep driver to take me to the CP and to return. Upon reaching the CP I talked to a major about what was going on up there. Then I went into the kitchen, and was offered a cup of coffee. I was shaking so bad that I could not hold it. I sat down on a box and was handed it again, placing it between my knees. It was no use, I was shaking too badly. Then the Medic (I don't remember his name) gave me a shot of morphine. It had some

calming effect on me, but not enough. Later on the same Medic gave me
some more. I think enough to put me to sleep.[17]

The group on the trail did not recover Lt. Hensen's body, but returned
to the schoolhouse. Drake knew Hensen was a very aggressive young officer
and was not surprised when his sergeant told him of his attempt. Drake
searched the mountain country to the northeast with binoculars, eventually
spotting Hensen's body propped against a tree in a sitting position, his rifle
in his lap. Drake assumed that the Chinese had set a trap, hoping that
Americans searching for Hensen would walk into it. He did not respond.[17]

Before he left for Hagaru-ri, Hodes, realizing that the Chinese in the
high mountains on the northeast had perfect observation of the 31st Rear
CP at Hudong-ni and after dark might make an effort to overrun it, decided that it should have a perimeter defense. He told Major Witte, the
regimental S-2, to lay out a perimeter, and he then walked over it with him.
Witte had no regular infantry for the perimeter, so he used an engineer
platoon and regimental service troops. Hodes asked Witte whether there
was any reason why he should not leave Lt. Col. Berry K. Anderson, the
regimental S-3, in charge at Hudong-ni. Neither Hodes nor Witte knew
Anderson well, but Witte replied that he knew of no reason to deny Anderson his seniority.

In the afternoon of the 28th, therefore, Anderson became the acting commander of the 31st Rear CP, pending any change that Colonel MacLean might
make. But MacLean was never again in communication with Anderson or
the 31st Rear CP. During the 28th, Service Battery of the 57th Field Artillery Battalion, which had spent the night about a mile south of Hudong-ni,
moved up to the 31st Rear CP and joined the group. There were now 150
miscellaneous 31st regimental headquarters and service troops at Hudong-
ni. Counting Drake's tank company of about 176 men, the total number
of troops there was approximately 325.

The Chinese did not attack Hudong-ni while the 31st Rear CP and the
tank company were there, possibly deterred by the presence of the tanks.
But they did infiltrate snipers to within small-arms range and placed long-
range machine-gun fire on the area, causing some casualties.[18]

During Drake's tank action on the 28th at Hill 1221, he had in view the
entire mountain mass of Hill 1473, 1½ or 2 miles eastward. There on the
high ridgeline he could see long lines of horse-mounted Chinese moving
steadily southward. Drake estimated that he saw several hundred who had

already bypassed the 31st RCT forward and inlet positions and now also Hudong-ni. Whether they were parts of the CCF 80th Division that had attacked the 31st RCT or were from another major enemy formation is not known.[19] It is reasonably certain, however, that they were on their way to East Hill, which dominated the east side of Hagaru-ri, and possibly other positions farther south along the X Corps MSR, which was under attack all the way to Sudong. Very likely many of them participated in the Chinese attack on Hagaru-ri that night.

During the tank action at Hill 1221 on November 28, Drake had no communication of any kind either with the 3rd Battalion, 31st Infantry, and the 57th Field Artillery at the inlet, only 2 miles northeast, or with Faith's 1st Battalion, 32nd Infantry, 4 miles farther north. Nor did anyone at the inlet perimeter hear any sound of the tank battle. The infantry and artillerymen, only a mile or two away, had no knowledge of the armor effort being made to reach them.

At the Inlet

When the Chinese overran the 81-mm mortars and A Battery's 105-mm howitzers, they neither destroyed nor removed them. When they withdrew at daybreak, therefore, these weapons were still in place, and the artillerymen and the infantry reclaimed them during the morning. After the last Chinese had been driven from the battalion CP and the communications huts in Lieutenant Traywick's dawn counterattack, the 3rd Battalion reoccupied its original CP. During the day with the help of air strikes the infantry troops occupied their original ridgeline positions on the east side of the perimeter. Stragglers from the rifle companies continued to filter into the perimeter throughout the day from their places of refuge during the latter part of the night. M Company improved its position for an expected continuation of the fight after dark. This was difficult work because the ground was frozen.[20]

The artillery changed its position during the day so that it did not coincide with the emplacements of the two batteries the first night. First Lieutenant Paul C. Smithey, B Battery, said that he talked to one of his ROK soldiers, who in turn talked with several Chinese prisoners. They told him that the next night (November 28–29), after the Chinese launched their first attack, they planned to follow it up by moving on B Battery, where they had been stopped the first night.[21]

One unfortunate thing had become clear in the artillery positions during the night of November 27–28 and the day of the 28th: Captain Theodore C. Goss, commander of B Battery, was not performing up to the standard of a battery commander. He acted more like a case of "combat fatigue," and was not in the fight.[22] In contrast to Goss, Capt. Harold L. Hodge, A Battery commander, has been praised by all his officers and men who left any record of their views. Lieutenant Thomas J. Patton, of A Battery, said of Hodge that his "leadership proved to be of an outstanding quality, giving courage and inspiration to the men of the battery. His coolness under heavy fire was almost unbelievable." Patton said that on the second day Hodge told him that "the Battle of Bastogne was a picnic compared to this." Hodge had been decorated for bravery at Bastogne, according to Patton.

Although the Chinese withdrew from close contact at the inlet at dawn, they did not cease hostilities during the day. They deployed out of range to take control of the high ground around the small perimeter of the inlet. From the northern slopes of Hill 1456 they continued a harrassing sniper fire from the ridges on the east and the slope south of the perimeter. Several officers and men were killed or wounded by this fire during the day.

The command situation at the inlet perimeter seemed uncertain throughout the day. Both Colonel Reilly and Colonel Embree had been wounded during the night, though Reilly remained in command after he regained consciousness in the morning. Reilly, according to Captain Jordan, was able to sit up and carry on a conversation. It is not certain whether Embree relinquished command of the 57th Field Artillery on the 28th after being wounded. If he did, it is probable that Maj. Robert J. Tolly, the S-3, assumed command. Reilly's condition must have worsened, because when Major Curtis, of the 1st Battalion, 32nd Infantry, saw him the next day in the aid station, he thought Reilly appeared to be in a daze and could hardly talk.[23]

The most important event affecting the 31st RCT at the inlet during the 28th was Colonel Embree's order in the morning for the 57th Field Artillery Headquarters and Headquarters Battery, together with Captain McClymont's AAA AW weapons, to move into the 3rd Battalion perimeter. In making the move, McClymont had to leave one knocked-out M19 dual-40 behind in the little valley. The rest of his antiaircraft weapons, three M19s and four M16s, were taken into the 3rd Battalion perimeter, together

A Far East Air Force airdrop in the southeastern part of the inlet perimeter, November 28–29, 1950. The photographer is unknown. Photograph courtesy of Col. Ray O. Embree.

with a 2½-ton truck. It is not known how many vehicles of the artillery headquarters were operable and made the short trip into the inlet perimeter. The move was completed about 1:00 P.M. without enemy interference. Air cover and the lethal power of the M19s and M16s made the situation unappealing to the Chinese. The American dead were left behind, and the wounded were taken to the middle of the perimeter.

In the afternoon McClymont took one of his half-track M16 quad-50s with its crew and went back to their recently abandoned bivouac. He wanted to be sure that no stragglers or wounded had been left behind. He made a circuit of the area but found no one. Enemy were present in the hills, however, and some small-arms fire came from a few of them. It caused no damage.[24]

The M19s and M16s were the most effective weapons for defending the inlet perimeter. Without them it is unlikely that the troops could have survived another night. McClymont describes how he positioned the AAA weapons: "When we arrived at the 3/31 perimeter, I placed my weapons around the edge, with fields of fire such that the northern, eastern, and southern solid ground areas were covered by overlap—one M19 and one M16 also could cover the arm of the reservoir."[25]

In the late afternoon C-47 aircraft tried to drop 16 tons of supplies to the 31st RCT at the inlet, but strong winds carried much of it to the Chinese on the southern slope.

7

The Second Night,
November 28–29

Throughout the 28th the Chinese watched the inlet from the high ground. They saw the M19s and M16s of McClymont's D Battery move into the perimeter and carefully plotted the position of each of the dreaded weapons. They noted the reorganization of the position and the composition of infantry put into the front lines, roughly at the same places K and I companies had occupied the first night. Captain Kitz still commanded K Company, but it now included remnants of both K and L. The L Company troops occupied the lower section of the line next to the Pungnyuri-gang, below the bridge and causeway.

The main defense still faced east, positioned along the spur ridge that came down to the stream east of the southern end of the bridge and causeway across the Pungnyuri-gang. The 3rd Battalion line ran up this ridge about 800 yards along its lower, gentler crest. From that point the Chinese held the upper and sharply steeper portion of the ridge to the crest of Hill 1456. During the day the 31st Infantry troops in the low ground frequently saw enemy groups higher up, south and southeast of them.[1]

The CCF resumed the battle at the inlet perimeter before dark on the night of November 28–29, so eager were they to finish off what they had nearly accomplished the night before. The attack began against the infantry line on the east side of the perimeter. There the Chinese captured a machine gun and for a time achieved a penetration of K Company. Members of the gun crew ran up to the K Company CP to report the incident. Captain Kitz at once set off to get mortar fire to stop the enemy. Many of his men criticized him for leaving his company at this point, thinking that he should have stayed with it and sent a runner back with his request.

There is no explanation why a telephone line was not in to the 81-mm mortars. It was probably Kitz who ran up to Sfc. Robert M. Slater, who commanded an M19, and ordered him to move his weapon to stop a CCF attack. Slater thought that a captain had abandoned his company. He did not move his M19.[2]

The Chinese who had overrun the machine gun on the infantry line were subsequently killed inside the perimeter. During the night some of the enemy penetrated as far as the artillery, but the artillerymen stayed with their pieces and, aided by the fire of the M19s near them, killed or drove off the Chinese. At the inlet, the battle lasted all night and at times was furious. There were many temporary enemy penetrations, but they were all liquidated. At daybreak the perimeter still held, though shakily.

New and ominous features of the fighting in the hours before dawn were the enemy attacks coming from the west, on the approach along the inlet by the road and the railroad. These enemy troops had come from the *south*. The attacks at the western part of the perimeter by these Chinese lasted the longest. Before they withdrew just after daylight, they had occupied land between the inlet and the perimeter.

Many within the perimeter saw that the Chinese had made the M19s and M16s their special targets and had attacked them at close quarters in an effort to destroy them. The antiaircraft guns played a dominant role in holding the main part of the position. First Lieutenant Patton, of A Battery, speaking of the heavy combat that night, said that the enemy attacks "were repulsed with credit due mostly to the men of the 15th AAA AW Bn who manned the M16s and M19s."[3]

The main enemy close-in attack against the antiaircraft weapons guarding the artillery came after midnight and was preceded by a salvo of mortar shells and heavy small-arms fire. Sergeant Grantford R. Brown's M19, near the artillery, came under close attack, and a number of Chinese succeeded in infiltrating right up to it. Captain McClymont was in his foxhole about 35 yards from Brown's dual-40. Brown had been firing the two Bofors guns toward the hill southward, and his heavy fire of high-explosive 40-mm shells, at the rate of 240 rounds a minute, which included tracers, briefly lighted up the area.

McClymont realized that Brown's M19 was under attack and started toward it, even though he felt that it was defending itself adequately. Before he got to it, the firing stopped, and all was darkness again. Then one of the nearby quad-50s opened up, sweeping the area in front of it. When

McClymont arrived there, the crew was reloading the gun. These enemy attacks, and the responding fire of the antiaircraft weapons, continued at intervals throughout the night.

At daybreak McClymont walked over to Brown's dual-40. He saw a trail of Chinese bodies beginning at the very side of the M19 and leading up the hillside out of sight. Brown had fired most of his ammunition during the night. He told McClymont that he had something to show him. He pointed out the body of a Chinese soldier lying beside the full-track, killed by small-arms fire. He said, "That fellow came in with the second rush. I was up on the turret directing fire when he climbed up alongside of me. I saw he was carrying something and he looked Chinese to me, so I hit him with my fist. Almost broke my wrist, I did, and he fell over the side. One of my ROK soldiers under the M19 shot the Chinese as he hit the ground." McClymont said that Sergeant Brown "reached down on the top deck of the M19 where spare barrels were kept and raised the end of a 6 inch (in diameter) bamboo tube. There were two fuses running into this homemade 5-foot Bangalore torpedo. Had the Chinese been able to find his matches, or had Sergeant Brown been less alert, that M19 would have been blown sky high and the perimeter would have been breached."[4]

McClymont and some of his men gathered up the Chinese bodies and put them in a pile. Two were still alive and told a ROK soldier that 4,000 Chinese soldiers surrounded the Americans. Whether they meant the inlet perimeter or all the scattered groups was not clear. Their leader had placed a big price on the antiaircraft full-tracks and half-tracks, promising a great prize to any soldier who knocked out one of them.

McClymont started on a round of his other AAA vehicles. At one of the other dual-40s the crew were standing at the rear of the full-track, pointing to the twin 40-mm guns. There McClymont saw an unexploded 60-mm enemy mortar shell wedged between the barrel jackets.

He fashioned a noose from a length of field wire, climbed on the M19, and gingerly slipped the wire noose around the mortar shell to catch on the fins at the end. After one effort to jerk the shell loose, which would have brought it straight to him, he was glad that the effort failed. He then slipped the wire through the towing eye of the M19 and went to the other end of the vehicle. From there he gave another jerk on the wire. The mortar round came loose this time and went flying to just about the spot where he had been standing. But it did not explode.

A little distance away the D Battery mess tent was a shambles. Parts of the field kitchen were angling out in all directions. Over the rear of the truck bed was a stovepipe from the immersion heaters. Pointing straight up out of the stovepipe was another unexploded Chinese mortar shell. The mess personnel lassoed and dragged away the stovepipe and the mortar round after McClymont showed them how to do it.[5]

How did the night battle look to the survivors in the foxholes? Each had his own experiences and impressions. John C. Sweatman, an assistant mess sergeant of K Company, gives a vignette of his: "The second night we were there, just before sunset, we dug a foxhole, took our position there, and every now and then they banzaied. These kept up all night about every half hour. During the course of the night there were 3 jeep drivers that got caught outside their foxholes. Two of them fell on top of us and died. Just about that time we were hit by white phosphorus. There was one Hawaiian boy there shot in the back and also burned with white phosphorus. Another was burned up by white phosphorus."[6]

When daylight came, the Chinese in contact at the perimeter began to withdraw, as they had the morning before, fearing air strikes, which would bring decimating casualties. But action was still heavy at the southwest corner, where there had been no enemy the first night. There were also large numbers of Chinese between the perimeter and the arm of the reservoir—the inlet—on the north side of the perimeter. It is apparent, therefore, that either the position did not go down to the inlet shoreline or that part of the perimeter had been lost in the night's battle. It is also apparent that the Chinese had completely surrounded the inlet perimeter.

The Chinese in this area withdrew west at daylight along the edge of the inlet, moving on the road and the railroad leading south. This showed a new development and directness in the approach march of many of their assault forces. Here the AAA automatic weapons had killed many Chinese near and along the side of the inlet.

First Lieutenant Paul C. Smithey, assistant executive and motor officer of B Battery, 57th Field Artillery, said that he and Lieutenant Magill went out and checked the perimeter to estimate the destruction they had wrought on the Chinese during the night. He said that he counted 750 Chinese bodies.[7] This figure probably included a somewhat exaggerated estimate of casualties in some places that could not be examined closely. There was ample testimony from others who saw parts of the enemy dead within and outside the inlet perimeter that there were many casualties.

At the Forward Perimeter

The second night started off quietly at the forward position of the 1st Battalion, in contrast to the situation at the inlet. There was time for the kitchen and mess personnel of D Company to prepare a hot meal.

Several officers gathered at the battalion CP hut, where a gasoline stove gave some warmth. Captain Raymond Vaudreaux, the battalion S-4, came in to report that ammunition had run low and an airdrop would be needed the next day. MacLean and Faith went into a small side room to try to get some sleep. But Faith apparently could not sleep and about 8:00 P.M. returned to the main room and began telephoning his company commanders. They reported that the situation was quiet.

The heavy mortars about two miles behind the 1st Battalion front lines had delivered heavy fire the first night and during the day just ended. But several of them had broken or cracked standards because of the heavy use and maximum rate of fire with extreme charge in the cold weather. The 1st Battalion, therefore, would have reduced heavy-mortar support during the second night.[8]

Lieutenant Colonel Faith had had to put some troops in position at the gap in the line that Mortrude had left at the extreme western end of C Company's sector, next to the road, when on orders he had taken his platoon to the company's right flank during the day. Faith asked 1st Lt. Hugh May, the motor officer, to gather about a platoon-size force of men from Headquarters Company and take them up the hill to fill Mortrude's former position. May assembled about 40 men and arrived at the gap in the line just before dark.

May appears to have been the oldest man in the 1st Battalion and also had perhaps as much varied experience, much of it in combat, as any other man in the battalion. He had obtained a battlefield commission as a second lieutenant when he was a member of a tank battalion in the Italian Campaign of World War II, and his long and varied career in the Army included training as an artilleryman and tanker. But at Chosin he served largely as an infantry platoon leader. He had seen enough service and combat that he had no trouble performing the role with distinction.

May was first assigned to the Far East in 1948. In Korea in the fall of 1950 he was reassigned to Headquarters Company, 1st Battalion, 32nd Infantry, as its motor officer. All who have written or spoken of May have admired him as a competent and experienced officer, a dependable soldier in combat.[9]

The wait in the 1st Battalion for the enemy attack ended at midnight. First there were a few probes. Then quickly the Chinese attack developed all around the perimeter. By 1:00 A.M. it was in full force, and at once the battalion was in trouble. On the battalion left in A Company's sector the Chinese moved around the west end of the company line and attacked from that side. They cut off the left-flank 1st Platoon and threatened the entire company rear, killing the 1st Platoon leader. A counterattack failed to restore the position. The Chinese success against A Company came at the point where the battalion perimeter made its closest approach to the reservoir, about 1½ miles west over rough terrain. The Chinese could now infiltrate around A Company's left flank and reach the battalion CP and Captain Bigger's 81-mm mortars, less than a mile to the rear.

At the same time more Chinese attacked up the road against Lieutenant May's improvised platoon, which now held the east side of the road in the battalion line. When he went into the line just before dark, May had arranged with Lt. Cecil Smith, commanding A Company, that he, May, would assume responsibility for the road during the night. May said that he made this arrangement because A Company informed him that they had every man on their front line for the night's expected action.

May comments:

> I arrived at the ridge line above (north) of CP to take over the position held by the left flank platoon of "C" Company, and on the right flank of "A" Co. I established contact with both "C" and "A" Cos. We set up with "A" Co's right platoon for my unit to cover the road. The road proved to be the point to defend during the night. The road was covered by 2 30 cal. M.G.'s one light and one heavy, plus one recoilless rifle.
>
> Using these weapons plus some rifle fire we beat back 2 attempts of the CCF to penetrate during the night. Also some probing action along our front on the steep forward slope.[10]

After May had repelled the enemy attacks up the road, the Chinese tried to mount an attack frontally up the draws of the steep northern slope. May and his men could hear the Chinese troops below them. May adjusted 81-mm and 4.2-inch mortar fire on their assembly areas, preventing any further attacks on his front during the night.

From their position on A Company's right May and his men could see the battle continuing against A Company westward on Hill 1316. On orders from battalion May directed observed mortar fire in front of A Company's position.[11]

At the right (east) of A Company and May's platoon, C Company was hard pressed. The critical point was still the Chinese-held knob and the high ground on its right flank at the boundary with B Company. There 2nd Lt. James G. Campbell, from the Weapons Company, had two machine guns emplaced downslope from the enemy-held knob. He expected the Chinese to extend their hold farther down the ridgeline during the night, so he selected alternate positions for the guns and was prepared to displace them so that they could cover the Chinese if they made a penetration. During the night Captain Bigger had been able to get a telephone wire run from his command post to Campbell's position to adjust on enemy mortar fire on his front. When the enemy began mortar fire, Campbell was able to see the tube flashes on the hill mass to his southeast but could not adjust on them because he could not differentiate the mortar ranging rounds from other indirect fire impacting on his front.

The expected CCF attack from the knob came during an enemy mortar barrage and pushed C Company's right-hand squad off its position. Campbell moved one of his guns about 30 feet to the alternate position and reoriented the other gun's field of fire. These changes limited further enemy penetrations and prevented the Chinese from exploiting the situation.[12]

Lieutenant Mortrude, a little farther east, received enemy sniper fire in his platoon area from the ridge and knoll in front of him. He requested mortar fire, and it came in on target. According to Mortrude, "The first ranging round fell over and behind the target ridge line and resulted in loud cries of distress. I then requested 'Fire for Effect' at repeat range. The next few rounds resulted in more cries of pain, as though the fire for effect was falling in an assembly area. In any case, the fire from the ridge line at that point ceased and all remained quiet thereafter."[13] During these attacks on C Company's right flank Capt. Dale Seever had his CP only 15 yards behind his frontline riflemen.[14]

The Chinese persistently attacked B Company's left flank, adjacent to the C Company boundary where B Company's line bent south. At the same time they penetrated C Company's line below the high knoll. Lieutenant Mazzulla, on the line there with B Company, reported to battalion that the enemy had broken through the line and were headed down the draw leading directly to the battalion CP. On receipt of this message Faith sent all remaining battalion headquarters personnel into the draw east of the CP.

But B Company quickly closed the gap in its line, and the Chinese never reached the battalion CP.[15]

Tension built at the CP after midnight as the Chinese assaults increased in intensity and severity. Shortly after midnight, Colonel MacLean joined the others in listening to reports on company situations. Faith seemed on edge and about 1:00 A.M. ordered many of those sitting or standing in the room to go outside to help in the defense of the CP.[16]

Outside the men took up positions near the hut and listened to the ever-increasing level of noise at the front lines. Spent bullets whistled overhead. A 4.2-inch mortar round fell short and landed 50 yards from the CP, knocking out one of the defenders' machine guns emplaced there. Major Robbins, one of those who had just left the CP hut, has given his impressions of that moment:

> All weapons of the battalion were apparently firing as fast as they could be operated from the din going on about us. The mortars were throwing out their incessant bursts. Shadowy figures kept coming and going about the entrance of the CP as wounded were helped or carried bodily into the relative safety of the area. Company runners made their way into and out of the building. A ghostly light pervaded the whole scene as a light snow began to fall and through this curtain a faint moon tried vainly to shine. Flashes of fire from bursting shells and flares intermittently lighted the area and added to the weird effect.[17]

The firing died down to sporadic bursts. Lieutenant McNally, the 31st communications officer, was among those outside the CP. Suddenly he was called into the building. He soon came back out and told Major Robbins that Colonel MacLean had ordered the 1st Battalion to prepare to withdraw and to attack if necessary to reach the 3rd Battalion at the inlet perimeter. It was 2:00 A.M.[18]

The details of the discussions between MacLean and Faith and the reasons for the order to withdraw are uncertain. Curtis has written that Faith was afraid that the Chinese, having turned the left flank of A Company, could reach the 81-mm mortar position and the CP and cut off all the troops to the north and northeast. According to one source, MacLean left the decision to Faith as a battalion decision.[19]

Whatever the details of discussion leading to the decision to withdraw, Colonel MacLean must have agreed with Lieutenant Colonel Faith's opinion. He was the senior officer on the ground and would hold the responsibility. One should remember that, after MacLean and Hodes arrived at

the reservoir on November 26, the 1st Marine Division ceased to command
the 1st Battalion, 32nd Infantry, or any other parts of the 31st RCT as they
arrived at the reservoir. Nor did the Marines try to exercise any command
over these troops. The 31st RCT was under the command of Maj. Gen.
David Barr, of the 7th Infantry Division, and through him the X Corps
commander. This command situation remained unchanged until the X Corps
order on November 29 gave command over all troops in the Chosin Reservoir area to Gen. Oliver Smith and the 1st Marine Division beginning at
8:00 A.M. on November 30.

The order to withdraw, decided on at the 1st Battalion CP about 2 A.M.
on November 29, did not reach all the troops on the perimeter until two
hours later. At 2:45 A.M., for instance, 1st Sgt. Richard S. Luna, of B Company, received orders to take all the Headquarters Company personnel and
cooks to the line to fill a gap. He did so, and he and that group were at
the front when the withdrawal order reached them at 4:30 A.M.

Meanwhile, in the continuing action on the C Company front, Cpl.
James H. Godfrey, of the Heavy Weapons Company, gunner of a 75-mm
recoilless rifle, again distinguished himself as convincingly as he had the
previous night. The Chinese in their attacks the first night had captured
the second 75-mm recoilless rifle in C Company's sector. In the ensuing Chinese effort to use this weapon, they found themselves engaged in a duel
with Godfrey. He and his crew demolished the captured gun and killed its
Chinese crew. In this encounter Godfrey expended all his ammunition, and
the rifle platoon to which he was attached was reduced to three men. He
was able to get his recoilless rifle on a truck and successfully evacuate it. He
then continued the fight with rifle and grenades as C Company withdrew.[20]

About 3:00 A.M., Major Miller, the battalion executive officer, climbed
the spur ridge to the C Company CP. There he talked over the situation
with Captain Seever, the company commander. Seever had been slightly
wounded in the leg the day before but had remained in command. With
Seever, Miller could hear the din of the battle increase in the A Company
sector westward on the battalion left flank. About 3:30 A.M., Miller received
a call on the company line from Faith, who relayed to him the details of
the projected battalion withdrawal, saying that the battalion would join the
3rd Battalion, 31st Infantry, at the inlet, starting at 4:30 A.M. Faith ordered
Miller to organize and conduct a rear-guard action with A Company during
the withdrawal.

Miller walked westward toward A Company. On the way he passed through Lieutenant May's position. Miller told May to withdraw to the 1st Battalion CP. He then crossed the road into Lieutenant Smith's A Company CP. There the company was still under attack. Its 1st Platoon was still cut off on the left flank. Smith had unsuccessfully counterattacked in an effort to reach the platoon, and he was about to counterattack again when Miller arrived. Miller discussed the situation with Smith and then told him to prepare to withdraw A Company down the draw in the company's rear.[21]

MacLean and Faith wanted to start the withdrawal at 4:30 A.M., completing it during the hours of darkness, and to enter the 3rd Battalion inlet perimeter at daybreak. There were about 4 road miles to cover between the two positions. Flank infantry guards on higher ground on the east would cover the vehicles' passage on the road. No one knew whether there were enemy troops on the high ground who would have to be driven off before the vehicles could pass.

Faith and his staff sent the verbal orders to the units by field telephone, by radio, and by messenger.[22] The general terms and conditions governing the withdrawal were as follows: it would be executed in blackout, which precluded the burning of abandoned equipment and supplies; all kitchen trucks would be emptied to carry wounded; and part of Headquarters Company would serve as advance guard on the road with the battalion headquarters and the vehicles, with Captain Turner's B Company on the left flank on ground east of the road and C Company east of B Company on still higher ground. Since an uncertain overland movement of the company was involved, Captain Seever, because of his leg wound, turned over C Company to Lieutenant Mortrude, his 3rd Platoon leader; Faith ordered Major Curtis to accompany C Company; Major Miller would command A Company, the rear guard. The 1st Battalion informed the 3rd Battalion by radio that it intended to join it at the inlet during the morning.[23]

In giving orders to his units, Faith talked directly with some unit commanders. Lieutenant Hugh May was one of these. He commented about Faith's instructions to him: "During the preparations for the withdrawal, Lt. Col. Faith instructed me to remove parts from any vehicle we could not evacuate, the object being to cripple the vehicle but not to destroy them, as it was *the intent to re-occupy these positions within 24 hours* [italics added]. This crippling was done by removing coils, coil wires, and other items, so the vehicles could not be operated under their own power."[24] In pondering this order, one wonders whether Colonel MacLean still intended to attack north after his 2nd Battalion, which he still expected, arrived.

The 31st Regimental Combat Team Consolidates at the Inlet

Lieutenant Colonel Faith ordered all trucks regardless of their cargo to be unloaded and the wounded put in them preparatory to the withdrawal. The vehicles of the 31st RCT that Major Robbins had brought into Faith's perimeter would therefore have to abandon all the field desks and contents considered essential to the operations of a command post. Robbins estimated that there were about 60 vehicles in the convoy. He wrote of preparations at the CP:

Already the headquarters personnel and the medics were busily assisting the ambulatory patients onto the trucks and carrying stretcher cases out of the tents which had been their shelter for the past 24 hours. The snow was now coming down in earnest and the footing had become extremely slippery. Drivers . . . began the task of starting frozen engines, and, once having them turn over, driving the trucks out onto the road. Since our own jeep driver was out in a foxhole defending part of the perimeter, I tackled the job of getting our own jeep going which boasted a nearly dead battery to begin with. . . . McNally came out of the CP and joined me as I wheeled into the column ready to move out.

Columns of foot soldiers formed on the road on each side of the vehicles and moved on out to the front. All preparations had been completed by around 0430. The column began to crawl forward. Many vehicles which simply could not be started because of the cold had to be left behind, but none of the wounded were without transportation, and that was the imminent thing at the moment. It was strangely quiet behind us as we moved on down the road towards the 3rd Battalion.[1]

This view, looking southwest, was taken on the morning of November 29 from a point on the causeway just north of the bridge over the Pungnyuri-gang. The crest and western slope of Hill 1221 are in the distance near the right edge of the photograph. The mass of men huddled under an embankment at the edge of the inlet (center) and others walking southward beyond them are members of the 1st Battalion, 32nd Infantry, crossing the inlet and joining the 3rd Battalion. Hill 1250 is the closer hill mass near the center. The photographer is unknown. Photograph courtesy of Col. Crosby P. Miller.

In the frontline companies the scene was not so orderly. Although B Company, for example, had received instructions to be ready to move at 4:30, it was 5:00 A.M. when First Sergeant Luna got the word to move out, leaving everything behind, including supplies and bedding. At 5:30, Luna actually started skirting the higher hills on his left. In C Company, Mortrude's 3rd Platoon was the first to leave. Subsequently, instead of platoons moving out in a scheduled rotation, one man would leave his hole, and others who saw him did likewise and made for the rear. There was even a semblance of panic as the men evacuated their positions. Lieutenant Campbell, at the right flank of C Company, thought that there was no panic but that "it was hasty." He engaged in a shouting argument with an adjacent C Company platoon leader over who would withdraw first, the infantry platoon or the Weapons Company section. Campbell argued that the D Company weapons section should withdraw first, since they could not just run off the ridge at the last moment carrying their heavy machine guns but would need some protection from riflemen at the beginning of their withdrawal. He persuaded the infantry platoon leader that this was the proper course. Campbell then had his machine gunners fire, in a sudden burst, the ammunition that they could not carry. This heavy fusilade of fire may have caused the enemy to think that an attack was being mounted and may have thrown them off balance, because when the weapons section began its withdrawal, there was no enemy pursuit or even fire. Campbell said that after they got off their position "it was a walk in the sun," and they reached the battalion CP and the line of vehicles forming there with no trouble.[2]

In Lieutenant May's sector there was a Chinese prisoner. What should they do with him? The man's hands and feet seemed to be badly frozen. May examined him and assured himself that this was indeed the case. He gave the Chinese prisoner rations and cigarettes and motioned him northward. May then led his men down the hill toward the battalion CP. There he took a position near the rear of the column. He and his men stayed at the rear of the 1st Battalion column throughout the withdrawal, forming a road rear guard.

On the battalion left flank in A Company's position the situation was bad. Lieutenant Smith's second counterattack to reach his cutoff 1st Platoon on the extreme west flank had failed. Major Miller thought that he could wait no longer. The protection of the battalion rear was more important, he knew, than trying harder to reach the 1st Platoon. He ordered Lieutenant Smith to move out. South of the point where the draw behind A Company's front met the road, Miller ordered Smith to keep one platoon about 100 yards west of the road. Before Smith could get his company in motion, the Chinese launched an attack. Most of the enemy were silhouetted clearly against the snow and made easy targets. Many were killed or wounded, and their attack was repulsed.[3] A Company now began its withdrawal.

The withdrawal was generally under way by 5:00 A.M. Perhaps the first unit out of the line was C Company, which was to act as the advance guard on the east. As C Company moved out, B Company held its place on the high ground. When C Company cleared, B Company followed. C Company, as it arrived abreast of the CP, was to remain east of (above) the road. Likewise, B Company, trailing C Company, was to remain on still higher ground east of the road to protect the motor convoy on the road below. But in the movement south Faith shouted to Mortrude at one point to move higher up the hill slope, and as it turned out, before the column reached the inlet, B Company was closer to the road on the left. Headquarters and D companies accompanied the battalion headquarters on the road. May and his improvised platoon from Headquarters Company closed the column.

Faith had ordered Major Curtis to accompany the troops on the high ground east of the road. He accordingly joined Lieutenant Mortrude's unit there. With Major Miller accompanying the rear guard, Faith had his two ranking staff officers in the most dangerous places from which to give leadership if trouble developed. Captain Bigger, Major Jones, Captain Stamford, and Lt. Henry Moore, of the A&P Platoon of Headquarters Company, were with MacLean and Faith in the command group.

The locations of the troop units in the withdrawal were logical in view of their positions on the line. Headquarters and D companies were closest to the battalion CP and could be most quickly assembled with it on the road. While B Company, closer to the withdrawal route than C Company, covered that company's withdrawal, it could follow after it, both staying on high ground east of the road. A Company, which was hardest pressed by the Chinese at the time, might have trouble. But with a machine gun at the rear, which let loose intermittent bursts of fire, the Chinese were kept from closing, and the company got away without serious trouble. But it left its 1st Platoon behind.[4]

One of the men in the command group, as it went ahead of the road column to find the rumored enemy roadblock near the inlet perimeter, was a young, boyish-looking former paratrooper, now the commander of Faith's Weapons Company, Captain Bigger. He was considered a special officer in the 1st Battalion as an acknowledged expert in the use of 81-mm mortars. Faith used him to coordinate all supporting artillery fire—not just armament of the Weapons Company, the recoilless rifles, the heavy machine guns, and the 81-mm mortars.

Bigger graduated from Castle Heights Military Academy, in Lebanon,

Tennessee, in 1938. He was called to active duty in January, 1942, as a second lieutenant and sent to the Infantry School at Fort Benning, where he graduated in April. He also attended the Airborne Parachute School at Fort Benning. Thereupon he was assigned to the 504th Parachute Infantry Regiment (PIR), which later became part of the 82nd Airborne Division, commanded by General Ridgway. Bigger made the assaults with his regiment at Gela, Sicily, and Salerno, Italy. Bigger's 504th PIR landed at Anzio on D Day and was there for 62 days. After World War II, Bigger eventually found himself in the 1st Battalion, 32nd Infantry, 7th Division, in Japan. By the time of Chosin, Bigger was an "old-timer" in the 1st Battalion. He had activated the battalion's Heavy Weapons Company and had trained the men who formed its ranks. He said unabashedly, "They knew their job and I knew mine." Faith had a close personal relationship with Bigger and relied heavily on him. Bigger and Jones, the latter also an airborne combat soldier in World War II, appear to have been Faith's closest friends in the 1st Battalion.[5]

Except in the A Company area, the Chinese did not react aggressively to the 1st Battalion's withdrawal. They may have been taken by surprise. There was no pursuit, and only a little small-arms fire fell anywhere near the withdrawing column. The most important factor in the failure of the Chinese to follow up closely on the withdrawal was perhaps the great amount of plunder they found all along the front line just vacated, and even greater amounts of food, supplies of all kinds, and various kinds of equipment in the vicinity of the battalion CP. To freezing and starving Chinese all this must have been temptation beyond the power of resistance. For the battalion it may have been worth all that was left behind to gain an unmolested withdrawal.

The men of C and B companies encountered no enemy on the hills east of the road as they moved south toward the inlet. This was the greatest good fortune. If the Chinese on the north and east sides of the perimeter had launched a determined close pursuit, or if they had emplaced troops and roadblocks between the battalion and the inlet, the going might have been very rough indeed. But there was none of this.

The road column progressed halfway to the inlet and halted opposite the 31st Heavy Mortar Company and near Colonel MacLean's former advance CP. There Capt. George Cody, commander of the Heavy Mortar Company, had, in the words of Major Jones, "the force drawn up in a circle 'Wagon Train style!'" Some vehicles from the road column were directed into this circle of vehicles, including the Weapons Company jeeps.[6] It was daylight when the battalion column stopped at Cody's position. The Chinese had never attacked the heavy-mortar position, although it must have been known to them. In its stop the 1st Battalion column picked up Cody's mortars.

From their position in the flat ground at the mortars members of the column could see the A Company rear guard moving downhill toward them from the northwest. They could also see a Chinese force following closely. First Lieutenant Robert Reynolds, platoon leader of the 32nd Heavy Mortar Company's 4.2-inch mortars, hurriedly set up two of them. He first set them to fire over the heads of A Company into the Chinese. Then he fired some rounds over the crest of the hill. This caused the Chinese there to run over the crest toward A Company. He immediately set to fire shorter, putting the rounds on the enemy troops, causing heavy casualties.

A Company came on, relatively free from pursuing Chinese. All the firing should have alerted everyone that the company was approaching. Despite this, a machine gun with the column opened up, but someone quickly stopped it. The gun then shifted its fire to a group of Chinese far in the rear of A Company.[7] When A Company joined the battalion, the battalion's rear vehicles were a mile from the inlet. Major Miller said that he had had no real trouble in the rearguard withdrawal, even though Chinese followed closely, blowing "weird calls on their bugles."[8]

During this stop the column reorganized to incorporate the heavy mortars and A Company. The leading vehicles were not far from the inlet. MacLean and Faith went ahead with a small party to reconnoiter the approach to the 3rd Battalion perimeter. They discovered a roadblock of logs on the south side of the bridge, covered by enemy automatic and small-arms fire. Faith kept the column stopped where it was and ordered some infantrymen to climb the hill to the east above the bridge to attack the enemy roadblock from above it.

When these orders were given, Lieutenant Campbell, at the heavy-mortar position with the halted column, asked permission to take a machine-gun section and a 75-mm recoilless rifle to the high ground of Hill 1324, east of the road, to give supporting fire to help reduce the roadblock. He and his men started to climb the western slope of the hill, well north of the inlet. In his climb he did not encounter any other American troops on the high ground, so he knew that they must be farther east on the hill.

Above the 1,200-meter contour line on this long spur ridge above the mouth of the inlet, Campbell had an excellent view of the 3rd Battalion, 31st Infantry, perimeter below and saw the havoc the enemy had caused within it, especially in the artillery positions. He saw fighting still in progress in the southwestern part of the perimeter and enemy troops moving southwest on the road west of the perimeter. He saw and heard some artillery pieces within the perimeter still firing, the explosions of the propelling charges and detonations on impact almost simultaneous, indicating close direct fire. But he could not see the enemy roadblock or the bridge and causeway from his position, since folds of ground on the mountain blocked the view to the southeast.

Campbell did try a few rounds of 75-mm recoilless-rifle fire and long-range machine-gun fire on the Chinese he could see at the southwestern edge of the perimeter, but the range was too great. He then heard the convoy on the road below begin to move, so he took his men and weapons down the finger ridge, which offered easy access to the road. Arriving at the road, he crossed the frozen inlet from a point near the mouth of the inlet in a long slant in a southeasterly direction to a point on the south side within the 3rd Battalion perimeter. At that time there were no vehicles on the road where he crossed it.[9]

On the high ground east of the road and north of the inlet parts of B and C companies were screening the left flank of the road column and moving toward the inlet along the high spur ridges of Hill 1324. Before Sergeant Luna's party of B Company on Hill 1324 reached the overlook site north of the inlet, a runner brought word from Lieutenant Colonel Faith that they were not to cross the inlet on the ice. Luna was told that there was a 25- to 30-foot drop to the ice, that there was a log roadblock at the causeway, and that enemy fire covered the entire causeway approaching the bridge.[10]

Somewhat higher on the hill, east of Luna's group, Lieutenant Mortrude led two platoons of C Company southward on the high ground of Hill 1324 toward the inlet. He describes his route, which had changed abruptly when Faith had earlier shouted an order to him to climb higher on the hill in proceeding southward:

> This we did without enemy resistance but with much slipping and sliding around in our shoe pacs and overshoes on the hillside. After a mile or so, we were hailed by our Battalion Commander, Lt. Col. Faith. Upon identifying me by voice, he shouted for me to lead my column over the high ground and attack the enemy roadblock down in the valley beyond the turn

of the road ahead of us while he hit it frontally. After a much longer, slower climb than I had anticipated, we finally gained a high, snow covered ridgeline. Here there were numerous prepared but abandoned positions. From the "C" rations scattered about (but too frozen to eat) we assumed these positions must have been previously occupied by US troops, perhaps the Marines. Well after daylight, we reached a position high above the enemy roadblock overlooking the frozen arm of the reservoir and the 31st Regimental positions. I formed the two platoons with me as skirmishers with orders to initiate marching fire on my command. However, just as we broke out of our attack position over the final military crest, Col. Faith's troops attacked down the road below and seized the road block with seeming ease. Perhaps the enemy had also detecked our impending "vertical envelopment" and lost some of their resolve in the face of being "pinchered."[11]

Just how the logs at the southern end of the bridge were removed and how the enemy positions covering the roadblock by fire were neutralized is a bit uncertain. These tasks were probably carried out by a small group of soldiers, with Faith among them, aided by artillery fire from within the 3rd Battalion perimeter. One observer wrote that "Lt Moore, 1st Bn A.P. Platoon Leader, got across and with about six men proceeded to knock out the enemy positions on both sides of the bridge."[12] One must also consider the comment written at Hagaru-ri a few days after the event by First Sergeant Luna of B Company. He wrote that he and his party from B Company had reached the ridgeline of Hill 1324 above the inlet and had come down from the cliff above the road not far from the bridge. In descending, many men were bruised and injured and broke or lost weapons and ammunition. Luna implies that he and some of his men met Faith on the road near the bridge and that some of them, including himself, with Faith leading, got to the logs on the far side of the bridge. They removed the logs, according to Luna, before enemy fire drove them to cover on the west side of the bridge abutments. It is possible that Lieutenant Moore with some of his A&P Platoon were with Faith. Luna and a few B Company men may have joined Faith and Moore in the attack on the roadblock.[13] Luna gave credit to some of the 105-mm howitzers inside the perimeter in delivering direct fire on enemy east of the bridge and giving them effective cover while they removed the logs.

Faith told the B Company men now streaming off the ridge and others coming up the road from the west that they would have to cross the ice on the inlet below the bridge for it was too dangerous to use the bridge. Faith placed riflemen on the west side of the bridge abutments and behind the causeway to fire on enemy east of the bridge up the Pungnyuri-gang Valley to prevent them from seizing the bridge or establishing a strong fire-block of automatic fire near it.[14]

Mortrude and his two platoons of C Company apparently were not far behind Luna and his men in reaching the road near the bridge. Mortrude wrote: "When we finally broke over the military crest [of Hill 1324] above the roadblock Col. Faith and his troops were already closing on it. We came directly down the hill and joined them. I do not recall seeing any friendly or enemy casualties at that junction as we paused under cover of the West Bank of the causeway awaiting placement in the new perimeter. . . . The numerous enemy KIA [killed in action] found later in our new position along the south shore of the inlet appeared to be the result of the larger caliber antiaircraft weapons."[15]

During the reduction of the roadblock the convoy remained halted. Major Robbins went to Colonel MacLean's jeep and learned from the driver that MacLean was ahead making a reconnaissance of a reported roadblock that had caused the command group to halt the column. Robbins went back to his jeep. Someone then shouted that the vehicles were to get off the road and disperse in an open area left (east) of the road. They did so, expecting a Chinese attack. Suddenly a squad of Chinese came double-timing around a bend in the road from the north, no more than "twenty feet from our nearest vehicle." Firing started at once, seemingly from everywhere. The startled Chinese turned and took to their heels, and soon all was quiet.[16]

Again, Robbins said, he walked forward toward the inlet to Colonel MacLean's jeep. He said, "This time his bodyguard and radio operator, who rarely left the colonel's side, were there looking concerned and talking excitedly among themselves. I was told that the colonel had not gone with the enveloping company toward the flank of the road block, but had gone boldly down the road directly towards the obstacle when last seen and had not returned."[17]

The halted column at the bend of the road was about a mile from the causeway and bridge roadblock. While Robbins looked up the inlet to the bridge and waited there, Faith came up the road and told him that the men he could see were his troops holding the bridge and that the vehicles were to dash across it to the 3rd Battalion perimeter, although there were still some enemy and enemy fire nearby. The vehicles were to cross the bridge one at a time, for the roadway across the bridge was only one lane wide, and any stalled vehicle on the bridge would block it.[18]

Faith then started the vehicular column forward, placing Major Jones at the mouth of the inlet to control movement from there. Major Miller was to take a place at the north end of the causeway where the road turned to cross the Pungnyuri-gang to the south side and into the 3rd Battalion perimeter. He was to send the vehicles across in a dash, one by one, and to prevent a jamming of traffic at that key point. Enemy small-arms fire still peppered the crossing area.

The column moved up the inlet under this control, and under Miller's direction they got across, some unscathed, some hit but not immobilized. All crossed except two 2½-ton ammunition trucks, whose drivers abandoned them on the north side of the causeway. Sergeant Charles Garrigus, assistant motor sergeant, 1st Battalion, on his own initiative left the perimeter later in the day and drove both trucks inside, the second one under small-arms fire, an extremely heroic action.[19]

The men of the 1st Battalion, first those of C and B companies, crossed the ice of the inlet below the bridge into the 3rd Battalion lines, some as early as 9:00 A.M. First Lieutenant Thomas J. Patton, of A Battery of the 57th FA, inside the perimeter, wrote: "At approximately 0900 hours we saw the first elements of the 1st Bn 32 RCT coming across the frozen part of the reservoir to join us. Lt. Col. Faith took charge of all the forces in our sector and reorganized the perimeter defense."[20]

Lieutenant Campbell, who, as described earlier, descended from the point of Hill 1324 and crossed the inlet on a long slant into the 3rd Battalion perimeter, may have led the first group from the 1st Battalion into the inlet perimeter. Most of the members of the 1st Battalion were in the 3rd Battalion perimeter by 10:00 A.M., except for the vehicle drivers, the officers left on the north side to control the movement of the motor column, and Captain Stamford, who remained with his TACP near the mouth of the inlet on the north side to direct air strikes. It was early afternoon before all the vehicles had closed. The entire battalion crossing lasted from about 9:00 A.M. to 1:00 P.M.

Some accounts have Faith sending or leading parts of two companies across the ice in the early morning to attack Chinese still on the southern side of the inlet, killing many and driving the rest away. I do not believe that such an attack ever happened. Faith may have sent some troops across the inlet to the south side after the bridge roadblock was removed to determine whether any enemy were on the south side at that point. The evidence does not support the alleged attack. Both Major Jones and Captain Bigger say that Faith did not lead an attack across the inlet, although Jones says that he did send a force across to check out the situation. Captain Bigger, commenting on the alleged movement across the inlet says: "I recall no such attack taking place. I crossed the ice with Col. Faith and would have been in on it. We skirted the ice as unobtrusively as possible into the railroad cut where we began setting up a CP."[21]

Lieutenant Mortrude and his two platoons of C Company were at the bridge and causeway. He says that he saw no attack, and his troops would likely have been involved had it been made. Lieutenant Campbell and Major Curtis, who were on the scene at the inlet early, say that they saw no attack. Captain Kitz, commanding K Company, 3rd Battalion, within the perimeter, saw the 1st Battalion cross the inlet into the 3rd Battalion's perimeter but does not mention an attack. Nor did Lieutenant Patton, who saw the beginning of the crossing, mention an attack.[22]

That there were many Chinese dead in the area when the 1st Battalion crossed the inlet on the morning of November 29 is true. But the evidence is strong that these Chinese had been killed during the night battle. Mortrude said that the dead were killed by antiaircraft weapons fire. Major Curtis noticed that the dead faced the 3rd Battalion perimeter, not the inlet, indicating that they died while attacking the perimeter and not facing an attack from across the inlet behind them. It is evident that there were no Chinese soldiers along the inlet when 1st Battalion troops crossed it and that the CCF troops who had been there when the 1st Battalion came into sight about dawn withdrew to the west along the road and railroad.

Captain John D. Swenty, of the 1st Battalion, provides a typical first impression of the 3rd Battalion perimeter when the 1st Battalion men entered it. He wrote: "It was easy to see that their position was almost overrun. Within a small sector of their perimeter I counted over fifty (50) dead Chinese. All the dead had infiltrated to within 100 yards of the task force CP. Some even got within 25 yards of the CP."[23]

Another first impression of the south side of the inlet was recorded by Captain Stamford, the FAC, who was near the head of the vehicular column. Two months later, he recorded his observations: "I observed troops across the finger of water moving south on the road and shoreline. They were carrying mortars and heavy MG's and on the hill I observed a mortar in the dawn. . . . I could get no permission to run strikes, because Colonel

MacLean and Faith thought they were friendly, and before it got light enough to see well they both moved down the road with troops to reconnoiter a crossing to the 3/31."[24] Later that morning Faith told Stamford to direct air strikes on the enemy mortar emplaced on Hill 1250 south of the inlet, which was registering on high ground north of the inlet. Faith also had Stamford run strikes behind A Company, the battalion rear guard with aircraft early on the scene. He then used all available aircraft to cover the troops crossing the ice west of the causeway and bridge. Afterward he shifted the strikes east of the causeway and bridge to suppress enemy fire there.[25]

When the 1st Battalion troops first saw the south side of the inlet, they looked at a battered battlefield. From Hill 1324 the view was panoramic. Major Curtis was one of many who approached the inlet from near the crest of the hill, descending a spur ridge running south. From this spur, where it dropped precipitously toward the inlet, he had a good view of the 3rd Battalion perimeter. He wrote:

> The "perimeter" of the 3/31 and 57th F.A. when I first saw it from the ridge line was a scene of destruction. It had been effectively "reduced" and was offering no organized resistance. There was smoke, fog, and very limited visibility. There was a sizable column of troops moving down the road to the southeast [Curtis subsequently corrected this to *southwest*] along what had been a part of the perimeter. I recognized them as Chinese troops— and assumed (correctly I think) that they were by-passing the perimeter and moving south since the perimeter had been reduced.[26]

Campbell, who had viewed the scene below from near the same point, agreed with Curtis, saying that the 3rd Battalion area "appeared a scene of total devastation."

Captain Bigger was with MacLean and Faith in the command group when it reached the inlet. He wrote of that moment:

> As our Bn Command Group arrived on the north side of the Inlet we could look across the ice and see that the 3rd Bn., 31 and 57 FA were heavily engaged. Chinese were pouring down the surrounding hill toward the perimeter of the units. The quad 50 machines guns and the dual 40 mm anti-aircraft weapons of the 57th FA were taking a heavy toll of the Chinese columns. It was like being a spectator at a large screen movie for a moment. It was about this time that we observed a column of troops approaching the perimeter of the 31st *from the south* along the road.[27]

Colonel MacLean Disappears

Colonel Allan Duart MacLean, 43 years old, commander of the 31st Infantry Regiment, 7th Infantry Division, disappeared at the Pungnyuri-gang Inlet of Chosin Reservoir during the early morning of November 29, 1950. The Department of the Army carried him as missing for nearly three and a half years. Only on March 17, 1954, was he officially declared dead. What happened to him? Several eyewitnesses saw him crossing the frozen inlet a few minutes before he disappeared near the western edge of the 3rd Battalion perimeter on the south side of the inlet. From then on, there was only silence.[28] In the few months that Colonel MacLean commanded the 31st Infantry, he had acquired the reputation of being aggressive and perhaps a bit impulsive. Captain Robert E. Drake, commander of the 31st Tank Company, said that MacLean "was a very aggressive commander and wanted to be in the position as forward as possible."[29]

At dawn on November 29 the command reconnaissance party had only a short distance to go from the halted motor column to reach the inlet, where the road turned east along the inlet toward the causeway and bridge. Visibility was still poor. Where the road turned east along its north bank, the inlet was 500 yards wide but narrowed to a small stream near the causeway and bridge. Along the stream were places where backup water from the reservoir had pushed into low ground on the south side, and there were marshy, brush-covered islands in the inlet. A few logs were also frozen in the ice.

The command party traveled some distance down the road before fire came its way, either directed fire or spent bullets from the fight in progress on the other side.[30] As the command party moved up the road alongside the inlet, it split into two or more parts. Faith was in front with a small group. Bigger and MacLean with a few others were some distance behind Faith. It was at this time, Bigger said, that "we observed a column of troops approaching the perimeter of the 31st from the south along the road. Col. MacLean was at first overjoyed for he felt that that was the remainder of his regimental combat team he had been expecting [2nd Battalion, 31st Infantry]."[31] Bigger said that the column coming from the south was approaching but had not yet reached the western end of the 3rd Battalion perimeter. There was firing from this group toward the perimeter, and there was return fire from the edge of the perimeter toward the marching column. Mac-

Lean looked at the scene for a moment and then shouted, "Those are my boys!" He thought that the column of men marching east toward the perimeter was the vanguard of his 2nd Battalion, which he had been expecting since the 27th. His immediate impulse was to get across the inlet to stop the firing, in which his two battalions, he thought, would cripple each other.

MacLean turned to Bigger and said, "Here, take this order and give it to Faith." He rapidly delivered an oral order to Bigger that generally followed the usual five-point field order. He then turned and strode out onto the ice of the inlet, headed for the other side. Bigger watched. After MacLean got some distance out on the ice, Bigger could see that men on the other side were firing at him and saw him fall several times, but each time MacLean got up and continued on. Bigger could not tell whether MacLean was hit each time he fell or whether he was slipping on the ice. As MacLean neared the other bank, Bigger could see Chinese soldiers come out to the edge of the ice, where they took hold of MacLean and pulled him to the brush-covered ground. They led him up the bank and onto the road and then away westward. That was the last Bigger could see of MacLean as the party went out of view. Bigger said that the incident took place about half a mile west of the bridge, about halfway between the turn of the road eastward along the inlet and the bridge.[32]

Concerning the nature of the oral order MacLean gave to him, Bigger wrote in answer to a question from me: "Col MacLean's oral order to me just prior to his striking out across the ice consisted in general of what he thought the enemy situation was, where our bn should tie in with the 31st and the fact that he thought the relief column was in sight. He wanted to secure the high ground around the perimeter of the location of the 31st and 57th FA. His CP was to be in the remains of a house and that is where Faith was to meet him when the 1/32 entered the perimeter."[33]

Bigger's sketch map of MacLean's course across the Inlet shows him proceeding almost straight south from his point of departure until he reached one of the many marshy, brush-covered islands near the south side of the inlet. Then his course veered sharply southwest over marshy but frozen ground to the bank of the inlet. The point where he reached the bank was west of and outside the 3rd Battalion perimeter and was held by the Chinese.

Others saw MacLean cross the frozen inlet and saw him fall to the ice several times when Chinese fire from the south bank hit him. Faith, Jones, and Curtis saw the crossing in full or in part. Each saw him from a different vantage point along the inlet. All of them have left accounts that verify Bigger's more detailed version. Faith said that he saw MacLean fall four times. Curtis saw him fall twice in the latter part of the crossing. Faith gave his account to General Barr when the latter visited the inlet perimeter on the 30th, the day after the event, and subsequently General Barr included the account in a letter to Mrs. Don C. Faith, Jr.

Later in the morning, after he had crossed the inlet, Faith ordered a search for MacLean. C Company made the search since it was to take over the shore of the inlet as its sector in the new perimeter organized that afternoon. It reported that it found no trace of MacLean. The search necessarily was made in the low ground along the inlet and did not include the CCF route of withdrawal or the high ground behind the perimeter, all of which was held by the Chinese.

Inquiry disclosed that no one in the 3rd Battalion or the 57th Field Artillery had seen MacLean or witnessed his capture. This is not surprising when one realizes that the incident took place outside their perimeter, that there was much brush and low scrub along the shore of the inlet where the Chinese captured MacLean, that they had just undergone an ordeal for survival during the night, and that at the western end of the perimeter the men were still in their holes fighting off the Chinese at dawn. Also, visibility was not good from their position to the area where MacLean was captured. The topography along the edge of the inlet there was masked by rough, broken ground above the bank and was screened from much of the perimeter by folds of ground and the high weeds and brush lining the inlet at that point.[34] The Chinese soldiers who captured MacLean quickly left the area soon after daybreak.

Colonel MacLean's fate was unknown until an American prisoner released by the Chinese said that in early December, 1950 he had been a prisoner along with many others, including MacLean, who were being moved north from the Chosin Reservoir to a prison camp. He said that the Americans cared for and helped the wounded colonel all they could but that he died of his wounds on the fourth day of the journey. His comrades buried MacLean in a grave alongside the road.[35] Eight months after his disappearance Colonel MacLean was awarded the Distinguished Service Cross for his personal heroism and leadership of troops under his command November 27–29, 1950.[36]

What Colonel MacLean might have done with his troops if he had been allowed another day or two to bring them together cannot be known. If he had not disappeared into the enemy's hands, he might have withdrawn them or parts of them successfully, though with heavy casualties, to Hagaru-ri, as the Marines did with their regiments cut off at Yudam-ni. At least we know that this Army officer, the highest-ranking combat leader of the US Armed Forces to lose his life in enemy action in northeast Korea, would have set a personal example as a hard-driving, courageous leader, inspiring his officers and men to their best effort.

Captain Stamford, the FAC, remained on the north side of the inlet until shortly after noon, directing Corsair strikes to help the trucks cross the bridge. He then crossed with his radio jeep and TACP. He wrote two months later, "The dead were everywhere when we joined them." He also said that he saw American soldiers dead in their sleeping bags. Captain Bigger confirmed that "in the 31st Infantry and 57th FA . . . many men were killed by the Chinese as they (US soldiers) slept in the bedrolls."[37]

Stamford needed to know the condition of the 3rd Battalion's TACP and on inquiry learned that Lieutenant Johnson, USAF, the FAC, had been killed and his radio equipment wrecked. Thus the full burden of close air support for the combined forces fell on Stamford and his TACP. He wrote that he

> looked for a place to sit and relax while I ate this rare repast [a can of rations]. A few feet away there were two CCF corpses. One was in a position to afford me a place to sit. The other was in a kneeling position, sitting on his heels and resting on his elbows. The top of his head had evidently been removed the night before while fighting for possession of the perimeter. As he froze, his brain expanded and rose up out of cranium until it looked like a piece of pink coral on a South Pacific reef. The hoar frost that fell during the early morning hours covered the top of his brain and sparkled in the sunlight. Too hungry to wait for a collecting detail to remove these corpses from my area, I opened the can of rations and using the "coral" as a centerpiece I sat down on the other and wolfed down my rations.[38]

Major Robbins tells of his first minutes in the perimeter after floorboarding the accelerator of his jeep when he crossed the bridge. He said: "I set out for the 3rd Battalion CP to find Colonel Reilly propped on a stretcher with a bullet hole through his leg and grenade splinters lightly sprinkled in his arm and shoulder. He was in good spirits and chatted with me about the situation in general. Colonel Faith came in at this time and went into immediate conference with Reilly as they laid plans to consolidate the two battalions and the field artillery, gathered in a tight circle of defense."

Robbins searched out Capt. Bob McClay, the 3rd Battalion adjutant, to learn about the beating the perimeter had taken from the Chinese the night before. He commented: "One had only to look about as he told the story to confirm everything he said. Dead and wounded GIs lay in and around the Korean mud house that served as a CP and just a few yards beyond I counted twenty dead Chinese in their now familiar quilted jackets and tennis shoes. In fact they were strewn throughout the area giving evidence of their penetration into the very foxholes of the beleaguered battalion and its command post."[39]

Pausing at the aid station, Robbins found Captain Adams, the 3rd Battalion S-4, dying of wounds, and Lieutenant Dill, executive officer of M Company, apparently mortally wounded. Captain Henry Wamble, of the Medical Company, an old friend, lay with a bullet through his lungs, able to speak only in a whisper. None reached Hagaru-ri. Robbins took over Colonel MacLean's jeep and crew and dug a cavelike hole in the side of a small embankment with an overhead cover of logs. He then went in search of Faith and Miller. After Faith had his conference with Reilly, he had assumed command of all troops in the perimeter. When Robbins found Faith, the latter appointed him "Task Force S-4."[40]

Faith, with Miller and Curtis, spent the rest of the morning, in Curtis's words, "trying to find out what was left of Companies I and K of the 31st (there was no Co. L left)—tying them in with our Cos A, B, C to form a perimeter."[41]

During the morning Lieutenant Mortrude held his two platoons of C Company in safety behind the west side of the causeway after he met Faith at the inlet. He waited there until he received instructions to go into the C Company line in the new perimeter. Mortrude describes his own 3rd Platoon role:

Our platoon was deployed to defend the northwest portion of the task force perimeter blocking the road approach from the southwest with our right flank on the southern bank of the frozen arm of the reservoir. We spent the remainder of [the day] preparing our platoon positions with emphasis on the road leading into us along the reservoir from the southwest. Also, I directed that the many Chinese dead within and in front of our area be searched for grenades to be salvaged and then the bodies be collected together to prevent confusion in any further night attacks. In addition to salvaging many "potato masher" grenades, we also acquired a healthy respect for the effects of our 40 mm automatic weapons fire which had apparently destroyed this unit the night before our withdrawal to the area. In anticipation of a cold night, I even salvaged a greatcoat from an unusually large enemy KIA. This supplemental item fit quite comfortably, if not stylishly, beneath my parka, but it was to be a source of considerable concern to me.[42]

Mortrude's position was on the north side of the road along the inlet, opposite A Company, and he had a recoilless rifle on the southeast shoulder of the road where A and C Company boundaries met. A Company had responsibility for the roadblock, but Mortrude's platoon shared it during the fighting of the next two days and nights. From his northwestern platoon boundary Mortrude's position "extended northeast down to and along the ice of the reservoir." The rest of C Company extended the line toward the causeway and bridge.

In forming a new perimeter, Faith tried to include some high ground on the south as part of A and B companies' side of the perimeter. They failed in their efforts during the afternoon to wrest it from the Chinese. So, in the end, Faith had to settle for a very restricted, unsatisfactory perimeter, all of it dominated by higher terrain.[43]

In addition to the high ridge rising to its crest at Hill 1456, south of the perimeter, long finger ridges from that peak came down on both the east and the west sides to the railroad, the road, and the shore of the inlet. The high ground formed roughly a flat U around the restricted American perimeter, with the open side of the U pointed north at the shore of the inlet.

The eastern spur ridge from Hill 1456 descended abruptly to the inlet about 500 yards east of the causeway and bridge, ending in a knob named Hill 1210. Its crest was 390 feet above the Pungnyuri-gang, and it dominated the eastern end of the perimeter.

At the other, western, end of the perimeter a spur ridge from Hill 1456 dominated the low ground there. This ridge spread out just above the inlet in a wide knob, named Hill 1250. Its steep northern slope dropped sharply to the edge of the reservoir. The narrow-gauge railroad had been cut into its lower slope to make the turn south. Hill 1250 rose nearly 530 feet above the level of the inlet and the reservoir, dominating the western side of the perimeter.[44]

Lieutenant Colonel Faith organized the units in the perimeter into a

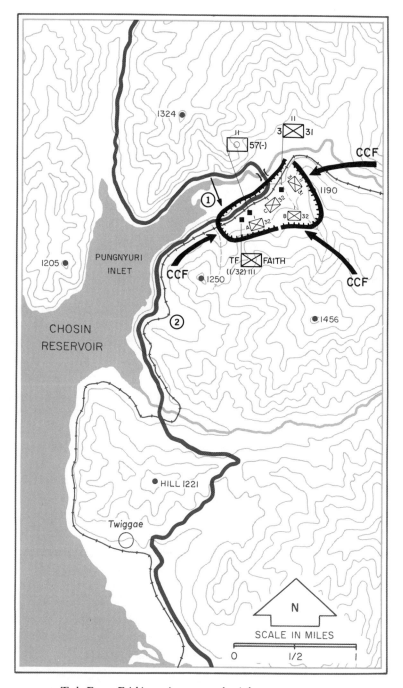

MAP 9. Task Force Faith's perimeter at the inlet.

unified command that thereafter was informally called "Task Force Faith" but did not include Captain Drake's 31st Tank Company or the 31st Rear CP at Hudong-ni. This reorganized perimeter had the 3rd Battalion of the 31st Infantry on the east and the 1st Battalion of the 32nd Infantry on the north, west, and south flanks, with the heavy mortars, the 57th Field Artillery Battalion, and the 15th antiaircraft guns in the center.[45]

Faith's reorganized perimeter departed little in dimensions and physical features from the original perimeter of the 3rd Battalion. The ground on the south side of the inlet and the Pungnyuri-gang did not allow any great changes once B and A companies had failed to gain high ground from the Chinese south of the inlet. The south bank of the inlet from a point east of Hill 1250 and extending eastward up the Pungnyuri-gang to a point 500 yards beyond the causeway and bridge was the northern side of the perimeter. There, at its eastern extremity, a spur ridge from Hill 1456 came to the edge of the stream. It climbed from the river slightly east of south toward the rounded crest of Hill 1456. The lower reach of this ridge was gentler in incline than higher up, where it was sharply steep as it neared the crest. The 3rd Battalion (I and K companies combined all the remaining infantry) held the lower part of this spur ridge, which formed the eastern side of the perimeter for a distance of about 800 to 1,000 yards. From that point the slope of the ridge became steeper, as did all the mountainside westward, and it could not be included in the perimeter. Enemy forces held the higher ground.

The lower ground just south of the inlet was an uneven, semilevel, elongated area sloping gradually northward down to the inlet's edge. This stretch of ground became narrower as it extended westward. An erosional drainage draw ended this western low ground at the eastern base of Hill 1250. The draw was the west border of the perimeter. The perimeter in general outline resembled a bow with the bowstring drawn taut. If an arrow had been fitted to the bowstring, its flight would have been southward. The road and railroad at the north could be considered the taut bowstring of the perimeter.

The horizontal dimension of the perimeter could hardly have been more than 1,400 yards wide, with the deepest part at its eastern end no more than 800 yards. From there its depth gradually decreased as it extended westward, until it was no more than 300 to 400 yards deep. The western boundary of the perimeter was just in front (east) of the draw on the east side of Hill 1250 and the spur ridge that ran down to the railroad and the vehicular road.

Task Force Faith's troop disposition along the perimeter was as follows: beginning at the northeast corner of the perimeter, the 3rd Battalion, 31st Infantry, held the line from the river's edge up the spur ridge. A remnant of L Company under Capt. William W. Etchemendy, now part of a consolidated K Company, apparently held the lower part of this line where it met the boundary of C Company at the river. Captain Kitz still commanded K Company, including the L Company remnant that had been consolidated with it. Above K Company Captain Marr's I Company carried the line to its upper and southern limit, where it met B Company, 32nd Infantry. From this point, the boundary of I and B companies (and of the 1st and 3rd battalions), the 1st Battalion was responsible for the remainder of the perimeter. Captain Turner's B Company carried the line westward along the lower slope of Hill 1456, following the 1,160-meter contour line for perhaps 800 yards. A Company then picked up the line and carried it in a curve down to the railroad and road, where it met the C Company boundary. From there, just east of the drainage draw near Hill 1250, C Company had the line along the inlet to a point about 500 yards east of the bridge. There it met the beginning of the 3rd Battalion line and closed the perimeter.

The C Company portion of the perimeter, less than a mile long, was the longest section held by any of the rifle companies, but it was also the most easily defended, with the inlet to its front. The boundary between A and C companies at the road at the western end of the perimeter was perhaps the single most important defensive point of the perimeter. A Company was responsible for the road there, but throughout the battles of the perimeter C Company helped in its defense. In effect it became a joint responsibility.

Within the perimeter the 3rd Battalion command post remained in the hut near the bridge. Captain Jordan's M Company, the weapons company for the 3rd Battalion, remained in its initial position, which it never had lost, just behind the I Company infantry. Major Miller, who now commanded the 1st Battalion in a delegation of command Faith made when he assumed the role of Task Force commander, had a new improvised CP near the western end of the perimeter. Faith's Task Force CP and that of the 57th FA were about in the middle of the perimeter area, where they had always been—Faith's in the cave hole in the side of one of the railroad cuts. Captain

Bigger's Weapons Company was behind (north of) A and B companies. Faith ordered a platoon-size force of D Company to be kept uncommitted as a task-force reserve. While there were eight 105-mm howitzers within the perimeter, only four of them were now operational. Most of the heavy mortars were in the center of the perimeter. The antiaircraft weapons did not change location; they remained in a circle around the artillery and as a group were capable of firing in any direction with their revolving turrets.[46]

Faith's new perimeter included both the road and railroad where they ran near the edge of the inlet. Of the two the road was closer to the inlet; the railroad was just above the road. The road made a sharp bend to the left when it entered on the bridge; the railroad continued on eastward up the valley of the Pungnyuri-gang. The railroad for most of the distance through the perimeter was on a slightly raised embankment above low ground on both sides and gave some protection to troops behind it. In other places the railroad made cuts 3 to 6 feet deep and 20 to 30 feet long in the irregular ground.

In his task-force reorganization at the inlet, Faith had his ad hoc CP and three battalion CPs. Major Miller commanded the 1st Battalion; Maj. Harvey H. Storms led the 3rd Battalion; and Maj. Robert J. Tolly, S-3 of the 57th FA, took command of that battalion. Faith's old battalion staff continued to serve him as task-force commander. It was an informal arrangement, and there never was time to institutionalize it. All units continued to function along their traditional lines for the two days the arrangement existed, except that everyone recognized Faith as task-force commander.[47]

Captain Stamford, in his radio contacts with Corsair pilots, told them that the troops were short of ammunition and all kinds of supplies and needed airdrops. Major Robbins, as the newly appointed task-force S-4, began collecting all the supplies in the perimeter to make an equal distribution. Stamford's request for airdrops brought results at 3:00 in the afternoon. Two C-119s ("flying boxcars") came overhead and after two trial runs dropped their cargoes of ammunition and rations. One of the parachutes failed to open, and the heavy package dropped like a stone. It hit a group of ROK soldiers about 20 feet from Robbins, killing one of them. After that, when a drop was pending, a warning was given, and everyone watched the sky for falling cargo.

Not all the drops landed inside the perimeter; many fell outside and went to the Chinese. Stamford was not pleased with the equipment supplied in the drops. He said that it was "standard emergency equipment which included unnecessary items such as castor oil [these emergency drops were prepackaged in Japan]. We never got enough bandages, morphine, or ammunition in sufficiently varied types. The most noted shortage was in 40 mm ammunition for a dual self-propelled gun we had which would have been most useful for the next couple of days."[48]

An hour after the airdrops a helicopter sent by General Hodes, who was at Hagaru-ri, landed at the inlet. He had been able to get this Marine air evacuation mission sent to the inlet to evacuate wounded. It took out two men, Lieutenant Colonel Reilly, 3rd Battalion commander; and Lieutenant Colonel Embree, 57th Field Artillery Battalion commander. It returned a second time, taking out two more unidentified wounded, but that was all — four men — before darkness fell. Hodes made an effort to get the helicopter the next day, but his request was denied because there was a higher priority for its use, presumably evacuation of critically wounded Marines at Yudam-ni.

The failure of the airdrops to deliver the right ammunition and supplies to the intended area had serious results. Captain McClymont's dual-40 guns did not receive a single resupply shell during the entire time they were in the Chosin Reservoir battles.[49] From his position at Hudong-ni, four miles south of the inlet, Captain Drake could see cargo planes fly over them and the mountain on the north to make drops at the inlet. Cargo drops for resupply of the 31st Tank Company and the 31st Infantry Rear were received. There were mixups, however: a large drop of 40-mm ammunition, intended for the dual-40s at the inlet, landed instead at Hudong-ni. In turn, Drake did not receive 105-mm and 76-mm shells he needed for his tank company. Drake blew up the large stack of 40-mm shells the next day shortly before his armor withdrew to Hagaru-ri.[50] If this 40-mm ammunition had been available to the dual-40s, it might have made the difference between success and failure in achieving a breakout of Task Force Faith to Hagaru-ri.

It is appalling that there was no communication between Task Force Faith at the inlet and Drake's tank company and the 31st Infantry Rear, only 4 road miles apart. One reason was the high mountain mass of Ko-bong and Chokpo-dong between the two positions. The radios in both positions were World War II models, rebuilt in Japan, that functioned poorly in mountainous country. Also, these infantry radios could not net with Drake's tanks at Hudong-ni. Neither of Drake's two attacks toward the inlet from Hudong-ni was known at the inlet. Nor did the 31st Rear or Drake know of the destruction within the 3rd Battalion and artillery perimeter. Information coming from Corsair radio to Captain Stamford's TACP that tanks were making an effort to reach them led many to believe that General Hodes was organizing a Marine tank-led force at Hagaru-ri to reach them.[51]

The weather remained an overriding factor in the battle situation. Temperatures were always below zero at night and occasionally dropped to −30° F. The strong winds out of Manchuria added to the cold. During the daytime the weather was tolerable, sometimes rising above 20° F, but at night it was almost unbearable. Automatic weapons had to be fired every 15 to 20 minutes to keep them operable. One night, Captain Kitz said, of nine Browning automatic rifles (BARs) in K Company not one would fire on automatic.

From time to time during the day targets of opportunity on the hills around the perimeter came into view, and the dual-40s hit them with deadly effect. When night approached on the 29th, McClymont told all his gun crews to be very alert. The Chinese knew their locations and would try hard to destroy them. He and Lieutenant Chapman dug a big foxhole on a little ridge in front of them facing the reservoir. Then he had the driver of the only M19 personnel carrier drive the vehicle over the foxhole. The full-track covered his D Battery CP.

Captain Drake's Second
Tank Attack, November 29

When Faith reorganized the new inlet perimeter late in the afternoon of November 29 and prepared for another night of battle, he did not know that during the day Drake had tried to join them at the inlet but could not get past Hill 1221. After his return to Hudong-ni on the 28th, Drake spent the evening and part of the night preparing for a second try the next day with infantry support. He planned to leave the same number of tanks at Hudong-ni for protection of the 31st Rear CP and to take the rest up the road to the Chinese position. Because he had lost 4 tanks the day before at Hill 1221, Drake had only 11 tanks with 76-mm guns and a command tank with a 105-mm howitzer. He counted on the infantry troops to make a difference. Unless they could help control Hill 1221, Drake realized, his attack would go nowhere because one of his tanks now effectively blocked the road, and there was no alternate route to the inlet. He did not consider using the narrow-gauge rail track.

Lieutenant Colonel Anderson and Major Witte had few troops of any kind to send with Drake. They apparently did not draw on the approximately 100 troops of Service Battery, 57th Field Artillery, who had joined them on the 28th. This left only part of the 31st Infantry Headquarters and Headquarters and Service Company, an engineer platoon, a detachment of the Heavy Mortar Company, a detachment of the Medical Company, and some attached South Koreans (KATUSA).

The exact number and makeup of the foot force is not known. Captain Drake said that there were "about 50 to 75 men who assaulted the ridge with tank fire support on 29 November." Nearly 30 years later Ma-

Maj. (later Brig. Gen.) William R. Lynch (*left*) and Capt. (Chaplain) Martin C. Hoehn. Photograph courtesy of Brigadier General Lynch.

jor Witte, the 31st Infantry S-2 (and Acting S-3) at Hudong-ni, recalled that there were about 3 officers and 30 enlisted men from the service troops.[1]

On the 29th the tank and "infantry" force left Hudong-ni about 8:00 A.M., with good visibility and advanced the short distance north to the turn of the road and Hill 1221. This time Drake directed his entire attack against the south face and crest of Hill 1221. The tanks again tried to climb the slope in support of the makeshift infantry force, but again they slipped and could not get traction. He had only one mortar, with which he tried to reach the CCF positions just over the crest of Hill 1221, but he had no artillery support. The air support he had asked Hodes to arrange arrived, but there was no FAC with Drake, so the necessary information and directions for effective air attack could not be given to the Corsair pilots. As a result, when they made their strikes, their fire hit among the Americans as well as the Chinese.

At the height of the effort to get to the top of Hill 1221 the chaplain,

Capt. Martin C. Hoehn, accompanying the foot soldiers in their attack, became so incensed at the Chinese, who fired on the tankers whenever they dismounted, that he took a submachine gun from a soldier and fired clip after clip as he moved forward with the others, all the time asking God for forgiveness. An officer at X Corps who knew Hoehn remarked that in the Middle Ages he would have been a Knight Templar and a great threat to the Saracens. The fight at Hill 1221 lasted about four hours, but in the end the attack failed. The CCF held all their positions, and the tank-infantry force withdrew to Hudong-ni.[2]

No tanks were lost on November 29. No precise figure can be given for casualties in the composite body of foot soldiers, but Captain Drake said that "they were heavy—not many killed, but many wounded. They were not well trained—there were KATUSA along also. We lost track of the latter."[3] A 7th Division document said that 20 men were lost in this attack.

This was the last effort armor made to join with the 31st Infantry at Chosin. Captain Drake's tanks remained at Hudong-ni one more day, until November 30, when they were ordered to withdraw to Hagaru-ri. There never was any Marine effort from Hagaru-ri, either with infantry or with armor, to assist the 31st Regimental Combat Team or Task Force Faith east of Chosin. The Marines at Hagaru-ri were fully occupied holding their own precarious perimeter.

10

The 2nd Battalion, 31st Infantry, Fails to Arrive

At this point in the story of Task Force Faith at the inlet, the story of the 2nd Battalion, 31st Infantry, which Colonel MacLean anxiously awaited at Chosin Reservoir to complete the infantry element of his RCT, should be told. His expectations in this respect were a significant factor in his wounding and capture by the Chinese on November 29. The Marines' situation at Hagaru-ri and General Hodes's efforts to help Faith should be also noted.

When MacLean passed through Hamhung on the way to Chosin, he understood from X Corps that the 2nd Battalion of his regiment would follow rapidly behind the 3rd Battalion and that it might arrive at the reservoir the night of November 27–28 or the next morning. It never reached Chosin Reservoir, so the 31st RCT there never reached regimental strength.

Lieutenant Colonel Richard R. Reidy, commanding officer of the 2nd Battalion, received orders on November 27 at Pukchong, the 7th Division Rear CP, to take his battalion, less E Company, to the Chosin Reservoir to join MacLean. The battalion left Pukchong for Hamhung by train in open railway cars on November 28, its vehicles going by road. The battalion reached Hamhung that evening and awaited further orders.

The next day, Colonel Millburn, G-3 Section, X Corps, ordered them to proceed by train to Majon-dong (or Santong), 22 miles north of Hamhung, where X Corps trucks would provide transportation. The battalion's own trucks would follow and join it later. Reidy and his command group went forward by jeep and arrived at Majon-dong at 9:00 A.M., November 29. The other troops arrived there by train in two increments at 9:30 and 10:15 A.M. But no trucks were available there for the battalion's march north.

Major Fairbanks, of the G-4 Section, X Corps, went up the MSR to find the trucks allotted for the battalion. The 2nd Battalion's own trucks arrived during the morning, but they could not be used without a change in X Corps orders. The 2nd Battalion went into a perimeter defense at Majon-dong and remained there overnight on November 29–30.¹ Major Fairbanks learned that the X Corps trucks were not at Majon-dong to carry the 2nd Battalion forward because they had reached Majon-dong earlier on the 29th loaded with ammunition and had continued north with it.

According to Reidy's version of events, when the trucks arrived that morning, they were ordered off the road. There is no doubt that military traffic northbound was heavy and difficult to control. The Chinese were causing havoc among all the units at the reservoir, and there were priority demands from the Marine and Army troops at Chosin and elsewhere below the plateau for reinforcements and supplies.

The confusion in the 2nd Battalion, 31st Infantry, at Majon-dong during the 29th was unraveled that evening by new X Corps orders: the battalion would leave for the reservoir the next morning, November 30. At 6:45 A.M., loaded on its organic transportation and trucks from X Corps, it started north once again, reaching the foot of Funchilin Pass without incident.

Beyond Chinhung-ni, about a mile into the pass, the enemy brought the battalion column under fire at 10:00 A.M., destroying two lead jeeps. Soon two 2½-ton trucks were also destroyed. Troops deployed and returned enemy fire, forcing the Chinese back. But the enemy threatened to envelope the column on the east. Chinese forces holding high ground north and northwest of the column were held in check by 57-mm and 75-mm recoilless-rifle fire. The battalion sent an officer back to report to X Corps that the pass was not secure. A battalion TACP joined the troops at noon and called for two air strikes. One came late in the afternoon. Lieutenant Colonel Reidy ordered an all-around defense where the battalion was stalled and prepared to stay there during the night. The battalion was about three miles from Koto-ri, one mile from the top of Funchilin Pass.

During the afternoon of November 30, Marine air reconnaissance reported to Hagaru-ri that the 2nd Battalion, 31st Infantry, was pinned down partway up the pass, that several of its vehicles were wrecked on the road, and that it was making little or no effort to move forward. At this time, General Almond, X Corps commander, was in Hagaru-ri in a conference that he had called with his commanders, Generals Smith and Barr.

General Almond reacted violently to this news. His diary entry for November 30 tells the substance of what happened: "By telephone CG X Corps ordered Chief of Staff X Corps to send an immediate message to Lt. Col. Reidy, commanding the battalion enroute to Koto-ri to join Col. Puller immediately at Koto-ri." Chief of Staff Maj. Gen. Clark L. Ruffner knew exactly what Almond meant. He immediately chose Maj. Joseph I. Gurfein, X Corps Headquarters, G-3 Air, to go as a personal messenger up the road with Almond's orders to Reidy and see that they were executed.

Gurfein arrived at Reidy's stalled position at 5:30 P.M. He gave Reidy Almond's orders—to move out at once, attack the enemy if necessary, and join his regiment north of Hagaru-ri.[2] Reidy then issued a battalion order to his company commanders at 7:00 P.M., but the attack, with F Company leading, did not start forward until an hour before midnight. A heavy snow had begun falling, reducing visibility. The battalion in close formation encountered a booby-trapped roadblock. Major Gurfein, who was present throughout, has the best account of what happened:

> Colonel Reidy collected his staff and company commanders at once, and by 1915 had issued orders for the movement. The time for the movement was 2100. The battalion moved out at 2330. At approximately 2345 a booby trap on a bridge in front of the column exploded, wounding one (1) man. The leading company started rumors that it was an antitank gun, that it was the enemy shooting, that the Chinese were coming, and they were ordered to move to the rear. Within 10 seconds a near rout had started with the tail and lead companies turning to the rear and starting to overrun the battalion command group. Jeep drivers turned their jeeps around and headed to the rear. The driver of a ¾ ton truck started to unhitch his trailer to turn around. Not an NCO nor junior officer raised his voice to stop the rout. The battalion commander, pushed aside by the troops, stood there silently. I had to personally step in and stop the men, order them to halt, and turn them around. That started their moving forward again. By this time the battalion commander was moving back with the column. To the best of my knowledge he did nothing to stop the rout, or to control his men. During this commotion not a single shot had been fired by the enemy or us.[3]

About 1:30 A.M. on December 1, as the 2nd Battalion column neared the top of the pass, Chinese attacked and split it in two. According to the battalion report, made up later by a few of the officers, most of the front troops of the column abandoned their vehicles about two miles south of Koto-ri and made their way on foot to the lines of the 1st Marine Regiment at Koto-ri. The first of them arrived there about 2:30 A.M. Throughout the night other survivors came into Koto-ri, the last, from the rear part of the battalion, arriving about 9:00 A.M. on December 1. Gurfein, who saw it all, gives a different version of what took place when the Chinese opened fire near the top of the pass:

> At 0130 on 1 December the enemy commenced firing on the tail of the 2nd Battalion, 31st, as it moved up the road. The company in the rear of the column immediately returned the fire, the lead company continued to move on down the road, the next company dispersed, and the following company abandoned its vehicles and left the road. The battalion commander, near the head of the column, continued on down the road. I again had to personally come back on the road, collect the men, and move them off in an orderly fashion. The firing stopped within a half hour. The company who had set up the machine gun dug in defensive positions and stayed there the remainder of the night, instead of continuing up the road, as was their mission. This group attacked up the road the following morning.[4]

Asked whether the vehicles abandoned by one company were later recovered, Gurfein replied that "a tank force went back and did get some of them," but others were still there five days later. Asked about the reaction of the junior officers and noncommissioned officers when the rout started after the booby trap exploded at the bridge, he said, "Neither the junior officers or noncommissioned officers said a word, nor took part, except to obey my orders." The battalion staff did not assist Gurfein at the time. Gurfein made an oral report of the episode to Lt. Col. John H. Chiles, the X Corps G-3, and to Lieutenant Colonel McCaffrey, deputy chief of staff, X Corps. Subsequently he submitted a written report to Chiles.[5]

Upon his arrival at Koto-ri, Reidy reported to Col. Lewis B. Puller, commander of the 1st Marine Regiment. Puller informed Reidy that he and his battalion were attached to the 1st Marine Regiment and were given a sector of the Koto-ri perimeter. Puller also directed that the battalion assume control of all Army personnel, about 1,800 men from 44 different units who had piled up there, unable to go farther. The 2nd Battalion remained at Koto-ri as part of Puller's command until the Marines and Army troops withdrew to Hamhung, closing there on December 12 in midafternoon.[6]

The 2nd Battalion, 31st Infantry, was not the only Army unit intended for MacLean's RCT that did not arrive. Captain Charles Peckham's B Company, 1st Battalion, 31st Infantry, was supposed to replace E Company, 2nd Battalion, as its third rifle company. On its way to Chosin it was in advance of Reidy's battalion and had arrived at Koto-ri in the evening of November 28, having traveled from Hamhung during the day. Unluckily, the next day B Company was made part of "Task Force Drysdale," named for Lt. Col. Douglas B. Drysdale, commanding officer of the British 41st Independent Commando, Royal Marines. This task force included the Royal Marines; Capt. Carl Sitter's G Company, 1st Marines; B Company, 31st Infantry; and a Marine tank company. It was formed when General Smith ordered Colonel Puller on the 28th to send him "desperately needed reinforcements" to hold Hagaru-ri. Smith wanted reinforcements, although it meant that they would suffer heavy casualties in reaching Hagaru-ri. Task Force Drysdale numbered more than 900 men with armor support. Its mission was to cut through Chinese forces along the 11 miles of road between Koto-ri and Hagaru-ri. The Chinese ambushed Task Force Drysdale about halfway to Hagaru-ri in what became known as "Hell's Fire Valley" and cut it to pieces. Only a few of the commandos, Sitter's G Company, and the tanks fought their way into Hagaru-ri. Peckham's B Company was caught in the ambush and cut into segments. It lost heavily.

During the night 1st Lt. Alfred J. Anderson, of B Company, regrouped into a defensive perimeter all the men of B Company that he could find. Armed only with his .45 pistol, he set an example of leadership throughout the night. Twice he closed with enemy soldiers who entered his perimeter and killed them at arm's length, deflecting their weapons with one arm as he used his pistol in these close encounters. At 6:00 A.M. on November 30, Anderson received orders to withdraw that part of B Company under his control. He led them back safely through enemy opposition to Koto-ri.[7]

B Company's losses were 100 killed or missing in action and 19 wounded — a total of 119 battle casualties. This company, another of MacLean's intended units, never saw the waters of Chosin Reservoir, but it knew the same ferocity of battle that engulfed MacLean's men on the east side.[8]

No matter what criticism might be made of X Corps's delays and confusions in handling the movement of the 2nd Battalion, 31st Infantry, from Hamhung toward the reservoir or the ineptness in the command of the 2nd Battalion itself, it is clear that it would not have reached the reservoir and the 31st RCT if its movement had been a model of planning and expeditious execution. The reason is simple enough. The enemy controlled the road between Koto-ri and Hagaru-ri from November 28 on, and also the road up the pass from Chinhung-ni to Koto-ri to some degree after November 28. This meant that from Koto-ri neither B Company, 31st Infantry, nor the 2nd Battalion, 31st Infantry, could have reached MacLean on the east side of the reservoir any time after the night of November 27. When General Hodes at Hagaru-ri sent a radio message to General Barr at 6:30 P.M. on the 28th urgently asking him to hasten forward the 2nd Battalion, it was already too late.

Colonel MacLean and Lieutenant Colonel Faith knew nothing of this. For the Army troops east of the Chosin Reservoir the failure of higher command to establish and maintain communications with them from November 27 through December 1, 1950 was of fatal importance.

Hodes and Lynch Serve as 31st RCT Liaison at Hagaru-ri

When General Hodes left Hudong-ni in one of Drake's tanks in the early afternoon of November 28 to go to Hagaru-ri to seek help, he found on arrival that Maj. Gen. Oliver P. Smith had just arrived to establish his 1st Marine Division CP. Hodes told him that the 7th Division battalions on the east side of the reservoir had 400 casualties and no way to get to safety.[9] Smith, however, learned that he had only a few troops at Hagaru-ri to defend it against Chinese attack. They were certain to attack Hagaru-ri because it was the kingpin of the entire American deployment around Chosin Reservoir. Smith was startled at what he found at Hagaru-ri and told Colonel Puller at Koto-ri to rush reinforcements to him the next day at any cost. Task Force Drysdale was the result. Thus, Hodes learned that immediate help for the 31st RCT was out of the question.

The next afternoon, November 29, Hodes sent a radio message to Hudong-ni ordering Major Lynch and his two sergeants to join him in Hagaru-ri. They made ready as quickly as possible and about 3 P.M. set out in Lynch's jeep for Hagaru-ri.

As they moved along the twisting road southward, Lynch was amazed to see columns of Chinese moving in the same direction on the ridges 500 to 1,000 yards east of the road. He said: "The pucker-factor [tension] was quite high but we disturbed them not nor did they us. I recall meeting Gen. Hodes at the perimeter of the Marine defense which was under fire from Chinese coming from the E."[10] Darkness had begun to fall when Lynch reached Hagaru-ri.

Sergeant Cox busied himself finding places for General Hodes and Major Lynch to sleep. They finally slept in a tent occupied by two Marine lieutenants who were on duty that night. The tent was near the 1st Marine Division G-3 van, the sole means of sending or receiving radio messages. Lynch said that he spent much of his time outside the van, trying to learn what was happening.

The CCF attacked Hagaru-ri the first night Hodes and Smith were there (November 28–29), the night before Lynch arrived. The CCF first attacked from the southwest and during the latter part of the night from East Hill, which dominated the east side of the Hagaru-ri perimeter. The CCF and the Marines spent all of the 29th in sporadic fighting for control of East Hill. This situation continued into the evening of the 29th, with the Chinese in control. That evening, shortly after his arrival, Lynch was sitting with Hodes in the G-3 van when a bullet passed through the side of it, hit the metal rail, head high, and dropped between them. Hodes picked up the spent slug but said nothing.[11]

Hagaru-ri, as the Marine and Army men knew it at the end of November and early December, 1950, was a tent city. The native town had been reduced to rubble by UN air power. When General Smith indicated on November 28 that he was moving his division CP to Hagaru-ri, the Marines prepared for him one of the few huts still standing. Smith arrived about noon on the 28th and established his forward CP there. Lieutenant Colonel William J. McCaffrey, deputy chief of staff, X Corps, at the same time began setting up an X Corps Advance CP just outside the Marine perimeter, but it never became fully operational.[12]

When Major Lynch arrived at the Marine perimeter, General Hodes was there to meet him. They went directly to General Smith's covered "hootch." It was now dark. Smith and Hodes talked for about ten minutes, but Lynch did not hear what they said. It seemed clear, however, that Hodes informed Smith of conditions on the east side of the reservoir. Hodes and Lynch can be thought of as a 7th Infantry Division liaison group with the 1st Marine Division at Hagaru-ri, a relationship that Hodes established to communicate with X Corps and through it with his own division. He would also have tried to obtain from the Marines any assistance they could provide for the Army troops cut off on the east side of the reservoir, including maximum Marine air support.

According to Lynch, Hodes felt frustrated since there was little he could do. He believed that, as long as he lived, Hodes suffered from the knowledge that he was not able to save his men. Smith felt that he could not send a Marine infantry-tank force up the east side of the reservoir to help the 31st RCT without seriously endangering his own incompletely defended perimeter. In fact, the 31st RCT at first had about as many combat troops as Smith had. When Smith arrived at Hagaru-ri, his force consisted of two infantry companies and the Weapons Company of the 3rd Battalion, 1st Marines. After the first Chinese attack on the Hagaru-ri perimeter during the night of November 28–29 it was under constant siege and in jeopardy. Any force from Hagaru-ri strong enough to fight its way through to the Army inlet perimeter would have left the vital Marine perimeter vulnerable.

By the end of November General Barr had moved his 7th Division CP to the port city of Hungnam but later relocated it in Hamhung, closer to X Corps. For any communication with General Barr, Hodes had to go through the 1st Marine to X Corps, which would relay any message he wanted to send. If Hodes wanted to communicate with the 31st Infantry Rear CP at Hudong-ni, his only means of doing so was by his tank radio to other tanks of the 31st Tank Company there. Hodes had no communications of any kind with the combat battalions and the artillery farther north. Nor could 31st Rear at Hudong-ni talk with these units. Communication from higher authority to the forward units east of Chosin was, therefore, nonexistent after November 28, except that from FAC Stamford with the 1st Battalion, 32nd Infantry (and later Task Force Faith), to the Corsair fighter-bombers and the resupply-drop planes.[14]

One cannot overemphasize the significance of the lack of communications from the battle area—from the forward perimeter and the inlet perimeter 4 miles farther south and with all points south of the inlet. Even the 31st Infantry Rear at Hudong-ni, approximately 4 miles south of the 3rd Battalion and the 57th Field Artillery, knew only in a general way that a fight was going on north of them during the first night of battle. Major Lynch, who was at Hudong-ni during this period, has written that after midday November 28 "information dwindled progressively to zero. Communications were never established with the 1st Marine Div CP."[15] According to Lynch, about the only—and last—things that General Hodes did for Task Force Faith were to send a Marine medical evacuation helicopter to the inlet, which in two trips evacuated four wounded men, as mentioned above, and to have an L-5 liaison plane from Hagaru-ri drop a supply of morphine, both on November 29.

Macarthur Calls a Conference, November 28

By the afternoon of November 28, four days after he had confidently launched his attack to the Manchurian border to unify all of Korea, General MacArthur in Tokyo decided that a crisis existed in Korea. He and his staff had been reluctant to recognize that the Chinese XIII Army Group was defeating the Eighth Army in western North Korea. A long message that General MacArthur sent to the Joint Chiefs of Staff on November 28 and a communiqué he issued late that afternoon in Tokyo indicated that he had reached a personal decision about the nature of the crisis. This was one day after the Chinese opened their attacks against X Corps in northeast Korea, but it was three days after the Chinese attacks first struck Eighth Army in the west. The issue might not yet be clear in the X Corps area and around the Chosin Reservoir, but it was becoming frighteningly clear in the west on the Chongchon River front.

MacArthur's long radio message to the Joint Chiefs of Staff struck officials in Washington, D.C., right up to the president, like a thunderbolt. It showed a clear about-face in MacArthur's opinion of the war and posed the possibility that the American and UN forces might have to evacuate Korea. The message said in part:

> All hope of localization of the Korean conflict to enemy forces composed of NK troops with alien token elements can now be completely abandoned. . . . No pretext of minor support under the guise of volunteerism or other subterfuge now has the slighest validity. We face an entirely new war. . . . It is quite evident that our present strength of force is not sufficient to meet this undeclared war by the Chinese with the inherent advantages which accrue thereby to them. . . . This command has done everything humanly

possible within its capabilities but is now faced with conditions beyond its control and its strength.[1]

After sending his message, MacArthur issued his Communiqué No. 14 for worldwide consumption as his explanation of what was happening in Korea. It said that a major segment of the Chinese continental armed forces in army, corps, and division strength of more than 200,000 men were now committed against the United Nations in Korea. The communiqué continued: "Consequently we face an entirely new war. This has shattered the high hope we entertained that the intervention of the Chinese was only of token nature on a volunteer and individual basis as publicly announced."[2]

At the same time MacArthur decided on a third step: to call Generals Walker and Almond, his field commanders in Korea, to Tokyo that same afternoon. But MacArthur had made up his mind about the situation in Korea before he met with them that night. When Almond arrived, the others were waiting. The conference got under way at the American embassy, MacArthur's residence, about 9:50 P.M. and lasted until 1:30 A.M., November 29.[3] Walker's and Almond's flights to Tokyo had been kept secret. Those present at the conference were as follows:

General MacArthur
Vice Admiral Charles Turner Joy, commander, Naval Forces Far East
Lt. Gen. George E. Stratemeyer, commander, Far East Air Force
Lt. Gen. Walton H. Walker, commander, Eighth Army
Maj. Gen. Edward M. Almond, commander, X Corps
Maj. Gen. Doyle O. Hickey, Far East Command chief of staff
Maj. Gen. Charles A. Willoughby, Far East Command G-2
Maj. Gen. Courtney Whitney, Adviser on MacArthur's staff
Brig. Gen. Edwin K. Wright, Far East Command G-3[4]

MacArthur asked many questions, mostly directed to Walker and Almond. Occasionally some of those present would offer a remark or a suggestion or ask a question. Wright seems to have been the most active participant in the conference, other than MacArthur, Walker, and Almond.

The most surprising element was the optimism of both Walker and Almond concerning the military situation in Korea. Heavy fighting had been in progress in the Eighth Army zone since the evening of November 25 — three nights and three days — and one night and one day in the X Corps zone. The military situation had developed further and was clearer in Eighth Army than in X Corps. When MacArthur asked Walker what he thought of the situation on his front and where the Eighth Army could make a successful stand, he replied that he expected to hold Pyongyang and to establish a defense line north and east of the city.

When MacArthur asked Almond a similar question relating to X Corps, Almond answered euphorically that he expected the 1st Marine and 7th Infantry divisions to continue their attacks west and north from the Chosin Reservoir and cut the enemy line of communications in their rear, at or near Mupyong-ni, below Kanggje and the Yalu River. This was the main mission of X Corps in helping the Eighth Army. On the night of November 28–29 in the Tokyo conference Almond expressed the same view that he had expressed to Colonel MacLean and Colonel Faith that afternoon.[5]

Almond's unrealistic belief that he could continue his attack is hard to explain. That day he had visited the 7th Division on the east side of the reservoir and the day before had visited the 1st Marine Division at Yudam-ni on the west side. At neither place was there any reason for optimism. He had badly misjudged the situation. MacArthur hoped that Walker could hold Pyongyang, but did not agree with Almond that he could continue to attack successfully to Mupyong-ni. He had already stated his view in his message to the Joint Chiefs of Staff that afternoon.

General MacArthur expressed no decisions or orders to Walker or Almond during the conference. However, before they left Tokyo about noon on November 29 he gave them his instructions. He asked General Walker to hold the Pyongyang area if he could do so but to withdraw as needed to prevent Chinese forces from moving around his right flank and into his rear. He ordered Almond to end offensive action, withdraw, and concentrate the X Corps in the Hamhung-Hungnam area. Although he probably contemplated evacuating X Corps from northeast Korea and moving it by sea to join Eighth Army, he did not include that in his instructions to Almond.

Almond left Tokyo at noon on the 29th to return to Korea. Lieutenant Colonel McCaffrey, Lieutenant Colonel Glass, and Major Ladd were on the plane with him. During the trip the men discussed the situation. Almond, acting on MacArthur's orders, told McCaffrey and Glass to prepare a X Corps order to concentrate the corps forces at Hamhung "and action against enemy wherever possible within good judgment."

After arriving in Korea, Almond, accompanied by McCaffrey, flew to the X Corps CP. An hour later he conferred with his chief of staff, General

Ruffner, and the rest of his staff. This resulted in Operational Order No. 8, which called for a discontinuance of the X Corps attack to the northwest and a withdrawal of its forces. This carried out MacArthur's instructions.[6]

The Joint Chiefs of Staff on November 29 approved MacArthur's plan to pass from the offensive to the defensive in Korea. They said, "Strategic and tactical considerations are now paramount." But they also asked, "What are your plans re the coordination of operations of the 8th Army and X Corps and the positioning of X Corps, the units of which appear to us to be exposed?"[7]

None of the troop units east of Chosin knew anything about the fast-changing high-level decisions for the war. In any event, those decisions would not immediately change what was taking place on the battlefield.

12

The Third Night—Task Force Faith at the Inlet

Contrary to expectations, the early hours of the night of November 29–30 proved to be relatively quiet at the inlet perimeter. From dark until nearly midnight silence reigned, except for the distant sound of artillery fire from the west, across the reservoir near the Marine perimeters at Yudam-ni, and occasional bugle sounds on the north. A bright moon illuminated the landscape, but as the night progressed, the sky clouded over and it began to snow.

The tense quiet ended before midnight as artillery and mortars within the perimeter began to fire. Soon machine guns and rifles added their clamor, and fire from attacking Chinese passed overhead.

The first attack came over the ridge and descending slope at the south side of the perimeter, where B and A companies held the line. Lieutenant May, Headquarters Company, helped repel one enemy attack that came down a ravine at the southeastern edge of the ridge. This clash lasted about an hour. If the Chinese wanted to test the newly arrived troops, they did so to their regret. They were harshly received, with many killed and wounded. They did not enter the perimeter and finally withdrew from contact with a lot of bugle blowing. Quiet settled over the area once again, with infrequent firing from outpost positions and an occasional mortar round at a suspected enemy position. All within the perimeter were surprised at the lack of a general enemy assault.[1]

We do not know what the Chinese did after Faith led the 1st Battalion to the inlet. They probably spent the day pillaging the area. Although there was no coordinated assault on the perimeter during the night, there were infiltration attempts and probing along the lines all night long and two or three sharp attacks. One of these attacks was especially vicious, though it did not last long. It was directed against both ends of the perimeter where the road entered and exited. The worst part of the attack was at the southern end, where A Company had established a roadblock to anchor its western boundary road. There an assault party overran a heavy machine gun, and a mortar shell exploded on a 75-mm recoilless rifle, wiping out that position. These two weapons had provided most of the American firepower in that sector. The Chinese captured some of the crew members.

The enemy made special efforts against the antiaircraft weapons, causing some damage. In placing his quad-50s around the artillery, McClymont put one of them close to his CP with the cab away from the direction of the intended main area of fire, toward the inlet. The M16 could fire better over the tailgate, for the turret had more freedom to traverse.[2] There was concern that the enemy might attack over the flat frozen area of the inlet. Mortars walked a barrage up the inlet and then pulled their rounds to within 100 yards of American foxholes. These shells did not break the ice and expose running water as hoped, to inhibit an enemy attack across the inlet. From time to time mortars fired illuminating shells over the perimeter.

McClymont happened to be gazing out toward the inlet when one of the illuminating shells opened in the sky over a part of the inlet. In the sudden light he saw a group of men on the ice, crossing toward the perimeter. Then the anticlimax: they were American stragglers cut off the night before when the 1st Battalion withdrew from the forward perimeter. When they entered, McClymont said, "How they hollered, laughed, and were glad to see us."

After this brief, tense incident, things quieted down again. McClymont remained in his foxhole underneath the half-track with a confiscated tommy gun at his side and a row of grenades on the lip of his foxhole. He had pulled his sleeping bag over him and was about to drop off to sleep. Suddenly shooting started at a foxhole near the edge of the inlet. McClymont and his two buddies were immediately awake. He grabbed his glasses and could just make out figures running on the ice, coming toward the perimeter. A star shell rose into the sky over the inlet. The quad-50, about 10 to 20 yards to his right, opened up. The running figures had reached the south side of the inlet and the foxholes at the edge of the perimeter.

By now the four machine guns of the quad-50 were raking the edge of the inlet and the ice. Each gun fires 450 rounds a minute on full automatic, and every fifth round is a tracer. The tracers showed the fire cutting into a bank and working over the edge of the ice at the inlet. Then suddenly it stopped firing, and the illuminating shell burned out. Relative darkness and quiet once more prevailed.

McClymont could make out movement, closer to him than before, but he did not know whether it was friendly or enemy. He and the two men with him pointed their guns toward the movement but held their fire. Rifle fire was still coming from friendly foxholes in front of him. This led him to conclude that the moving shadows he saw were enemy.

At this point a soldier climbed into his foxhole from the rear. He told McClymont that the edge of the inlet was "crawling with Chinese." McClymont picked up his gun; the others seized their weapons, and all fired into the mass of moving shadows below them. The nearby quad-50 had by now reloaded and came to life with a swath of .50-caliber bullets along the edge of the inlet, only 40 to 50 yards away. After this moving scythe of fire passed along the edge of the inlet, things became quiet. This is the only recorded enemy attack across the ice of the inlet from the north to the south side. It came to a bloody end.

McClymont used the ensuing interval of inaction to go to the quad-50 and check on its status. The last stoppage of its fire was caused when the gunner was hit in the head as he sat in the turret. He was a tall man, and the crew had not been able to remove him because his feet were entangled with something inside. McClymont crouched down until he could feel the gunner's feet and slowly was able to turn them around. Then the crew lifted the gunner from his place, and laid him down alongside the quad-50. A new gunner slid into the empty place in the turret.

The soldier from the inlet who had crawled into McClymont's foxhole had other information. He said that a Korean house near the inlet held Chinese soldiers. McClymont went to one of his dual-40s and directed fire on the house. The 40-mm shells soon made a wreck of the hut, killing a squad of Chinese inside it.[3]

During the night the Chinese attacked the M19 dual-40 commanded by Sgt. Harold B. Haugland, going for a knockout there, and a penetration of the perimeter. Enemy squads attacked it repeatedly before midnight. Haugland was able to direct the dual-40 fire against the assault groups, killing most of them. But in the action Haugland suffered a serious foot wound and was carried to the aid station.

In the early hours of November 30 enemy groups renewed the attack on the M19. Haugland wrapped his foot and wedged it into an empty ration box, using it for a shoe, and under fire hobbled back to his M19 and re-sumed command of it. Enemy mortar fire now set the M19's ammunition trailer ablaze, causing the 40-mm shells to explode. Despite this, Haugland went to the front of the dual-40 and guided the driver in moving the vehicle to a new position away from the trailer. The M19 continued in action and during the night was the dominant factor in preventing an enemy penetra-tion of the perimeter at that point. But in the nightlong duel the M19 suf-fered serious damage, which rendered it immobile, although still able to fire its guns. The destruction of the trailer also meant the loss of invaluable 40-mm shells.[4]

After the attacks against the antiaircraft weapons, enemy activity for the rest of the night was confined to harassing with machine-gun fire, blowing bugles and whistles, and setting off flares. The latter were probably used as signals in the regrouping of forces.

During the night an American soldier froze to death in a sitting posi-tion in his foxhole.[5]

Daylight at the Inlet, November 30

Ground fog during the morning of November 30 slowed the arrival of day-light. The fog began to dissipate about 8:00 A.M., and by 10:00 A.M. the skies had cleared. Airdrops then brought supplies, but ammunition was still critically short. Stamford asked the pilots to bring in more ammunition. Later there was a drop of .50-caliber machine-gun ammunition, but there was still no resupply of 40-mm shells for the dual-40s.

After dawn the men built fires to warm themselves and heat water for coffee. Thus fortified, they worked on improving and deepening their posi-tions. The Chinese on the high ground did not interfere and seemed to give no heed. After the fog burned off and the sun came out, some optimism developed in the perimeter, primarily because the scale of enemy activity had dropped off during the previous night from that of the first two nights. Many thought that the worst was over. Some still expected that a relief force from Hagaru-ri would reach them during the day. But by midafter-noon it was obvious to all that they would have to stay another night. An-other airdrop during the afternoon improved the ammunition situation for the perimeter forces, especially for the 4.2-inch mortars.

Early on the 30th, Lieutenant Mortrude was ordered to clear the shore-line of the inlet in his platoon area for a helicopter landing site for the evacuation of casualties. The work was finished before the only helicopter ever to use it arrived shortly before noon—with an unanticipated visitor, Maj. Gen. David G. Barr, commander of the 7th Infantry Division.

Earlier, from Hagaru-ri, General Hodes had made it clear to Barr that all 7th Division troops east of the reservoir were in jeopardy. On the morning of November 30, Barr had flown from Hungnam to Hagaru-ri after an early-morning conference with General Almond. He also had a brief meeting with General Smith at Hagaru-ri before boarding a helicopter for the short flight to the inlet.

When Barr stepped out of the helicopter, Mortrude and some of his men were there to greet him. Mortrude wrote, "He quickly discouraged our enthusiastic welcome with a brusque and unsympathetic response and stalked off to locate Col. Faith." Barr went into immediate private conference with Faith, the meeting lasting about half an hour. What passed between them is not known, and Faith did not disclose it to his staff. From remarks that Barr made later in the day to Smith at Hagaru-ri, however, Faith told him that in any breakout attempt he would have 500 wounded to bring out. This figure did not include casualties that the task force might incur at the perimeter or in the breakout effort. He also told Barr about Colonel MacLean. This was the first information that higher headquarters had of the loss of the regimental commander on the 29th and of Faith's assumption of command.[6]

The next day, when Faith called a meeting of his officers to tell them of his decision to try a breakout, all he said of his meeting with Barr was that he had received no instructions on what he was to do. But when Barr met Faith before noon on November 30, he no longer had authority to give Faith orders. General Almond's X Corps Operational Instructions No. 19, effective 8:00 A.M. on 30 November, placed all elements of the 7th Infantry Division north of Koto-ri under the command of Maj. Gen. Oliver D. Smith, 1st Marine Division commander.[7] Barr could make recommendations to General Smith upon his return to Hagaru-ri on what he thought would be best for his troops cut off in the inlet perimeter, and he no doubt did so. For two years Barr had headed the US Military Advisory Group assigned to help Chiang Kai-shek in the civil war against the Communist Chinese and should have known as much as any other man in the US Department of Defense about the Communist forces and their capabilities.[8]

Stamford got in a good day's work on the 30th. He had planes on station as soon as it was light enough to see. The Corsair flight leader reported that east of the perimeter he had spotted vehicles, tents, and enemy soldiers dragging away their dead. He reported that the center of activity seemed to be what looked like a CCF regimental CP, which he and his flight attacked with good results. Stamford thought that the supporting arms on the ground—the mortars, the artillery, and the AAA AW weapons—did a good job in helping the infantry defend the perimeter, considering the shortage of ammunition.

By now three main avenues of enemy attack toward the perimeter had become apparent. The first, which had been used each night, was from the northeast along a shallow draw upstream from the bridge and causeway leading into the northeast corner, down the valley of the Pungnyuri-gang. The second approach was down a draw that entered the perimeter at its southeast corner from the ridge on the south. The third approach, an increasingly frequent avenue of violent attack, was along the narrow-gauge railroad and the road passing through the perimeter from the southwest.

About noon, after the early Corsair and supply-plane flights to the inlet, Stamford's high-frequency radio ceased to operate. Stamford thought that parts of Lieutenant Johnson's equipment, damaged when Johnson was killed in the first night's attack on the 3rd Battalion, might be salvaged to repair his set. Johnson's equipment lay about 500 yards from Stamford's position. Corporal Myron J. Smith, the radio operator, and Pfc. Billy E. Johnson, another member of the TACP, volunteered to cross the area under enemy fire to bring the equipment to Stamford. They succeeded in rescuing it and then worked four hours with bare hands in freezing weather to make the radio set operable.[9]

The prevailing practice was for the 1st Marine Air Wing and the Fifth Air Force to send all the planes they could make available from Yonpo Airfield near Hungnam, the Marine Air Field near Wonsan, and carriers off the coast near Hungnam to Hagaru-ri every day to support the 1st Marine Division and the 31st RCT. A dispatcher at Hagaru-ri would direct the planes to points where they were most needed. The repaired radio set enabled Stamford to reach the dispatcher at Hagaru-ri by relay through the pilots in the air over the inlet. The expert repair work done under adverse conditions by Smith and Johnson thus enabled Task Force Faith to continue to receive the help of a forward air controller. It is sad that neither Corporal Smith nor Private Johnson survived Chosin.

In view of the disastrous effects of the lack of communications between the cutoff battalions at the inlet and the 31st Rear at Hudong-ni and the

Marines at Hagaru-ri, it is regrettable that no one took steps to reestablish communication. It was Army practice at that time that responsibility for reestablishing broken communications rested with the higher command. But in this instance nothing was done by higher headquarters. Therefore, common sense should have dictated that a lower-level commander of cutoff forces would take the initiative in getting communications reestablished if it was in his power. There is no evidence that any effort was made by Faith at the inlet to establish communications when the means were at hand to do so through the daily radio contact of the TACP with pilots overhead. According to Stamford, he had the means to communicate if he had been given the proper radio frequencies. He said: "My AN/FRC-1 was capable of tuning any high frequency used by US forces air or land. Had we been given a frequency by a pilot or had Gen. Barr brought one with him, or someone air dropped one, we could have been in business. The 1st Mar Div Air Section knew what kind of equipment I had."[10]

It apparently never dawned on Faith or his principal staff officers that this means of establishing communication with the 1st Marine Division at Hagaru-ri, and through it with the 7th Infantry Division and X Corps, was feasible. According to Curtis, who admits his own lack of foresight in the matter, he knew of no such effort in the 31st RCT.[11]

During the late afternoon of the 30th, Faith and Curtis worked out a detailed plan for counterattacks that might be needed to close penetrations at any part of the perimeter. The counterattack forces were taken from the 57th FA Headquarters Battery, the 1st Battalion Headquarters, and the Heavy Weapons (D) Company. Wire communications within the perimeter were improved, and ammunition was redistributed.[12]

Major Miller explains how he improved his medical operations: "The aid station was set up under a tarp stretched across the railroad culvert or cut, with other canvas hung on the sides to cut the wind and a makeshift stove set up inside to dispel some of the chill. A standard GI field range was in use to heat soup for the wounded. The Bn CP was of the same makeshift construction and was set up about 20 yards from the aid station in the culvert. Two sets of telephone wires were run from the Bn CP to each company and to the Task Force CP."[13]

Miller was especially concerned about frostbite, and he ordered all the men to change socks before nightfall and keep an extra pair of socks under their shirts to dry out from body heat. So far there had been few cases of frozen feet because, as mentioned earlier, Faith did not favor wearing the shoepacs but believed that the ordinary combat boots with overshoes were better. Most of the men who went through the winter in North Korea in 1950 agreed with that judgment.

Throughout the day parts of the perimeter received sporadic, light-caliber enemy mortar fire. Mortrude's platoon CP had been discovered by the Chinese, and it was one of the targets. The mortar fire spurred Mortrude's men to dig deeper into the cutbank of the railroad. Once during the day they observed an enemy group approaching up the roadbed but dispersed them with long-range rifle fire.

Lieutenant May relates an unusual incident that occurred at his corner of the perimeter on the morning of November 30:

> I observed a lone man out on the ice coming toward our positions. We put our glasses on him and found he was in an American uniform. Col. Faith told me to get a ¼ ton M.G.veh. and pick him up.
>
> Our point of departure was from the west corner of our position at the edge of the ice. Sgt. Rule of Dog Company drove the vehicle. The north side of the reservoir Inlet was controlled by the CCF and required we stay as far away from them as possible. I decided to go along the south side of the inlet to open ice. I think we took the CCF to our west by surprise as we had very little fire from them at this time.
>
> We traveled southwest until out of rifle range, then cut west and picked up a man from our HQ. Co. The man had been cut off at the time of our withdrawal from the forward positions.
>
> We returned with the rescued man by the same route we used going out. We did get a lot more small arms fire on our return trip. Yes, we took a chance on this venture and were lucky in the rescue.[14]

After returning from this mission at noon, May was given one of the more difficult and dangerous jobs on the perimeter. He was to cover the road and the railroad leading south out of the perimeter. This was the boundary between A and C companies, A Company having originally been responsible for the line across the railbed and the road. The repeated enemy attacks made it necessary to reinforce this critical point. May recruited his force from drivers, cooks, and other Headquarters personnel. His role here was almost identical to the one he had had in the forward perimeter. In addition to their individual weapons, the men of his makeshift force were provided with a rocket launcher, two .50-caliber machine guns, and two .30-caliber machine guns. The Chinese continued attacking the line during the afternoon, not waiting for nightfall. May tells about this action:

The Chinese continued to make attacks from around an embankment approximately 100 to 150 yards southwest of our road outposts. The outposts had to withdraw to the perimeter boundary and we set up a strong point there. These suicide attacks, of the Chinese along the road, continued all that afternoon and night. At times they got so close we used grenades. Due to this action, the Chinese KIA was extremely heavy, while we suffered only a few KIA and wounded. The Chinese had a strong point set up behind the curve in the road out a few hundred yards, which later proved to be an obstacle, requiring an air strike to remove.[15]

As darkness settled over the perimeter, word was passed to those within it, "Hold out one more night and we've got it made!"[16] Those words may have held out hope to some, but to others they seemed to mean that the situation was desperate.

Commanders' Conference at Hagaru-ri

In a meeting on the morning of November 30, General Almond explained to the X Corps staff the changed policy of operations resulting from the conference in Tokyo and MacArthur's instructions to him on the morning of the 29th before he returned to Korea. A little later, at 9:00 A.M., Almond conferred with General Barr. Barr left immediately for Hagaru-ri to confer with General Smith and made a brief visit to Faith at the inlet. In the meantime Almond had lunch at Hamhung and at 1:40 P.M. departed for Hagaru-ri in an L-17 plane, accompanied by his senior aide, Major Ladd.[17]

Sometime during the afternoon, after returning to Hagaru-ri from the inlet, Barr told Smith about the 500 wounded to be brought out in any breakout attempt from the Task Force Faith perimeter and said that this would be his biggest handicap. In his discussion with Smith, Barr is said to have agreed that Faith could improve his situation and probably succeed in a breakout effort with strong Marine air support.[18]

That morning at his CP, General Almond had received from his staff, and especially from Col. Edward H. Forney, USMC, a frightening account of the Chinese roadblocks and attacks on the MSR to the reservoir. The report heightened Almond's concern about the danger to the 31st RCT. Pursuant to MacArthur's instructions to abandon offensive action in the Chosin area and concentrate the corps, Almond had issued the X Corps Instruction No. 19 ordering the 1st Marine Division to redeploy one regiment immediately from Yudam-ni to Hagaru-ri and gain contact with the 31st RCT.[19]

Upon arriving at Hagaru-ri, Almond at 2:10 P.M. began a conference with his commanders in the joined pyramidal tents that had been erected at the airstrip. His main purpose was to impress them with his views in the changed situation.[20] Almond told the assembled group, which included Generals Smith, Barr, and Hodes and Colonels Williams and Forney, that the corps would abandon the Chosin Reservoir area and that all the troops would be concentrated immediately in the Hagaru-ri area. Once concentrated there, they would be withdrawn to the coast. Almond not only was acting to carry out MacArthur's instructions to him but also showed genuine alarm at recent events at the reservoir. He was an entirely different man from the one who had visited his troops there two days earlier. He knew now that the survival of X Corps itself was at stake. He told Smith that he would resupply him by air if he felt it was necessary to burn or destroy some supplies and equipment to hasten withdrawal to the coast. He stressed the need for speedy action. Smith responded that he felt that there would be no need for destruction of supplies and equipment and that he would need everything he had to fight his way to the coast. He said that the care and evacuation of the wounded would be the biggest obstacle to a speedy withdrawal. Almond ordered Smith and Barr to prepare a plan and a time schedule for getting the Army units east of the reservoir withdrawn to Hagaru-ri.[21]

No transcript or record was made of the November 30 command conference at Hagaru-ri. An entry in Almond's diary concerning the conference reads as follows:

> 1410 – Conference with Generals Smith, Barr, Hodes and Colonels Williams and Forney on the present situation. CG X Corps stressed the urgency of withdrawing the 5th and 7th Marine Regiments to Hagaru-ri immediately and ordering Generals Barr and Smith to submit a plan for the withdrawals of the elements of the 31st and 32nd Infantry Regiments from the present position east of the lake to Hagaru-ri. By telephone, CG X Corps ordered Chief of Staff X Corps to send an immediate message to Lt. Col. Reidy, commanding the battalion enroute to Koto-ri to join Col. Puller immediately at Koto-ri. Lt. Col. Carlton was ordered to proceed to Hagaru-ri for the purpose of providing airlift of supplies specifically desired by the 1st Marine Division and arranging for their proper packing and delivery.[22]

The conference lasted 1 hour and 20 minutes. At 3:30 P.M., Almond flew back to the X Corps CP in Hamhung to confer with his chief of staff and the G-4 concerning supply to the Hagaru-ri forces. He then drafted a message to General MacArthur on the X Corps's situation.

Meanwhile, back in Hagaru-ri, after Almond had left, Generals Smith and Barr discussed how they could best implement his order to extricate the 7th Division elements east of the reservoir. They agreed that not much could be done with the troops available at Hagaru-ri. Every man there was needed to hold that position. Lieutenant Colonel Thomas Ridge, USMC, the defense commander, desperately needed reinforcements if he was to have a chance of holding Hagaru-ri against an expected strong enemy attack, which came that night. Smith and Barr agreed that before anything could be done the Marines would have to be withdrawn from Yudam-ni to Hagaru-ri. Smith told Barr that Marine air support would be allotted the next day on a preferential basis to help Faith fight his way out of the inlet perimeter and try to reach Hagaru-ri.

Smith subsequently discussed the situation with General Hodes, directing him to prepare a message to Faith ordering him to fight his way out of the perimeter to Hagaru-ri the next day but not to jeopardize the safety of his wounded.[23]

General Almond's order to bring a Marine regiment from Yudam-ni to Hagaru-ri for the rescue of the Army troops on the east side of the reservoir is a perfect example of a moment in battle where a higher headquarters can issue commands but subordinate ones are powerless to carry them out. In this case the enemy controlled the situation on the ground. The Marines at Yudam-ni were cut off from Hagaru-ri as completely as were the 7th Division troops on the east side of the reservoir. It would take them four days and three nights to fight their way to Hagaru-ri. The situation was worse for the Army troops than for the Marines at Yudam-ni since there was no communication between Hagaru-ri and the Army units. Also, the Marines at Yudam-ni were more concentrated and in greater strength.

13

Withdrawal from Hudong-ni to Hagaru-ri

On the afternoon of November 30, the 31st Infantry Rear and Captain Drake's 31st Tank Company were ordered to withdraw from Hudong-ni to Hagaru-ri. Until then the presence of the tank company at Hudong-ni had kept the Chinese off the road south of the big roadblock and fire block at the hairpin curve at the east side of Hill 1221, two miles south of the inlet perimeter.

Until November 29, Captain King's A Company, 1st Engineer Marine Battalion, was stationed about two miles north of Hagaru-ri at a sawmill near Sasu getting timbers to repair the blown concrete bridge over the Paegamni-gang. For use until this could be accomplished, an easy ford around the west side of the damaged bridge had been built by the Marine Engineers. They also had an outpost on Hill 1203, just south of Sasu, from which they could see Hagaru-ri. On the 30th the need for troops to bolster the Marine perimeter defense at Hagaru-ri was so great that General Smith ordered them back to Hagaru-ri. First Lieutenant Nicholas A. Canzona's 1st Platoon led the way back without incident and was committed that night to the fighting on East Hill.[1]

The recall of the Marine Engineers to Hagaru-ri, together with the withdrawal of approximately 325 Army troops from Hudong-ni to that point, left no American units between Hagaru-ri and the cutoff troops of Task Force Faith at the inlet. The 325 Army troops at Hudong-ni belonged to three units: 44 in the 31st Infantry Headquarters and Headquarters Company and Service units who had remained at the 31st Rear CP, 176 in Drake's 31st Tank Company, and 105 in the 57th Field Artillery Headquarters Battery who got no farther north.[2]

183

Lieutenant Colonel Berry K. Anderson, S-3 of the 31st Infantry, who was the senior officer present at the 31st Rear after General Hodes left for Hagaru-ri on the afternoon of November 28, assumed command at Hudong-ni. Lieutenant Colonel George E. Deshon, the 31st Infantry executive officer, had remained behind at Iwon with the main regimental rear. Major Carl G. Witte, the 31st Infantry S-2, was the next-ranking officer at Hudong-ni. When Anderson became commander, Witte assumed the duties of S-3 as well as S-2.

On November 26, Colonel MacLean had established a supply dump at Hudong-ni, and by the evening of November 27, about 260 tons of miscellaneous supplies had been brought there by truck. After that there were airdrops of supplies and ammunition, but the tank company did not get the 105-mm and 76-mm shells it needed or any .50-caliber machine-gun ammunition. It did receive a generous airdrop of 40-mm ammunition, for which it had no use.

The 31st Rear Command Post area encompassed about 25 acres of relatively flat land below the schoolhouse on the north side of the Paegamni-gang with the vehicular road on its west side. Chosin Reservoir lay about a mile west of the CP and could easily be seen from it, down the valley of the Paegamni-gang. The Chinese never attacked Hudong-ni, probably because they were busy elsewhere and perhaps because they did not want to face Drake's tank company. Enemy snipers did get within range, however, and at times delivered harassing fire into the perimeter, as did some machine guns at long range. This fire did no serious damage, though a few men were wounded by it. The area was under enemy observation from higher ground on the north and northeast.[3]

Vehicular traffic reached the 31st Rear and the tank area from the Hagaru-ri road a short distance north of the blown bridge over the Paegamni-gang. As long as the tank company and more than 300 soldiers remained at Hudong-ni, it constituted a strong way station between Hagaru-ri and the 31st RCT infantry and artillerymen four miles north.

One particular feature of the terrain at Hudong-ni was especially important. Directly north of Hudong-ni a long ridgeline descended from Ko-bong (or Nopun-bong), 1,473 meters high, in a southwesterly direction to end in a high knob, Hill 1239, about one-third mile north of Hudong-ni. From it a sharp finger ridge descended to end directly above the road about 300 yards west of the 31st Rear CP and just north of the turnoff from the road into it. That finger of ground was to be the final critical point in deciding the fate of Task Force Faith.

Because the removal of the 31st RCT Rear and the 31st Tank Company from Hudong-ni occurred in the late afternoon of the day before Task Force Faith undertook its breakout from the inlet perimeter, and the end of that effort came virtually at the position those troops had held, the question presses: If they had still been there on December 1, could they have saved Task Force Faith from destruction? And if this question is pressed, then it would be useful to know who decided to withdraw those forces from Hudong-ni just when their presence there became most crucial.

Let us consider for a moment what answers there are to these questions: *Who ordered the 31st Rear and the 31st Tank Company to withdraw from Hudong-ni? When was the order delivered? What were the reasons for the order?* These remain questions for which only uncertain answers are available, but some rather direct evidence and much circumstantial evidence exist to warrant speculative conclusions.

The 7th Infantry Command Report for the period says that at 11:00 A.M. on November 30, 1950, the 1st Marine Division ordered Anderson and Drake to withdraw to Hagaru-ri. On December 12, 1950, Captain Drake in a memorandum to the commanding officer of the 31st Infantry Regiment stated that he received the order to withdraw at 4:00 P.M. on the 30th but does not say who gave him the order. It would seem that the order would have had to come directly or indirectly from Lieutenant Colonel Anderson. Colonel Witte (then Major), many years later said that he could not recall how or from whom the order was received. The communications situation would indicate that the order would have had to come from Hagaru-ri, and from there it could come only by 31st Tank Company radio. General Hodes at Hagaru-ri had the only 31st Tank Company radio that could communicate with Hudong-ni, and then only with other tanks of the 31st Tank Company under Drake's command.[4]

If the order for the 31st Rear and the tank company to withdraw came at 11:00 A.M. on November 30 as the 7th Division Command Report states, it would have had to come from the 1st Marine Division, since all troops in the Chosin Reservoir area north of Koto-ri were under its control after 8:00 A.M. that morning by X Corps order. If General Smith or his operations officer, Col. Alpha Bowser, issued an order at 11:00 A.M., the order could have been delivered only over the radio in the tank that Hodes had brought to Hagaru-ri.[5]

It is important to remember that General Barr, the 7th Division commander, was in Hagaru-ri during the morning and most of the afternoon of that day, and he would have been in communication there with both Hodes and Smith, who now commanded all UN and X Corps troops north of Koto-ri. Barr or Smith could have had Hodes transmit the order verbally to the 31st Rear CP over tank radio. If General Barr gave instructions to Hodes to transmit the order, he could have done so only with General Smith's oral or tacit approval. The Marine Operations Journal for the day shows no order from the Marine division. General McCaffrey, deputy chief of staff, X Corps, at the time, has told me that the order for the 31st Rear to withdraw to Hagaru-ri originated with General Barr. He said that when General Almond heard about the withdrawal he asked General Barr for an explanation and that Barr replied that he could not see any good coming from losing more men in behalf of those already lost.[6]

General Lynch (then Major) states that he did not relay the withdrawal order to Anderson on behalf of Hodes or anyone else. He thinks that all the circumstances in the situation indicate that General Hodes transmitted the order.[7] I agree with that judgment, but it is impossible now to determine on whose instructions Hodes transmitted the order or precisely when it was received at Hudong-ni. It is possible, and perhaps probable, that in discussions with General Barr, General Smith or Colonel Bowser had agreed to delegate their authority concerning the 7th Division elements east of Chosin Reservoir to him and through him to General Hodes. I believe that the decision was made by the higher command of the 7th Division, although General Smith could not ignore or escape his responsibility in the matter under X Corps order. He had to approve the order in some way, and probably did so verbally. The order may have been issued in his name by General Hodes, who acted as either Smith's or Barr's agent, by tank radio to Anderson at Hudong-ni.

One further development of some importance occurred at Hagaru-ri on November 30 that does not appear anywhere in the official records. This was a decision made by General Barr when he told General Smith that, to avoid possible embarrassment to all concerned and to avoid the semblance of a conflict in command, he would recall General Hodes from Hagaru-ri to 7th Division Headquarters.[8]

The troops began their withdrawal from Hudong-ni about 4:00 P.M. on November 30, with some tanks in the lead and others covering the rear. The march order included foot soldiers moving on either flank as the motor convoy and tanks followed the point down the road. Most of the troops rode in trucks, with Lieutenant Colonel Anderson commanding the movement. About one mile south of Hudong-ni, at a sharp switchback in a saddle of the first ridge south of the Paegamni-gang and east of Hill 1167, Anderson ordered Drake to abandon two disabled tanks that he was towing. He foresaw difficulties getting the towed tanks around the sharp road turns that would delay the movement of the convoy. This made 6 tanks that Drake lost or had to leave behind east of Chosin. He continued the movement with 15 tanks.[9]

The 7th Infantry Division After Action Report for the period states that the convoy had a running fight with the enemy on its way to Hagaru-ri, but this was not the case. Captain Drake reported that there was no significant enemy action directed at the movement to Hagaru-ri. There was occasional small-arms and automatic-weapons fire, but at such a great distance that it did no damage. No tanks or trucks were lost to enemy action, and there were no personnel casualties in the movement. Major Lynch and General Hodes met the tanks when they reached the Marine perimeter at Hagaru-ri. Lynch stated that he understood at the time that there was no enemy action.[10]

Drake and his tanks reached the Marine perimeter about 5:00 P.M. Darkness was near, but Drake had time to place his tanks in the perimeter in its northeastern arc before daylight faded entirely. Sixteen tanks were deployed along the base of East Hill at a sector of the Marine perimeter that had been poorly defended. Drake now had these 16 operable tanks under his control. He recalled: "We were in a tight formation—50 to 110 yards apart—thus we covered about 1,000 yards of the line. Our tents were within running distance from our tank line."[11]

That night Drake's tanks played an important role in turning back a massive Chinese attack from East Hill. The Chinese at one point broke through Drake's tank line and reached the tents in his rear, but they were killed there or escaped back to East Hill. A body count in front of two of his tanks the next morning showed 200 dead Chinese.

By dark of November 30, Task Force Faith at the inlet perimeter was isolated and alone. There were no friendly forces between it and Hagaru-ri.

The Fourth Night at the Inlet, November 30–December 1

For Task Force Faith the long, 16-hour night of darkness on November 30–December 1 was almost certain to bring renewed Chinese attacks at the inlet. The troops were short in all kinds of ammunition and were weary after three days and three nights of fighting and trying to stay awake at their posts.

Enemy mortar fire began about 8:00 P.M. and built up to barrage level, lasting about 45 minutes. These experienced soldiers took it to be the prelude to an infantry assault, and everyone in the perimeter stayed low in his foxhole, seeking to escape a direct hit. Many heard the repeated sound of steel on steel as mortar fragments struck nearby vehicles and other metal objects. There were two near misses at the 3rd Battalion Aid Station that wounded some medics and gave fresh wounds to men who were already casualties. Under the barrage enemy assault teams crept close to the perimeter, and those inside finally heard the sound of rifle and submachine-gun fire. The enemy had begun to clash with the infantry in the outposts.[1]

One of the early attacks came from the southwest along the road. It was headed for the boundary between A and C companies, where Mortrude's 3rd Platoon held the western end of the C Company line. Mortrude wrote of the attack:

> Shortly after dark, my forward positions on the road approach reported hearing voices and observing enemy crawling to their immediate front. I requested and received mortar fire 100 yards to our front. Upon warning my front line people down in foxholes and reducing the range by 50 yards with a "Fire for Effect" we heard much crying and shouting. Thereafter, there was no further pressure in this area.

An aerial view of the right (east) side of Chosin Reservoir, looking northwest over the middle and lower (northern) parts of Chosin Reservoir. It was taken on November 1, 1950, from a point over the Paegamni-gang Valley, with Hudong-ni at the lower-left corner. Hill 1221 is the hill mass in the lower-left center. All the terrain on which the 31st RCT and Task Force Faith fought their battles from November 27 to December 1, can be seen in this photograph. The inlet perimeter is the frozen-over shallow water of the Pungnyuri-gang at the right center. US Army photograph SC 363267.

Throughout the night . . . I continued to walk the line of the platoon positions to ensure that one man was awake in each hole and that no one was freezing. Fortunately, the platoon sergeant and his Korean counterpart were able to prepare some "C" ration coffee on a squad burner. This coffee, though only lukewarm when distributed to the troops, was greatly appreciated, more, I think, for the effort than the sustenance. All through the night we heard cries from our friendly wounded within the perimeter who were suffering from the cold. Also, the fighting with infiltrators in other areas of the perimeter had apparently resulted in US stragglers drifting into our more stable area. During one of my platoon rounds I was threatened by a hysterical battalion truck driver who was frenzied by the bizarre appearance of my improvised helmet cover (a pillow case) and my salvaged Chinese greatcoat. After he refused to be reassured by my voice, I was rescued by one of our automatic riflemen who in turn threatened to cut him "in half" if he didn't "leave the lieutenant alone."

Toward dawn . . . enemy mortar fire increased in the vicinity of the Platoon CP. First, my acting Korean platoon leader was slightly wounded in the legs and back, and next, our platoon sergeant, SFC Campbell was killed. This left only the platoon medic, Camoesas, with some battalion wounded still awaiting helicopter evacuation, and myself in the CP area.

Sometime in the early morning . . . Capt. Seever came to my CP and informed me of the increasing infiltration of other portions of the Task Force perimeter and of the possibility of a counterattack to clear the area. However, this mission never materialized for the 3rd Platoon.

Also, during this busy period, I injured my knee while launching a rifle grenade flare from a kneeling position on the icy ground. I don't know if the butt of my carbine slipped across my knee or if I carelessly placed it against my knee before firing. Thereafter it became difficult for me to walk.[2]

By shortly after midnight the Chinese attack had built up to an intensity not known in previous nights. Major Curtis thought that the enemy was determined to overrun the perimeter at any cost. Only the determined holding of their positions by A and C companies prevented the perimeter from being overrun. Even though there was more need for antiaircraft automatic-weapons fire than ever, McClymont had so reduced its volume that his quad-50s were firing only two of their four machine guns and the dual-40s only one of their two guns. Their ammunition had been so reduced by this time that he had to take this conservation measure to keep the invaluable weapons in the fight.

One enemy penetration swept the infantry from in front of one of the quad-50s and beyond, but the crew stayed with their weapons and kept on firing. The penetration was sealed off largely because of the heavy quad-50 fire, and the enemy who had penetrated were killed inside the perimeter.[3]

After midnight the Chinese attacked the south and southeast sides of the perimeter simultaneously and penetrated the east side in the sector held by the 3rd Battalion, 31st Infantry. Strangely, however, their attacks did not appear well coordinated, nor did they concentrate on crucial points, though some received stubborn and repeated attacks.

Early in the night there was much blowing of bugles and whistles and launching of flares on the north. To those inside the perimeter this appeared to be a logical approach of any new attacking force: all it had to do was cross the ice at the narrow neck of the inlet and come directly to C Company's position. Heavy snowfall that began after dark made visibility poor.

On the second night of battle Captain Jordan tried to confuse the Chinese in their use of signals by having his M Company mortars fire different-colored flares. Captain Bigger used the same tactics in his D Company on the night of November 30. When the enemy blew a whistle, he had his men blow one; when the Chinese shot a flare into the sky, his mortars fired one.[4]

One of the most persistent points of Chinese attack during the night was the boundary of A and C companies at the road at the western end of the perimeter. The A Company roadblock and Lieutenant May's improvised Headquarters Company group that reinforced them took the brunt of these attacks. May said his force killed a Chinese soldier within 50 feet of their position when 40 enemy made a desperate attempt to break through along the road about 6:00 A.M. on December 1. After daylight May discovered that the soldier carried a .50-caliber American machine gun wrapped in burlap. But he had no tripod for the gun and no ammunition, nor could any ammunition be found on others in the party who were killed in front of the position.[5]

Major Miller in his statement on the fighting during the night of November 30 commented about the terrible destruction the AAA weapons wrought on the Chinese. He wrote: "Two dual 40-mm guns and two multiple caliber 50 MG self-propelled AA Carriages [M16 quad-50s] of the 15th AAA located within the perimeter inflicted terrific casualties on the enemy, particularly a multiple mount which had been laid on the road in front of C Company. The Chinese made repeated attempts to knock out these self-propelled vehicles."[6]

Major Curtis also commented on one of the Chinese attacks against the A Company roadblock at the western end of the perimeter. He said that "a body of enemy troops charged down the open road in such a manner that our men at first identified them as other friendly troops. This attack, however, was repulsed with great casualties to the enemy. Fighting became very close, and in some instances hand-to-hand in other parts of the perimeter." He added that "occasionally a Chinese soldier would infiltrate inside the perimeter and run about like a madman spraying with his burp-gun until he was killed. . . . Between 0400 and 0600 every man in the perimeter was in a defensive position operating a weapon. The question was whether the perimeter could hold out until dawn."[7]

From the very first night of their attacks on the inlet perimeter the Chinese had struck at the northeast corner from the valley of the Pungnyuri-gang above the bridge. There they had good approaches to the 3rd Battalion, 31st Infantry, holding the eastern side, and L and K companies suffered heavy losses. In the renewed Chinese attacks against this part of the perimeter in the predawn hours of December 1, Pfc. Stanley E. Anderson, of L Company, distinguished himself with a 3.5-inch rocket launcher, succeeding in turning back one of the enemy assaults.[8] But the CCF kept hitting this part of the perimeter repeatedly throughout the night, seeking a breakthrough.

About 3:00 A.M. on December 1 the Chinese finally penetrated the northeast corner of the perimeter. Previous penetrations elsewhere had been sealed quickly when Faith sent his preplanned counterattack force to the spot. This last breakthrough at the northeast corner was not closed, however, and it gave the enemy control of a high knob overlooking the perimeter below it to the west. The site was just east of the point where the road crossed the inlet on the bridge and causeway.[9]

When it became apparent that the Chinese would continue to hold this high ground, Faith called D Company, ordering a counterattack force to recapture the hill. First Lieutenant Robert D. Wilson, company reconnaissance officer, volunteered for the job and got together about 20 men. Just after daybreak he set off from the D Company area for the objective. His force was pitifully armed for the attack, but its condition was no worse than that of anyone else still able to fight in the perimeter. His group had a total of three hand grenades, only small-arms ammunition, and no rifle grenades. Wilson carried a chrome-plated Thompson submachine gun, captured earlier from the Chinese. The men had individual weapons, most of them rifles or carbines.

Wilson moved eastward from the D Company CP, passed through Lieutenant Campbell's machine-gun platoon position just north of (below) the road and slanted northeast toward the causeway and the point of high ground beyond it. Campbell saw him pass through his position just after daybreak. Wilson soon moved from Campbell's sight, dropping below one of the hummocks of ground near the inlet. Since Campbell could not see the attack against the knob, he moved to his northeast gun position at Bigger's request, so that he could report back to him on Wilson's counterattack. From this gun position he could see the enemy-held knob. When Campbell got to the observation point, he could see no movement on the objective. His gun crew there told him that they saw Wilson's attack, which did not get very far.[10] Their comments and later evidence from survivors indicated that Wilson reached the base of the knob and started up the slope with his men. Enemy fire soon hit him in the arm, knocking him down. He rose and continued on. Another bullet hit him, but he kept advancing. Almost immediately a third bullet struck him in the head and killed him. Then Sfc. Fred Sugua assumed command and climbed on with a small remaining group, but enemy fire killed him within a minute or two. The leaderless men continued the fight and reached part of the knob but were unable to gain control and restore the perimeter. The Chinese continued to hold the crest.[11]

The Chinese did not pull back from the perimeter everywhere at daybreak as they had on previous days. Many of them stayed in the low ground within the perimeter. Others withdrew only a few hundred yards, within small-arms range. From these positions they delivered small-arms grazing and some machine-gun fire. Also, enemy mortar fire picked up and continued with increasing accuracy. This daytime fire caused more casualties.[12]

The Chinese made some desperate efforts at a final breakthrough after daylight. An assault force of 40 to 50 soldiers tried again to rush the 75-mm recoilless rifle posted on the road at the boundary of A and C companies. As before, the attack came up the road from the west, this time along the ditch on the south side of the road. Corporal Armentrout used a heavy machine gun, damaged during the night by an enemy mortar round, to hold off the enemy for a few minutes. Then the gun jammed. He sent his assistant gunner back for the only other heavy machine gun available. It arrived in time, and Armentrout killed about 20 enemy soldiers with it, repulsing the attack.[13]

The increasing difficulty of taking care of the wounded is illustrated in Major Miller's statement that "during the night the Bn Aid Station had received a direct mortar round hit which wounded all the Aid Station medical personnel including Capt. Navarre, the battalion surgeon. Medical supplies were completely exhausted by dawn."[14]

Daylight revealed low clouds and fog. The prospect for receiving desperately needed air support during the day was not good. Curtis described the situation after daybreak:

An attempt to describe accurately the scene inside the perimeter of Task Force Faith on the morning of 1 December 1950 runs the risk of appearing macabre. Very probably, however, even Hollywood will not be able to duplicate it in stark tragedy and horror. . . . By dawn on 1 December members of the Task Force had been under attack for 80 hours in sub-zero weather. None had slept much. None had washed or shaved; none had eaten more than a bare minimum. Due to the season of the year, darkness covered about 16 hours of each 24 hour period—and during the hours of darkness the enemy exploited his terror weapons such as bugles, whistles, flares, burp-guns, and infiltration tactics. The ground was frozen so solidly as to hamper digging, so riflemen and weapons crews occupied very shallow trenches.

The dead, concentrated in central collecting points, had to be used as a source for all supplies including clothing, weapons, and ammunition. Everyone seemed to be wounded in one fashion or another and to varying degrees of severity. Frozen feet and hands were common. The wounded who were unable to move about froze to death. Trucks and jeeps and trailers were ransacked for ammunition and any kind of fabric that would serve for bandages or clothing.

But the factors that discouraged and disheartened most were these: Everyone could see that the weather was growing worse, which meant the loss of air support and aerial resupply; that relief from Hagaru-ri in any force less than regimental size could never reach us; that another night of determined attacks would surely overrun the position.[15]

As the dead accumulated, there was at first some effort to dig graves and bury them just below the bridge and causeway in the low ground along the inlet. But the frozen ground made this difficult, and other pressing matters and the near-exhausted state of the troops led them to abandon it. Most of the bodies were carried to a sheltered place under a low embankment along the inlet not far from the causeway. There, frozen stiff, they were laid in rows and stacked about four high. Only the recent dead were in the aid station at the end.[16]

15

Breakout from the Inlet Perimeter, December 1

Dawn on the morning of December 1 came to the inlet with low-hanging clouds completely covering the perimeter. Snow flurries added to the dismal scene. All this was most discouraging to the men. They would desperately need air support during the day. If the weather remained this way, they would get none.

Those who could find a ration tried to eat the frozen food. Major Robbins told of breakfasting on a can of beans, frozen as usual. He started a small fire, but it soon went out for lack of fuel. No one was willing to expose himself in the open to scavenge for something to burn. So the group ate their frozen beans mixed with ice crystals.

Caring for the wounded was a top priority after daylight. But it was hard to do anything for them since medical supplies were exhausted. There was neither morphine nor bandages, so reasonably clean cloths and towels were used for bandaging. A Korean shack served as the principal aid station. Two stoves from the Headquarters Company kitchen had been saved. They provided hot soup and coffee for the wounded.[1]

Shortly after 9:00 A.M., in heavy clouds, a lone Marine fighter-bomber appeared over the inlet. The pilot came from the carrier USS *Leyte*, and must have made many previous trips to the inlet. However he managed it, his performance was of utmost value to the task force. The pilot established radio communication with Captain Stamford and told him that if weather permitted he would guide a flight of Corsairs to the perimeter about noon. Stamford gave this information to Faith and then told the pilot to relay to the 1st Marine Air Wing dispatcher at Hagaru-ri Faith's request for heavy air support during the day and to notify General Barr, the 7th Division commander, of Faith's intention to try for a breakout. Faith's decision that early was probably influenced by the pilot's remark to Stamford that the weather report received that morning on the *Leyte* was that sunshine and broken clouds would most likely prevail about noon.[2]

In the meantime, Majors Curtis and Miller had been conferring with Faith, and they urged him to try for a breakout during the day, for they did not think the task force could hold the perimeter another night. Faith seemed to agree. He called a conference for 10:00 A.M. with his battalion commanders and other staff officers at his CP. There is no record of all the men present, but some who attended recalled that the group included Major Miller, Major Storms, Major Tolly, Captain McClymont, Lieutenant May, Captain Stamford, Major Curtis, and Major Jones. Captain Bigger most likely was also present.

When his officers had assembled at his CP, Faith told them that he had decided on his own initiative to order a breakout from the perimeter during the day in an effort to join the Marines at Hagaru-ri. He said that there was a chance the weather might improve by noon and that aircraft might arrive to help them in the breakout. They were to make preparations for the breakout in case the support aircraft arrived. He said that no help could be expected from the Marines on the ground. He also said that he had had no communication with higher headquarters. The task force would be on its own, except for the close air support it expected to receive. Major Tolly reported that the artillery had only a few rounds of 105-mm howitzer ammunition left. Captain Cody reported the same situation for the 31st Heavy Mortar Company. Captain McClymont said that he had very little ammunition for the antiaircraft automatic weapons.

Faith then issued his verbal orders:

1. The 1st Battalion, 32nd Infantry, would lead off, opening the way through the enemy position known to be just west and south of the perimeter along the road and clear the road and roadsides for passage of the truck column.

2. The 57th Field Artillery Battalion and the 31st Heavy Mortar Company would expend their remaining ammunition just before the breakout in support of it and then destroy their pieces and mortar tubes. The personnel would fight as riflemen in the center of the vehicular column.

3. The 3rd Battalion, 31st Infantry, would follow the vehicular column and protect its rear.

4. Jeeps and their trailers would be destroyed, except certain radio and machine-gun jeeps.

5. All 2½-ton trucks would be unloaded of whatever cargo they might have, and the wounded would be loaded in them. All inoperable trucks would be destroyed.

6. All operable antiaircraft weapons carriers would be in the column.

7. All supplies and clothing and unused equipment were to be burned or otherwise destroyed.[3]

Faith told Stamford to ask for at least 10 aircraft to be over the breakout column at all times to cover the withdrawal.

Major Miller asked Faith for an M19 full-track dual-40 to lead the point of the breakout. He wanted it not only for its formidable firepower but also because with its full track it would be the best equipment in the convoy to push obstacles off the road and extricate any vehicles that got stuck. Faith approved the request.

Faith said that the breakout would start on his order after the aircraft arrived. He gave specific orders to a few officers in the meeting. He told McClymont to place one M19 at the point, as Major Miller had requested, to place another at the rear of the column, and to intersperse the M16 quad-50s in the column. Lieutenant May said that Faith told him to "prepare cargo vehicles, plus machine gun vehicles, and to move only the wounded. These vehicles were to be put in a column out on the road. . . . I was instructed to remain in the rear of our column and to see all vehicles fall into the column."[4] McClymont commented that Faith's order to him was the only time he received instructions of any kind from anyone while he was in the perimeter. There is some confusion about who had the responsibility for destroying vehicles that were not to be in the convoy. In any event, many of the vehicles were not burned or destroyed.[5]

Major Miller returned to his CP and called his company commanders together. His improvised staff consisted of Major Jones, Captain Bigger, Captain Bauer, and Warrant Officer Wester. He ordered his company commanders to destroy all jeeps and trailers and unload the remaining vehicles and destroy the contents. The wounded were to be made ready for loading on the trucks. All available blankets and sleeping bags were to be used for them. When the air strikes started, signaling the breakout, C Company would lead off down the road as point, followed by B, D, and A companies. The truck column was to follow C Company. Miller's plan was for C Company to overcome initial enemy resistance and allow the truck column to move out of the perimeter and then to fall back as reserve. The next rifle company behind C would then take the lead, and this process would be repeated by successive companies if the lead company became bogged down or suffered heavy casualties. Miller ordered all ammunition to be picked up from the dead or wounded for use by able-bodied men.[6]

Presumably Major Tolly informed his artillery headquarters staff, the A and B Battery commanders, and others of their duties and places in the march order. It is assumed that Major Storms did likewise with the 3rd Battalion, 31st Infantry, outlining their duties as task force rear guard.

Captain Jordan, commanding M Company of the 3rd Battalion, however, said that he learned of the projected withdrawal on a visit to the 3rd Battalion CP and thereafter prepared for movement. He expected to receive further details later but never received additional information and only by watching the 3rd Battalion CP move out was he able to get his company into the column. Had he gone to sleep, he said, presumably he and his company would have been left behind.[7]

Apparently there were not enough operable 2½-ton trucks to carry all the wounded, and some ¾-ton trucks were used. Each of the trucks was loaded with 15 to 20 wounded—more would have meant uncomfortable overcrowding. But Jordan's M Company had only one truck for about 50 wounded who could not walk, according to Cpl. Helmuth Bertram, the company's acting reconnaissance sergeant. Bertram said that Jordan built three decks in the truck and placed the wounded in the truck in three layers. This was probably the heaviest-loaded truck that left the perimeter.[8]

During the morning of December 1, Lieutenant Mortrude was exhausted. So were many others. When Captain Seever summoned him to the company CP for the breakout order, Mortrude had difficulty finding the CP. Of his condition then he wrote:

> I hardly remember receiving the withdrawal order now, and perhaps barely focused on it then. I do remember discussion about my impaired mobility which terminated in a decision that I was to command my platoon from an automatic weapons tracked vehicle. I also remember experiencing a moment of panic in not being sure I could find my way back to my platoon area from the company CP. I do not recall my order to my platoon but it must have been, at best, a brief fragmentary one, perhaps as I led them out of our positions to the head of the column forming for the breakout. I also vaguely recall the confused situation of trucks being lined up under occa-

Capt. (later Lt. Col.) Earle H. Jordan, Jr., in Korea, early 1951. Photograph courtesy of Lieutenant Colonel Jordan.

sional mortar fire. I specifically noticed our Battalion Surgeon [Vincent Navarre] supervising the loading of the wounded.[9]

Not even all the officers knew that a breakout had been ordered. Capt. John Swenty of the 1st Battalion wrote: "I first noticed men from the 31st and artillery were burning clothing. Men were changing tires on 2½-ton trucks and destroying motors and burning ¾-ton and ¼-ton trucks. While this was going on we were still drawing enemy mortar fire. I made contact with Maj. Curtis, 1st Bn S-3, and he told me we were getting ready to pull out about noon."[10]

The breakout orders and preparations for it by subordinate units of the task force were hurriedly made and, as in many other matters relating to battle and war, imperfectly executed. It is not known precisely how many vehicles there were in the column. Major Curtis estimates 25 or more 2½-ton trucks, but about 30 vehicles is closer to the mark, as it turned out. There was only one M19 dual-40 in the column, for the other one that was still mobile and operable could not be started when the column left the perimeter. When the column was forming on the road, this M19, intended to be the last vehicle in the column and to cover it with its firepower, had to be jump-started. After idling the motor a while as the column waited, the driver shut off the motor to save fuel. Later, when the column started, the M19 would not start because of a dead battery, and the crew had to abandon it. Lieutenant May saw it and asked the crew about it. Captain McClymont, at the head of the column, did not know that the M19 had been left behind until midafternoon. There had gone half of the M19 firepower and the ammunition. It was a disaster.

There were only two M16 quad-50s interspersed in the column. McClymont states that two of the M16s would not start when the column was forming and had to be left behind. All the antiaircraft weapons in the column ran out of ammunition and fuel before they got past Hill 1221. At the time of the breakout the point M19 had only a little ammunition, perhaps enough for a few targets of opportunity.[11]

Concerning destruction of what was left behind, Captain Stamford wrote two months after the event: "Not all equipment was destroyed. Much clothing and nearly all baggage was left intact. I burned all my confidential publications, but I believe much was left by the units. . . . Time did not permit its destruction."[12] Lieutenant May confirmed this about the rear units.

The enemy, watching from the high ground around the perimeter as

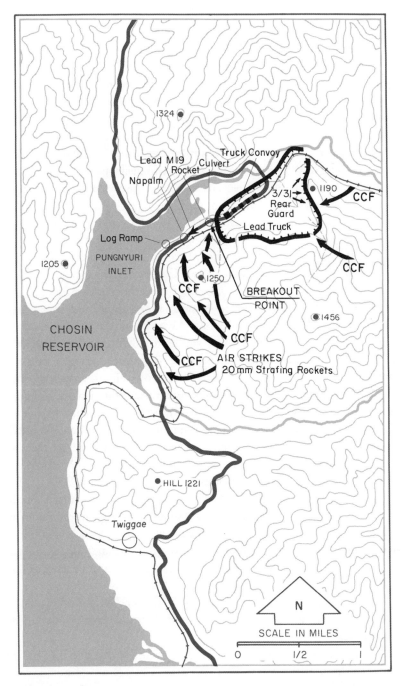

MAP 10. The situation at the beginning of Task Force Faith's breakout attempt.

the vehicles formed on the road and the wounded were loaded, could readily surmise that the men in the perimeter were getting ready for an attempted breakout. At 11:00 A.M., Sergeant Luna, of B Company, holding a temporary position on the railroad track, could see Chinese soldiers half a mile in front of him coming off the hills to go into position along the road and the breakout route.[13]

Seldom critical of anyone, Captain Jordan, of M Company, 31st Infantry, said: "The breakout effort was, and I am not happy to say, poorly organized, if at all, as regards rear guard. My unit was a part of the 3rd Bn. and I received no instructions or mission whatever. As a matter of fact we would have been left in position if we had not observed the people between us and the lake pulling out. I then ordered my people to follow."[14]

As Stamford recalled it, the troops were ready to move at 11:00 A.M., with the truck column on the road and artillerymen, mortarmen, and the walking wounded Headquarters men lined up as foot soldiers on either side of the trucks. It was now a matter of awaiting the arrival of air cover. Very few machine guns were mounted on vehicles, Stamford said, because .50-caliber ammunition for them was almost nonexistent. The shortage of .50-caliber ammunition for heavy machine guns, including the guns of the M16 quad-50s, and the 40-mm shells for the M19 dual-40s, was a serious matter—gravely threatening the prospects for a successful breakthrough to Hagaru-ri.

Seeing the preparations for the breakout attempt, the Chinese increased their mortar fire into the perimeter, and this caused many late casualties. Ten minutes after Robbins received word from Faith that the breakout attempt would be made, and while he was walking to the 57th Field Artillery CP, he was hit in the arm and legs by fragments from a mortar shell that landed only a few feet from him. He could reach the edge of its crater from where he lay on the ground. He saw his assistant, Lieutenant McNally, hopping around on one leg, wounded by the same mortar round. The blast had knocked Robbins's carbine from his hand and rendered it useless as shells in the clip exploded and damaged the slide. Sergeant Major John A. Lynch, Jr., of the 31st Infantry, got Robbins into a slit trench, bound his wounds, and then placed him in one of the slat-sided 2½-ton trucks being loaded with wounded.

Another mortar shell made a direct hit on the 1st Battalion aid station. Two more mortar shells hit the 1st Battalion CP, just after Faith's meeting ended and the officers were dispersing. Lieutenant May, Captain Bigger,

Capt. Jack Thompson, Captain Vaudreaux, Lieutenant Campbell, and an unidentified truck driver from B Company were standing in a group outside the CP when one of the mortar shells hit in the center of their circle. May was the only one who was not hurt by the explosion. The B Company driver was the most seriously injured. Both of Thompson's legs were broken. Campbell received mortar fragments in his left leg, his left shoulder, and the left side of his face. Bigger had mortar-fragment cuts on his face, one eye was blown from its socket, and he had serious leg and back wounds. A medic put the eye back in place and fastened a patch over it. Bigger afterward hobbled around with two canes he had used as mortar aiming stakes. All the wounded men were placed in trucks. At least one of them, Thompson, did not survive Chosin. May said that he saw his body later in the day.[15]

Another mortar shell landed about 10 feet from where Major Curtis and Captain Seever were sitting on the edge of a foxhole, but neither was injured. Only two weeks earlier Seever had learned that his wife had given him a first son. Already wounded in a leg at the forward perimeter, Seever had remained in command of C Company in the days that followed. Now, escaping further injury from the mortar shell, Seever said to Curtis, "I feel like I am a thousand years old." Did he feel that his luck had run out? By 3:00 P.M. that afternoon he was dead.[16]

As the morning wore on, the Chinese began pressing on the perimeter, and Faith began to fear that they might break in and wreak havoc before the expected air support arrived. Because of this threat Faith went to the 1st Battalion aid station and appealed for all the wounded who were able to do so to get weapons and go back on the defense line. A few made the effort. One of them, Lieutenant Campbell, recently wounded, describes that moment:

> I recall feeling as though I had been hit with a log and falling like a sack of rocks. Someone, I believe Cpt May dragged me under a nearby 2½-ton truck. I was later carried to the railroad or road cut outside the Aide Station where I was given the morphine surette from my aide pouch and the aid kit bandage compress applied to my head. My shoulder and leg were checked to ensure that the bleeding had stopped. There appeared to be no other dressings available. I was taken then to rest in the makeshift tent in the cut which was even then filled with wounded. I recall being on my back looking at the hole in the tent roof where apparently a mortar round had entered. Later I remember LTC Faith coming to the tent entrance and en-

couraging all that could move to help out. Several of us made our way out. I found a carbine in a pile of discarded weapons near the tent entrance. I crawled to a firing position in a ditch about 20 yards away. I was groggy and my leg had stiffened and would not support my weight. That was as far as I could go. Later I was policed up and put on a truck with the other wounded from the area of the aid station. In retrospect it is amazing and a credit to the unsung heroes in the medics that the care of the wounded continued right up to the time they were loaded on the trucks for the breakout.[17]

The trucks with their wounded from the 57th Field Artillery Battalion were placed in line behind those of the 31st Heavy Mortar Company. As in all other units, all spare blankets and sleeping bags were put on the trucks with the wounded to keep them as warm as possible.

During the preparations Curtis kept up his practice of visiting the artillery-fire direction center and some of the howitzer crews. He said that the 57th Field Artillery Battalion CP "was always a scene of confusion when I was there. . . . From my rather limited close observation, I got the impression that most of the firing was being directed by Section Sergeants. . . . There was a lot of firing and empty shell cases and ammo boxes were used to build parapets and shelters."

The morale of the artillerymen was as good as, if not better than, that of the average infantryman on the day of the breakout, if Curtis's experience was typical:

I remember one Section Sergeant in particular on the morning of 1 Dec. I walked by his position—he handed me his binoculars and pointed out his target to me, a large group of Chinese on the mountain side to the NE—in plain view, but at long range. He was adjusting his own fire at them and he was making them scatter. He said he was starting to run low on ammunition. I asked him if he knew how to destroy the block of his howitzer if we had to pull out and leave it behind. His answer was quite emphatic: (paraphrase) "I'm not leaving this piece. If they (the Chinese) get it, they're going to have to take me with it." For all I know he may have stayed with his piece. I never saw him again.[18]

Sergeant Major Lynch, of the 31st Infantry, said: "By the 4th day of the battle so many officers and noncoms had been killed or wounded that I could not get an accurate check on our casualties and fighting strength. The day we started our retreat south I personally counted 200 dead Chinamen inside our perimeter. And they were stacked four or five deep for four to five hundred yards around the perimeter."[19]

As preparations for the breakout ended, drivers of vehicles on the road began draining gasoline from inoperable vehicles to fill their own tanks. Gasoline was at a premium, and not all the drivers could fill their vehicles' tanks. Small-arms ammunition was distributed to the men, but there was not much of it; some men had only one clip each.

The short supply of small-arms ammunition was due in part to a mishap in the airdrop the previous evening. In a brewing snowstorm Stamford lost radio contact with planes coming in after dark, and the drops from the plane loaded with rifle and carbine ammunition fell to the Chinese outside the perimeter.[20]

Several persons later asked, "Why did not X Corps, the 1st Marine Division, or the 7th Division rescue the stranded troops east of Chosin by using the frozen surface of the reservoir, or why did not Task Force Faith itself take its convoy of vehicles over the ice from the inlet?" The question of using the ice was discussed at several command levels but was always rejected as impracticable. The Chosin Reservoir was not frozen solid to a great depth, as most persons have assumed. There was considerable open water at the reservoir, and much of the ice close to the shoreline was treacherous. X Corps at one time made a proposal to use seaplanes, landing on open water to rescue the men, but nothing came of it. The 1st Marine Division Headquarters considered the possibility of using the reservoir surface but could not find a workable plan.[21]

Faith also considered the ice-crossing option. He rejected it because he was not willing to trust 2½-ton trucks loaded with wounded to the uncertain reservoir ice.[22] Major Curtis was also much opposed to the idea of using the ice of the reservoir as a passageway to Hagaru-ri. He pointed out that the trucks did not have chains, and he considered it highly irresponsible to try to get the trucks out on solid ice and then hope that it would sustain them the 7 to 8 miles to Hagaru-ri. These fears were well founded. We know that when Captain Kitz with K Company went out on the ice at one point it broke in a few places, men fell in the water, and some of them drowned.[23]

Breakout

Everything depended on the Corsairs from the USS *Leyte* getting into the air, having good enough weather to reach the inlet, and once there having visibility to give close ground support to Task Force Faith. They found the inlet, arriving there just before 1:00 P.M. Visibility was improving, just as forecast. The stage was now set for the breakout.[24]

The 1st Marine Division Special Action Report (SAR) for the day states in part:

> At 1100 on 1 December, RCT-31(–) USA, having passed to operational control of the 1st Marine Division the previous day, was ordered to make every effort to secure necessary exits from its position east of the Reservoir, and move south to Hagaru-ri at the earliest. In view of the critical requirements for holding Hagaru-ri, CO, RCT-31 was notified that no actual troop assistance could be furnished, although maximum air support would be immediately available. RCT-31 initiated movement to the south at noon with an air cover of 20 VF.[25]

This passage would make it appear that Task Force Faith was acting on Marine orders when it made ready to start fighting south shortly after noon on December 1. That was not the case, however, for, as stated earlier, Faith ordered the breakout on his own initiative. Major Curtis stated that General Smith's order was not received until about 3:00 P.M., two hours after the breakout had begun and when the column was approaching the first bridge south of the inlet. More will be said later about the manner in which this order was received. At 11:00 A.M. the 1st Marine Division decided to order Faith to break out but, because it lacked adequate communications, was unable to get the order to Faith then or while his force was still within the perimeter.

To visualize events associated with the breakout, one should remember that A Company, 32nd Infantry, manned the perimeter defense line on the south side from the east across the railroad and vehicular road to the edge of the inlet. Meeting it there, on an east-west line along the inlet, was the western boundary of C Company. These two companies would necessarily be involved in the initial fighting to break out of the perimeter. After breakout the task force would follow the road west for half a mile along the inlet and then turn south along the reservoir toward Hagaru-ri. C Company was to be the lead breakout unit down the road. Because no enemy line was facing it along the inlet, that company could most easily be withdrawn from its defense line for the effort. A Company held the defensive roadblock on the road. About 100 feet farther west Chinese foxholes on the rising ground promised immediate resistance once the breakout started. A Company was to advance on the high ground just east of the road as C Company cleared the road itself. Behind A Company and farther uphill, B Company was to join in clearing the high ground east of the road as the attack progressed and thus enable the column to move southward.

There was little to fear on the right or west flank, since the edge of the reservoir nearby gave natural protection, allowing only a limited place for enemy action. This protection, however, was not complete until the road turned south at the junction of the inlet with the reservoir about half a mile west of the perimeter. Then the right-hand flank protection continued for about two miles until the road circled the high hill that came down steeply from the east to the edge of the reservoir and reached a valley tributary to the reservoir.

The breakout plan called for Lieutenant Mortrude to form the point with his 3rd Platoon of C Company with an M19 dual-40 AAA full-track vehicle in the lead. The rest of C Company would follow as the breakthrough rifle unit on the road. Because of Mortrude's injured knee, it was decided that he would ride the dual-40 and command his platoon from it. Behind the M19 was a jeep mounting a .30-caliber machine gun. Then came the truck column, with troops on either side of it on the road.

The command group was behind Mortrude's platoon. Captain Stamford, with VHF radio and his TACP, took his station about 20 yards behind the point. He was to control air strikes and direct the Corsairs on Faith's orders. Faith was in the same approximate position as Stamford in the column. Captain McClymont, commander of the other AAA vehicles, was a short distance behind the lead M19. Major Miller, as commander of the 1st Battalion, was also just behind the point.

Captain Stamford has left a precise description of the western end of the perimeter. On a 1:50,000–scale map of the inlet area the location of the breakout spot and the western limit of the perimeter can be identified (see map 10). The inlet, Hills 1306 and 1250 south of the inlet, and a prominent draw or drainage from the east side of Hill 1250 to the inlet locate the place. The draw running down from Hill 1250 crossed the railroad and the vehicular road at a right angle before dropping off to the inlet. A culvert carried it under the railroad and the road. A large, blunt spur ridge just west of the draw ended short of the reservoir, and the road and rail track passed around its terminal nose. The task force's roadblock at the perimeter's western end was about 100 feet east of the point where the draw passed under the road. Beyond the draw, west of it, was enemy territory. Chinese were in the draw in strength and on the high ground that rimmed the reservoir westward, south (or left) of the road. This high ground overlooked both the railroad and the road. For half a mile the fight initially was along the shore of the inlet east to west and the high ground south of it.

The overriding mission of Task Force Faith in the breakout was to protect and escort the truck convoy with its hundreds of wounded. Stamford moved up the road to take his place near the point. Eight or nine dead Chinese lay in a row in the roadside ditch within the perimeter, so neatly in order that he thought that they had been caught in a burst of enfilading machine-gun fire. Mortrude took his platoon forward past the forming truck column to the M19 waiting at the point. He got on the M19, and his platoon formed on either side of it.

The Corsairs came on station. The artillery and the mortars within the perimeter now began firing rapidly to expend the last of their ammunition. Some were still firing after the point started forward.[26]

The time was just before 1:00 P.M. Two entries in the 1st Marine Division G-3 Journal fix the time. An entry at 12:05 P.M. reported the 1st Battalion ready to move out. A later report, at 12:50 P.M., read, "1/31 Moving out at 1245 is making some progress" (there was no 1/31 in the force—the message had to refer to the 1/32).[27]

When the Corsairs first appeared, Stamford instructed the pilots to make a dummy run or two on the enemy positions just ahead of the panels marking the American perimeter. They did so, diving with guns silent. This kept the Chinese down in their holes.

On Faith's order Mortrude's 3rd Platoon started forward with the M19 and passed through A Company's roadblock. About 20 yards beyond the roadblock Chinese machine-gun and small-arms fire hit the point. Men began to drop from the fire.

Captain Seever had started the main body of C Company moving up behind the point platoon. As C Company reached the A Company roadblock, some A Company men close to the road on its east side joined it in an enthusiastic rush. The Chinese on their side did not hesitate but came right out on the road and moved in. The Americans were no more than 50 yards out of the perimeter when they were in the midst of a violent fire fight at close quarters, closing with the Chinese in a fan-shaped formation with assault fire. The two American units became interspersed near the draw and the forward Chinese line. Faith called on Stamford to bring in an air strike on the Chinese.[28] Mortrude, riding on the M19, had a view

A Marine Corsair, F4U, in flight, responding to a call for infantry ground support, Korea, 1950. US Marine Corps photograph A 133540.

from the very tip of the point. When Faith gave the order to move out, here is what he experienced:

> As we lurched off down the road to the southwest, the troops of my platoon were deployed on either side of my mobile command post. At this time the supporting US Marine Corps aircraft began flying directly over us from the rear to strike the enemy positions on the road ahead of us.
>
> We had proceeded only a short way beyond the perimeter when a furious burst of enemy automatic weapons fire drove me and the gunner down behind the shield of our open turret and the vehicle stalled. While I was exhorting the driver to restart the vehicle and the gunner to return fire, I hopefully watched a Marine aircraft making a low level run toward us from the rear. As the aircraft approached us, however, I saw his napalm tank fall away. Realizing it was a premature release, I crouched against the rear of the turret. A sheet of flame burned overhead momentarily with a sensation of heat and then dissipated. With the vehicle stalled, its weapons inoperable, and my own mobility remotivated, I tumbled over the rear of the turret

to the ground. Some small fires were still burning. Lt. Foster [2nd Lt. George E. Foster, platoon leader, 2nd Platoon, C Company] of our company was standing nearby with face and clothing blackened [and charred] and in a seeming dazed condition. Also some of my platoon members were writhing on the ground. I dashed down over the (north) shoulder of the road followed by several of my platoon.[29]

Lieutenant Foster undoubtedly was the man mentioned in stories circulated later of an officer who, burned black behind the M19, walked up to a soldier, asked for a cigarette, and walked away, never to be seen again.[30] Both Foster and 2nd Lt. Herbert E. Marshburn, Jr., a platoon leader in A Company, who was killed a few hours later at Hill 1221, were graduates of the 1950 class at West Point. They had been sent straight to Korea, missing the usual infantry course at Fort Benning.[31]

No two observers near the point saw everything the same way. Some saw and remembered certain details. Others noticed and remembered other things. But all the survivors of the group near the point will never forget the first air strike Stamford called in that afternoon. A flight of four Corsairs came roaring down the valley of the Pungnyuri-gang to the head of the inlet and on down above the road to the point where the breakout fight had been joined; their flight was from east to west. Stamford was calling the strike and was in a good position to see the action. His description follows:

> At the start of the breakout from the perimeter at the Inlet I was about 20 yards behind the point and ran a napalm drop which landed short causing some casualties among our own personnel on the left side of the road. The main part of this burst, because of the speed (in excess of 33 K) of the corsair (F4U) splashed onto the target of intention. The part that hit our people was of lesser duration and volume [but] is just as hot as any other part of the burst.
>
> There is no explosive device in the napalm tank other than an incendiary device as part of the tank cap to ignite the napalm on impact. When the major portion hit the Chinese, it caused terrific casualties. I saw many on the higher ground to our front come up out of their holes as flaming torches and die immediately. A ROK soldier who dove in the drainage on my left as I bellowed "Stay on your feet," caught the full force of the backwash of the napalm ignition, came up out of the drainage, took three faltering steps toward me and collapsed and died on the road. He had inhaled the heat blast as it traveled down the drainage.

At this time I called the pilots to bring their 20 mm fire to bear on the Chinese evacuating their position to our left front. Later they told me that had been the first time they had actually seen the enemy they were shooting at since they had been in Korea.

As I moved forward, Capt. Seever turned to me and told me to get those Chinese about 20 yards to the front of him in the drainage that crossed the railroad and road via a culvert. I looked back and picked an F7F (twin engine fighter) just rolling into his strafing run and told him I wanted a rocket and to start strafing the road right in front of our troops. I never told him his target. He was 200 yards long and as I kept telling him to shorten up he obeyed me as if I had strings on him. As his tracers started hitting in the drainage I quickly told him that's the spot—give me a rocket. By this time he was very close and all I heard was a sound as if someone had torn a long piece of canvas followed by a sharp bang. The Chinese who had been in the drainage throwing grenades among us were no more.

Later, talking to the pilot in Japan I was told, "if you had not kept talking to me and I had a split second to think I would not have fired that rocket." When I asked why he said, "You know as well as I, an HVAR is not that accurate. I could see your helmet on my 20 mil ring on my sight, but I was excited and when you said give me a rocket I automatically pressed the trigger. I knew I had killed you."

I bought him a drink and commented that I didn't think that I would be any deader if he or the Chinese killed me but if he hadn't fired on my command I didn't think I would have been around to buy him a drink for saving my life (and how many more?).

As C Company surged forward Don Faith grabbed me by the arm and ordered me into the low ground to the right of the road along with my radio man PFC Myron J. Smith, USMC, and Faith's radio man. He said he didn't want me on the road getting myself killed. We moved parallel to the road about 1–15 feet below its surface through a grassy and bushy area about 20 yards apart, in order me, Smith, the CO's radio man. It was uneventful until I approached a log ramp slanting toward the shoreline from the road. About 20 yards from it where the logs' ends slanted onto the ground I saw a gun barrel pointing at me and the lower legs and feet of someone crouched close to the gun. I walked without varying my pace, climbed up on the ramp right beside the gun, and then waved to Smith and pointed between my feet at the gun. He waited until he was no more than 5 to 10 yards from me and fired a burst from his burp gun and successfully secured the position. We pulled the gun out (it looked like a Bren gun) and threw the charging handle away. At the time I was carrying my radio and armed with a .45 but thought it the better part of valor to get the radio by the gun. Then we proceeded around the curve and I climbed up onto the

road. Again Faith ordered me off the road and I refused. I told him I was
unable to keep up with the TF stumbling through the brush over frozen
ground.[32]

Stamford says that he saw only one soldier, the ROK, killed among the
Americans in the napalm burst, that he does not know how many American soldiers were killed or died of burn injuries, but that he saw 8 to 10
men who had been burned in the napalm put into a truck. He was busy
directing more strikes and had no time to assess the damage.[33]

When the breakout started, Major Robbins was riding with other
wounded in a truck at the head of the column behind the M19 and the
jeep with the machine-gun mount. He was lying on his stomach, peering
out between the slats on the side of the truck. This is what he saw:

> Our troops on either side of the road moved forward but were dropping
> from withering fire laid down by the Chinese as we moved into their sur-
> rounding ring.
>   Then came one of the most horrible sights and incidents I ever hope to
> witness. A Marine Corsair diving towards the enemy line just ahead of our
> troops loosed a tank of napalm which slammed into our staggered front line
> of advancing GI's through his error in aim. A wall of flame and heat rushed
> out in all directions, enveloping about fifteen of our soldiers in its deadly
> blanket. As I peered out at this spectacle the heat and flash caused me to
> duck momentarily. Looking back up I could see the terrible sight of men
> ablaze from head to foot, staggering back or rolling on the ground scream-
> ing for someone to help them. This, coupled with the steady whack of
> enemy bullets into our ranks, stopped our advance. I am quite sure now
> that I recognized the helpless and blazing figure of Sgt. Dave Smith, my
> assistant sergeant major, and one of the finest men I have ever known. He
> wasn't more than ten yards off the side of the road on my side of the truck
> and I was powerless to do a thing for him. I had to turn my head. Officers
> and noncommissioned officers through superhuman efforts rallied their men
> and soon our line of GI's began to move forward again, filling the black-
> ened gap which had been blasted open minutes before.[34]

Many other witnesses of the napalm drop have left accounts of what
they saw, including Lt. Cecil Smith, A Company commander, who said
that 5 men burned to death; 1st Sgt. Richard S. Luna, of B Company, who
said of the napalmed soldiers, "You could see them running all around just
ripping their clothes off, just keep on running"; Dr. Lee Yong Kak, assistant
battalion surgeon, 1st Battalion, who saw the burst hit Lieutenant Moore,
of Headquarters Company, and 9 or 10 other men.[35] Lieutenant May said

that he did not recognize Moore after the napalm burst until Moore spoke to him and that Moore "was burnt about the upper torso. His hair was gone, eye glasses gone, and most of his clothes burnt off from his waist up. He was parched a dark brown, & in places black and open burns."[36]

First Lieutenant Henry Moore, A&P Platoon leader of Headquarters Company, 1st Battalion, 32nd Infantry, was one of the leaders of the breakout effort. That he continued on foot in the fight after being burned in the napalm incident is in itself a remarkable testimony to his courage and leadership. His reputation as one of the ablest and most courageous young officers of the task force stands high among the survivors of Chosin. There is contradictory evidence about his end.[37] One account has him killed on Hill 1221; another holds that he was killed early in the breakout (an account possibly based on his being burned by the napalm). He did not survive Chosin, but was carried as missing in action. He assuredly was one of the many heroes east of Chosin.

Major Miller certainly saw the whole thing and as commander of the breakout 1st Battalion was in a position to know the result of the napalm drop on the battalion. He wrote subsequently: "Eight or ten men in 'C' Company were set on fire by the flaming gobs of jellied gasoline. Most of these men were seriously burned before they could be rolled in the snow and their burning clothing extinguished."[38] Miller also appraised the effect on the Chinese of the napalm strike: "I was in command of the battalion at this time and feel that Capt. Stamford's cool control of our aircraft, in which he directed the dropping of napalm not more than forty yards to our front, started the Chinese on the run and allowed the First Battalion to inflict tremendous casualties on the enemy in our immediate follow-up."[39]

Captain Swenty saw the episode from some distance back in the column, but he appears to agree with Miller on the effect of the napalm drop on the Chinese. He wrote:

The napalm did the trick, as the advance guard began to move immediately. I could observe our men moving off the road and moving on the reverse slope toward the reservoir's edge. I was moving with HQ Co in the march column. When I approached the point where our troops were pinned down initially, I observed the results of the napalm. Our troops had been pinned down less than ten yards from the enemy. The napalm got at least forty of the enemy lying in the ditches but it had taken its toll on our own men. The motor column began to move slowly. You could hear firing from the advance guard but movement was being made. The enemy was firing from across the finger of the reservoir and we received fire from the hill to the left of the road. The rear guard was taking up the fight in our abandoned area. Our men began laying fire to the hills but they were moving and the motor column gained momentum.[40]

It seems true that the task force breakout brought forth perhaps the closest air support in a moving column engaged with an enemy in the Korean War. A Marine report of a later study of the subject commented on the strikes called for by Stamford on December 1. Stamford's radio code name was Boyhood 14. A Corsair pilot was quoted in the Marine report as saying, "Boyhood 14 kept calling for closer and closer support to less than 50 feet. The pilots could observe people practically clubbing the Reds off the trucks."[41]

When the napalm dropped, panic began among the American infantrymen at the head of the column. Officers and noncommissioned officers had a hard time bringing the troops back to their task. Foremost among them was Lieutenant Colonel Faith, who immediately undertook to rally his men. Stamford witnessed Faith's part in the action at this critical moment. He included the following in his report to the commandant, US Marine Corps, in February, 1951: "I saw him in one act that showed him as a true leader. On 1 December when the troops were on the verge of running away from the area where a napalm tank had landed and injured some troops, he moved out among the men and met the enemy with drawn pistol as they took advantage of this confusion to make a counter-attack. By this demonstration of courage he rallied the men and put the enemy to flight, thus averting disaster."[42]

Stamford said later that immediately after the napalm drop Faith saw some Chinese jump from their holes and start a counterattack against the American point troops, who had momentarily stopped. "Some of these men turned around and started back," Stamford said. "It was at this point that Faith rushed to the fore and drew his .45 pistol. He pointed it generally at the retreating men, but did not fire, and shouted for them to turn around and face the enemy. They did so."[43]

Captain Bigger also saw Faith turn the faltering troops around. He wrote of him: "He was all over the place, exhorting, ordering, threatening. . . . But the incident was very demoralizing to us. We had started a beautiful assault, with much enthusiasm. Our spirits had been raised by the appearance of the Corsairs. We were ready to get out of this situation."[44]

Nearly all survivors of Task Force Faith agree that with the napalm drop a demoralization set in among the troops that was never wholly overcome. It grew worse as the afternoon wore on. Major Miller, however, said: "I do not believe that the napalm drop itself had the long term effect. I believe that for most of us it was just another terrible part of an already unbelievable situation which progressively worsened. Everyone knew without question the value of the air support."[45]

Smith kept his promise to Barr. Task Force Faith did get air priority on December 1; Smith allotted 20 planes to it. They came in flights usually of 4 or 6, and in relays. Beginning with the initial strike, the Corsairs and a few other types of planes were over the task-force convoy all afternoon until darkness prevented further support at Hill 1221. They swept the road ahead of the task force and strafed, rocketed, and bombed the high ground on the left of the road column, while one or more planes covered the rear. The survivors generally agreed that without this close air support the task force might never have been able to clear the perimeter. Had the task force been willing to leave its wounded and abandon all vehicles, its men could have walked out over the hills and the ice, and most of them would have escaped. But its mission was to escort the truck convoy with its wounded.

The fight down the road was particularly intense for the first half mile outside the perimeter. There the black-painted Corsairs must have looked to the Chinese like so many huge birds of prey, but to the Americans they were birds of hope. Perhaps it would not be Black Friday after all.

We return to Mortrude to learn what happened to him and members of his point platoon after he rolled off the M19 and dropped over the western embankment of the road. Once defiladed from enemy fire, Mortrude stopped to gather his wits. A battalion staff officer ran up to him and said that the entire task-force column had stopped and that he must get moving. Mortrude replied that he would try to flank below the road along the ice and get behind the enemy's front line. He and several of his platoon started west below and parallel with the road. In a few moments he saw an enemy immediately above him. Mortrude threw one of his salvaged enemy grenades at him. The grenade fell short and started to roll back toward him. Mortrude ducked behind a rock as the grenade exploded. When he looked up, he saw the Chinese running away down the road. In this flurry of activity Mortrude's white-camouflaged helmet and fur cap fell off and rolled toward the inlet. He ignored them and led his men back up to the road. There he saw a Chinese soldier on the elevated shoulder of the road trying to put some kind of ground-mounted weapon into operation. Mortrude said:

I attempted to fire at him at close range, my carbine misfired, he abandoned his position but returned immediately and then ran again. At which point I manually chambered a round, fired, and hastened him on his way. Thus encouraged and enthused, our little group of five or six people including two BAR men ran screaming and cursing down the road shooting at everything. This included one Chinese who crawled out from under a disabled US vehicle and a communications lineman up a telephone pole. As our targets and endurance exhausted, we stopped to regroup and rest. . . . One of my platoon members came up with my helmet and cap which he had salvaged from the ice. As more members of the platoon rejoined us and other battalion troops appeared to be closing on us we resumed our march. This time we proceeded without incident to the mouth of a large valley where a collapsed concrete span crossed a gulley and the road was intercepted by another trail or road leading up the valley. . . . There were only four or five of us advancing abreast on the road to the blown bridge at any one time with some occasionally falling out and others filling in. I suspect that we had avoided the main enemy strength at the first roadblock by leaving the road and working along the shore of the reservoir ice. Those few enemy we encountered when we first came back up on the road were, very likely, only in supporting positions backing up the main road block and were surprised by our accidental initiative in leaving the road in a flanking maneuver. After these people broke and ran, no other established positions or determined return fires were encountered.[46]

After the temporary chaos and confusion following the napalm drop, Captain Seever led C Company down the road, despite his four-day-old leg wound. The Corsairs were now engaged in a furious assault on the fleeing Chinese and their position on the left side of the road. Their fire slaughtered most of the enemy ahead of C Company as they broke and ran. Many Chinese ran to the south and southwest on the road and in the railroad bed just east of the road. If the Corsairs did not get them, American small-arms fire accounted for most of them. C Company was soon ahead of the rest of the task force. It was commonly believed by survivors of the company that Captain Seever was killed in this phase of the fight, but Lieutenant May said that he saw him hobbling with a cane in the approach to the first blown bridge. If the latter is correct, he did not live long afterward.

When C Company charged into the Chinese following the napalm burst, Major Miller ran forward on the road with them. He climbed the bank on the left to reach the railroad bed to see what the situation was there and looked down into the cut. He said:

Not ten yards away were three Chinese manning a heavy machine gun and firing into B Company on the left flank which now was moving forward on my orders to help clear out the enemy positions. I fired one round from my carbine and it jammed. However, a BAR man sprayed them and put the MG out of action. The fight was over in a matter of seconds and C and B Companies moved out down the road and on the right side of the road. At the first slight turn of the road was a log barricade of three or four eight inch logs. I signalled up the SP [the M19 dual-40] which moved the logs diagonally and nudged them far enough to one side to allow the trucks to clear.[47]

When the trucks started moving after the road had been cleared ahead of them, they moved in "jerks and halts," with some frightened ROK soldiers trying to climb aboard. Americans moving alongside the trucks pulled them off. Most of the wounded in the trucks lay quietly and "stared into nothing." Major Robbins lay at the side in one of the trucks where he could look out between the side slats. He wrote of this part of the breakout:

> From my peephole I could see dead Chinese and American soldiers alike lying in little sprawled heaps on the side of the road and in the ditches, their blood forming pools from which steam rose into the freezing air. I remember staring at this in complete realization of the fight those GI's were making. Soldiers passing our truck called out encouragement to us and grinning as they went on forward to blast more Chinese or fall themselves. The enemy was giving way now and our guys sensed it, following them more closely and with greater courage.[48]

But it was not clear sailing by any means for the truck column. Chinese were on every nose of ground east of the road, their small-arms and automatic fire killing and wounding despite the ferocious air attacks. The task force was under heavy fire as it moved slowly south. But with effective air support there seemed a chance that the column would make it to Hagaru-ri. This prospect depended primarily on two factors: (1) that the column would not be stopped for any great length of time by enemy roadblocks and could reach Hagaru-ri before dark, when vital close air support would end, and (2) that enough officers and noncommissioned officers would survive to exercise control over the men to keep them protecting the vehicular column of wounded, without degenerating into a mob seeking their own survival.

The tendency of the men on foot to rush ahead of the trucks was apparent early after the breakout. It was partly exhilaration in reaction to the

A view looking north along the narrow-gauge railroad track. Hill 1250 is on the right, and Hill 1324 is on the south side of the Pungnyuri-gang Inlet in the distance (*left*). The photograph was taken in the early afternoon of December 1, 1950, during Task Force Faith's breakout from the inlet. The men shown are probably members of the 3rd Battalion, 31st Infantry, the designated rear guard. The vehicular road is immediately left of the railbed under the embankment. Both railbed and road are at the edge of Chosin Reservoir to the left. The photographer is unknown. Photograph courtesy of Col. Crosby P. Miller.

initial breakout, and partly the men on the higher ground east of the road wanting to drift down to the road for cover from enemy fire from the east. The officers and noncommissioned officers did not have much success keeping the infantry on the high ground where they could protect the roadbound column. Most wanted to get to the head of the column on the road and stay ahead, thinking thereby to improve their own chances of reaching safety.

Sergeant Luna of B Company was on the road with the trucks. Two or three days later at Hagaru-ri he wrote a statement of what he saw on the road in the breakout. He said that 500 to 600 yards outside the perimeter, beyond the site of the napalm drop and the dead of both sides in the initial clash, there were many enemy dead in the road, so many, he said, that one had to step over them, and that in some places they had to be removed so that the trucks could pass. As the trucks moved forward, he and others put many newly wounded Americans on the trucks. He wrote: "We got what wounded we could out. I mean just kept loading them on and on the trucks. It was impossible to get all of them on. I do not recall now just how many were left behind. You couldn't possibly back up and take them with you. . . . They [the trucks] just kept moving forward."[49] Luna added that the ROK soldiers were a continuing difficulty. They kept crowding down on the road and would not stay on the high ground east of the road. He said that Faith was on the road constantly ordering them back to higher ground.

After Major Miller had called up the M19 and cleared the small roadblock of logs from the road half a mile west of the perimeter, he noticed that the infantry were leaving the trucks behind. By this time his two radiomen were missing, and he could not communicate with the forward platoons. He wanted to slow them—they were getting beyond his control. He sent runners ahead to B and C companies with orders to keep the troops on the left of the road. He saw that

> the troops were giving way to the right of the road and the shelter of its embankment. I do not believe the runners were able to accomplish their mission as no change in troop disposition became evident either then or later. In retrospect, I believe that at this point (the Chinese encirclement had been broken and troops and trucks were on the move) for the first time, loss of control began to creep into the picture. The leading troops were moving very rapidly and elements of B and C Companies were becoming mixed together. It was here that a brief reorganization or slowing of the leading elements would have helped to retain the control which was slipping away. I started trotting forward to catch the leading company.[50]

Major Curtis saw it much the same. He said that after the initial success of the breakout the troops "flooded down the road like a great mob and tactical control broke down almost immediately. Officers tried frantically to re-establish control and to order men up on the high ground where they could protect the truck column. . . . Enemy small arms fire was encountered all the way, but men attacked and overran enemy positions frontally with seeming disregard for basic tactical principles and their own safety. The aircraft were having a hey-day strafing and bombing in front of the troops."[51]

Lieutenant Thomas J. Patton, of A Battery, said that he had a group of 15 men of Headquarters Battery who helped cover the left flank of the column where enemy had concentrated to stop the breakout. It was a rough place to be. Patton gives a sampling of what happened to units there in the first part of the breakout. He wrote: "By the time we had reached the old Headquarters Battery area [about one road mile] there were only 3 men left along with myself. The others were wounded and placed on trucks. 2 of them dead."[52] Captain Hodge, of A Battery, played an active and courageous role in getting his battery ready for the movement and leading it thereafter. The commanders of both A and B batteries were apparently killed in the breakout.

At the rear of the column the situation was also deteriorating. Faith had instructed May to stay near the rear to make sure that all vehicles got in line. May said that as the column moved down the road after the breakout it took a great deal of rifle fire from the high ground on the left. He was in a good position to know the amount of damage to the vehicles between the perimeter and the first blown bridge, where the convoy had a prolonged stop. He said, "I saw no vehicles knocked out from the Inlet south to Hill 1221. . . . But many of our drivers were badly hit and had to be replaced." Private Edward E. Bilyou, L Company, 31st Infantry, was in the rear guard, behind the trucks, but he was called on to replace a driver who had become a casualty, and he drove a truck until well after dark. He said that one of his wounded in the truck was hit three more times by enemy fire. The drivers, on the left side of the trucks, were exposed to enemy fire, which came almost entirely from that side, until the convoy reached Hill 1221. It was hard to find replacements for killed or wounded truck drivers in the convoy, for nearly all the soldiers on foot considered the job a form of suicide.[53]

Lieutenant Smalley was one of those killed by enemy small-arms fire as he lay, already wounded, in a truck. Concerning him, May wrote: "I was with Lt. Smalley when he was killed. He was in the rear of a 2½-ton truck, a casualty from wounds in the legs. Lt. Smalley was shot through the head by rifle fire coming from the CCF on high ground to our east. This shortly after the breakout from the Inlet."[54] Enemy fire hitting wounded in the trucks a second and a third time, killing many of them, was a dismal occurrence that became more pronounced later in the afternoon.

In the running fight from the breakout to the first blown bridge, enemy opposition was intense. It was in this part of the breakout that the M16s were able to counter the enemy. May said of them: "The Quad 50's played a very important role in the Inlet area prior to the breakout. During the breakout they placed withering fire on CCF troops trying to overrun our column. Until they ran out of ammo they were our most deadly defensive weapons." Unfortunately, they were out of ammunition before the column reached Hill 1221.

Captain Jordan's M Company, 31st Infantry, was near the end of the column. About a mile down the road Jordan found that the foot troops had stopped and were bunching up because an enemy machine gun was firing from the east down a draw and across the road to the ice of the reservoir. This draw was the shallow valley east of the road where the 57th Field Artillery Headquarters and Headquarters Battery, together with Mc-Clymont's AAA AW weapons, had bivouacked the night of November 27–28. For the enemy it was an ideal site for a strongpoint along the withdrawal route. Earlier Stamford had had to call in an air strike on this area to help the men in front get past it. Now there was considerable pressure from rear elements crowding forward, which only made the bunching worse. Jordan sent his Sergeant Pruitt with a squad of men to take out the enemy machine gun while he worked to get the column moving again. Jordan wrote: "At this point there were few officers to be found and not much leadership. So many had become casualties and fatigue was taking its toll."[55] Once past this point, Jordan said, the rear of the column closed up and moved ahead at a reasonably good pace until it reached the valley north of Hill 1221. For the Chinese this last mile to the valley was difficult terrain; they could find few strongpoints from which to harass the column. The slope of Hill 1456 was steep and came down abruptly to the road and the reservoir.

Captain McClymont, who had been near the point during the breakout, stayed there until the column had covered the first mile to the cove where he and his antiaircraft battery had bivouacked and fought the first night. There he decided to walk back along the column and check the condition of his remaining weapons. He found that the first quad-50 in line was in good condition. He continued on, looking for the M19 that was supposed to bring up the rear. Instead, he came on his sergeant with the other crew members walking along with the foot soldiers. He was shocked and dismayed when he learned what had happened and that the M19 was standing back in the perimeter with half the priceless 40-mm shells they had remaining at the beginning of the breakout.[56] He told the M19 crew members to stay with the convoy. As he walked back toward the front of the column, he found that he could walk faster than it was moving.

The 3rd Battalion, 31st Infantry, was the convoy rear guard. The three rifle companies of the battalion, I, K, and L, were now so reduced in strength that their able-bodied men, those who could walk and carry a weapon, had been combined into one company. It was called K Company, with Captain Kitz, of the original K Company, commanding. It left the perimeter at the rear of the column but must soon have moved to the right side of the road, where it would be defiladed from most enemy fire. Kitz, in a statement made a few days later at Hagaru-ri, said that K Company moved mostly on ice. This meant that his company moved far enough to the right to get onto the ice of the reservoir where the going would be easier, but it is hard to see how moving there would serve his mission of acting as rear guard for the column.

While K Company was on the ice, presumably close to the edge of the reservoir, the ice broke in one or two places, and some men, including Kitz, fell into the water. Some of them, Kitz among them, got out, but others drowned—Kitz did not say how many.[57] After regaining the road, Kitz led his company south on it and the railroad bed, following the trucks.[58]

According to Major Curtis, about 3:00 P.M., after the column had traveled approximately two miles from the perimeter and was nearing the valley north of Hill 1221, a "jeep mounted radio picked up the following message in the clear, 'To Colonel Faith: Secure your own exit to Hagaru-ri. Unable to assist you. Signed Smith, CG 1st Marine Division.'"[59] This message was received over the artillery observer's jeep radio. It had been prepared that morning by General Hodes at Hagaru-ri and signed by Smith.[60] The task-force withdrawal had now been in progress for two hours. Curtis learned of this message firsthand, at the time it was received, from the operator of the jeep radio.

In the meantime, Lieutenant Mortrude and his point men arrived at the blown bridge about an hour after the breakout started. It was another hour before the convoy began arriving there. Mortrude remembered the blown bridge as being a short, single concrete span about 20 feet across, broken in the middle and collapsed into the gully below with the ends still tilted skyward on their abutments. He and his men found shelter in the ruins of a house beyond it, near the junction of two trails, one from the east in the valley, the other slanting down from the side of Hill 1221. The latter was the main road.

Soon after Mortrude and his men stopped there, Lt. Herbert E. Marshburn, Jr., a platoon leader of A Company, arrived with a group of his men and joined Mortrude. While they discussed which route to follow, a Marine Corsair came over and strafed the house but caused no casualties. The Corsair strafing, however, reactivated the two lieutenants, and they led their groups outside and began moving ahead on a course east of the blown bridge. Mortrude describes what followed:

> From this new vantage point, our direction was determined by the sight of many Chinese advancing toward us from a considerable distance up the valley [to the east]. We, of course, decided to continue across the valley, on what we now realized was the main road, to the opposite high ground which we had once before occupied [Hill 1221]. At this point, I was struck heavily in the left temple by a sniper's bullet which I imagined I felt passing through my head (actually only a glancing blow). When I regained consciousness, Lt. Marshburn said that my wound was bleeding and needed attention. He suggested he take all the people available and keep moving and that I catch up when I could. I agreed and staggered back to the vicinity of the ruined house where our platoon medic, Cpl Camoesas, cleaned and bandaged my wound suggesting I wait there for the trucks. After a brief rest I regained my mobility but apparently lost or abandoned my weapon and stumbled after the lead troops moving south across the valley.[61]

It would appear from this episode that Marshburn was the first officer with a body of troops from the 3rd Platoon, C Company, and his group from A Company to reach Hill 1221. Although he did not know it at first, the Chinese held Hill 1221 in force, and he was moving into a hornet's nest. Marshburn was mortally wounded at Hill 1221.

On his way across the valley toward the opposite hillside Mortrude passed some American dead and wounded. At the time he did not know what had happened. On the south side of the valley he caught up with a large number of troops huddled in the roadside ditch where the road slanted up the north side of Hill 1221. The men there were receiving fire from the enemy on the hill just above them and from others on the northeast in and across the valley they had just crossed. The latter were the Chinese that Mortrude had seen earlier at a distance.

Mortrude had regained consciousness about 3:00 P.M., soon after the head of Task Force Faith reached the blown bridge. There the vehicles piled up on the north side while most of the foot troops moved around the bridge and started up the road at Hill 1221, toward the saddle. Captain Swenty arrived at the scene after the advance units and the front of the truck column reached the bridge:

> The advance guard was receiving small arms fire from the hill directly in front of the bridge. I moved to the bridge and observed our companies moving approximately 300 yards to the left of the bridge along the railroad track and on the reverse slope of the hill to our front. There they were receiving fire from the bend in the road and it seemed their advance was stopped.
>
> The motor column was stopped approximately 150 yards short of the blown bridge. The terrain to the left of the bridge was a frozen swamp and could be used as a bypass.[62]

Now began a critical period for the task force. A pressing need was to get the convoy of trucks around the blown bridge and across the frozen stream and marshland east and south of it.[63] Darkness and the end of air cover were only an hour or two away.

The First Blown Bridge

The head of Task Force Faith's motor column arrived at the blown bridge about 3:00 P.M. The rear end of the column had closed on the rest in 15 minutes or so, certainly by 3:30 P.M. The M19 in front had crossed the steep banks of the small stream and the partly frozen clumps of marsh grass and frozen earth and had climbed to the road again on the other side with no difficulty. But behind it the first truck trying to cross became stuck at the stream when its wheels broke through the crust of ice.

Major Curtis said that it was a surprise to all the task-force staff that the bridge was blown. He knew of no previous planning or reconnaissance to find out whether the bridges south of the inlet up to the Paegamni-gang were intact. It would seem that a simple request over Stamford's radio to the pilots that were overhead daily could have received a report from them that would have disclosed the situation. Apparently neither Faith nor his staff thought of obtaining such intelligence.[1]

Major Miller was among the first of the officers, after Mortrude and Marshburn, to arrive at the blown bridge. He took in the scene:

When I reached the first major stream crossing the road (5379), I could see that the bridge was blown and could see our troops moving up the valley below and to the left of the road which ran diagonally up the hill (1221) on the far (south) side of the valley where the road disappeared over the hill through a small saddle (5478). Fire was coming from this hill. As soldiers were working up the lower slopes of the hill, I was hopeful that, by the time the truck column could be gotten across the stream, the hill would be cleared. The dual 40 mm SP easily crossed the stream, but the trucks, rocking bumping over hard hummocks of swamp grass and dirt, were unable to cross the stream. It was deep and very narrow and effectively trapped their front wheels. I immediately turned the SP back to throw a cable on each truck and tow them through. All this time scattered fire was striking the hill to our front (south). I moved forward to a small house on the far side of the valley where I found Major Wesley Curtis, Bn S-3, now Executive Officer, with a small group of men preparing to move directly up the hill.[2]

Captain Swenty arrived at the blown bridge soon after Miller and saw the trucks in the process of crossing the swampy stream:

The trucks carrying wounded started through the frozen swamp, full of clumps of what looked like johnson grass and each clump was about two feet high. All the time we were still receiving small arms and mortar fire. As the trucks were running the bypass you could hear the screams of wounded men within the trucks. Many had broken bones and I am sure several died from the shock of crossing the swamp. Progress was slow as the trucks would have to be backed up to the bank to get back on the main road. It seemed as [though] breakthrough was stalemated until we could get the motor column through the swamp. When a truck did get on the road the driver would take the truck up the road about 250 yards and halt it and wait. When a driver would get hit trying to run the pass, the truck was a pigeon for the enemy. Time was lost getting another to take his place. . . . Somewhere along the route of withdrawal we had picked up about a hundred refugees, mostly women and children and they were staying close to the trucks. . . . The delay in crossing the swamp afforded the enemy time to move from our abandoned positions to a new position directly to our left. The positions they now occupied were on the military crest of a hill paralleling our halted trucks that had crossed the swamp.[3]

Lieutenant May arrived at the blown bridge with the rear of the column, took charge of the bypass operation, and fearlessly exposed himself in directing the crossing of each vehicle. He was at this task for about two hours. Meanwhile, the troops with the column had crossed the valley and were bunching up on the road, dug into the slope of Hill 1221. Nearly all the officers were there also, preparing to attack the hill.

Major Miller started up the road ahead of Curtis and his group. In Curtis's group there were casualties almost at once. About 3:30 P.M., Curtis received a rifle slug in the right leg near the knee. Major Bob Jones was with Curtis at the time. He put a pressure bandage on the wound and found a broken tree limb for Curtis to use for a crutch. With this stick Curtis could hobble along, and he proceeded painfully up the road. Jones soon outdistanced him as he hurried on ahead to help with the fight that had already broken out farther up the hill.[4] Faith, in his jeep with sirens blaring, passed Curtis on the road.

Meanwhile, May was acting as a traffic cop at the blown bridge.[5] From his vantage point, Curtis said, he could see May in the middle of the road, ignoring the small-arms fire that had now begun hitting the bridge site, directing the movement of the trucks across the stream. May, who is the main witness to what occurred at the bridge bypass, had this to say:

> . . . we attempted to ford the small stream. Being a marshy area, the trucks broke through the layer of frozen crust. Almost every vehicle had to be winched through this stream. During this time I was met by Lt. Col. Faith. He had come to the bridge to see what our situation was. When he left, it was the last time I saw him.
>
> The rear guard troops passed us and left the rear of the column exposed. I collected a few men and put them in the RR cut to fire on the Chinese on the hill to our rear. I then returned to trying to get the last two (2) trucks across the stream. After getting them across, one was knocked out by small arms fire and the driver of the other truck was killed. I unloaded the wounded who could walk, and sent them on ahead. With some help from the half-track crew, we transferred the remaining wounded to another 2½-ton nearby. One of the crew members from the half track drove the truck out. By this time it was nearly dark and the Chinese riflemen were not able to place accurately aimed fire on us. This relieved the situation somewhat and allowed me to close up the remaining vehicles into our column, which was halted on the winding, uphill road.[6]

May subsequently amplified his comments about the difficulties at the bypass crossing and the failure of the rear guard to do its duty:

> There was so much happening at this time, and I was trying to do a little bit of everything at the rear of the column. Trying to maintain some control and to keep things from getting completely out of hand. . . .
>
> The 3rd Bn., 31st Inf. was assigned as the rear guard unit. At the time we were attempting to cross the last few vehicles at the blown bridge we started to get an awful lot of enemy small arms fire, from our rear and the high ground to our northeast.
>
> At this time I found the 3rd Bn., 31st Inf. were deserting their mission and were streaming past our position. There were some junior officers strung out among the troops and completely ignored my plea to stop and start firing on the CCF.
>
> I did manage to get some troopers and Sgt. stopped and into a railroad cut and to build up a base of fire on CCF to our rear and on hill to our

east. However as soon as I returned to the job of getting the last vehicles over the bog and stream these troops pulled out, up and over Hill 1221. [Elsewhere May says that they went "up southwest over hill 1221." This would be not up the road but over or near a trail that climbed Hill 1221 from a point almost directly south of the blown bridge. All 1:50,000-scale maps of the Hill 1221 area show this trail.][7]

During the stream crossing, Sgt. Charles Garrigus, assistant motor sergeant, 1st Battalion, 32nd Infantry, was responsible for driving two trucks across the stream. He had already distinguished himself several times as he moved two abandoned ammunition and ration trucks across the bridge at the inlet on the 29th, and earlier on this day (December 1) he was the machine gunner who had turned back one of the Chinese assaults on the A Company roadblock at the western end of the perimeter. A few hours later the valorous sergeant was killed in another attempt to run the final enemy roadblock.[8]

Major Jones called the crossing at the blown bridge "a very rough and difficult by-pass." He confirms May's and Curtis's statements that it took until dark to get all the trucks across.[9] This means that the task force spent its last two hours of daylight getting the vehicles with the wounded on the road south of the blown bridge and ready to continue the run toward Hagaru-ri. It should be recalled that at that time of year darkness came between 4:30 and 5:00 P.M.

To show what a painful experience this was for the wounded riding in the trucks, perhaps nothing could be more compelling than the words of one of them, Major Robbins:

> . . . we came to a bridge which had been destroyed and our motor column turned off the road and into a wide river bed to bypass the obstacle. Great mounds of frozen earth covered with a tough grass carpeted the river bed over which we now bounced. For about 100 yards we bounced and crashed up and down over those hummocks with the wounded screaming in anguish as they were jostled and slammed into one another on the truck bed. I luckily still had on my steel helmet and thus was able to protect my head from a banging against the front and sides of the truck bed which might have knocked me out otherwise. At that I had a bruised head for days afterwards. We came to a final jolting crash and stopped. Our front wheels were down through a crust of ice in a small creek and no amount of effort on the part of our driver could move that truck. Other vehicles began to come abreast of us and with more caution ford the creek and go on for-

ward. Again I began to sweat—was this going to be the end of the road?

After what seemed hours but was actually but a short time, the tracked vehicle backed up to our truck, hooked on a tow rope and pulled us up through the creek and onto firm ground again. Our driver returned to take over and once more we moved slowly forward. We reached the road again and after a halt to allow other following vehicles to cross the difficult by-pass, we got under way. The hills were now on the right side of the road and on our left the ground fell sharply away to form a valley paralleling our course along the road south. Heavy small arms fire was coming down at the column from the high ground on our right and the continual smack of slugs slapping the truck was unnerving to me as I expected any minute to be hit by the next one. . . . Again our truck came to a halt. This time the word came back that another road block which was heavily defended by the Chinese was holding up the column.[10]

Lieutenant May has told how he had no protection at his rear while he was trying to get the truck column across the stream. At the same time, the trucks that had crossed to the south side of the stream and started up the road with the walking soldiers began receiving an ever-increasing volume of machine-gun and small-arms fire from the north side of the valley east of the bridge. The stream there flowed generally west from its source southeast of Hill 1456, a two-mile-wide mountain separating this valley from the inlet area on its north side. Increasing numbers of Chinese appeared on the high ridges north and northeast of the valley and in the upper reaches of the valley itself. They fired into the truck convoy on the south side with increasing effectiveness. Some of them appeared to be forming for a direct attack from the valley up the slope to the road. They apparently came from the main force that had been attacking the perimeter during the past several nights.

What was the rear guard of the task force doing? The situation in the valley and on the ridges east of the blown bridge and north of the road was getting serious. Faith had designated the 3rd Battalion as the rear guard —in effect, the infantry remnants of the battalion now combined into K Company. They had no great trouble reaching the blown bridge and were not engaged in any important action between the perimeter and the blown bridge, though there was continuing harassing fire when they were east of the road.

When they reached the blown bridge, they were ordered to move up the valley to the east and protect the column and the bypass area from the large numbers of Chinese who could be seen approaching from that direction. At the same time the 57th field artillerymen, on foot behind the truck column, moved off to the ridgeline north of the valley and northeast of the blown bridge for the same purpose. Most of these troops were ineffective, which resulted in dire consequences for the task force.

Just about all of the 1st Battalion, 32nd Infantry (A, B, and C companies), were on the road leading to the saddle of Hill 1221 or attacking in groups up the slope of the hill. From his position south of the bridge at the foot of Hill 1221, Stamford was running air strikes on the surrounding ridges where Chinese had shown themselves. He gives his version of the initial attack of the 1st Battalion, 32nd Infantry, on the roadblock at the saddle, Hill 1221, and the movement of the rear guard up the valley to help in this effort by reaching the enemy's right flank at the roadblock. As he saw it:

> The troops of 1/32 moved up the road toward the road block and the troops of 3/31 moved up the valley below the road to force the roadblock. The attack was moving along, but 3/31 was under heavy fire from the other side of the valley and from enemy troops to their northeast. I saw at least 300 enemy to the northeast of 3/31. 1/32 succeeded in forcing the road block and it seemed they would go on but they evidently ran into resistance and fell back. It looked as if they had lost their leaders. The retirement looked like a rout. The enemy again occupied the road block and inflicted heavy casualties on 1/32 with rifle and machine gun fire and was then able to do the same to 3/31 on the slopes below the road causing them to withdraw. The troops of 1/57 had gained the high ground over the road to the north in an attempt to silence machine guns firing from that area, but were unable to do so because of the danger of being cut off by the several hundred enemy to the northeast of us, in and at the foot of the hills.[11]

From the road ascending Hill 1221, Major Miller saw the same troop movements that Stamford described, but with certain differences. He too, without knowing the facts, had to draw some inferences about why the 3rd Battalion troops abandoned their positions. One of the big problems here, as almost everywhere else during the breakout, was the lack of communication between parts of the task force with each other and between the task force commander and the several parts, except those he could personally reach. Efforts could not be coordinated and mutually supported. Miller tells what he saw after he went up the road about 3:30 P.M.:

> I moved up the road to find out what was going on there. By this time several trucks had gotten across the stream and joined me on the road

sheltered from fire from the hill crest by the steep bank to the right (south) of the road. I noticed, at this point, that friendly troops (3rd Bn, 31st Inf) on the high ground across the valley (north side) were leaving the hill (5479) and moving down to the road. I assumed that Colonel Faith, whom I had last seen at the blown bridge in the valley, had ordered them forward to assist in clearing the hill from the right flank. These troops, however, were promptly replaced by Chinese who opened up with long range fire across the valley into the exposed left flank of the truck column. Captain Stamford, FAC, was able to get an air strike in on the Chinese across the valley that helped.[12]

Meanwhile, Lieutenant May stayed at his task of getting the last of the trucks across the bypass around the bridge. He and his helpers were now fully exposed to enemy fire from the hill to their rear and from the valley. May summed up his view of the 3rd Battalion, 31st Infantry, role as rear guard: "During the time I was at the bridge by-pass, the Bn that had the mission of rear guard security completely deserted the rear of the convoy. The net result was an extremely high casualty rate among personnel involved in the vehicle crossing and many riding wounded were KIA."[13]

Captain McClymont had returned to the head of the column by the time it neared the bridge site and was present when it came to a halt at the blown bridge. He said of the stream crossing, "My M19 crossed again and again, pulling the trucks through the water and to the other side." While this was going on, he and two of his sergeants crossed to the other side of the stream, where he saw Chinese up the valley on the northeast, a marching formation. He organized a group of men nearby and began firing at the Chinese with M-1 rifles. The range was too great, however, and the Chinese showed no reaction to their fire.[14] In the events that followed as this force drew closer, Major Miller, who was watching from the road slanting up Hill 1221, agreed with May that the rear guard abandoned its mission at the first blown bridge and Hill 1221.[15]

With the high ground northeast of the road and the valley below the road now unprotected, the Chinese moved across the valley and began climbing the slope to the road, where the convoy of wounded, fully exposed, was stalled. Captain Stamford saw this threat and was able to bring in an air strike on them before they got to the road. The strike was successful. It scattered the Chinese, who fled back to the valley and thereafter were ineffective.[16] Major Miller, now lying badly wounded in the roadside ditch, saw this strike. He wrote: "Chinese troops tried to close on the column along the hillside by moving up from the valley toward the road. Just before they overran us an A-26 aircraft [an F4U Corsair, according to Stamford] came out of nowhere and strafed twice just below the road effectively driving back the enemy."[17]

By now there was enemy mortar fire as well as machine-gun and small-arms fire on the stalled truck column. There was no effective response. Casualties mounted by the minute.

After receiving his leg wound at Hill 1221, Major Curtis hobbled up the road to the point where the truck column was collecting. There he sat in the roadside ditch for a time and noted that the column was stalled. It occurred to him that it might be useful to make a reconnaissance of the railroad bed as a route of travel if the enemy continued to block passage of the road. He found a few men to accompany him, including a wounded first lieutenant chaplain from the 3rd Battalion and three or four enlisted men whom he did not know.

They moved slowly westward on the narrow-gauge track that curved around the west side of Hill 1221 in a cut just above the edge of the reservoir. They reached and passed the point where the track rounded the northwestern edge of the hill and turned south along the reservoir. About 300 to 400 yards down this stretch an enemy mortar round landed near them. With this Curtis knew the Chinese had the railroad under surveillance and covered with fire, which meant that the convoy could not use the railbed.

Curtis and his group turned back, knowing that the road up and over the east side of Hill 1221 offered the only chance to move south. When he got back to the blown bridge after an hour, it was dark. When he caught up with the column, the trucks were moving forward on the north side of Hill 1221.[18]

17

The Chinese Block at Hill 1221

The Chinese positions on Hill 1221 and the high ground immediately east of the hairpin turn in the saddle of Hill 1221 were for the most part the same positions that elements of Lt. Col. Raymond Murray's 5th Marine Regiment had occupied about 10 days earlier when that regiment first arrived east of the reservoir. Major Curtis called Hill 1221 and its environs the best defensive position on the road east of Chosin Reservoir.

When the 5th Marines first prepared this area for defense, the positions faced north and northeast. It is not known just how much the Chinese improved or extended them after they seized the area on the night of November 27. They did blow the bridge across the stream at the north side of the hill and constructed a roadblock of logs on the road at the south end of the hairpin turn in the saddle where the road crossed Hill 1221 and started the southern descent. The orientation of the old Marine positions fitted perfectly the needs of the Chinese when they made it the centerpiece of their defensive positions of fire blocks and roadblocks behind the cutoff 31st RCT. They did not occupy the southern face of the hill but could defend it as long as they held the crest and its immediate reverse slope.

There is only a fragmentary record of Lieutenant Colonel Faith's movements and actions in the early part of the attack on Hill 1221. Enlisted men on the road saw him near the head of the column. It is probable that he led and directed the first attack against the enemy positions in the saddle at the hairpin turn. When that attack took place, Faith had few if any of his staff with him. He was with those troops who had moved around the blown bridge and climbed up the slanting hillside road toward the turn in the saddle. They knew little of what they would find there, except that a heavy volume of automatic and small-arms fire was being directed down the road from that vicinity and the hill on the right. At the time of the first attack most of the officers were still arriving at the scene or were scattered about at the blown bridge and on the lower reaches of the road trying to organize the hundreds of troops who crowded the right-hand side of the road between the trucks and the embankment cut into the side of Hill 1221. There they had some protection from heavy enemy fire directed at them from the surrounding high ground. No one seems to know what happened at the enemy fire block in that first effort to reduce it—only that the troops who reached it seemed for a moment to have succeeded but were then driven back.

The only available report of a participant in that first attack is that of 1st Lt. Thomas J. Patton, of A Battery, 57th Field Artillery. When he left the inlet perimeter, he was in charge of 15 men, who formed part of the left-hand guard for the convoy. By the time he reached the blown bridge, he had only three men left with him; several had been killed, the others wounded and placed in trucks. At the bridge an infantry captain ordered Patton to go to the far left up the valley to the north side of Hill 1221 and then climb the slope toward the saddle and attack the enemy fire block at the road from the flank. Patton was told to collect what men he could for the effort. Said Patton:

> There was no organization to be seen as the men were mostly on their own. I was able to get about 15 men to go with me, most of them from the 57th FA Bn.
> A Marine Corsair strafed my group once by mistake wounding Sgt. Poor in the left leg. He was bandaged and continued with us for some 25 yards when he was shot in the right leg. Sgt. Compos was wounded in the eye and five others received body wounds. There were about 30 men in the ditch at the log road block. We were receiving fire from the front of the road block, the top of the hill above the road block, the high ground to our rear, the left side of the valley and the east end of the valley. We were unable to round the bend of the road at the road block because of the heavy automatic fire. Then ten men and I went up the hill above the road block. A Sgt. from the 32nd Infantry Regiment knocked out a machine gun nest with a hand grenade enabling us to reach the top. We then received rifle fire from both sides forcing us to take cover in holes on the far side of the hill. Some stragglers were coming up to join us from the road block. The firing eased up on us and we found that we were very low on ammunition, each man having only a few rounds left. We went down to the road on the far

side of the hill where there were several knocked out vehicles and tanks which had tried to reach us several days before.

We attempted to work our way up to the rear of the road block and began receiving heavy fire causing several casualties. We were forced back to the knocked out trucks [from the ambush of the medical company on the night of November 27–28] and it was decided to try to reach friendly forces to our south to get reinforcements. Only four of us had ammunition left, about 25 rounds, both M-1 and carbine.

We started down toward the valley, with stragglers running to join us from the hill. Six CCF's ran from our right front down to our front to cut us off. They were all killed. We received fire from our right, left and rear, causing us to head toward the frozen reservoir. We started out on the ice angling to the southwest. We were about 500 yards out on the lake when CCF's began coming out after us. They didn't fire, several didn't even have weapons. I saw a C-47 circling in the distance approaching us and I stamped off in the snow "WHICH WAY." The C-47 circled and flew south circling a town in the distance. The C-47 then came back and dropped a canteen containing a note which stated "Keep to the center of the reservoir—UN troops holding Hagaru-ri—Have requested air cover—Good luck fellows."

The CCF's had caught up with the end of the column and had bayoneted one ROK. At this time two F-51s arrived and the CCFs broke and ran. The 51s began strafing them and killed them all. We continued on toward the town of Hagaru-ri where we were met by the Marines at approximately 1800 hours.

There were approximately 85 men in the column, nearly ¾'s of which were wounded. They were taken to the hospital and the ones that were all right were put in marine tents. I requested aid for the column which was back on the road and was told that they didn't have sufficient forces to go out to help and still hold the perimeter.[1]

Some of the 1st Battalion troops whom Stamford saw attacking up the road to the hairpin turn in apparent success and then turned back in rout must have joined Patton's group; it was a large force when it arrived at Hagaru-ri.

After the first attack up the road was turned back, it was hard to get the troops to move from the partly protected area of the ditch on the right-hand side of the uphill road. It appears that Faith either was far enough forward in this initial attack to see the enemy fire block and roadblock or had reports of it from soldiers who had been in the forefront of the attack.

In all this turmoil on the slope of Hill 1221 the men who were least protected from enemy fire were the wounded in the trucks. There the situation was rapidly turning into a long-range slaughter. More and more Chinese were taking up firing positions in and across the valley to the left of the road and firing directly into the stalled trucks. Captain Swenty wrote: "It was during this time I think we received our greatest portion of casualties. Air was called to strafe and napalm the houses and area from where this new fire was coming from. This was done immediately and with a few direct hits with napalm, broke up this new enemy position. In fact it was so good the enemy broke from their positions and ran. It was heartening to all men and they lay down a barrage of small arms fire on the enemy."[2] But this success did not last long. The Chinese were soon back in even greater numbers, and their fire from across the valley was greater than before.

This dreadful situation on the left of the road was caused by the failure of the rear guard to check the advance of the Chinese down the valley. The words of two members of the rear guard who participated in that action disclose its nature. Private First Class James R. Owens had been a member of a rocket-launcher team and a machine gunner during the battles of the inlet perimeter but in the breakout served as a rifleman in the rear guard. He said that when his unit reached the bridge "an officer told us to take a hill on the left side of the road. We took the hill and by the time we got to the top of the hill the Chinese were coming and they told us to *retreat from the hill* [italics added]. After we retreated off the hill we crossed an open field and were told to try to take another hill. I witnessed the overrun of the rearguard."[3] Owens and many others of that unit soon got to the reservoir and made their way to Hagaru-ri.

Master Sergeant Ivan H. Long, intelligence sergeant of the 31st Infantry, appears to have been in the same unit of the rear guard as Private Owens. Their experiences in meeting the Chinese in the area across the valley from Hill 1221 seem to mesh. When the breakout from the perimeter started, Long attached himself to "the left flank company and moved forward with them." He was with the troops that went up the valley from the bridge to defend the task force rear and to help reduce the Hill 1221 roadblock from the left flank. He describes the situation in the late afternoon when the Chinese mounted what he termed a company-size counterattack against his unit in the area east and northeast of the blown bridge:

> *The outfit I was with took to their heels* leaving me with only two men I could persuade to stay and face the attack. I am not sure, but I think they were headquarters [31st Infantry Headquarters] men having recognized me. We were exhausted from fighting but we fixed bayonets and took cover behind a wood pile in a farmyard. We got in a few good licks before my carbine

jammed from snow and mud. We were all wounded and just overwhelmed by the onrushing Chinese.

We were relieved of our weapons and ammunition. One Red soldier took my mittens, but I refused his demands for my jacket even when he threatened me at gun point. We were assigned a guard detail of 3 or 4 men and marched up a mountain trail to a lookout post and forced to lie on the snow-covered ground. Climbing the trail was extremely difficult for me. One of my wounds was a chest wound and breathing presented a big problem. With help from the other men and determination on my part, we kept up with our captors.

The temperature was freezing and I could feel my sweat-soaked socks freezing in my boots. After soaking my underwear with blood, my wound clotted which slowed the bleeding. By now nightfall had arrived and the moon was shining brightly. Our captors did not bother us. One Chinese soldier having stopped one of my bullets, was in bad condition, but received no attention from the others.[4]

Back on the road at Hill 1221, when the rear guard abandoned its mission, Major Robbins, still in one of the trucks near the head of the column, described how the situation appeared to him at this juncture:

Looking out to our left I could see ragged lines of Chinese troops forming up in the valley below and this despite the continuous fire from our air cover of planes which dived time and again upon them. The Chinks were too far away for any effective rifle fire to get them but seeing them reforming for new attacks on our column was no comfort. On our right the slant eyes were in the commanding spots on the ridges and were having a field day firing into our column and its escorting guard of troops. Wounded in the trucks began to get additional wounds and set up a mournful racket for someone to help them or get them out. There was nothing could be done for them at that time. Officers began forming their groups to flank the road block up ahead but had the prospect of taking the menacing Chinese-held hillside [Hill 1221] overlooking our column. The men were reluctant to get going when they looked about and saw men on all sides of them being shot down from the fire from the Chinese above them. At first a few began to inch their way up the steep hill which began abruptly at the roadside, then others, noting that the few were still going, joined them. This action had a snow-balling effect and a platoon soon took the top of the ridge and went over the other side blasting away at the retreating Chinese. This at least cleared a part of the ridge but fire was still coming in from where none of our guys had yet reached.

Dozens of soldiers huddled and crouched around the trucks seeking their protection and not heeding the call of their officers to charge on over the

hill to support the initial group of GI's which went over. The dull boom of
enemy mortars began a new tale. Out to our left their bursts began to creep
closer to our column of trucks. Included in this fire [were] the deadly and
much feared white phosphorus shells which can burn the flesh right off
one's bones in a matter of seconds. About this time a wild-eyed ROK soldier jumped in the truck and flung himself down on top of the wounded
guys causing them to yelp in new pain. He wasn't wounded—just out of his
head, I guess. He wasn't so far out of his head that he failed to recognize
what I wanted of him when I picked up a carbine and shoved the barrel
in his face yelling at him to get the hell out of the truck. I was so mad at
that s.o.b. for jumping in like that I would have gladly blown his head off.
He got out pronto and lost himself in the crowd of others milling around
the area.

As those mortars continued to come closer and closer I made up my
mind right then and there to get the hell [out] of that truck despite my
aching leg and try to get out somehow. We had been stalled too long now
and it was growing darker by the minute as the late afternoon came on. No
progress had been made in reducing the road block and the Chinese were
still pouring in a deadly fire from their positions forward and above us. I
pulled myself out between the other wounded in the truck and dropped to
the ground behind the truck. I had in my hand the carbine I had come
upon in the truck and checked it, finding I had a full clip of ammunition
ready to shoot.[5]

During this period many officers were killed or wounded on the road
near the truck column. Major Harvey M. Storms, commanding the 3rd Battalion, 31st Infantry, was seriously wounded and placed in one of the trucks.
Major Crosby P. Miller, commanding the 1st Battalion, 32nd Infantry, was
critically wounded, escaping death by an eyelash. In his words:

I moved up the road [after leaving Curtis and others at the foot of Hill 1221]
to discover if the high ground covering the road had been cleared, spotted a
heavy machine gun trained on me from just above the road, dove for cover,
but was too slow. Just before I reached cover I was hit in the upper left leg
(three bullets later removed from leg) and, at the same time the last three
fingers of the left hand were neatly removed by a bullet which I believe
came from across the valley. As my First Aid packet had been expended
long ago, I removed the glove from my right hand and pulled it down over
the wounded hand to stop the bleeding. The soaked glove soon froze and
effectively cut off the flow. Nothing could be done about the leg, so I lay in
the ditch taking stock of a very sorry situation. I sent a lieutenant lying in
the ditch near me back to Colonel Faith to tell him I was hit and that the

only way to clear up a desperate situation was to get troops up to clear the high ground above the road. . . . The ditch and road around me were dotted with dead and wounded with casualties increasing every minute. I tried to get men around the trucks to move directly up the hill and clear it, but each man who tried it became a casualty. Chinese troops tried to close on the column along the hillside by moving up from the valley toward the road. Just before they overran us an A-26 aircraft came out of nowhere and strafed twice just below the road, effectively driving back the enemy.[6]

The bullet that clipped off three fingers of Miller's left hand (he was left-handed) took with them his Virginia Military Institute class ring and his wedding band. The little finger was hanging by a shred of flesh, which Miller had a soldier cut off.[7]

Lieutenant Marshburn, who must have been the first officer of the task force to reach the road slanting up the north face of Hill 1221, was mortally wounded by an enemy bullet between his eyes during the heavy fire on the stalled truck column. Private First Class Wendell P. Shaffer, one of Stamford's TACP, was slightly wounded by the same burst of fire that hit Marshburn. It was his third wound at Chosin. For a brief time he cradled Marshburn's head between his knees as the lieutenant seemed to be dying. He then took cover in the ditch. After a time he recuperated enough to join a party that attacked up the hill. He survived to reach Hagaru-ri. He and Cpl. Gerald R. Thomas, the TACP leader, were the only members of Stamford's TACP other than Stamford to escape with their lives. TACP members Cpl. Myron J. Smith and Pfc. Billy E. Johnson were missing in action the next day, December 2, but Major Miller told Stamford that he had seen them dead.[8]

At the foot of Hill 1221, Stamford noted that the late afternoon was turning to dusk and that his air cover was thinning. He said that the aircraft stayed on station as long as possible but that no more arrived. In the gathering dusk his radioman, Cpl. Myron J. Smith, who had been carrying the AN/TRC-7 radio on a packboard, was wounded by enemy fire. Stamford took the radio packboard from him and put it on his own back and lifted Smith into the TACP jeep. Stamford decided that in the deepening gloom it was time for him to join the other vehicles. As the jeep moved forward up the hill, Stamford walked alongside it. By this time he had lost track of Lt. Colonel Faith. On the way up the hill Stamford came upon Major Miller in the ditch. Miller later wrote, "Fortunately for me, Captain Stamford came by walking beside his jeep, spotted me and had me loaded across the hood."⁹ The hood was a good place to ride. The engine kept the hood warm and helped keep Miller from freezing. The time was now about 5:00 P.M., and it was getting dark.

Stamford continued on up the road with some infantry, expecting, he said,

> to find our troops on the hill [the slope of Hill 1221] moving toward the road block. About halfway up I noticed it was too dark to run any more air strikes so I threw away my binoculars, removed the packboard and destroyed the radio because I knew if we did not get out that night we would be captured. I continued up the hill [not on the road but on the hillside to the west of it] and tried to organize the troops and keep them moving toward the road block. They continually tried to drift down to the road south of the road block.¹⁰

Before Stamford went up the hill, and before dark, Faith went to the stalled truck column and again tried to get soldiers out of the ditch and away from the shelter of the trucks and the embankment. He attempted to organize assault parties to attack the slope and crest of the hill to clear it of enemy so that the truck column could move forward. He found dogged resistance to his efforts. He was especially infuriated by the ROKs, who, prodded to join parties starting up the slope, immediately came back down to the road.

The situation was truly desperate, and if attack parties could not be made to clear the enemy from their firing positions on Hill 1221, the truck convoy could not move. The fire block and roadblock had to be removed from the flank and rear; frontal effort had failed. Faith came on ROK soldiers tying themselves to the undercarriages of trucks so that if the trucks got through so would they. Faith ordered two ROKs to come out from under the trucks and rejoin the fight. They refused. He shot both of them with his .45 automatic.¹¹

Finally Faith, with the help of officers, some of whom were wounded but still able to move, did get various groups of men started up the hill to clear it sufficiently to permit an attack on the roadblock. But it was an uncoordinated, disjointed effort. It was a case of each officer working with those men who were close to him and whom he could motivate. The groups were of varying size, ranging from only 3 or 4 to a squad to a platoon or more. One or two attack groups at first consisted of 100 or more men.

These individual attacks were made from various points along the road below the roadblock up the north face of Hill 1221 to the crest or high points on the long finger ridge that ran down eastward to the saddle and the road at the hairpin curve. The great majority of the men who reached the crest of the finger ridge continued on over it down the other side to reach the road on the southeastern slope south of (below) the roadblock. Most of them crossed the finger ridge along a line that brought them to the road near the point where the Chinese had earlier knocked out two of Drake's tanks and ambushed the medical company. When they gained the crest of this ridge, they did not try to turn down it and attack toward the enemy fire block and roadblock at the hairpin curve. Only one group, led by Capt. Earle Jordan, did that.

Lieutenant Campbell had a good view of the effort that Faith and other officers made to rally the men along the road. He had been dazed when he was placed in a truck at the perimeter after being wounded that morning. His memory of events remained fuzzy for hours from shock, fatigue, and a Syrette of morphine. After the convoy reached the bridge and moved around it, his head began to clear. He was relatively alert by the time the trucks stopped on the side of Hill 1221. He realized that small-arms fire was hitting wounded in the trucks. The thud of impacting rounds and the moans of the wounded were unforgettable, he said. He rolled out of the truck and into the ditch alongside. From there he had a good view up the road.

He saw Faith striding up and down the road near the front of the column exhorting everyone in the ditch to get up and attack the hill. Every time Faith passed his own jeep, he stopped long enough to fire a burst from the .30-caliber machine gun mounted on its side. Campbell realized how hard a time Faith and other mobile officers were having mounting an attack. If the hill could be cleared, it would be possible for foot troops to pass over it and attack the fire block from its flank and rear.

A major problem facing Faith was the shortage of ammunition for the troops. One of Stamford's requests to the pilots making the strikes at Hill 1221 and in the valley in the late afternoon was to bring in a drop of rifle and carbine ammunition. In a subsequent flight relay a Corsair pilot came on station and reported that he had the ammunition. Stamford said: "I requested the pilot to drop the ammunition on the road at the side of Hill 1221. The pilot brought the Corsair in from the direction of the reservoir. I asked the pilot to make the drop on the outer side of the road where the trucks were lined up. The drop was nearly perfect. It landed on the northern edge of the road opposite the trucks. The troops in the vicinity rushed to grab the ammunition. Some men divided with others, but there was no effort at a systematic distribution to all."[12]

Lieutenant Cecil G. Smith, commander of A Company, 1st Battalion, 32nd Infantry, was one of the first to lead a sizable group up the slope of Hill 1221. Smith said that the men bunched badly along the road and many were hit there. He organized as many near him as he could and led them up the slope. Their immediate objective was an enemy machine gun that had been firing on the road, but they did not attack it. In going up the hill, they bypassed the machine gun and thus did not help the rest of the troops on the road. When they reached the top, his point men went on over it and headed south. Smith with some 15 men followed and continued south toward the road on the south side of the fire block. They made no effort to turn back and attack the enemy roadblock from the rear but simply continued down the road toward Hagaru-ri. For a mile not a hostile shot was fired at them. This kind of action at Hill 1221 unfortunately became the common pattern thereafter, with no benefit to the stalled truck convoy.

After Smith's groups reached the bottom of the hill on the south side and passed Twiggae, it turned toward the reservoir. A force of about 25 Chinese soldiers came from east of the road and chased them but stopped at the edge of the reservoir. A wounded man fell behind the others, who moved out on the ice about 500 yards. A Chinese soldier followed and caught up with the wounded man and bayoneted him.[13] Smith's group may have joined with Patton's artillerymen, mentioned earlier. Neither Patton nor Smith mentions the other, but both tell the story of one man at the end of their column who was bayoneted by a Chinese soldier and was identified by Patton as a wounded ROK.

Captain Bigger led one of the more successful attacks on Hill 1221, but success was brief. Bigger had been severely wounded in the leg by a mortar burst at midmorning at the inlet. When the breakout came, he was riding in a jeep. But he soon gave up his place to other wounded along the road and hobbled along using the two canes his mortar section had used as aiming stakes. Near the bridge he met Faith, who told him about the roadblock ahead at the hairpin turn that was holding up the column. Bigger said that he would go up to see if he could help:

> As I drew near the column, I observed that the trucks with the wounded were stopped; that the soldiers on foot were trying to take cover between the trucks and the embankment where the road had been cut out around

Hill 1221. But the road was exposed to a murderous fire from the Chinese from the high ground to the East. I began shouting to the dead tired soldiers, "If you are going to die, do it while in the attack. Let's get moving and secure this hill." I began flailing at them with my canes. Captain Vaudreaux came up and joined in. Another group that I later learned belonged to Captain Earle Jordan and under his leadership also moved out. We mounted a pretty good attack and seized Hill 1221. We were trying to get organized and set up a defensive perimeter on the hill when the Marine fighter-bombers mistook us for Chinese and began strafing us. I stood up to wave them off (I came within ten seconds or less of being killed by this mishap, for someone called to me and as I turned to see who it was, trajectories began hitting my former position). At this point we lost control of those who had responded so valorously moments before. They began streaming down the west side of Hill 1221 away from the Chinese and toward the reservoir. I went with them. . . . It was my intent to hold this hill until we could get the trucks moving. . . . this inadvertent strafing of our positions by the Corsairs threw the men into a panic. . . . the harm had been done, the men took off toward the reservoir. It was a case of leading where they were headed. We walked south [on the ice] and shortly darkness fell. The Marine Air had spotted us, notified the 1st Marine Division who sent line crossers (Blue Boys) out to lead us in through the anti-personnel mine fields.[14]

One can appreciate what this effort cost Bigger, considering the many wounds he had received earlier in the day, including a wound in one eye, over which he wore a patch. In a letter to Captain Stamford less than a year later, Vincent J. Navarre, the 1st Battalion surgeon who had treated Bigger when he received the mortar wounds, asked, "How in the world did Bigger make it? His leg was a bloody mess the last time I saw it."[15]

There was a big surprise for Bigger and the others in his party as they approached Hagaru-ri: "As we moved down the ice toward the south end of the reservoir, we could hear the sound of revving airplane motors. At first we couldn't believe it for there had been no completed airstrip as we passed Hagaru-ri several days prior."[16] This unexpected accomplishment, completed just that day, was to save hundreds of lives among both Army and Marine wounded.

It was probably Bigger's group whom Lieutenant Mortrude joined in the assault on Hill 1221. After Mortrude hobbled across the valley to join the mass of troops assembling in the road and the ditch alongside Hill 1221, he took part in an attack up the hill:

Someone initiated movement up the hill which quickly became a spontaneous attack under the rallying cry of "come on GI." Somewhat recovered by
this time, I salvaged an M-1 rifle from a wounded Korean auxiliary and
followed the movements up the hillside which was now dotted with our
casualties. This attack carried to the crest of the hill into the very midst of
the Chinese occupied positions which had been originally prepared by the
US Marines and temporarily occupied by us on Day One. The Chinese
broke under the pressure of our assault and ran down toward the saddle
where the road crossed the high ground. Those that did not run were
quickly killed in their holes and I have heard that at least one was choked
to death by an enraged American. During this melee on the hill, we were
again struck by the US Marine air support, this time by rocket fire. Fortunately we had the abandoned positions as refuge and I saw no casualties. It
does, however, give our platoon the dubious distinction of being hit by
friendly napalm, machine gun, and rocket fire, all in one day, in the course
of one operation. Obviously, these experiences were the function [result?] of
our close engagement with the enemy rather than any ineptness on the part
of the Marine fliers. Even if I had a choice I would certainly have chanced a
few stray rounds for the benefit of the remarkably close support.

With the line of trucks now moving across the valley and up the road to
our rear, the movement of our troops (I doubt that any one was really in
command) continued south off the high ground to intersect the road as it
now curved back to the west. Once down on the road again, I observed at
least one disabled US tank and several friendly KIA as I followed the line of
march down to the reservoir.

Although my memory is now vague, and very likely my observations
were at best hazy then, it seems to me that we converged into a sizable
group of perhaps 50 or more people as we moved out on the ice of the
reservoir. In recall, it seems we were led by a wounded officer who was familiar to me and that it was Capt. Bigger. . . . I do recall, that as we moved
across the ice, groups of Chinese would attempt to intercept us but we
would drive them back to shore with much shouting and shooting. Also,
we came across one wounded US soldier and one wounded and one dead
Chinese, all literally frozen to the ice of a watering hole location. The US
soldier said the Chinese had shot him after initially indicating friendship as
they hosted him to a drink from the water hole. Subsequently, the
wounded US soldier had retaliated by shooting both of them.

Just prior to darkness we observed a friendly air drop of supplies in what
we assumed to be the Hagaru-ri area and I was heartened by the assurance
of our direction of our march.

Sometime after darkness, it seemed to me that we were moving through a
built-up area and in my state of exhaustion I wanted to fall out and rest in

one of the houses. Fortunately, someone of more presence of mind convinced me my "buildings" were merely rocks and that I must keep moving.

Upon reaching Hagaru-ri, we were individually passed through the friendly forward US Marine positions in a most professional manner. My impromptu camouflage and again my expropriated Chinese great coat occasioned some concern and curiosity among the Marines. I was, however, able to identify myself. Since there were infiltrators in the area and their troops were nervous, they insisted on divesting me of my coat and remaining "potato masher" grenades before escorting me to the aid station.[17]

First Sergeant Luna, of B Company, in his statement, made at Hagaru-ri on or about December 3, 1950, does not mention taking part in any attack on Hill 1221, but he did lead a party of about 25 men, 15 from B Company and 10 ROKs, to Hagaru-ri from the roadblock area.[18]

The 1st Battalion assistant surgeon, Korean doctor Lee Yong Kak, joined a group attacking up Hill 1221, but he could not make it and had to drop back to the bottom. He said that some ROK soldiers were with the group that made it to the top. There one of the ROKs pushed his carbine into a gunport in a Chinese bunker and on automatic fire sprayed a 30-round clip into it and secured it. It had contained 16 Chinese soldiers.[19]

When Major Robbins crawled out of the truck in which he had been riding, Lieutenant Curtis, of Jordan's M Company, called to him from the roadside ditch. In a quick conference they decided that there was only one thing to do—go up and over the hill as others had been doing. The two officers rounded up about 20 other men to go with them and began scrambling up the slope, firing as they went. Robbins's carbine fired twice and then jammed. He threw it down and picked up another from a dead American soldier. Most of the group reached the top and started down the southern side toward the Hagaru-ri road. While he was still on the hill, Robbins came upon Captain Jordan and a group who were preparing to attack down the spur ridge toward the enemy roadblock. Robbins came out on the road where Drake's knocked-out tanks stood. They paused there and joined about 30 more men, who were sitting around or milling about trying to decide what to do next. Major Robbins wrote:

> There was no organization left. Men of all units were mixed up at this stage. Again [Lieutenant] Curtis [not to be confused with Major Wesley Curtis] and I came to our decision as to what to do; we were going on to Hagaru-ri where the Marines were holding, or where we thought they were

holding. What lay between we could only guess. Major Jones of the 32nd Infantry and Capt. Goss from the 57th FA Battalion came up about this time and joined up with a few men [more than a few were with Major Jones when he left Hill 1221] they had led out. We formed two long lines of soldiers on each side of the road and moved out quietly down the road to the south. As we moved along the group swelled in size until there must have been a hundred or more GI's moving along the road.[20]

Captain McClymont remembers the experience he and two of his sergeants had on Hill 1221:

The short day was beginning to wane as the convoy started up the switchback of a hill I later learned was Hill 1221. I was about halfway along the column, when the convoy slowed. I started forward. As I started to cross an open space between two trucks, someone else also decided to cross that space and elbowed me aside. The man was about three feet ahead of me when there was a thunk and a bullet tore through his head. He slumped to the road, rolled on his side, and died. For a moment I was afraid, afraid because that man had taken my place!

By the time I made it to the head of the column, I realized that the whole convoy was being fired upon from the hill above us, small arms fire was hitting all about us. . . . I took my two sergeants, [Grantford R.] Brown and [Robert M.] Slater, and several other men I could get together and we started up that snow-covered hill. The climb was steep and for a while, in the darkness, the Chinese didn't seem to be aware of my small group.

Then we came over a crest and the high hill mass loomed up, perhaps a hundred or so feet higher than we were. A sloping field-like area extended to the top of the hill and as we came in sight, several dark figures literally dropped out of sight on top the hill. We began to draw fire from the hilltop. I loaded my Tommy Gun with a fresh clip, yelled at my group to follow me, and began walking up that hill, firing at anything that looked like a target. On my right and my left I could hear similar firing. Two thirds of the way up the hill I looked back and only my two sergeants were with me. The rest of the men had turned back.

The three of us were too far up the hill to turn back. We kept moving and firing. To the left a dark shadow became a man [lying] on his stomach, hastily swinging something towards us. I turned my fire control lever on FULL and sprayed him, but there [were] only about three rounds in that clip. I grabbed another twenty round out of my Chinese apron, dropped the old clip on the snow, slammed home the new clip. My target wasn't moving, though. I kept on walking upwards and there I was on the gently rounded top of the hill. Like perfect little golf holes on a putting green, there were several absolutely round foxholes. A figure jumped out of one, ran for another, didn't make it as we cut him down.

As far as I knew, every one of those foxholes held a Chinese soldier—what to do? I had a grenade taped to my Chinese apron. I took that in hand, went close to what looked like a larger foxhole, pulled the pin, counted this time one one thousand–two one thousand–then I rolled that grenade towards that round hole like a golfer on the 17th hole in a Master's tournament. That grenade rolled around the lip of that hole and didn't go in. It exploded there and we three hit the dirt [another grenade did the same thing].

I rose to my feet, took my Tommy Gun at the ready position and walked towards that infamous foxhole. Someone popped up from another hole, but one of my sergeants picked him off. As I walked forward, I could see farther and farther into the hole. A shot came from the hole. I could see the muzzle flash, but I didn't hear the bullet go by. I raised my Tommy gun high with the muzzle pointing down into the hole and the trigger guard high and I began spraying that hole. I put a whole clip into that hole and nothing moved then. I turned, reloaded, and walked to the next hole, spraying downward. I was tired, exhausted, mad, a little crazy. My sergeants either joined me or covered me and all of those foxholes were sprayed. . . .

The three of us had captured our part of the hill. From both sides of us, along the crest of that hill, there were dug in Chinese troops and they began to fire at us. We went over the flat part and on down the other side of Hill 1221. Sliding and crashing our way, we went rapidly down the slope. About halfway down we intercepted the road switchbacking down toward Hagaru-ri.[21]

McClymont's description of the top of Hill 1221 is unlike that of any other of the participants. Only his and Bigger's groups seem to have reached the crest; the others crossed the long spur ridge running from the crest down to the saddle and the enemy roadblock at some point short of the crest.

After regaining the Hagaru-ri road south of the saddle, McClymont, joined by other troops, led the group south until they were challenged in Chinese, whereupon all of them jumped over the embankment in the direction of the reservoir just as a machine gun opened fire on them. They decided they had better get out on the ice. They took their direction from the North Star and with it at their back walked into the Marine perimeter at Hagaru-ri.[22]

The movements of Captain Kitz and his composite K Company in the late afternoon of December 1 are ill defined. When they abandoned their mission as rear guard east and northeast of the bridge, some of them may have gone directly south over Hill 1221 to the vicinity of Twiggae and then on south over the ice toward Hagaru-ri. But Kitz and some of K Company went up the road to the truck column. He spoke of his men at this time as being hard to handle. Two or three days later at Hagaru-ri he wrote a statement that gives some information about his and his company's role at Chosin. He wrote: "The men were damn hard to handle. You couldn't get them to move . . . you couldn't control them. . . . The men just wouldn't function as soldiers should. They didn't go up to the high ground. They were tired and wanted to huddle together and thought there was more protection in numbers and very few of them would listen to reason. They just looked at you when you tried to get them to move."[23]

Eventually Kitz and several other officers got groups together and attacked the hill, knocking out several enemy positions, and reached what he called the top. He thought that they had taken the hill. It was nearly dark by this time. He sent two messengers back to the truck column with orders to start moving, and then he and his men began moving "across country" with Chinese at their heels. Actually Kitz had not taken the hill as he thought. Perhaps he had cut a way through some of the enemy forces or found a way through them or some enemy pulled aside to let him through. But he had not cleared the hill. He said that he looked back to see whether the trucks were moving around the bend of the hairpin curve, but they were not. Some wounded had dismounted from the trucks when he started, he said, and had joined him. Kitz had about 210 men with him when he struck out for Hagaru-ri, arriving there about midnight.[24]

Captain Swenty was among those who were still with the trucks as darkness came on. He saw that the column remained immobilized. He went back down the column, talking with some of the men about what they knew of the situation, especially about Hill 1221. One group in the ditch said that two groups of men, each of about platoon strength, had attacked the hill an hour earlier but had not returned. Swenty went back along the trucks and ran into Captain Bauer, whom he found badly wounded. Swenty said: "There was little to do for him as he had bled badly and the hole in him was pretty big. His talk was incoherent but I could make out he was asking for a first aid man. I could see he was in great pain and I proceeded to look at his wound. All I could do was to pull him to safety. I looked for an aid man. I found a couple that were hit but all their equipment was used up. I could not even find any dressings."[25]

Swenty decided to try to go up the hill to see if he could make contact with any American soldiers there. He talked to some men in the ditches, asking them to go with him. They refused to move. He then started by himself, but soon others were following him. Near the top, enemy in a fox-hole on their left fired on them. Two of the soldiers deployed around the foxhole and knocked it out. Swenty and his group searched for more enemy but found only eight positions where the Chinese had already been killed or the holes were empty. The group then went cautiously down the south side of the hill, where they could hear voices of men who had crossed the hill earlier. They were a mixed lot of stragglers from virtually every unit in Task Force Faith. In talking with the men along the road, Swenty had learned from them that Captain Turner, of B Company, and Captain Seever, of C Company, had been killed and that Majors Miller and Curtis had been wounded.

When Swenty heard the truck motors start up, he thought that the con-voy was ready to come across Hill 1221 and head for Hagaru-ri. On the south side of Hill 1221 he gathered up the wounded who could walk and started south. Half a mile down the road he was suddenly challenged. Startled, he asked, "What?" The challenge was repeated. An ROK soldier quickly responded in Korean or Chinese, Swenty did not know which. Word passed back down the line that the men were to cross the road and get to the rail-road. They crossed the trestle at the Paegamni-gang under fire but without casualties. Continuing south along the railroad, they reached the sawmill at Sasu, where they stopped to make a check. Swenty counted about 60 men who had joined his group after it started, so that now there were about 100 men with him. They moved onto the road and made it to Hagaru-ri. One man hit over the heart would not accept help, saying that he could make it to Hagaru-ri. About 40 of the group had been wounded. Swenty himself was uninjured except for frostbite on feet and hands.[26]

By 6:00 P.M. the enemy had been more or less cleared from their posi-tions on Hill 1221, except in the strong fire-block and roadblock area at the hairpin turn at the saddle through which the road passed. Faith and Jones agreed that it must be attacked from the south, or rear. They agreed to gather up individually all the men they could find on Hill 1221 and its south side, meet on the road south of the saddle, and then jointly attack it from the rear. Lieutenant May was still at the bridge finishing the work there.

Faith and Jones set about their job and soon met on the Hagaru-ri road south of the hairpin turn, just above the point where Drake's knocked-out

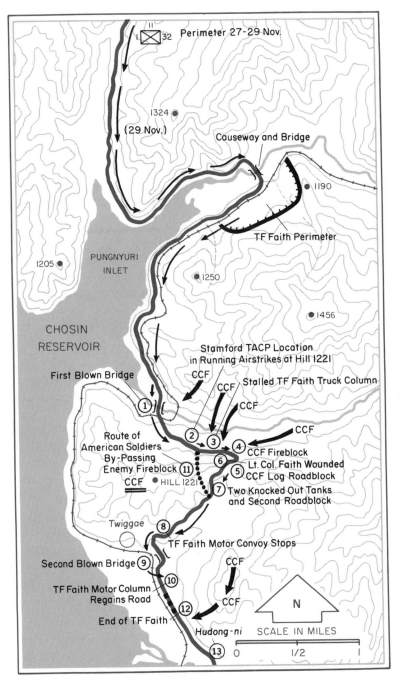

1324 (29 Nov.)

Causeway and Bridge

1190

TF Faith Perimeter

PUNGNYURI
INLET

1205

1250

1456

CHOSIN
RESERVOIR

Stamford TACP Location
in Running Airstrikes at Hill 1221

First Blown Bridge

CCF

CCF Stalled TF Faith Truck Column

CCF

Route of
American Soldiers
By-Passing
Enemy Fireblock ⑪
CCF HILL 1221

CCF

② ③ ④ CCF Fireblock
⑥ Lt.Col. Faith Wounded
⑤ CCF Log Roadblock
⑦ Two Knocked Out Tanks
and Second Roadblock

Twiggae ⑧

TF Faith Motor Convoy Stops

Second Blown Bridge ⑨

CCF

TF Faith Motor Column
Regains Road ⑩

⑫ CCF

N

End of TF Faith

Hudong-ni   SCALE IN MILES

⑬ 0   1/2   1

MAP II. Step-by-step sequence of Task Force Faith's breakout attempt.

tanks blocked the road 400 to 500 yards south of the saddle. About this meeting and their subsequent action Jones wrote:

Having only passed through the area of Hill 1221 once previously, and then after dark, I was not as familiar with the terrain as the others in the group. However, upon reading my memo of 4 Dec 50 and looking at the map accompanying it, to refresh my memory, I recall that I went due south up Hill 1221 slightly left (east) of its highest point, gathering up men along the way and attempting to clear the hill by fire. When I arrived at the top of the hill all enemy had been cleared from it. I then turned and proceeded southeast toward the main road. According to the sketch on the 1950 map, I came out at the second roadblock, or a few yards south of it. I turned left (NE), as I recall, to proceed up the road toward the hairpin turn to meet LTC Faith. I met him very shortly and we formed up our men on each side of the road just north of the second roadblock and made the attack.[27]

... By the time dark fell most of the officers and NCO's had become casualties along with many of the enlisted men. Units were intermingled and ceased to exist as organizations. Leadership provided by the officers and NCO's in the line units had ceased to exist. Many of the wounded were climbing the ridge and Hill 1221 west of the CCF roadblock and continuing southward individually and in small groups. When LTC Faith and I formed the two groups with which we attacked the Road Block from the south, those groups were formed by us standing on the road and getting people to stop and join us for the attack. Since it was dark and because the units were nonexistent (as organizations) we had no way of identifying the people who stopped or those who continued on down the road toward the Marine lines. There were many who did not stop even though we pleaded, ordered or tried to influence them of the importance of knocking out the road block. If LTC Faith or I had decided to shoot anyone in order to get their attention — it wouldn't have worked—those people were too far along from injuries, freezing cold, shock, fear and confusion to care. It was a matter of degree — those soldiers whom we were able to gather together and to whom we could explain our plan were also scared, shocked, injured and cold, but they still retained discipline, and the realization that an effort had to be made to reduce the road block so the convoy of wounded could proceed toward the Marine Lines. Most of them I believe were members of the 32nd Inf and knew us and thus stopped because they recognized a remnant of the chain of command still existed, whereas the others neither knew or cared. This might seem like a condemnation of the people of this task force, but it is not. At this stage of affairs, with no organization, no crew served weapons, no communications, no NCO and officer leaders to look to, the fighting units came apart, and left individuals who were in the main looking for aid, medical care and safety. When LTC Faith was hit, the Task Force ceased to exist.[28]

In this effort on the road south of the enemy fire block and roadblock after dark, Jones collected about 200 men, and Faith had about 100 men. Faith then organized both groups on either side of the road for the attack. Jones with his group was on the right (east) side of the road; Faith was on the left (west) side. This put Faith on the Hill 1221 upslope side of the road.

Both groups started toward the roadblock, traveling in the brush and scrub-tree growth along the sides of the road. The ground on the left rose steeply from the road; on the right the slope was gentler and easier traveling for most of the distance. Both groups fired small arms and threw grenades as they advanced, but apparently there was no attempt to coordinate their advance, nor was there any communication between them. Perhaps in the circumstances there could have been neither. Jones's group, which rapidly shrank in numbers, reached the roadblock area first. It seemed to them that they had knocked out the roadblock since there was no enemy reaction when they reached it. They did not stop to remove the physical block of logs. Jones continued on around the hairpin curve and descended on the other side to the head of the stalled column. He did not know where Faith and his group were.[29]

About the time Jones and Faith were organizing their attack on the enemy fire block from the south, Captain Jordan, commander of M Company, 3rd Battalion, 31st Infantry, was preparing to attack it from above. Jordan had arrived at the stalled truck column late, after most of the vehicles had crossed the bridge bypass. He was behind the column, near the end of the troops on the road. He and his men crossed the open valley, where he noticed many casualties. He said of that time: "Enemy fire was taking a heavy toll of the wounded in the trucks and the men who were gathered along the road bank as it hugs the nose of Hill 1221 just before the hairpin turn. . . . It was obvious the force was getting nowhere but more casualties." If many had thought that the crest and enemy firing positions on the hill had been eliminated earlier, it was now clear that the positions had been reoccupied or the earlier impression had not been factual. Jordan found many Chinese still on the hill. He did not hesitate; he prepared to attack the hill.

Jordan represented well the quality of many of the experienced officers of World War II who were present in the task force. One should remember that he had suffered grenade wounds during the first night battle at the inlet but had continued to command his company, which had held its original position until the breakout. Now he was still going to do a disciplined officer's duty. In his group Lt. Robert Schmitt, leader of the Heavy Machine

Gun Platoon, had one arm in a sling from a wound received at the perimeter and a weapon in the other hand. Lieutenant Gray, leader of the 81-mm Mortar Platoon, also wounded earlier at the inlet, got out of a truck and joined Jordan's group. Said Jordan:

> Along with Lt. Schmitt, Lt. Gray (both already wounded) we, through various means, assembled about 25 to 30 men from the ditch along the road and attacked up the N. slope of the nose of 1221. We took it and arrived at the top with 10 men and no ammunition. Lt. Schmitt was killed in this action and Lt. Gray wounded a second time. With the 10 men we moved down the nose toward the RB. We assaulted the RB by yelling, shouting and making as much noise as possible. We received a few rounds of S A fire and then we were on the RB which consisted of many logs piled across the roadway. We started to remove the logs and sent a man back to the column to get them started.
>
> It was at about this point that we heard a voice demand who was making all the noise. I responded and it was Col. Faith. He made a comment and along with the small party with him moved along toward the truck column. Just a few minutes later we heard an explosion like a grenade. There was loud talking so I asked what was going on. One of the party stated that Col. Faith had been hit and didn't know if he was dead or not. This took place just yards from the RB.
>
> There were enough people there to care for Col. Faith so we continued to clear the RB.[30]

Jordan was the only officer who attacked Chinese emplacements on Hill 1221 during the afternoon and evening, knocked them out (incurring heavy casualties in his own group), and then led a charge directly against the enemy strongpoint at the hairpin turn—without ammunition and with only a handful of men. His was quite a different story from that of the men who went up the hill, across the finger ridge to the south side, and then on to Hagaru-ri. Jordan's capture of the enemy's roadblock at the south edge of the hairpin curve, together with Major Jones's attack up the road against the enemy fire block just minutes earlier, set up the situation for the truck convoy of wounded to continue at last over Hill 1221 toward Hagaru-ri.

First Lieutenant Gray, wounded in one hand and in both legs two days before at the inlet perimeter and barely able to walk at Hill 1221, survived Chosin. Both he and Jordan received the Distinguished Service Cross for their actions at Chosin. So too did Jones.[31]

There had been no coordination between Jones's and Jordan's separate attacks, or even knowledge in the two groups of the other's progress and action. That they came almost at the same time and with success was co-incidental. Jordan's comments on Faith's arrival with a few men at the saddle sometime after Jones had passed it, and the manner of his injury at the moment of success at Hill 1221, are the most precise known to me. Faith was wounded by an enemy-thrown grenade just a few yards north of the log roadblock and a short distance—perhaps about 100 feet—up the slope of Hill 1221 from the road's hairpin turn. Jordan wrote: "Yes it was dark when we arrived at the RB. There was snow on the ground making it possible to make out moving objects at close range. Col. Faith was not on the road when he called to me. He was probably 50 to 75 yards off the road on the north side [probably northwest because of the hairpin turn at this point]. In this area there were scattered small trees, either birch or poplar in type. When I approached Faith he appeared to have a GI blanket wrapped around himself."[32] Apparently a lone Chinese soldier hidden in a hole in the brush threw the grenade at Faith or his group. Heavy grenade fragments struck Faith above the heart.

When these events occurred, Jones was at the head of the stalled column, about 500 to 600 yards below the hairpin turn. He knew nothing of Faith's arrival at the roadblock or of his being wounded there. Jones has written, "I didn't know then that he had become a casualty and had been put into a truck."[33] Jones apparently did not learn of Faith's injuries until after he arrived at Hagaru-ri, an indication of the chaos and confusion reigning at Hill 1221. Later, however, Jones was able to make an important addition to Jordan's remarks about Faith's injuries at Hill 1221. In his December 4 report to the G-3 Section, 7th Infantry Division, Jones said that in talking at Hagaru-ri with Lieutenant Fields E. Shelton, of the Heavy Mortar Company, 31st Infantry, the latter told him that he had been with Faith when he was struck by a grenade fragment above the heart and that he himself had received slight wounds from fragments from the same grenade explosion. Shelton told Jones that he "attempted to help Lt. Col. Faith down to the road, but couldn't make it. He wrapped up Lt. Col. Faith and went to the truck column for help."[34]

A message in the 11th Marine Regiment S-3 Journal file for December 2, 1950 is pertinent. This message, dated 020200 (2:00 A.M., Dec. 2, 1950) reads in part: "Approximately 200 more stragglers from RCT 31 picked up by Dog Battery [D Btry, 11th Marines]. . . . A Lieutenant Shelton reports 31st ran into heavy resistance at roadblock located at TA 5478 George. Stopped again by roadblock constructed of damaged tanks pulled onto road 400 yards to the south. Col. Faith wounded above heart and left with two enlisted men."[35]

Second Lieutenant Campbell, wounded and riding in one of the trucks, saw Faith carried to his jeep sometime later. He wrote:

> ... his [Faith] being brought back to the convoy wounded had quite an effect on the survivors there. His jeep (quite distinctive with the radios and side mounted 30 Cal LMG which he earlier had been firing) was about three vehicles up the convoy from where I was then located. Most of the other jeeps had stretchers placed across their hoods to carry the most severely wounded and it was there I recall he was initially placed. I did not talk to him nor did I see him later being placed in the cab of a truck nor did I ever personally see him in a truck cab. . . . I didn't see Bob Jones at this time nor was I aware of his actions. . . . The people down on the road at the time were largely a mixture of walking, non-walking wounded and dead from all the participating units. It became increasingly so as nightfall set in and whatever leaders were left could not be recognized.[36]

When Faith was wounded, Major Jones was at the head of the stalled column below the hairpin turn at Hill 1221, from which the enemy fire block was substantially cleared. This is confirmed by what Lieutenant May relates happened after he had seen all the vehicles in the column move around the blown bridge and back onto the road south of it. This difficult operation had kept May at the bridge for about two hours. It was dark when he moved up the road to the stalled trucks. He wrote of his next duties:

> After closing up the column, I went forward to see what the delay was. Upon arriving near the front of the column, Major Robert E. Jones instructed me to unload the wounded from some 2½ ton trucks that were knocked out, and to prepare the column for movement. This we did by overturning the empty knocked out trucks and letting them roll down the hillside. When the column was ready to move, I reported to Major Jones and received the following instructions: take about 20–30 riflemen and proceed through the pass at the top of the hill, continue along the road and open the road for the column. I picked a Sgt Clark, the Charley Company Supply Sgt., and Cpl. Swenson of Dog Company to form up the point. One was placed on each side of the road and we moved out.
> We went about 100–150 yards when we were ambushed from the high ground to our left front. I had instructed the men prior to moving out that in case of an ambush, to hit for cover first and then to bring fire upon the flash of the weapons firing on us. When the Chinese opened up, they got off only about 3–4 rounds from a MG when we knocked it out and moved on.[37]

Upon being asked how he and his men had knocked out the enemy gun, May replied:

> I split the team, had a column on each side of the road, the men to stay at 5 to 6 paces apart. At the first sign of movement or fire from the road block to hit the ground and to fire directly into and above and below the gun flashes. The CCF . . . could hear us but could not see us as they were looking into the darkened road, and we were moving in a crouched position. The CCF got off only one short burst from the M.G. as the point on right column saw movement and opened fire at about same time they did. We hit them with about 10 or 12 rifles at the same time, we hit something at their position that caused an explosion such as a grenade or small prepared charge would make. We moved in on the position, found 2 or 3 dead CCF.[38]

May's account shows that the enemy fire block near the hairpin turn had not been entirely reduced when Jones and his group attacked up the road from the south earlier or that enemy gunners had moved back to at least one of their machine guns after he had passed. May's group destroyed the last operable machine gun at the fire block.

The long-stalled task-force column was now able to start moving again. The time was between 7:00 and 8:00 P.M. on December 1.

The Chinese Destroy
the Convoy

Captain Stamford had discarded his binoculars and pack radio, joined some soldiers, and climbed with them to the ridgeline of Hill 1221. He tried to lead the men down the hogback toward the enemy roadblock at the hairpin turn, but they had no stomach for that and kept veering south. As a result they arrived at the Hagaru-ri road about 400 to 500 yards south of the hairpin turn. To their surprise they found there a second roadblock consisting of two knocked-out tanks and some destroyed vehicles. To this wreckage the Chinese had added some logs piled on the road below the tanks. Stamford has provided the most detailed description of this second enemy roadblock:

> I found a second road block and several disabled vehicles and at least 2 burned out tanks. These vehicles were of the medical unit that was caught unexpectedly when enroute to our position. The tanks evidently were of a relief column which came later because the tanks were beside the ambulances and there were a few ¼- ton 4 × 4's and trailers in front of the tanks. One tank was overturned about 25 yards down the slope and both were burned. The second roadblock had evidently been constructed after the tanks had been knocked out because it was south of them. There were several men there and I organized a working party of the slightly wounded and got the rest to move up the road.[1]

After removing the logs, Stamford started up the road with some men. Before reaching the hairpin turn, he heard sounds of a few shots from what he thought was an automatic weapon and then a louder report. He then met Lieutenant May and his point men coming down the road. May told him that they had just knocked out the last enemy machine gun at the fire block. When he reached the hairpin turn, Stamford posted some soldiers in his party to watch the draw that came down from higher ground east of the saddle to the turn, to prevent the Chinese from reestablishing their fire block before the column could pass. Stamford then went down the road toward the stalled trucks.[2]

Two months later Stamford wrote what he found:

> Maj. Jones of 1/32 staff was at the head of the convoy and I went to work to clear 2 damaged trucks of wounded [at the rear of the convoy] and get them over the side of the hill below the road. After working some time I found myself alone with the convoy of wounded. . . . The only officers I saw were the artillery liaison officer of 1/32 [Lieutenant Barnes], who was wounded, and our battalion surgeon, Doctor Navarre, who was unable to walk without aid. I pushed him in an ambulance and that was the last I saw of him until I found he had been evacuated to the U.S. from the 101st Station Hospital in Yokohama.[3]

In writing to Maj. Gen. Field Harris, USMC, about Stamford's role in the breakout attempt, Navarre commented:

> . . . the last time I saw him [Stamford] was in the early evening of 30 November [December 1] 1950. The enemy had caught the withdrawing Task Force in a small valley, and we spent most of the afternoon fighting off annihilation. There was some respite as evening fell, and the vehicles clogged the road, while the able bodied men attempted to load newly wounded on the already overflowing trucks. It was almost impossible to find any more space on the transports, until Captain Stamford came along. He quickly organized things, and began to force space for those recently wounded. Without his leadership and initiative, many of us (I was wounded and benefited directly by this action) would have had to hobble along the road with help from walking wounded. I don't know how this would have been possible; certainly it would have added to the mortality and frost bite.
>
> It is difficult to express the value of this man's leadership in that dark hour when leadership was needed so badly. Only those that were there can understand its worth.
>
> After he shoved me into an ambulance, and made certain other wounded were cared for; he moved on to other vehicles doing the same. I did not see him again.[4]

Later, in a letter to Stamford, Navarre said, "I'll never forget your organizing that dilapidated convoy and getting me into the ambulance; I would never have made it otherwise."[5]

While Jones and May at the front and Stamford at the rear were unloading inoperable trucks and removing them from the road, the column became divided into at least two parts. Jones's front part of the column moved off around the hairpin turn and down the south side of Hill 1221 to the second roadblock before Stamford had the rear part of the convoy ready to move. Jones's report to the G-3 Section of the 7th Infantry Division three days later tells about his part of the column:

> By this time so many wounded were without transportation that even though the column was started, many hundreds would be left where they lay. . . . decided that the only solution was to leave guards with the wounded and taking as many able bodied and walking wounded as possible.
> . . . Approximately two hundred men were put on the road. . . . instructed the group of guards with the lead vehicles to attempt to remove the roadblock. The column then moved down the road toward Hagaru-ri catching up with several groups of men who had already struck out and picking up stragglers all along the way. . . . [Later] it was decided that it would be more advisable to cross over to the RR track and follow it south.[6]

From Jones's report it appears that "many hundreds" were left "where they lay" on the north side of Hill 1221 because there was no room for them in the remaining operable vehicles. Jones and his party unloaded three trucks of wounded at the head of the column and reloaded them on other trucks that were already full, and Stamford and his helpers did the same for two more trucks at the rear of the convoy.[7] This made at least five trucks that were unloaded of their wounded and pushed over the edge of the road, the wounded from them being placed in other trucks that were already loaded to capacity. There undoubtedly were many wounded scattered around the slope of Hill 1221 who could not get back to the road and were never rescued.

In many of the trucks the wounded were piled 2 and 3 deep when they came to their last stop. Sergeant Jessie R. Dorsey drove a truck in the breakout. There were about 15 or 20 wounded in his truck when he left the inlet perimeter. He estimated that there were about 40 to 50 wounded in the truck when the Chinese stopped the convoy near Hudong-ni, and many of them were dead by that time.[8] Probably the other trucks were overloaded to a similar extent. Dorsey said that of the wounded men on his truck at the end only 5 or 6 got out to the ice and made it to Hagaru-ri.

When Stamford arrived at the rear of the road column, he found two inoperable trucks loaded with wounded. They had to be cleared from the road before others behind could move. Stamford found some walking wounded to help unload them and reload them in other trucks. Pushing the inoperable trucks over the side of the road proved almost beyond the men's capability. Most who helped in this work were wounded, weak from loss of blood, and completely worn out. All the men with any strength tried to help Stamford get the trucks off the road, but effort after effort failed. Many of the soldiers, unnamed to this day, reopened wounds and bled while they exerted what strength they had. Stamford and a few able-bodied men strained to the utmost and finally got the trucks to the edge and toppled them over the side. Stamford said that never in his life has he had to call on his last reserves of strength as he did in helping clear the road at Hill 1221. He commented: "Getting the road cleared I got the convoy moving and passed the word back to stay closed up and move slowly. I caught the lead truck [Jones's front section] about 400 yards down the hill south of the block and found they had picked up Col. Faith who was very seriously wounded in the body. I led the convoy down the hill by walking in front of it and held them up at the bottom while I checked a bridge, point G, ahead, to see if it was passable."[9] Of about 35 vehicles that were in the column as it left the perimeter, only about 25 were still moving at the hairpin turn and on down the south side of Hill 1221.[10]

Stamford and the rear part of the column found the road clear at the second roadblock of knocked-out tanks, and Major Curtis, who had rejoined the rear part of the column as it was moving out, also stated that the road was clear when he passed that point. It is not known precisely what the guard Jones had left with the convoy had done to free the road, but Campbell's comment on this point may provide the answer. He wrote: "At the time we passed around the K.O. tanks in the road (one was clearly in the road, the other slightly off to one side), we went off the road and back on without difficulty; a bypass could have been constructed earlier but there is no way I could cast light on this (when the truck which I was in passed, it was quite dark)."[11]

The convoy had reached the bottom of Hill 1221, on the south face, near the village of Twiggae. Here a small stream from the east ran through the low ground to the reservoir. Across the stream were a bridge and a small trestle for the railroad. It was here that Stamford said he first saw Lieutenant Colonel Faith sitting in the cab of the lead truck.[12] One may speculate that Faith had been moved from the hood of his jeep to the first truck in line when the convoy started up again, after Jones had left, and passed around the tank block. For a considerable distance south of the Twiggae

bridge there was high ground on the left (east) of the road; only flat marshland, varying from about a quarter to half a mile wide, extending westward to the edge of the reservoir. The rail track followed the western base
of Hill 1221 at the reservoir's edge until it reached the south side of Hill
1221. There it turned east along the base of the hill, passed through Twiggae, and then, just short of the vehicular road, turned abruptly south again.
Then, with only a few yards separating the two, both took a southerly
course on flat ground of the Paegamni-gang estuary for about a mile. Hills
hugged the eastern side of the road; low ground of the estuary extended
westward to the reservoir. Hudong-ni lay on the east side of the road just
north of the Paegamni-gang. There the road and the railroad diverged again,
the track turning westward, the road bending southeast, the two crossing
the Paegamni-gang half a mile apart. The rail track crossed the Paegamni-
gang on a trestle half a mile from the reservoir; the road crossed it on a
bypass around the blown concrete bridge a mile from the reservoir. The
reservoir could be seen over the flat estuary from both crossing sites. This
stretch of terrain just south of Hill 1221 was the scene of the final enemy
fire block.

It took about an hour for the truck column to reach Twiggae after Lieutenant May and Major Jones had passed it. In May's words, after Jones's
group left the convoy at the second roadblock at the knocked-out tanks,

> We continued along the road past our first assembly area in this sector
> [south slope of Hill 1221]. Immediately beyond this point we were hit by an-
> other ambush that seemed to be composed of only two (2) or three (3) rifle-
> men. When we returned their fire, they fled. As the sound carried clearly in
> the extremely cold air, we were able to hear them running on the road. We
> moved out and down the road again.
> I realized we were approaching the river near Sasu-ri. Just short of the
> river, I halted and went back to check with Major Jones. As he had not
> been over this ground in daylight, I briefed him on the lay of the land and
> told of the high ground that would be on our left, a logical place for an-
> other ambush. I recommended that we cut down the RR for an estimation
> of the situation. Major Jones asked for a check of ammo and we found
> only a few rounds per man, in some cases, none. We made a redistribution
> of ammo, which amounted to four (4) or five (5) rounds per man. We could
> not hear the column moving at this time.[13]

Jones and May were now near Twiggae, where Stamford later stopped the
truck column while he reconnoitered the bridge just ahead. May picks up

his story from this place onward after his group had redistributed their ammunition:

Major Jones gave instructions to move out along the RR. After moving a short distance, we heard the movement of troops to our front. At this time we were on the RR fill and quite exposed from both flanks. The road was approximately two to three hundred yards to our left on higher ground and an open valley to our right. We halted the column and I moved out with the point and found these troopers to our front to be composed of personnel from the 57th FA Bn, who were part of the task force. I warned them of the danger of an ambush to our left flank, and suggested they fall in with our column. There were a few officers in this group but their names I did not find out. I instructed the point to stand fast and returned to bring up Major Jones and the main body. When I got back to the point, I found that the artillery personnel had moved out.

Our group moved along the RR only a short distance when flares were fired over the trestle to our front. At this time, we were just entering the RR cut leading to the trestle and took cover along the bank on the left. We could see the artillery personnel out on the trestle and had them under observation at the time the Chinese opened fire on them. At the same time some mortars started being fired from our left front over us and a long way to our rear. We could hear a large group of Chinese talking and calling back and forth on the high ground to our left front.

Major Jones said to me that we are "sitting ducks" in this cut if they catch us in it. However, there were flares still in the air, which would clearly outline us if we moved from our present position. Major Jones and I discussed our situation and decided to make a run for the darkness in the low land along the river [the Paegamni-gang]. At this time we could hear quite a lot of firing to our left rear and came to the conclusion that the convoy was again under attack. We also could hear quite a few Chinese on the high ground to our left, so Major Jones gave the order to move out. As we crossed the ice on the river, we were fired upon by the Chinese, whom we had heard on the high ground. Upon a later check we found no casualties from this action.

We moved across the valley in the general direction of the reservoir. Upon getting to the ice, we followed a route generally along the RR after coming back onto it short of the town of Sa-Su. Where the RR entered the town; I cut off to the right, by-passed the town and followed directly along the edge of the reservoir until the RR line followed the contour of the terrain back to the reservoir edge.

We followed the RR for a short distance and picked up the P&A Platoon Ldr from the 3rd Bn, 31st Inf, and a few of the wounded EM who then joined our column. The column continued along the RR for a short distance until the RR followed the terrain contour inland. At this point we came upon several civilians composed of women and children and some old men. After checking them for weapons, we let them join our column. At this point we had a clear view of the North boundary of the Marine perimeter. We called a halt to let our wounded rest and to check their condition, as a cook from our Hq Company had collapsed. We did not know he had been wounded until this time.[14]

When Jones left the side of Hill 1221 and started for Hagaru-ri, one of the groups that joined him was led by Major Robbins. Robbins's recollections of what the foot column met in going forward indicate that he and a group of about 30 men soon became separated from Jones's larger main group. Robbins wrote:

Crossing another bridge which had been severely damaged but not quite impassable we ran smack into an enemy outpost which immediately opened fire. Our troops dived off the road but kept on going forward. I was toward the tail of the column having dropped farther and farther back as my leg began to stiffen and retard my speed. I had become separated from Lt. Curtis by that time but Captain Goss stayed with me which I sure appreciated. Being left behind was no rosy prospect as far as I was concerned. When the group hit the sides of the road after being fired upon they broke in two units, one going on down a small-gauge railroad paralleling the dirt road and the other unit cut sharply to the right and hugged the frozen lake shore path. I was with the latter group. We had become about thirty in number and actually had a better chance to move undetected through the Communists' positions. We passed through a small logging village [Sasu] expecting any minute to be ambushed but got away to the other side without incident.[15]

Thus the remaining infantry and miscellaneous foot troops of Task Force Faith who had moved on ahead of the stalled motor column were now about three road miles south of the convoy temporarily halted at Twiggae. No word of the enemy fire block at the ridgetop overlooking the road and railroad just north of Hudong-ni had been sent back to the vehicular column.

When Stamford reconnoitered the bridge on the road just south of Twiggae, he found the bridge so damaged that vehicles could not cross it, but foot soldiers could. At the bridge Stamford was told by an American soldier coming back north that there was an enemy machine gun there. Stamford searched the vicinity of the bridge but did not find the gun. He crossed the bridge and went to the railroad, where he found the short trestle intact.

Back near Twiggae was a trail leading from the railroad to the road over which Stamford thought the vehicles could move.

Returning to the head of the column on the road, Stamford talked there with some of the men. They went into a small building, where he lit a cigarette and thought he saw an officer with the silver leaves of a lieutenant colonel, believing him to be an artilleryman. In addition to this officer, he said, many others were present. Not one of them, according to Stamford, made any attempt to take command of the truck convoy and the men with it. Stamford became impatient with them. Something had to be done. He wrote:

> In my annoyance I walked out of the shack and up to Col. Faith in the lead truck and asked him if he wanted me to try to continue on to Hagaru-ri tonight and he gave me a very weak "yes." He could barely talk, and seemed to be in extreme pain and on the verge of losing consciousness. I proceeded to carry out this . . . order. I placed myself in the point because there seemed no other way to get them moving and keep them moving. I do not know what the other officers did after this because I did not see them again. . . . I could only find a very few men who were unhurt in the vicinity of the lead vehicle. I led the convoy over the railroad and found a place to cut off back onto the road south of the bridge. Once on the road I stayed about 200 yards in front of the lead vehicle in the point with a few men.[16]

Behind Jones, May, and Stamford another officer of the 1st Battalion, 32nd Infantry, Major Curtis, moved with the motor convoy after night fell. Curtis had been absent from the motor convoy for something more than an hour in the late afternoon when he had made the reconnaissance of the railroad as a possible route of travel. By the time he returned, the convoy had begun moving forward, and he caught up with it near the saddle. Curtis gives his account of events he experienced thereafter:

> As we went up the road the trucks were inching forward gradually. I remember hearing wounded men asking that they not be left behind, and I tried to assure them that we were trying to move to Hagaru-ri.
>
> Though there were some gaps in the column, the column was not split or fragmented. I walked around the Hairpin Curve, noting the Chinese corpse with wire in his hand, and down to the trestle where several soldiers were assisting the passage of the trucks over the trestle. This was a time-consuming and tedious operation. I was there for some time. There were no other officers there. I went up to the nearby hootch to smoke a cigarette. I saw no officers there. There were 3 or 4 soldiers smoking, but not talking.[17]

Curtis estimated that it was about 7:00 P.M. when he arrived at Twiggae. According to his statement, some of the lead trucks were already trying to get onto the rail track to cross the trestle over the stream.[18]

In moving around the second blown bridge to the rail track near Twiggae, the convoy had little infantry protection. There were only the guard force that Major Jones had left with it at the tank block and some walking wounded. The convoy was vulnerable if it encountered an enemy attack on the road or another enemy fire block. By this time the convoy was more heavily loaded than ever with many newly wounded. Some of the less severely wounded clung to anything they could grasp on the outside of the trucks. For the wounded men in the vehicles it was another ordeal to endure the jolting and bouncing of this second passage around a blown bridge. There were 15 to 20 trucks left in the convoy by this time.[19]

Stamford stayed with the trucks at the rail track only long enough to show the drivers and guards where to get on and off the track and back to the road. After seeing the first two safely across the trestle, he cut across to the road, leaving to the guards and others the task of guiding the rest across. Arriving at the road, Stamford started south on it to scout the route to see whether it was clear of enemy and roadblocks. From this time on, Stamford assumed that Lieutenant Colonel Faith was in the cab of the lead truck. There is conflicting evidence on this.

After leaving the railroad trestle, Stamford with three or four soldiers took the point and moved about half a mile down the road. He came abreast of the high ridge nose that descended to the road just north of the schoolhouse, the former CP of the 31st Infantry Rear and Drake's 31st Tank Company at Hudong-ni. Suddenly a number of shadows emerged from the roadside. Stamford and his companions were surrounded. A group of Chinese took them prisoner before they could react. Stamford relates what happened afterward:

The soldier guarding me wanted me to [lie] down on the side of the road. Evidently I didn't move fast enough or he was scared too, and discharged his rifle in my face. We had a guard behind us and one across the road with automatic weapons. The enemy sent one man out to reconnoiter and a mortar fired a couple of rounds from a position alongside the road about 300 yards farther on. There was enemy on the high ground east of the road also. Someone fired several bursts with a weapon from the convoy and it passed over our heads as two of us lay on the roadside. The position of the enemy automatic rifleman was under fire so he moved farther down the road to the south. Soon after this the lead truck ran the blockade and seemed to draw little fire. The man beside me said he was going to try to escape at the first opportunity and I told him I'd try too. The guard behind us moved off firing at someone coming at him and I took this opportunity to leave telling the man beside me to go. I crossed the road and railroad and ran about 300 yards west, cutting south into a line of scrub for concealment. I then started moving south to the next town [Sasu-ri] and found it dead. I continued on south and as I started over a saddle on a path I saw someone coming. I changed direction and he pursued me so I went into some scrub pine and over the roughest terrain I could find. I came down the other side of the saddle and injured my ankle. I then worked my way toward Hagaru-ri being careful to stay off the road as it showed signs of being heavily travelled by foot troops. I infiltrated the Marine outguards at Hagaru and was picked up on the perimeter by the rocket battery under Capt. [Benjamin] Read at 0225 on 2 December.[20]

Stamford was captured at the foot of Hill 1239, the first high ground near the road north of the Paegamni-gang. He said that when he crested Hill 1203 after crossing the Paegamni-gang, Hagaru-ri "looked like New York City but the lights were mostly moving."

In my detailed interviews with Stamford in late September and early October, 1979, he added details that were not included in his report. He said that while he and his three companions were captives at the roadside the head of the truck column crossed the railroad trestle and regained the road south of the partly blown second bridge. One truck made a sudden dash ahead and passed Stamford lying at the side of the road. As it passed, one of the American prisoners jumped to his feet, ran after the truck, grabbed the tailboard, and got away. This sudden move caught the enemy fire-block soldiers by surprise, and there was not much fire on the escaping truck. A few seconds later a second truck tried the same dash ahead. It passed the fire block where Stamford still lay on the ground. About 75 yards farther down the road a Chinese rocket fired from the south hit the truck head on and stopped it. The other trucks waited on the road as word passed down the line that there was an enemy roadblock ahead. During this period there was exchange of fire between men at the front of the truck column and the Chinese who held Stamford.

While Stamford still lay at the side of the road, he saw the truck that had run the enemy block continue on to the flat area just north of Sasu-ri and stop. Stamford thought that the driver expected the rest of the convoy to run the block as he had done and join him. Assuming that it was the lead truck of the convoy, Stamford also assumed that Faith was in it.

After Stamford escaped from his captors, he began working his way south toward the truck. But it started up again, crossed the stream over the bypass, and continued through Sasu-ri and on up the road to a turn at the saddle. He did not see it again.

When Stamford went through Sasu-ri, there were no enemy soldiers there, though they were on high ground both north and south of it. He commented: "Sasu-ri. It was just south of the ford across the mouth of the Paegamni-gang. I know this place well. I sneaked back to the road trying to find the vehicle that Col. Faith was in that made it through the road block where I had been captured. I sneaked through the village and pro-pelled myself about 25 or 30 feet on my stomach across the icy surface of the Paegamni-gang, a shallow but wide river for this area."[21]

Stamford is speaking here not of the main branch of the Paegamni-gang but of a smaller branch running close to the base of Hill 1167. Sasu-ri stood between the two branches of the stream. Stamford crawled across the small southern branch after he had passed through Sasu-ri. He was still intent on reaching the truck, for he thought Faith was in it. He was working his way south when he ran into a Chinese soldier. Stamford's Chinese captors had taken his pistol, and now he was unarmed. He jumped off the trail and, as he reported, in his dash for safety badly sprained an ankle.[22]

Major Curtis has provided the most detailed account of the ordeal of getting the vehicles across the rail trestle south of Twiggae. He found the process slow and tedious. The men had little trouble getting the vehicles onto the rail track and headed for the trestle. They put only one vehicle on the track at a time, and only when it had moved across and out onto the adjacent rice paddy did they move the next one onto the track.

The real trouble came in getting the vehicles across the short, narrow trestle. The trestle was about 15 or 20 rail ties long, the ties spaced about 1½ feet apart, and the entire span of the trestle was about 25 feet long, sus-pended between two abutments, one at each end. The entire passage of the trucks on the rail track from entrance to exit was only 100 feet long. Once over the trestle there was little trouble getting the vehicles off the rail-bed and across the paddy to the road. But each vehicle had to be hand-guided across the trestle. Curtis watched the crossing of the trestle for at least an hour and saw only 2½-ton trucks cross. By good fortune there was

no enemy action against the convoy at this time. It was, however, very painful for the wounded in the trucks. Curtis said he could never forget their
screams and moans as the trucks jolted across the trestle. Seeing that the
trucks on the road were not moving, he decided to investigate the trouble.[23]

When he reached the road, the rest of the convoy was lined up on it
but not moving. Curtis started walking down the road and, he said, found
Lieutenant Colonel Faith in the cab of one of the trucks and spoke with
him briefly. He remembered the conversation: "Faith called me 'Butch'—I
don't know why, no one else did. I said, 'Colonel, this is Butch, how are
you doing?' He said, 'Let's get going.'"[24]

Farther down the column Curtis came on Major Miller lying on the
hood of Stamford's jeep. He said, "Dick, you're going to have to walk if
we get out of here." Miller replied, "I'm hurting too bad to walk."

Still farther along, Curtis talked with a sergeant of the 31st Infantry who
had a body wound but seemed well oriented about where they were. He
said he was hurt too badly to go himself but that someone should cut across
the ice to Hagaru-ri and tell General Hodes to "bring up the tanks at daylight."

Curtis estimated that it was about 10:00 P.M. He said that he did not
see any officers other than Faith and Miller. Before he reached the head
of the column, Curtis decided to leave it, go onto the ice of the reservoir,
and try to reach Hagaru-ri. By this time the enemy had begun to close on
the rear of the truck column, back near the place where it had crossed the
trestle. He heard firing there and saw white-phosphorus grenades exploding
among the rear trucks.

Although wounded in the late afternoon at Hill 1221, Curtis had never
ridden in any of the trucks. Now, nearing the head of the stalled column,
just short of Hudong-ni, and on the point of heading for the reservoir, he
saw the beginning of the end of Task Force Faith's motor column. It could
be said that technically, as senior officer present, and still able to move about
with the help of his tree-limb crutch, he was the commanding officer of
the task force at that moment.

Once on the shoreline of the reservoir Curtis used his improvised walking stick to move out on the ice, avoiding the shoreline. He was tired and
dehydrated and ate snow constantly. Once he became disoriented; he could
not find his compass but finally located the North Star and guided himself
south by it. After a short time he heard artillery fire and struggled on toward it. He entered the Marine perimeter at Captain Read's battery position. Stamford had arrived there just ahead of him.[25]

Lack of reliable information clouds the fate of many of the most capable and dedicated officers of the task force. One of them was Maj. Harvey H. Storms, designated by Lieutenant Colonel Faith as commander of the 3rd Battalion, 31st Infantry, for the breakout. Officially Storms was carried as missing in action. Several officers of the 3rd Battalion told of his heroism on December 1 and believed that he deserved the highest awards for valor and dedication to duty. One of them said that Storms led an attack on the left flank of the vehicular column at the first blown bridge, was wounded, kept on going, and was wounded again. Reportedly he was also burned in the napalm drop. After his second wound, near the first blown bridge, Storms was put in a truck, but he dismounted and tried to help get the convoy moving and keep it going in the passage around Hill 1221. Captain William W. Etchemendy, L Company commander, 3rd Battalion, tells how Storms died at the last roadblock near Hudong-ni: "Although wounded several times, he insisted on walking & did a magnificent job. We finally got him to ride near the last road block after we rode along those railroad tracks. He & I rode in the first truck when we tried to make a run for it & there he was killed."[26]

Major Miller describes the circumstances under which the motor column made this last effort to pass the enemy roadblock near Hudong-ni. During the slow passage of the trucks over the trestle Miller had remained on the hood of Stamford's jeep. With one hand shot up, the other frozen, and three bullets in one leg, it is a wonder that he was able to cling to the jeep as it made the rough detour. He wrote: "The column . . . moved slowly down the winding road . . . and over a section of narrow gauge railway trestle to the road again. Jolting over the exposed ties, coupled with wounds and cold, left me, by this time, in pretty bad shape. The column stopped on the road (5377) and I heard someone say there was another road block ahead. During an interminable wait, I checked the five or six soldiers near me and found that those who had weapons (2) had only one or two rounds of ammunition left. No other ammunition was available."[27]

Miller thought that the time was near midnight when the long wait on the road was interrupted by enemy fire. He said:

> The long silence was broken by two mortar round bursts to the right of the road opposite the truck column about 100 yards away. Very shortly two more rounds hit the right of the road but closer in. It became apparent that soon we would be bracketed. I could visualize the wounded hit again and possibly a truck set on fire making us an even better sitting target. The

leading truck driver came to me and asked permission to make a run for it. He said he had been forward 100 yards and had not seen nor heard any movement. It was a choice of the unknown against the known danger. I told him to move out.

The column moved out and proceeded about 200 yards down the road to a bend. As the lead truck started around the bend, a terrific blast of rifle and machine gun fire hit the column from a hill mass to the left of the road (5376) [Hill 1239]. The lead truck driver apparently was hit as the truck piled into the ditch and blocked the road. The column was stopped cold and being punished unmercifully by a hail of lead. I rolled off the hood of the jeep onto the road and into the ditch away from the hill.

The driver of the lead truck in this last breakout effort was Sgt. Charles Garrigus, the heroic and daring noncommissioned officer who had so often played a conspicuous role in perimeter defense and in the attempted task-force withdrawal. He had carried the bucket to the well once too often. The enemy blast that hit the truck killed him. The Department of the Army awarded him the Distinguished Service Cross, Posthumously.[28] Major Storms was in his truck and was killed at the same time, according to Captain Etchemendy.

Captain Harold L. Hodge, commander of A Battery, 57th Field Artillery, was carried missing in action on December 1 but apparently was killed at the final roadblock trying to defend the rear of the convoy when the Chinese closed in on it. Sergeant First Class Carroll D. Price, 57th FA Headquarters Battery, said that he was with Captain Hodge at the time.[29]

In like manner, Capt. George Cody, commander of the 31st Heavy Mortar Company, was killed on December 1, and, according to Cpl. Ambrose J. Feist, of I Company, 31st Infantry, his company commander, Capt. Albert Marr, was killed when the Chinese overran the convoy at this last roadblock.[30]

After the trucks had crossed the trestle and assembled on the road just north of the last enemy roadblock, Intelligence Sgt. Ivan H. Long, 31st Infantry, showed up. He had escaped from his Chinese captors during the long climb of the high mountain east of Hill 1221 after night had fallen. He had heard the distant sound of motors and assumed it came from the task-force convoy. He descended the rocky hill carefully and reached the trucks. No one was in sight except for the wounded. He walked toward the head of the convoy and found an officer, who told him to take a seat in a truck cab. Small-arms fire from the hillside was now hitting the convoy.[31] Long soon left the truck, crossed west to the reservoir, and escaped to Hagaru-ri.

While the convoy was still stopped on the north slope of Hill 1221, Lt. James Campbell, having taken cover in the roadside ditch, decided, after the enemy fire had been suppressed and the hill cleared, to work his way toward the front of the convoy. He was near the front when it began moving again. He hurriedly seized the tailgate of a truck and hung on as the convoy rounded the saddle and started down the south side. He remained with that truck to the end. Campbell recalls the bumpy, painful crossing of the trestle and the rough rice paddy and the return to the road. Back on the road, he remembered, the convoy stopped for what seemed a long time, and when it moved forward a short distance, it was stopped again by enemy small-arms and automatic fire from the high ground at the left front. Campbell estimated this nose of high ground to be about 150 to 200 yards ahead and just east of the road. The convoy had reached its final point of advance a short distance north of the nose of Hill 1239, a high mountain just north of Hudong-ni. Its western slope descended to the road just south of the spot where the motor column was stopped. Of those who survived the final moments before the Chinese overran the trucks, Campbell gives the best account:

> The muzzle flashes of the incoming were clearly visible. When I dismounted it was from the third truck—a 2½—in the convoy. Ahead of that was a ¾ and the lead truck was a 2½. I crossed in front of this truck, and pulled up to eye level on the left side of the open cab. (Why I thought I could get it going I don't know; I had never driven a 2½ before.) In any event I am absolutely certain there was no one in the cab—I remember that quite vividly. When SA fire began to impact on the front of the truck I moved to the rear, crossed over to the ditch on the right (west) side of the road opposite the rear of the vehicle. It was here that I was handed a carbine by an unknown person and began to fire on the muzzle flashes. I did notice that there was an overturned 2½ in the gully about 40 yards to the west approximately opposite the third truck (the road at this point was level but the ground dropped off to the west into a shallow draw where the drainage went under the RR through a cement culvert). It was at this time that the third truck moved forward and began pushing the ¾ which, with apparently no one at the wheel, veered slowly off the road to the right (west) and toppled in the gully. The 2½ did not continue in its efforts to clear the road for reasons unknown (driver may have been hit or effort aborted). At the time that the ¾ began to veer right and overturn into the

gully someone yelled and I scrambled forward, the left front wheel went over my boot but there was little weight on it as the truck was already starting to roll. Although there seems to be a lot of activity here, it actually took place in a very short time span, perhaps 5–10 minutes at the outside.[32]

With the warning Campbell almost got clear, but he received a badly bruised foot and ankle. Of the ¼-ton truck he said, "it tumbled down the incline and landed upside down, the wounded in it screaming in pain, throwing some of them out." After it came to rest, he heard someone inside kicking on the floor, now the roof.[33]

Campbell again:

Almost immediately thereafter the CCF began closing on the rear of the convoy. I could see WP grenades going off down at the end of the line of trucks. The trucks were in a straight section of road, approximately 10–15 yards between vehicles at the forward end. I could not have clearly counted the number of trucks in the convoy because of darkness but based on the road space that the convoy occupied I would estimate 15+ vehicles at this point in time. I cannot offer any personal knowledge on where Faith was at this time except in a negative sense—he was not in what was then the lead 2½ (he could have been in the third 2½ already in the gully, or in a truck that may have previously run the road block and proceeded southward past the nose) but I have no other firsthand knowledge.[34]

Sometime during these final minutes after the Chinese closed on the truck column and overran it, two of Stamford's TACP, Cpl. Myron J. Smith and Pfc. Billy E. Johnson, were killed in their jeep as enemy fire swept over the stopped column. Major Miller later told Stamford that both men were dead in their jeep when he finally left the scene.[35]

It will be recalled that Major Miller had rolled off Stamford's jeep into the ditch on the west side of the road, away from the high nose of ground from which enemy fire was sweeping the stopped truck column. His narrative continues:

A wounded soldier was already there. He started crawling across an open space to gain the shelter of the railroad embankment. However, he was silhouetted against the snow, was hit again and killed. It was here (about five miles from the Marines) that the efforts of many men and officers to fight off overwhelming numbers of the enemy and to get their wounded to safety finally collapsed. It is true that some broke earlier under the pressure but many fought well up to this point. There was no doubt in my mind when the column was hit this last time that the battalion was no more and it had become a case of every man for himself.

Soon the firing died down, and I realized that the Chinese would rush the trucks and, for the immediate time, the best bet was to get clear. I knew my hands would freeze while crawling if I didn't get gloves, so I crawled out to the dead soldier. I made sure he was dead, but, before I could get his gloves, a burst of machine gun bullets hit all around my head. Fortunately, none hit me, so I got back to cover. A few minutes later I crawled down the ditch to the lead truck where I found Lieutenant Mazzulla sitting in the back. He asked me to help get him loose as his clothes were frozen to the seat. I couldn't climb into the truck with the wounded hand and leg, but I was able to hand him my pocket knife. He was unable to cut himself free so he handed back the knife and thanked me. Knowing I could do no more with the help available, I crawled away from the truck toward a pile of ties.

A few rounds hit around me but I reached the shelter of the ties safely. Here I found two GIs both unhurt but unarmed. One started over the railroad embankment, but promptly dropped back, saying that some Chinks were moving toward us on the other side of the embankment. We started crawling down the ditch beside the road moving south away from the Chinese. The soldiers soon outdistanced me, but one came back to help. I told him to go ahead while they had a chance, and they both soon disappeared. A few minutes later someone shot at me from the direction I had come. I lay doggo and no more shots came my way. About ten minutes later I crawled on around the bend, found a stick, got to my feet, found I could hobble on the crutch and struck out across field toward the town of Sasu-ri, just beyond the Paegamni-gang. Having studied the terrain on the way up I knew the bridge was blown. I by-passed the school house near the bridge where the 31st Inf Hq had once been located, climbed up on the road and walked out on the bridge to the break. Then I realized that I was in pretty bad shape, wandering around without reason. Also, I realized my right hand was frozen stiff around the stick and the fingers were white and hard as a rock. From crawling in the snow, the remaining fingers of the left hand also were frozen. I retraced my steps to the end of the bridge, got down the bank to the water and started across the stream on ice and rocks. Almost across my foot slipped, and the left foot went in the water far enough to fill the boot with water. I kept on into the town which appeared to be deserted. I found a house with some comforters on the floor, sat down and, after what seemed hours, got out my penknife, opened it with my teeth, cut the left boot laces and got it off. The extra socks under my shirt were dry and I got one on the bare left foot. By this time I felt no pain, just an overall numbness, so I pulled a comforter over me and went to sleep. I woke up in daylight when a Korean woman and her son came in. She was quite frightened, but she dressed my finger stumps with some kind of powder, gave me some milk (GI, powdered, I think) and left hurriedly.[36]

Comments from a few of the men at the rear of the truck column who survived when the CCF overran that part of it give an idea of the situation there. Master Sergeant Carl A. Truett, platoon leader of the Machine Gun Platoon, M Company, 31st Infantry, wrote that the convoy ran into the last roadblock, which was defended with antitank rockets firing on the trucks. Vehicles in the lead were knocked out, and others to the rear could not move. The Chinese ran down the line of trucks, throwing white-phosphorus grenades into them.[37] First Lieutenant Paul C. Smithey, an artilleryman from B Battery, said that he saw one truck driver shot through the head at the last fire block and that enemy fire was hitting the column from its right rear as well as from the front and the hill on the left.[38] Sergeant Victorio R. Nonog, I Company, 31st Infantry, was on a truck when the column stopped for the last time. He played dead when the Chinese came up to the truck. He said that they took one enlisted man and one ROK from the truck but did not bother the others.[39]

Corporal Ambrose J. Feist, of I Company, wounded, stayed with the trucks, he said, until about 3:00 A.M., and during that time "The Chinese came, took some of our wounded's blankets and toward daybreak took off. I stayed there until the Chinese left. . . . I saw them kill three at the rear of the column. . . . I wouldn't say there were too many [wounded left alive], because it was cold there and clothes and blankets were taken by the Chinese. I started across the ice back to the Marine area.[40]

After midnight, Sfc. William C. Tillery, of B Battery, returned to the convoy and reported what must have been the situation thereafter. He said that he, Sergeant Wright, and Private Michell went back to the convoy about midnight and that nothing was left of it: "The CCF had come through. All I could see was people lying around in sleeping bags . . . dead."[41] Sergeant First Class William Mahon, of K Company, 31st Infantry, escaped when the Chinese came down to the trucks. He wrote: "I killed four (4) of them when I slipped and fell on the ice of a brook. I shot them with my carbine. The first two came at me. I was still sitting down when I shot. They were looking for me, and I opened up on automatic, on the other two. . . . I left and took off across a swamp and went on into Hagaru-ri."[42]

At the end each man had his own adventure, and some lived to tell them. Most of those who were not too badly wounded got out of the trucks during the night if the Chinese did not take them away. Those with severe body wounds or multiple leg wounds froze to death if the final Chinese assault did not kill them.

The Death of Lieutenant Colonel Faith

Darkness had closed on December 1, 1950, and Lt. Col. Don Carlos Faith, Jr., grievously wounded, blue with cold, was slumped in the cab of a 2½-ton truck. A piece of metal from an enemy fragmentation hand grenade had pierced his chest just above the heart.

The first information of record to reach the 1st Marine Division CP at Hagaru-ri that the commander of the 7th Division troops east of Chosin had been wounded was received at 2:00 A.M. on December 2 at the Marine perimeter, near the entrance of the Changjin River into the Chosin Reservoir, north of Hagaru-ri. The 1st Marine Division G-3 Journal file for December 2, 1950, contains a message from the 11th Marines (Artillery Regiment) that reads as follows:

S-3 11th Mar   G-3   020200

Approximately 200 more stragglers from RCT 31 picked up by DOG Battery coming across ice on Chosin Reservoir. Capt. Stamford, Marine TACP escaped successfully to our lines. A Lieutenant Shelton reports 31st ran into heavy resistance at roadblock located at TA 5478 George [Hill 1221]. Stopped again by roadblock constructed of damaged tanks pulled onto road 400 yards to the south. Col. Faith wounded above heart and left with two enlisted men. Trucks were burned. Hecklers checking area rept fires confirming this rpt. Wounded being abandoned. (Information given to Lt. Col. Anderson RCT 31 Hq and X Corps file)[43]   I
[Illegible–three initials]

On December 4, 1950, Maj. Robert E. Jones, S-1 of the 1st Battalion, 32nd Infantry, prepared a memorandum at Hagaru-ri, addressed to "Major Lynch: G-3 Section, 7th Division, APO 7," outlining the action east of Chosin Reservoir. In it he commented on the joint attack that he and Lieutenant Colonel Faith had made against the enemy fire block at the saddle of Hill 1221: "At this time Lt. Col. Faith was hit by a fragmentary grenade (Lt. Shelton HM Co 31st Inf confirmed this, as he was hit by the same grenade. He attempted to help Lt. Col. Faith down to the road, but couldn't make it. He wrapped up Lt. Col. Faith and went to the truck column for help)."[44]

When Jones reached the 32nd Infantry Service Company area at Hamhung on the afternoon of December 11, he decided to see General Barr and tell him all he knew from his own observation and what he had learned from others about Faith's final hours. Jones talked with Barr on the morning of December 12 and gave him all the details he knew.[45] Presumably Barr's December 13 letter to Barbara Faith from Hungnam about her husband's death was based largely on his conversation with Jones.[46]

Later Major Jones was in command of the remnant of the 1st Battalion, 32nd Infantry, and responsible for its rehabilitation. In late December, 1950, Col. Charles E. Beauchamp, the 32nd regimental commander, ordered WO (jg.) Edwin S. Anderson, assistant personnel officer of the regiment, to interview all the officers and men of the 1st Battalion who had escaped the Chosin disaster and were on the duty roster of the battalion—this did not include those who had been wounded or injured and air-evacuated from Hagaru-ri. The men to be interviewed were in a rehabilitation camp near Taegu, South Korea. The purpose was to reconstruct their personnel records, which had been lost at Chosin. There were 3 officers, including Major Jones, in command, and 73 enlisted men in this category, according to Anderson.

Before the interrogations began, General Barr ordered Anderson to go further than the reconstruction of personnel records and ask each man what he knew about Lieutenant Colonel Faith's death. He wanted to have all possible information before he wrote again to Faith's widow.

In the course of these interviews one of the men, Pfc. Russell L. Barney, told Anderson that he had driven the truck in whose cab Lieutenant Colonel Faith had ridden during the breakout effort from Hill 1221 onward. Barney said that in the truck Faith was wounded again by enemy small-arms fire and that when he left the truck Faith was dead in the cab.[47]

Warrant Officer Junior Grade Edwin S. Anderson's memorandum of January 9, 1951, to Maj. Gen. David Barr reported on his interview with Barney. In it Anderson said that Barney told him that he drove the truck to map coordinate CV 5373, where he left it with Faith dead inside the cab. Unfortunately, Barney did not give, or Anderson did not report, the reason Barney abandoned the truck. It may have run out of gasoline. The map coordinate puts the location of the abandoned truck about two and a half road miles south of the place the task-force convoy came to its end near Hudong-ni, north of Mulgam-ni and south of Pokko-chae, in hill terrain within a mile and a half of the Marine perimeter at Hagaru-ri.[48]

Captain Stamford believed that Faith was in the cab of the lead truck of the convoy and that this truck was the one that dashed past him when he was a prisoner of the Chinese at the edge of the road at the last enemy fire block. As related earlier, this truck, according to Stamford, went south through Sasu-ri, climbed the sharp grade beyond, and went into the road turn on top. It was the only vehicle to get past the enemy fire block near Hudong-ni. Barney's map coordinate and his story bear a close correlation with Stamford's account of what he saw of the truck's progress. When Lieutenant Campbell and his group of survivors came off the ice at Mulgam-ni to the vehicular road later that night and before dawn of December 2, they would have been south of the point where Barney abandoned his truck and thus would not have passed it on the road.

I give the weight of evidence to Stamford's and Barney's accounts of Faith's final hours and assume that his remains lie in the earth about two miles north of Hagaru-ri a little distance north of the village of Mulgam-ni.

After the remnants of the 1st Battalion, 32nd Infantry, arrived at their reconstitution site near Taegu, Major Jones prepared an award citation for the Congressional Medal of Honor, Posthumously, for Lieutenant Colonel Faith. He initially submitted it to a higher headquarters in late December, 1950. The recommendation was returned to Major Jones several times for rewriting. Eventually it was taken over by a still higher headquarters and progressed from one headquarters to another yet higher one. Each in turn rewrote it to satisfy what it considered would meet the requirements of granting the award. The citation was still undergoing this process when Jones was rotated back to the United States in May, 1951. The final draft bore little resemblance to Jones's initial draft.

Eventually President Harry S Truman awarded the Congressional Medal of Honor, Posthumously, to Lieutenant Colonel Faith. The award was presented to Barbara Faith in Washington, D.C., by Gen. Omar N. Bradley, chairman of the Joint Chiefs of Staff, in a ceremony on June 21, 1951. The official Department of the Army award and citation were published in its General Orders No. 59, August 2, 1951.[49]

19

Those Who Escaped to Hagaru-ri

Survivors from Task Force Faith arrived at Hagaru-ri by the hundreds during the night of December 1–2. More arrived every day thereafter until the reassembled 1st Marine Division and survivors of the 7th Infantry Division east of Chosin began their fighting withdrawal from Hagaru-ri on December 6. Most of the 7th Division troops came across some part of the Chosin Reservoir on the way.

The first more or less organized groups of survivors crossed the ice from the vicinity of Twiggae, at the southwest foot of Hill 1221. From there it was a straight-line distance of about four and a half miles to the Marine perimeter north of Hagaru-ri. Survivors who escaped from the trucks at the last enemy fire block later had a straight-line distance of about three and a half miles to the Marine perimeter. These men went through or skirted the village of Sasu, and most of them went on the ice for only a short distance before they returned to land.

The members of Task Force Faith who escaped to Hagaru-ri can be divided into two parts: (1) those who escaped in groups more or less organized under the leadership of one or more officers or noncommissioned officers during the period the task-force motor convoy was stalled at Hill 1221, from about 3:30 P.M. to about 7:00 P.M. (many of these groups left Hill 1221 while it was still daylight) and (2) those who escaped singly or in small groups after the Chinese halted the trucks at their fire block just north of Hudong-ni. The latter are the principal subjects of this chapter. Nearly all the men in this second category had wounds that did not render them completely immobile; they were able to walk or crawl away from the trucks to positions west of the road, where they found hiding places.

278

Survivors of Task Force Faith moving south across the ice of Chosin Reservoir toward Hagaru-ri. A large group can be seen in the distance. They seem to be near the southern tip of the reservoir and the marshland just north of Hagaru-ri. The ridgeline beyond the men appears to be on the west side of the reservoir. Photographed in the late afternoon of December 1, 1950, by an unknown photographer. Photograph courtesy of Lt. Col. Ivan H. Long.

The most reliable information on the time of arrival of several large groups of soldiers at Hagaru-ri from the 31st Infantry task force is found in the 1st Marine Division G-3 Journal and Message file. The first such message was a telephone call from the 1st Motor Transport Battalion to the Division G-3 at 1745 (5:45 P.M.), saying "About 100 men remnants of 2 Army Bns are at 3/1 CP" (the "3/1 CP" refers to Lt. Col. Thomas L. Ridge's 3rd Battalion, 1st Marine Regiment CP).

The second message of consequence in the Marine G-3 Journal and Message file reads: "About 350 more army personnel came into perimeter. Came in over the lake." The message was dated 012000I (8:00 P.M.). A third message came from the S-3 of the 11th Marines (the Marine artillery regiment) to the Division G-3 at 020200 (2 A.M. on December 2), reporting: "Approximately 200 more stragglers from RCT picked up by Dog Battery coming across ice on Chosin Reservoir. (Information given to Lt. Col. Anderson RCT 31 31st Hq and X Corps.)"

Some men like Captain Stamford and Major Curtis came in alone during the night. Some of the officers tried to induce the Marines to send rescue parties to the convoy. Curtis, for instance, upon arrival at the Marine perimeter, asked to see General Hodes, whom he supposed to be at Hagaru-ri, to get help for the motor column. But 1st Lt. Rollin W. Skilton, a 7th Division liaison officer with the Marines who went to the perimeter to give Curtis transportation, took him to an aid station and told him that "Hodes was attacking at sun-up."

Corporal Alfonso Camoesas, 3rd Platoon, C Company, the medical-aid man who had bandaged Mortrude's head wound at the first blown bridge in the afternoon, brought in a party of 15 men carrying 6 wounded. They followed the shoreline of the reservoir for a time but walked on the rail track most of the way to Hagaru-ri.

When the truck convoy came to its final stop, William J. Hingston, a wireman-runner with the Weapons Platoon, B Company, 32nd Infantry, was with the trucks. He had two leg wounds and shrapnel wounds in the face but was able to walk. He said that he had accompanied Captain Stamford when the latter reconnoitered the area of the second blown bridge near Twiggae. He tells of his escape from the trucks:

> The Chinese had us completely surrounded except for the way leading out onto the ice. At this time I was wounded in the face by shrapnel from a mortar round. I went back to the convoy and got mixed up with Chinese who were at that time all over the convoy. At that time, somewhere in there, I threw my rifle down for a few minutes rather than draw any more fire. No one was fighting back at this time. I thought twice about surrendering at this time, and began to think about escaping out onto the ice. The Chinese evidently had thought I had surrendered as I had thrown down my rifle. I picked my rifle back up and dived into a ditch. As I jumped into the ditch I resumed firing. I aimed between the back wheels of a six by [2½-ton truck]. I ran low on ammo and borrowed all that I could from the wounded on the truck. I let it be known that I was taking off as I considered it hopeless at this time to the men on the back of the truck, and that anyone who wanted to come could. I did not want to get captured and all resistance had stopped at this time except for myself and a few others. One person got off the truck and joined me in the ditch. I told him at that time

that I did not want any moaning and groaning. We made a break for the
ice. We got out maybe 200 yards and the bullets stopped coming at us from
behind. The man who was with me was hit at this time, again, before firing
ceased. He became troublesome at this time. I carried him across the ice,
heading in northerly [southerly] direction I believe. There were all kinds of
tracers down in that direction as that is where the Marines were. We
reached the shore and moved up about 50 feet. There was snow on the
ground and it was cold. The wind was blowing and I imagine it was around
50 below zero. I crawled around and saw that there was a house less than a
hundred yards away. . . . I carried him towards the house, dropped him
about 25 feet from the house and went down to the house by myself to
check it out. I kicked the door open and was ready to fire if anyone moved,
but there were several candles going. I saw several old men and women. I
tried to convince them that I would not hurt them. Two of the old men
helped me to carry the wounded man into the house. They helped him as
much as they could. I fell asleep and in the morning they woke me up.
They were completely trustworthy. Everything had quieted down by now.
The old man hooked up the ox cart and we put the wounded man on it.
They put all the blankets around him. We were drawing fire from a hill at
this time, but we were far enough away so that they could not hit us. We
made it to the Marines.[1]

After the Korean woman had dressed Miller's finger stumps in a house in
Sasu-ri on the morning of December 2 and then hurriedly left, Miller lay
quietly where he had slept some hours during the night. He continues his
story:

About 0900 (2 Dec) I heard shots in the village and realized that Chinese
were searching houses. But I had no place to hide so I lay there. Two Chinese soldiers came in, one armed with a rifle and the other with a typical
Russian tommy gun. They each took a cigarette from me, laughed when I
pointed out my wounds, and then left. Soon two more Chinese came in.
These took all my cigarettes and lighter, ransacked the house and left. A
third pair came in, took a can of meat and beans from my pocket, searched
the house and left. Nothing more occurred until about 1200 when a young
American soldier crept in the back door. No more Chinese were in sight in
the village but we could see approximately a company size unit digging in
astride the road on the high ground just to the south (5374). I decided to try
to walk around their left flank, advised the soldier to get a stick and hobble
as though he were wounded. I realize now that an attempt to get around
the enemy *left* flank was a bad choice, but it was a short-lived attempt at
any rate—we got no more than two houses down the street when two Chinese soldiers appeared, shoved me into a shed and marched the soldier with

me off up the road to the troops on the hill. I heard no shot so I assume he was held a prisoner. I can only assume that I was not taken prisoner throughout the whole time because of my appearance. Unshaven, dirty, covered with blood and with frozen fingers now beginning to blister and turn black, I believe I was being left to die. By this time I was again exhausted so I crawled into a shed behind a pile of wood and again went to sleep. I was awakened by being dragged out of the shed by two more Chinks who took my wallet, tore up my ID card in half, but gave me back my folder of family pictures. One Chink threw a round into the chamber of his rifle, pointed it at me, and, after what seemed to be an eternity, turned and walked away. At a temperature of at least 20 below zero, I still wiped sweat from my face. I picked up the largest piece of my ID card, found another house back off the street, and, entering it, found two soldiers hiding there. One was wounded in the back and the other in the foot. Again I slept.

The next morning, 3 December, I crawled out and took a look at the hill (5374) to the south where the Chinese had dug in. There was no sign of an enemy soldier. I estimated they had pulled out straight south along the road to Hagaru-ri or had moved out around the east side of that town and the Marines there. I knew that the odds were in favor of the Marines having to pull out that I'd better get moving or get left behind. Considering the condition of my leg and hands, I decided to use the road and move south until I ran across the Marines or more Chinese. I told the two soldiers what I intended to do, but they would not come with me. I hobbled down the road past a knocked out T-34 tank, up the hill past two M4E8 tanks to the top—no Chinese troops were in sight. I went down into the sawmill town of Sasu (5274). Here a North Korean man came out and led me into a house where another man and two women gave me some coffee (GI soluble) and gave me a pencilled note which said in both Korean and English, "Go to the edge of the reservoir and come down it to the Marines." One of the Korean men in broken English told me he would guide me down the road—that it was open. We started out but when we reached the south edge of the town, we spotted Chinese on the hill to the south. My guide left me and disappeared. I decided to go over to the railroad on the edge of the reservoir and try to get by the Chinese that way. As I reached the west side of the town, two corsairs made three passes at the town. I dropped into a ditch when 50-cal slugs [Corsairs strafe with 20-mm guns] tore up the house behind me. One napalm bomb went over my head, hit about 30 yards behind me—took some of the chill out of the air.

When the air attack was over, I moved on to the railroad and down the side of the reservoir, sweating out the high ground to my left—Hill 1203 (5273) [Pokko-chae]. I tripped and fell and almost quit because the snow seemed soft and warm. I felt as though sleep was all I needed. But I remembered a description of the symptoms of freezing told me by a friend of my father's who was an Alaskan expert. I realized I was freezing so I got up after what seemed hours of effort and stumbled on—I had lost my stick in the fall. Finally, I reached a point from which I could see Hagaru-ri with tanks spotted around it. This gave me enough strength to keep going until a jeep came out and picked me up.

The rest is routine—treatment in the Marine Aid Station, where I saw Captain Stamford and was told that Major Jones and Major Curtis had gotten out, was flown out by a C-47 to Hamhung, then to Osaka, Japan, and then to Camp Pickett, Virginia, by 19 December 1950. Thereafter, it was just a long siege (9 months) in hospital where the remaining fingers of the left hand and the first joint of all the fingers of the right hand were removed. The leg wound healed perfectly. Returned to duty at Fort Knox, Kentucky.[2]

Dr. Lee Yong Kak, the South Korean assistant battalion surgeon, 1st Battalion, 32nd Infantry, escaped from the final enemy fire block. Some days after his escape he wrote in part:

There was a full moon and the enemy found it extremely easy to observe us. . . . We attempted to escape by running our vehicles through at the fullest speed possible but we were stopped. Many of us were killed and wounded. . . . We were able to return only a small part of the fire and soon even that ceased. . . . I gave my good M-1 to a soldier and took his which failed to operate, wearing my white parka, I rolled about 200 yards to the edge of the reservoir and onto the ice. I found the southerly direction by the stars and from that direction observed red tracers first into the sky. These, I felt, came from our army so I walked on the ice in that direction. Soon, utterly exhausted, I fell upon the ice and . . . slept until awakened, perhaps ten minutes later, by two soldiers who had escaped from our convoy. We again began our walk south and at about 0500 on December 2, we arrived at the Marine base in Hagaru-ri. From that point, due to the annihilation of my own outfit, I joined with the 1st Marine Division.[3]

Ivan Long, the intelligence sergeant of the 31st Infantry Regiment, who was wounded during the afternoon of December 1, was captured, and later escaped, as previously described, reached the convoy after the Chinese had just stopped it at the final fire block. He saw the enemy's initial closing on the truck column rear and decided that he had to make an effort to get away to the reservoir. He wrote:

The loss of blood was beginning to have its effect. I felt light-headed and dizzy and felt I had better head for some medical attention. I crossed a swamp, drawing some fire, and headed across the reservoir. The snow-covered ice was trampled with hundreds of footsteps, leaving no doubt in my mind as to the destination of the troops assigned to protect the convoy. My strength by now, as I approached the Marine perimeter, was about gone and I folded and was carried to the aid station by the biggest Marine I ever saw. During my brief stay I was visited by Maj. Witte, but at this point I was not much help. My boots were cut off my feet and I was flown to a hospital in Japan. Subsequently I spent 9 months in the hospital.[4]

After watching Chinese grenades hitting the rear vehicles, Campbell fired off the remaining rounds in his carbine at the muzzle flashes on the nose of high ground east of the road. He then hobbled west across the low ground, crawled through the railbed culvert under fire, and came out on the other side of the track. There he encountered several wounded, mostly artillery-men and men from the 31st Infantry. A 17-man group soon gathered there and, with Campbell at the point, moved out onto the ice of the reservoir and started south. Being unable to fashion any kind of litter, Campbell in-sisted that the group carry and drag with them a man wounded in both legs who could not walk. The group left the ice and returned to the shore where the land flattened out south of Pokko-chae, near the small village of Mulgam-ni, about a mile north of the Marine perimeter at Hagaru-ri. Campbell's comments on the group he led describes well numerous small groups of survivors:

> I clearly recall that from where we started on the road [near Mulgam-ni] to the Marine outpost, it was essentially flat. . . . We encountered no trucks or other vehicles . . . and we were on the road less than half an hour or so before reaching the Marine outpost. Considering the somewhat cautious and slow movement of this group of walking wounded, we probably could not have been on the road for much more than a mile. The Korean house we entered shortly before starting on the road was one of a small cluster. As an aside, the discussion of the group in the house is perhaps an indicator of the degree to which the T.F. ceased to function within the accepted struc-ture and roles of a military unit. Up to that time I had unofficially assumed control of the group simply by being at "the point" and by directing that the wounded soldier incapable of walking be dragged with us. Getting peo-ple to help each other was difficult because of the lack of group structure and the prevalent "each man for himself attitude"; however, it appeared that

anyone at all who was able to exercise leadership would get a response. In the shack when one of the group suggested resting there until daylight, I briefly and forcefully vetoed the idea. I was challenged by an older member of the group who asked if I was an officer. I replied to the dissenting soldier giving my rank, name, and unit. The soldier replied, "That's OK for now but we'll have an election later." I didn't reply except to say "Let's move out now," and all did so including the dissenters. . . . Until reaching the marine lines, this group, and possibly others, thought of themselves as the sole group of survivors, functioning in isolation. . . .

After passing through the Marine outpost, we were helped back to a 2½ ton truck about 100 yards down the road from the outpost which transported the group to an aid station where wounds were dressed and antibiotics administered and hands and feet checked for the extent of frostbite. I was then taken [to] a pyramidal tent, already filled with wounded. We were given hot soup and rested until taken out to the airstrip in a Marine Ambulance truck that afternoon, where we joined a queue of ambulances waiting to load wounded aboard C-47s. After about an hour's wait, which seemed interminable—although the ambulances' engines were kept running because of the bitter cold, we were loaded on board for a quick flight to Hamhung, where we were quickly processed through an Army evacuation hospital near the airfield. Our wounds were again checked and in less than three hours we were on our way to Osaka, Japan. Looking out the window of the ambulance bus enroute to the 35th Station Hospital in Kyoto, it seemed unreal to see the lights, civilization and tranquility of Japan after having experienced the decimation of a fine unit in the frozen hell of Chosin less than 24 hours before, and you couldn't help but reflect on the hundreds of brave men who were still lying out there near that God forsaken reservoir.[5]

The treatment received by survivors after they reached the Marine perimeter described by Lieutenant Campbell above was standard for members of the 31st RCT.

At the final enemy fire block, the wounded 1st Battalion, 32nd Infantry, surgeon, Dr. Vincent J. Navarre, was still in the vehicle in which Stamford had placed him earlier in the evening. He wrote about his escape:

The ambulance was stopped right under the fireblock and I crawled out while they were still raking it; then hid in a foxhole right under their noses all night. Early in the morning while they were counting off & dividing supplies I grabbed a pole & walked out one step at a time down that railroad track over the frozen swamp. Any 5-year old could have caught me & the last part of my trip was in broad daylight. Spent the day in a N. Korean hut & at sundown the Koreans took me & 2 GIs on a sleigh ¼ mile to Marines [probably Lt. Col. Olin Beall and his helpers] who took us to Hagaru-ri & eventual evacuation.

The wound was right through the knee joint & the leg broken of course. Without the pole I couldn't have taken a step, but the pole was lying within easy reach. Also was shot thru the little finger of rt. hand & felt the bullet hit my hip. Later I learned the bullet must have hit the hammer of my .45 which was in my pocket, because it was broken off. That saved me from a bad abdominal wound.

Like everyone else I froze something; in this case it was the fingers of my right hand. Also had frost bite of all hands and feet.[6]

Sergeant Alex E. Stevenson, captured at the Chinese assault on the stopped convoy, later escaped. He said that the convoy carried 618 wounded. The Chinese held the convoy for about 10 hours and looted it. During that time they took off an unknown number of prisoners, most of whom could walk.[7] Some who could not walk or soon gave up to exhaustion were helped by friends and later were confined in prison camps.

The Far East Command Daily Intelligence Summary for December 24, 1950, says that Marine Corsairs strafed the convoy after the Chinese had left it, presumably on December 3. There were still Americans in the vicinity at the time, according to at least one witness who reported it later.[8]

When the convoy came to its final stop near Hudong-ni, wounded men and stragglers were scattered all the way back to the first blown bridge and even back to the inlet. One of these was Pfc. Glenn J. Finfrock, D Company, 1st Battalion, 32nd Infantry. He was wounded and lost a great deal of blood and as a result was unconscious until after sunrise on December 2. He was unaware of what had happened to the task force. He gained his feet and struggled down the road until he came in sight of the silent trucks. There he found some other wounded men trying to build a fire. Then he and another soldier tried to start one of the trucks. While they were busy in this effort, they saw some Chinese come out of the village in the distance (Sasu-ri) and head in their direction. Those who could make the effort to get away started for the reservoir; the others were captured. To the surprise of the soldiers, the Chinese administered morphine to some of the wounded and a few days later freed them.[9]

Among the wounded Americans freed by the Chinese were Maj. Robert J. Tolly, acting commander of the 57th Field Artillery Battalion, and

Lt. Lloyd Mielenze, of A Battery. They were released in time to reach Hagaru-ri before the troops there began their withdrawal to the coast on December 6.[10]

Looking ahead to events that happened later, one can record here what became of the American prisoners captured east of Chosin. Operation Little Switch, in which sick and wounded prisoners were repatriated, began on April 20, 1953. In the exchange several American soldiers of the 31st and 32nd regiments wounded at Chosin and in the Task Force Faith breakout on December 1–2, 1950, were returned to U.S. control.[11] They revealed what had happened to them and others captured east of Chosin in 1950.

The American prisoners were first taken a few miles from the battlefield to a holding area for a few days, until the American troops evacuated Hagaru-ri. Then they were taken, mostly by oxcart, to a place the prisoners called "Death Valley," 15 to 30 miles from the battleground, and held there until April, 1951, when they were transferred to Camp Changsung, across the Yalu River in Manchuria. One man, Pfc. Tully Cox, lost both feet, which had frozen and become gangrenous. Two of his prisoner buddies amputated his feet with a penknife at "Death Valley" and saved his life. In July, 1951, a Chinese woman doctor sewed up the stumps of his legs.[12]

Lieutenant Colonel Beall's Rescue Mission

No account of the survivors of Task Force Faith would be satisfactory without an account of the heroic and humanitarian role played by Lt. Col. Olin L. Beall, USMC, who commanded the Marine 1st Motor Transport Battalion, which held a segment of the Hagaru-ri defense perimeter on its northwest arc. In front of the perimeter at that point was an expanse of mined frozen marshland. Just beyond it the Changjin River emptied into the reservoir. Captain Read's H Battery held a section of the perimeter just north of Beall's battalion and on the east side of the Changjin River opposite Beall. Many of the American escapees came into the Marine perimeter through these two units.[13]

During the late afternoon of December 1 the command post of the 1st Motor Transport Battalion received word that pilots had spotted friendly troops making their way south over the ice of Chosin Reservoir toward the Marine perimeter. Just before dark Beall was told that a body of men was approaching his sector. He sent a squad through the minefield at his front to meet and identify the incoming group and guide them through the minefield.

Members of this group mistakenly told Beall that they were the sole survivors of the Army units on the east side of the reservoir. Beall said that of this first group only a few were wounded and that they were a disorganized mob, hysterical with fright, and only a few of them were armed. When he asked them where their weapons were, they replied that they had thrown them away because they were too heavy or were out of ammunition.[14] Another group, consisting of about 50 Americans and 50 ROK soldiers, came through Beall's lines about 10:00 P.M. on December 1. On December 2 and 3, Beall carried out an organized rescue operation of men who had been able to walk or crawl away from the destroyed convoy near Hudong-ni and some men the Chinese had captured and then released.

Lieutenant Colonel Beall was 52 years old at Chosin and had more than 30 years' active-duty service as a Marine enlisted man and officer. He was a Marine of the old school, with a sharp temper and a no-nonsense approach, intemperate in his judgment of troops who did not live up to the highest tradition of discipline and duty. He expressed a low opinion of the Army officers he rescued at Chosin.[15]

Beall wrote about the beginning of his rescue efforts on the morning of December 2, following the nightlong arrival of hundreds of survivors from the 31st RCT:

> The next morning at daylight, thinking that there must be stragglers from this mob of men, I went up to the reservoir to scout the place and while there found some more wounded. Brought in six, then took some trucks and men and went back. We went up the reservoir to Hudong-ni where we spotted a bunch of wounded men on the ice. We eliminated nine snipers on the shore on the way up and upon trying to enter the edge of the reservoir opposite Hudong-ni came under heavy sniper and automatic weapons fire, so we had to leave our jeep out on the ice about 300–400 yards and walk in. When coming under fire we would drop to the ice and they would not fire on us, so this we did and during the day we got out over three hundred (300) of the wounded from the convoy. . . . There were many brave men here this day, men shot through the body helping a buddy, men with hands frozen helping a buddy with a broken leg, men with both legs broken dragging themselves along with their hands and elbows.[16]

On one occasion, Beall said, he crawled to within fifty yards of a Chinese machine gun. The soldier he was trying to rescue yelled, "Go back, go back, they'll kill you!" He nevertheless reached the man, dragged him out, and carried him to the jeep.

Beall's unit had the help of some of the less badly wounded men in the convoy who had been hiding along the edge of the reservoir near Hudong-ni. Sergeant Joe A. Medina, a medical-aid man, said that when the rescue party came out "we had to carry the men from the trucks to the edge of the reservoir because the trucks could not get off the road. I was making my third trip when a Marine Lt. Colonel noticed my leg and arm wounds, ordered me into one of the rescue trucks."[17]

It appears that after daylight dawned on December 2, the Chinese did not search the area between the destroyed convoy and the shore of the reservoir for escapees and survivors from the trucks, nor did they make much effort to prevent Beall from taking off the wounded. After daylight they were largely in the villages of Sasu-ri and Sasu or digging in on the hilltops back from the reservoir along the road. Major Miller's account and the accounts of some others indicate that by December 3 they had left the villages near Hudong-ni and were moving to East Hill, overlooking Hagaru-ri. The Chinese in the vicinity of Hudong-ni on December 3 and later were probably stragglers.

When Beall made his first trip onto the ice on the morning of December 2, he was accompanied by two men, Pfc. Ralph Milton and Corpsman Oscar Biebinger. When he came back with his first group of 6 wounded men and prepared to return to the ice, he had 2nd Lt. Robert Hunt bring trucks to the edge of the reservoir, build fires there, and set up warming tents. Beall obtained a sled and attached it to his jeep so that he could evacuate 12 to 14 men at a time. On the second trip Beall's party came under fire. He halted the jeep and sled and walked by himself toward the shoreline, but the Chinese did not fire on him. Biebinger joined Beall at the shore, and they dragged 7 wounded Americans to the jeep and sled. Milton took these men to the evacuation point they had just established. Beal and Biebinger, meanwhile, continued to make trips to the shoreline to bring out more wounded.

Corporal Andrew Contreras and Lieutenant Hunt drove two more jeeps onto the ice and joined in the evacuation work. As long as the men left their weapons behind and went ashore unarmed, the Chinese did not bother them. Hunt even went inland some distance from shore and returned with wounded. Beall found one man who had compound fractures of both legs. He got him out by using an abandoned rifle sling, looping it around the man's shoulders, and skidding him across the ice. A group of 8 men came out saying that they had been prisoners but that their Chinese captors had brought them to the reservoir and freed them.

About midday a stranger with no rank came out on the ice and joined Beall's group. He was Buck Lefevre, the Red Cross field director for the area. Beall allowed him to stay on the ice, confining his job to directing walking wounded to the evacuation point. During the afternoon a strong, cold wind swept in from the north and made it increasingly difficult to continue the rescue work. With Lefevre now added to his party, Beall had six men on the ice: himself, Lieutenant Hunt, Corpsman Biebinger, Corporal Contreras, Private Milton, and Lefevre. The last stayed on the ice in bitter cold all afternoon until he collapsed from fatigue.

Late in the afternoon some Chinese soldiers on shore decided to interfere with the rescue efforts. Beall noticed them moving onto a finger of land that dominated the place where he had been leaving the ice to go inland short distances to get wounded men. Beall ordered a platoon to come onto the ice with automatic weapons, and the last evacuations before dark were made under their covering fire.

Beall and his men spent about 12 hours on the ice on December 2 in temperatures that reached −24° F. During that time they evacuated from the ice and the shore of the reservoir an almost incredible total of 319 American and ROK soldiers and brought them into Marine lines.[18]

On the morning of December 3 aerial observers reported more wounded men on the ice. Beall, Milton, and Cpl. William Howard went out on the ice. They found four soldiers huddled together under blankets in a fishing boat frozen tight in the reservoir. Enemy fire on Beall's group was heavier than at any time the previous day. The men told Beall that they had been prisoners, that two Chinese soldiers had taken them to the reservoir, and that when they started to walk away over the ice the Chinese had shot their legs from under them. The four wounded men had dragged themselves to the boat and had kept alive during the night by huddling together under the blankets. Beall later wrote of this incident:

> We came under heavy machine gun and sniper fire but an observation plane called in air to cover us and under close air support that came in at times less than ten feet off the ice we got the four men out, and this is the story of two of them. An officer and some men passed them and said that they could not help them off and left them there to die. Both of these men had both legs broken, one had sixteen bullets in his legs, the other twelve; the

other two men were severely wounded, one having both legs broken, the other one leg broken, three bullets in the other and a broken arm. These men were very bitter against their officers and freely said so. In fact, I had to order them to stop as it was getting them into a hysterical state.[19]

Beall sent the four men to the Marine lines in his jeep. Then, leaving his gun on the ice, he started alone for the reservoir shore. He was opposite Hudong-ni and still had air cover and was not fired on. Inland a short distance he came to the line of Task Force Faith's abandoned truck convoy. He later commented: "I went through that convoy and saw dead in each vehicle, stretchers piled up with men frozen to death trying to pull themselves out from under another stretcher. Yes, I saw this and I shall never forget it . . . (this statement later proven by the undersigned actually finding seventeen (17) stretcher cases in one 6 × 6 truck)."[20]

Beall went down the line of trucks from the first to the last but found no one alive. He returned to the ice, Milton picked him up, and they returned to Hagaru-ri over the ice. Thus on the morning of December 3, Beall and his helpers seemingly had rescued the last of the men who had escaped from the convoy.[21] The 1st Marine Division's official history of the Chosin operation refers to a Marine patrol that went to the destroyed task-force convoy. The reference must be to Lieutenant Colonel Beall's visit to it. I have found no report of a patrol to the convoy in the Marine G-3 Journal and Message file. The Marine official history gives an estimate of 300 dead men in the convoy, an estimate apparently given by Beall, though he does not give an estimate in his own written report.

If one adds the 4 men rescued on the morning of December 3 to the count of 319 rescued the day before, a total of 323 men were rescued from the reservoir and its shore near Hudong-ni. The estimate of some 300 dead left in the trucks indicates that about 600 men were in the vehicles when the convoy came to its final halt. The 1st Motor Transport Battalion report states that all these men were wounded, "with more than 50% with very severe wounds."

Major General Edward M. Almond, X Corps commander, presented Lieutenant Colonel Beall with the Distinguished Service Cross at Hagaru-ri on December 4, 1950, for his soldierly and life-saving rescue work at Chosin Reservoir, an award richly deserved.[22] There was no other rescue of so many men, with so many lives saved, during the Korean War. It was attributable largely to the initiative and valorous leadership of one man.

The last group of survivors from east of Chosin noted in the official records came into Hagaru-ri on December 5, the day before all the American troops there and in the Chosin area began their withdrawal to the coast. General Almond left his X Corps CP at Hamhung at 10:45 on the morning of December 5, and flew in an L-17 plane to Hagaru-ri. Coming in to land, he observed a scene which he recorded in his diary for the day: "A group of 30 individuals deployed around two vehicles or large sleds were observed making their way across the ice of Chosin Lake from the eastern edge toward Hagaru-ri. This group appeared to have four fighters protecting its movement."[23]

20

The Question of a Relief Force

The 7th Infantry Division Action Report for December, 1950, states that on the morning of December 2 a tank-infantry force tried to fight its way from Hagaru-ri up the east side of Chosin Reservoir to meet Task Force Faith but that heavy enemy opposition forced it back. The official US Marine Corps history of the Chosin Reservoir makes a similar statement: "A company-size task force of Army troops from Hagaru-ri, supported by tanks, moved out that day to bring in any organized units of the three shattered battalions which might have been left behind. Known as Task Force Anderson after Lieutenant Colonel Berry K. Anderson, senior Army officer at Hagaru-ri, the column met heavy CCF opposition and was recalled when it became evident that only stragglers remained."[1]

These statements are untrue. No such relief force ever left Hagaru-ri to help rescue Task Force Faith.

That a relief force was needed to rescue the 31st RCT on the east side of Chosin Reservoir was evident as early as midafternoon on November 30. At the commanders' conference that afternoon at Hagaru-ri, General Almond ordered General Smith to bring a Marine regiment from Yudam-ni to effect the rescue of the 31st RCT. After the conference ended, General Smith and General Barr, the 7th Division commander, agreed that no Marine troops could be spared from the Hagaru-ri defense perimeter, that it was already precariously thin, and that no rescue troops would be available until the cutoff Marine troops at Yudam-ni could fight their way through to Hagaru-ri. It would be December 4 before the vanguard began to reach Hagaru-ri. This left it up to Faith's troops to fight their way out on their own, with the help of Marine close air support.

293

Command arrangements in the Chosin Reservoir area suddenly changed on the night of November 29 when General Almond issued his Operations Instruction No. 19 at 8:47 P.M. It provided that as of 8:00 A.M. the next morning, November 30, all troops in the Chosin area north of Koto-ri would be under the command of the 1st Marine Division commander. Therefore, beginning on the morning of November 30, Task Force Faith at the inlet and the 31st Rear and the 31st Tank Company at Hudong-ni were under the command of General Smith.

This X Corps order led General Barr to discuss the matter with General Smith at Hagaru-ri on November 30 and to tell him that he would recall Hodes from the Chosin area to avoid any possible embarrassment for all concerned. It was also probably one of the reasons General Barr flew by helicopter that morning to Faith's CP at the inlet. Although we do not know any details of that conversation, we can speculate that Barr told Faith of the change in command that might affect him.[2]

Colonel Bowser, the 1st Marine Division G-3, told S. L. A. Marshall in an interview that X Corps sent the order recalling Hodes to the coast but did not state when it occurred—or at least it is not recorded in Marshall's transcript of the interview, nor is it recorded in any of the official records I have seen. Major William R. Lynch, Hodes's G-3 aide at Hagaru-ri, took Hodes to the airstrip on the morning of December 1 to meet an L-5 plane that General Barr had sent to pick him up. But Hodes returned to Hagaru-ri shortly after daylight on December 2. According to Lynch, Hodes returned to Hamhung again sometime after noon the same day.

Copies of all orders from the 1st Marine Division during the night of December 1–2 relating to a relief force for Task Force Faith were sent to Lt. Col. Berry K. Anderson, the senior army officer at Hagaru-ri from the 31st RCT and de facto unit commander of all 31st Infantry troops that had arrived at Hagaru-ri. As Marshall states in his interview notes, Colonel Bowser gave him the impression that "an attempt was made, however, by a 7th Div CP 'Task Force' under Lt. Col. Anderson to feel out the situation on to the north and was promptly met by CCF fire. Accordingly, Hodes was advised that 7th Div's elements would have to get out as best they could and he wrote the order so instructing them. The order was written by Hodes, but issued by Gen. Smith."[3] Either Bowser was wrong or Marshall misunderstood what Bowser said about "a 7th Div CP 'Task Force' under Lt. Col. Anderson" being sent out. The order referred to by Bowser as having been written by Hodes but issued by General Smith was the order that Task Force Faith received about 3:00 P.M. on December 1 after the task force had already been in its breakout movement for two hours.

There are two kinds of evidence bearing on the question of whether a rescue attempt was made from Hagaru-ri on the morning of December 2: (1) documentary evidence and (2) testimony of persons who would have been participants. Let us examine the documentary evidence first. A 1st Marine Division handwritten order, listed in the G-3 Journal as Serial No. 18, December 1, issued at noon to Lieutenant Colonel Anderson, reads:

> 01 1200
>
> Lt. Col. Anderson ordered to form Company sized Unit with tanks for operating on 2 Dec to render all possible assistance to Elements RCT-31 attempting to close Hagaru-ri. Troops to be drawn from Army personnel RCT 31 this vicinity. Air and Arty support for operations planned.
>
> Col. Anderson stated that he preferred for several reasons to take only equivalent of two platoons with tanks.
>
> Desires TACP and FO [word obscured] to accompany party. *Further arrangements—plus authority for a two platoon rather than one company unit to be made tomorrow* [italics added].
>
> Plans to jump off between 0930 and 1000 2 December.
>
> [three illegible initials][4]

For reasons unknown, Lieutenant Colonel Anderson wanted only two platoons of infantry-type troops to accompany the tanks, rather than the company-size force that the 1st Marine Division thought necessary. Since there was a difference of opinion on this point, the order said that a decision on it, and also on other arrangements, would be made the next day, December 2. I could find no further action by the 1st Marine Division on this tentative order on December 1 or 2 and must conclude that it was never completed in final form.

The next relevant message in the 1st Marine Division G-3 Journal is one dated December 1, 2115 (9:15 P.M.), Serial No. 37. It is a memorandum from Major Lynch reporting a telephone conversation with General Hodes, who was at the chief of staff's office, X Corps, at Hamhung. Lynch delivered this message to Lt. Col. J. L. Winecoff, assistant G-3, 1st Marine Division. This handwritten message reads in its entirety:

012115

Notes for G-3

The following information was given to Gen. Hodes in the C/S Office at X Corps.

1. Details of arrival of two groups from 7th Div under your comd.
2. That every arrangement possible is being made to Hosp—Feed—House this group.
3. That lookout is being maintained for the remainder of the 31st RCT including motor column.
4. That a complete issue of clothing and bed-sacks should reach here on 1st C-47 to re-equip this group. (Total 500 estimate) Gen H will arrange.

Gen. Hodes requested that you consider sending out an Armored-Inf Force at Day-light 2 Dec to intercept this Motor Clm of the 31st Inf. (Use our TKs) First locate the column by air.

[initialed by three sets   Lynch
of illegible signatures,   Maj. USA[5]
Marine personnel]

In the 1st Marine Division G-3 Journal and Message files for the period 4:00 A.M., December 2, only one entry, Serial No. 21, at 12:50 P.M., December 2, relates clearly to Task Force Faith. It states: "11th Marine Report of en positions firing on Army trps coming from north." Serial No. 34, at 1610 (4:10 P.M.), December 2, reads: "11th Mar—air strike just led [word seems inappropriate] in vic Army convoy to the North."[6] A truck driver in the convoy said that after the Chinese left the looted convoy Marine Corsairs strafed it.[7]

Now let us examine the personal testimony of those who would have been participants in a rescue effort. We know that Hodes left Hagaru-ri sometime during the morning of December 1 and was at Hamhung at 9:15 P.M. that night. After Lynch's report to him from Hagaru-ri by radio telephone at the X Corps Headquarters on the great number of 31st RCT soldiers arriving at Hagaru-ri in the early part of the night and their condition, Hodes must have thought that he should return as soon as possible to help the victims of the developing catastrophe. Most of the men would have to be reequipped to help fight the rest of the way to the coast. He was at Hagaru-ri shortly after daylight on December 2, according to the testimony of several reliable witnesses. Major Lynch confirms that Hodes was there on the morning of December 2. Lynch believes that Hodes took off from Hamhung in a light plane as soon as it was light enough to fly on the morning of December 2 and was at Hagaru-ri soon after daylight.

Lynch remarks on visiting, with General Hodes, the next morning, December 2, the men who had come in overnight: "The morning after I met the officers and men straggling across the ice from units east of Chosin, General Hodes, Anderson and I walked through the area where tents were being erected, officers and men were being counted and assembled in their respective companies, fed, and lost equipment noted."[8]

I sent an inquiry to Col. Thomas L. Ridge, USMC, Ret., who in 1950 was commander of the 3rd Battalion, 1st Marine Regiment, and designated Hagaru-ri defense commander, asking for his knowledge and recollection of whether a relief force left Hagaru-ri on the morning of December 2 to reach Task Force Faith. Ridge replied: "I do not recall that an attack was attempted. There was some discussion which, as I recall, I favored within bounds."[9]

According to Lynch, after Hodes arrived back at Hagaru-ri: "I was with Gen H [on] and off for the next two (+) hours, at the end of which time I took him to the airstrip for the last time. He talked with the men as he moved about. . . . On reflection, Gen H's main interest at that time was simply that this group had a fight ahead of them and they should get organized, weapons ready and be prepared for what then seemed a rough exodus for both Army and Marines."[10]

Evidence of Hodes's presence at Hagaru-ri on the morning of December 2 is confirmed by Major Curtis's statement that he and Captain Bigger saw General Hodes at the Hagaru-ri airstrip that morning when they were waiting for a C-47 plane to carry them to a hospital in Japan. Curtis said that Bigger went over to Hodes and spoke to him briefly. Captain Bigger in his own statement on this incident said: "General Hodes was in the perimeter on 1 Dec [Dec 2] as I met and talked with him prior to my departure 2 Dec by C-47. Hodes was sorely distressed and frustrated."[11]

In an interview with General Lynch, I asked him bluntly whether a relief force left Hagaru-ri on the morning of December 2. He answered simply, "No, there was no rescue force from Hagaru-ri that morning."[12]

Captain Robert E. Drake, commander of the 31st Tank Company, is another witness. His tanks would have been the ones used in such a rescue force. Drake says that he did not participate, nor did his tanks, in any relief force on December 2.[13]

It is evident that General Hodes consulted with General Smith and other members of the 1st Marine Division staff during the morning of December 2 on whether a rescue force, made up of Marine infantry and Drake's 31st Tank Company, could or should attempt to reach the stalled convoy at Hudong-ni. Factors that had to be considered included knowledge that, while Drake's tank company would be used for the armored element, there was no Army infantry to supply the infantry element. The only foot troops that Lieutenant Colonel Anderson had brought with him from Hudong-ni on the afternoon of November 30 were about 100 men from the 57th Field Artillery Service Battery and 34 men from the 31st Infantry Headquarters and Headquarters Company and Service troops (there were 176 officers and men in the 31st Tank Company), according to a count made on December 3. Lynch's note to the 1st Marine Division G-3 Section relaying General Hodes's telephone request on the evening of December 1 implied that the 31st RCT could not supply infantry and that the infantry element of a rescue force would have to be provided by the 1st Marine Division.

Another factor that entered into the consideration of a rescue mission was the report by night heckler aircraft that Task Force Faith's trucks were burning on the road. After daylight aircraft pilots were able to report the location of the looted and silent convoy.

All night long survivors of Task Force Faith arrived with their accounts of the 31st RCT dissolution as a fighting force. Their wounds and frozen and frostbitten feet and hands supported their stories. After midnight many of them came from the convoy's final encounter with the last enemy fire block at the site of the convoy's destruction. It must have seemed increasingly clear that a rescue effort, even if it reached the site, could do no more than pick up a few stragglers who had succeeded in hiding from the Chinese and wounded who had been left by the Chinese to die, and possibly to gain further knowledge of the end of the task force and of the dead in the trucks. The evidence available at the Marine Division CP at Hagaru-ri after daylight on December 2 must have convinced the commander that it was too late to rescue the motor convoy. But for many the frustrations ran deep.

In a review of the evidence, both documentary and personal, only one conclusion is possible: *There was no tank-infantry force, or any other kind of rescue force, that left Hagaru-ri to go to the aid of Task Force Faith's motor convoy on December 2 or any subsequent date.* Such a force had been considered on December 1 and that night, but the preliminary Marine order issued at noon on December 1 to Lieutenant Colonel Anderson of the 31st Infantry was never issued in final form or implemented. What role General Hodes played in the discussions with General Smith and his 1st Marine Division staff on the morning of December 2 is unknown. Possibly General Smith and his G-3 staff had already made the decision before Hodes arrived back at Hagaru-ri that the 1st Marine Division could not supply an infantry company from its own defense force and, further, that it was too late to rescue the convoy and that in trying to reach the convoy north of Hudong-ni the rescue force might be cut off or be severely mauled by Chinese now known to control high ground on the road from a mile north of the Hagaru-ri defense perimeter. The men who could clarify details of the final decision—General Hodes, General Barr, General Smith, and Colonel Anderson—have been dead for several years.[14]

On the morning of December 2, as he flew away from the Chosin Reservoir for the last time, General Hodes must have felt a deep sense of failure and heartache about his efforts to serve his 7th Infantry Division troops and comrades east of Chosin.

21

American and Enemy Losses

All the equipment and vehicles of two infantry battalions, the 57th Field Artillery Battalion and D Battery (−), 15th AAA AW Battalion, and the forward part of the 31st Regimental Headquarters and Headquarters Company were lost in the actions east of Chosin in the period November 27 to December 2, 1950. Not a single vehicle, artillery piece, mortar, or machine gun of these units was saved; only some small arms carried by individual escaping soldiers were brought out. Sixteen tanks of the 31st Tank Company and the vehicles of the 31st Rear that did not go farther north than Hudong-ni were withdrawn with accompanying troops to Hagaru-ri on November 30.

The number of troops in the 31st RCT east of Chosin on November 27, 1950, is not known precisely, but estimates range from 2,500 to 3,155. The 1st Marine Division and Major Curtis made the lower estimate. Several officers of the RCT estimated its number at Chosin to be from 2,850 to 3,000 men, while Major Lynch thought that the count was about 3,000.[1] I think that the number may have been marginally higher than 3,000.

Personnel losses in the 31st RCT were heavy in killed, wounded, injured, frozen and frostbitten hands and feet, and captured. All the combat units of the RCT except the 31st Tank Company were combat-ineffective by December 1. No attempt has been made to give American or enemy casualties day by day or for any particular phase of the fighting. They simply are not known. Losses for the enemy at any given time would be little more than guesses. One can be sure that Marine fighter planes killed and wounded hundreds and perhaps thousands of the CCF 80th Division, and ground fire of the RCT elements engaged also produced hundreds of casualties, but no exact numbers can be given.

Although the CCF 80th Division destroyed the 31st RCT as a combat-effective force, it itself became virtually combat-ineffective after winning control of the east side of the reservoir. Some parts of the division probably took part in the attacks on Hagaru-ri from the night of November 28 through December 6, and soldiers from it were identified later near Hamhung during the evacuation of X Corps from northeast Korea. On the basis of evidence known, it is my conclusion that the CCF 80th Division was the only enemy formation engaged against the 31st RCT.

Fortunately for the American wounded, the incomplete airstrip at Hagaru-ri became operational for C-47 aircraft on December 1. Thus hundreds of Task Force Faith survivors were flown out on December 2 and every day thereafter through December 5. Evacuation of wounded had become so critical that on December 1 General Smith authorized a trial landing of a C-47 transport plane on the new airstrip, which was only 40 percent complete. The strip was 50 feet wide and 2,000 feet long, with a 2 percent grade to the north. Earlier, from November 27 to December 1, the only wounded who could be evacuated from the Chosin Reservoir area were the critically wounded, who were taken out by helicopters and small planes. These earlier air evacuees numbered 152, mostly Marines from Yudam-ni.

At 2:30 P.M. on December 1 the first Far East Air Force C-47 made a bouncing but successful landing on the uncompleted airstrip. Half an hour later its pilot took off with 24 casualties. Thus began the massive air evacuation of wounded from the Chosin Reservoir combat area. Three more C-47 planes came in during the afternoon and left with about 60 more casualties. The last plane in, a Marine 4RD, brought a heavy load of ammunition, collapsed its landing gear on the rough strip, and had to be destroyed. But the way was open for a continuing evacuation of wounded by Air Force C-47 and Marine 4RD planes in the days that followed.

Only one four-engine plane ever landed at and took off from the Hagaru-ri airstrip. That was on December 1, the first day of the strip's use by transport planes, through a mistake made at Yonpo Airfield, on the coast. A Navy pilot, B. J. Miller, had flown an R5D plane to Yonpo from Japan. He learned about the numerous critically wounded survivors at Hagaru-ri and offered to fly a plane there to help get them out. The operations officer, assuming that Miller had a two-engine plane, gave permission. Normally

Miller's plane required a runway 4,000 to 5,000 feet long, but somehow Miller landed the plane at Hagaru-ri, to the astonishment of all. Then he loaded 39 wounded men on the plane and from the extreme end of the runway, and at full throttle, took off, clearing the first ridgeline by only 30 feet.[2]

On December 2, 960 casualties were flown out of Hagaru-ri, many of them 31st RCT men. The next day 464 casualties were air-evacuated; on December 4, 1,077; on December 5, 1,580—a total of 4,081 Marine and Army casualties in four days. The planes landed at Yonpo, and the wounded were delivered to X Corps clearing stations. Marine casualties went to the 1st Marine Division Hospital in Hungnam; Army soldiers went to the Army 121st Evacuation Hospital in Hamhung and to the hospital ship USS *Consolation* in Hungnam harbor. Wounded requiring 30 days' or more hospitalization were flown from Yonpo to Japan, but some more critically wounded were evacuated directly from Hagaru-ri to Japan. Major Curtis and Captain Bigger were among the Task Force Faith officers evacuated on December 2, while Captain Stamford left on December 3. From December 2 to 5 more than 1,500 wounded and frostbitten men of the 7th Division were flown from Hagaru-ri to hospitals in Japan.[3]

There is evidence that in the evacuation of 31st RCT soldiers from Hagaru-ri on December 2 some men, in their exhausted mental and physical condition, feigned wounds, frostbite, injuries, and illnesses beyond their actual severity to obtain evacuation, when they could have continued on duty with their units. This seemed to have happened only during part of one day, December 2. Captain Eugene R. "Bud" Hering, USN, senior medical officer of the 1st Marine Division, heard complaints that some men were being evacuated without sufficient reason. He began a close examination of men boarding the planes and weeded out those who were exaggerating their injuries, effectively stopping the practice.

Captain Hering and his C and E companies of the Marine Medical Battalion had the almost impossible task of treating the hundreds of wounded that poured into Hagaru-ri. His performance and that of the units he commanded were admirable. Within one 48-hour period he treated, processed, and evacuated by air 1,500 Army and 1,000 Marine wounded.[4]

After the evacuation of wounded from Hagaru-ri there remained 490 7th Division able-bodied soldiers, including 385 survivors from the 31st RCT. These men were organized into a provisional battalion under the command of Lt. Col. Berry K. Anderson and attached to the 7th Marine Regiment.

To the Marines this unit was known as 31/7. It participated in the 1st Marine Division breakout from Hagaru-ri to the coast beginning on December 6. The 385 men from east of Chosin, now a part of Anderson's provisional battalion, constituted what was left of the approximately 3,000 men who had been in the RCT on November 27. Adding to the 385 men the 1,500 who were evacuated makes a total of just under 1,900 men, indicating about 1,000 soldiers killed, captured, or left for various reasons in enemy-held territory. It is not known how many men were left along the road or on the hills in the roadblock and fire-block areas who later died of wounds and exposure. Nor are there reliable figures on the large numbers captured by the Chinese or the number of those who died during captivity. In the weather conditions it was inevitable that many wounded soldiers, who also had parts of their bodies frozen or frostbitten, died trying to escape from the battlefield.

On December 3, Major Lynch made a count of the American soldiers from the 31st RCT at Hagaru-ri and reported it by radio telephone to Maj. Gen. Clark L. Ruffner, X Corps chief of staff. This report shows Lieutenant Colonel Anderson, commanding; Maj. Carl G. Witte, executive officer; and Captain Dovell, S-3 of the group, which numbered 40 officers and 844 enlisted men, a total of 884 men. In this total Lynch had a count of 21 officers and 304 enlisted men, a total of 325 men, from the Hudong-ni schoolhouse perimeter area. Of these 325, 6 officers and 170 enlisted men had been in Drake's 31st Tank Company.

From the 1st Battalion, 32nd Infantry, there were 5 officers and 228 men; from the 3rd Battalion, 31st Infantry, 7 officers and 165 men; and from the 57th Field Artillery Battalion, including D Battery (–), 15th AAA AW Battalion, 11 officers and 197 men. Of the rifle companies in the two infantry battalions K and M companies had the fewest men, and the same count, 1 officer and 30 men each. Of the three rifle companies and the Heavy Weapons Company, 1st Battalion, 32nd Infantry, A Company had 1 officer, and the others none. Many of the men in the count of December 3 were air-evacuated on December 4–5.[5] When Hodes left Hagaru-ri, he ordered Lynch and Sergeants Cox and Hammer to remain behind, Lynch to act as a 7th Division liaison officer with the 1st Marine Division.[6]

Some members of the 1st Battalion, 32nd Infantry; the 3rd Battalion, 31st Infantry; and the 31st Infantry regimental staff and Headquarters Company in Lieutenant Colonel Anderson's provisional battalion were killed or wounded in the fighting during the withdrawal from Hagaru-ri to Koto-ri and on top of Funchilin Pass. Thereafter in the continued withdrawal to the coast the 31st RCT provisional battalion was in reserve and was not engaged in combat.

Many officers and men air-evacuated from Hagaru-ri from December 2 to 5 returned to their regiments after recovering from their wounds and frostbite, most of them in January and February, 1951. By then the 7th Infantry Division, still a part of X Corps, had entered the Eighth Army line in central Korea. Among the officers who returned were Major Curtis, Captain Bigger, Captain Vaudreaux, and Lieutenants May, Campbell, and Mortrude. Capt. Earle H. Jordan, promoted to major, returned to duty as the S-3, operations officer, 2nd Battalion, 31st Infantry. Major Lynch, promoted to lieutenant colonel, was assigned to command the 2nd Battalion, 31st Infantry. When he learned that Jordan's wounds had healed and he was returning to the regiment, he requested and was granted Jordan's assignment to his battalion.

Little is known of the CCF strength and losses east of Chosin. If the 80th Division was of average Chinese strength of those engaged in the Chosin Reservoir Campaign, it had 7,000 to 8,000 men at the beginning. The number of casualties it sustained during the actions against the 31st RCT east of Chosin is unknown, but it was a very large number, totaling in the thousands. It is known that the 80th and 79th Chinese divisions were so decimated that they were not combat-effective when they went into bivouac near Hamhung after X Corps evacuated northeast Korea. These Chinese divisions did not reenter combat until March–April, 1951, when they took frontline sectors on the central Korean front.[7]

Could Task Force Faith
Have Been Saved?

The fate that overtook Task Force Faith was one of the worst disasters for American soldiers in the Korean War. Could it have been avoided? I think that the answer is a speculative yes. If certain things had been done that were in the realm of the possible, then the story could have had a different ending. Few disasters occur spontaneously. Most are due to a chain of significant circumstances that build to a cumulative finale. Often a backward glance over the course of events seems to indicate that the result was foreordained. But a critical analysis will ordinarily reveal factors that might have been avoided or corrected to bring about a different outcome. Part of the answer is framed in Kipling's words:

> If you can force your heart and nerve and sinew
> To serve your turn long after they are gone
> And so hold on when there is nothing in you
> Except the Will which says to them: "Hold on."

That, however, does not say it all. In military affairs a big part of the answer lies in the wisdom of command.

The main adverse factors for Task Force Faith were: (1) lack of communications; (2) lack of effective ammunition and gasoline resupply; (3) lack of air-reconnaissance intelligence on physical obstacles on the withdrawal route; (4) short daylight period; (5) a breakout plan hastily decided upon and providing no options as it progressed; (6) depleted officer and noncommissioned officer leadership for troop control; (7) surviving troops exhausted by four days and five nights of battle in frigid weather; (8) and a

305

higher-command decision to withdraw the 31st Tank Company and the 31st Infantry Rear from Hudong-ni the day before the breakout effort. Without adequate communications in a military organization, both upward and downward in command echelon, in action a given unit becomes a struggling organism without its central nervous system. It flounders. The most powerful radio the 31st RCT had east of Chosin was the SCR 193 that Colonel MacLean had on the ¾-ton vehicle that he left at the 31st Rear at Hudong-ni. It failed about midnight on November 27 in the course of a brief radio conversation between General Hodes and General Barr.

The 31st Rear radios were not netted to the 1st Marine Division, and those CPs therefore had no radio communication with each other though they were only five miles apart. Only when General Hodes took one of the 31st Tank Company tanks to Hagaru-ri on the afternoon of November 28 was there any radio communication between Hagaru-ri and Hudong-ni, and it was limited to messages between the one tank Hodes had at Hagaru-ri and the 31st Tank Company tanks at Hudong-ni. Major Lynch wrote: "General Hodes had one of Drake's tanks and this was the sole means of communication with the School House [at Hudong-ni] from Hagaru-ri."[1]

The mountainous country and the extremely cold weather, which weakened batteries, rendered the infantry battalion and company radios all but useless. The radios were mostly World War II instruments rebuilt in Japan. Their life-span in Korea proved to be short.

Major Lynch remarked about the serious communications problem:

> There was no command and control setup established either at regiment with MacLean or with General Hodes which would enable either to get information and influence counter action. It was a case of the blind leading the blind so far as command control was concerned. Bits of unclear information came to us over a multitude of radios. Usually source was uncertain other than we got the picture that the units up forward were eyeball to eyeball with the Chinese. This communication garble lasted through midday on the 28th. After that information dwindled progressively to zero. Communications were never established with the 1st Mar Div CP.[2]

After late afternoon of November 28 neither of the forward infantry battalion commanders nor the field artillery commander could reach the 31st Infantry Rear at Hudong-ni, and they had never been able to reach the Marines at Hagaru-ri. The Fifth Air Force TACP attached to the 3rd Battalion, 31st Infantry, never had a chance to function during the battles with the Chinese. It was overrun at the communications headquarters the first night of the battle. Lieutenant Johnson, the TACP leader, was killed, and his radio equipment was damaged. The TACP thus had no opportunity to call in any air strikes at the inlet perimeter. Only from November 29, when Captain Stamford and his TACP with the 1st Battalion, 32nd Infantry, arrived at the inlet, did the 3rd Battalion and the 57th Field Artillery Battalion receive the benefit of a TACP. According to Stamford, the 31st RCT need not have been isolated without communication to the outside world. He said: "My AN/GRC-1 was capable of tuning any High Frequency used by U.S. Forces air or land. Had we been given a frequency used by a pilot or had Gen. Barr brought one with him, or someone air dropped one, we could have been in business. The 1st Mar Div Air Section knew what kind of equipment I had."[3]

The lack of communication applied also to a very large extent within the task force, especially when any of its elements were in movement. Curtis, the 1st Battalion operations officer, commented on the lack of reliable communications within the 31st RCT itself, which compounded its problems. "Wire communications within the perimeter were good," he said, "but during movement, radio communication from Bn to Co. to platoon was practically non-existent. This contributed greatly to the loss of control. Example: the movement from the forward perimeter to the Inlet. I was on the east flank—but out of communications with the command group and the company commanders. The Command Group was out of communication with Miller and the rear guard. Runners *could not run* in the snow in shoe pacs!"[4] The lack of communication by runners within the task force was disastrous during the breakout attempt from the inlet perimeter on December 1 and was one of the factors leading to loss of control of the troops early in the afternoon.

There is considerable evidence that coordination within the task force was not good. The lack of coordination is partly chargeable to Lieutenant Colonel Faith. Major Curtis, for instance, was never informed of Faith's action in placing Major Miller in charge of the 1st Battalion on December 1 with a staff of his own. Nor did Curtis know that Faith had designated Major Robbins, of the 31st Infantry, the S-4 of the task force. Some units of the 3rd Battalion, 31st Infantry, seem not to have been well informed on the breakout plan.

Colonel Embree has stated that "during the action on the east side of the Chosin Reservoir (in either the initial position area of the HQ and HQ Btry, or in the subsequent position area with the two howitzer batteries)

I had no contact, verbal or written with LTC Faith nor with LTC Reilly."[5] This is almost incredible when one reflects that Faith, Reilly, and Embree were within the same small inlet perimeter after the morning of November 29.

Major McClymont has said that he received orders or instructions only once from anyone within the inlet perimeter. That was on the morning of December 1 when Lieutenant Colonel Faith told him to place an M19 full-track dual-40 at the point of the breakout column, as requested by Major Miller. The lack of communication with Major McClymont in the form of orders and instructions seems strange, considering the vital role his antiaircraft weapons played in the defense of the perimeter.

In discussing with survivors the questions of coordination and communication in the task force and its several units at the inlet perimeter, I found almost all in agreement that they were poor. Hugh May has written of the situation: "In general terms there was very little of the who, what, why, when, and where forthcoming. . . . These five points of information failed to be issued from the inlet CP and in my opinion was partially responsible for the disintegration later. Some of the points were issued in the orders rec but not all and surely not adequately covered (in my opinion). Majors Miller and Curtis did their best to correct that mistake."[6]

After Colonel MacLean and General Hodes arrived at the reservoir and until the morning of November 30, the 7th Infantry Division had responsibility for the 31st RCT on the east side of the reservoir. It had to be apparent that the 31st RCT was isolated and had no communication with higher command. It should have been mandatory for higher headquarters to send a liaison officer, using a liaison-type plane from Hamhung to Hagaru-ri and a helicopter from there to Task Force Faith at the inlet daily from November 29 on to ensure that needs in ammunition, gasoline, batteries, spare parts, and food were known and delivered by airdrop. Such regular liaison would have provided a means of communicating information and orders for needed cooperative action. But such liaison was not established. Only once from November 27 through December 1 did an officer from a higher headquarters visit the inlet perimeter.

Regular liaison visits should have eliminated one of the causes of the ultimate disaster—the failure of ammunition resupply, especially certain ammunition for particular weapons that were vital for a successful defense of the perimeter and for a successful breakout. There were airdrops on several days, but some of them went to the enemy when high winds drifted the parachutes away from the intended drop zone and into Chinese-held territory.

The resupply of .50-caliber ammunition fell far short of meeting the needs of the M16 quad-50s with their tremendous automatic firepower, and not a single 40-mm shell was delivered to the perimeter for the M19 dual-40s, the most destructive weapon of all against close enemy attack and enemy close-in assembly areas. The one large airdrop of 40-mm ammunition on the 28th or 29th of November came down at the wrong place. The pilot carrying the 40-mm shells dropped them at Hudong-ni, where the 31st Tank Company and the 31st Rear had no use for them. The men stacked the 40-mm ammunition, and when the units left Hudong-ni on the afternoon of November 30, Captain Drake ordered it destroyed. That ammunition would have been invaluable for the M19s and Task Force Faith at the inlet and in the breakout attempt.

McClymont has commented: "I have always regretted that the re-supply of ammunition and gasoline [was] not received by us when we so desperately needed them. . . . perhaps with a little better planning we could have easily extracted ourselves, and there would have been no Chosin Reservoir incident for us to remember, to relive, and to write about."[7] Captain Bigger echoed that thought, saying: "The Quad 50 and the Dual-40 are magnificent ground support weapons. If a few more of these weapons with their tracked ability had been available with ammunition we could have made it."[8]

The troops at the inlet did not know about the drop of 40-mm shells at Hudong-ni, only three air miles south of them. When I first mentioned it to Major Stamford in 1979, he exploded with "Those d——— knuckleheads!" In correspondence with me Drake told about the airdrop of 40-mm shells at Hudong-ni and the failure to deliver to him the 76-mm and 105-mm shells he needed for his tank guns.

It is necessary to dwell a moment on what the lack of 40-mm shells for the M19s and belted .50-caliber ammunition for the M16s meant when the breakout started. Captain McClymont said, "The lead M19 twin 40 mm had precious little ammunition, perhaps enough for some targets of opportunity." By the time the M19 and the point of the motor column reached the first blown bridge two miles down the road it was out of ammunition. The M19 proved its tremendous value there in another way, however, for its full-track locomotion enabled it to pull the vehicles in the column around the blown bridge over an unimproved bypass. But just beyond, on the road climbing obliquely to the saddle of Hill 1221, the motor column and the foot soldiers were stopped by an enemy fire block.

In my view, if the M19 and the M16s had been well supplied with ammunition after reaching the blown bridge and the road beyond, they could have suppressed the terribly costly enemy fire from the valley and the ridges north of the road at Hill 1221 and very likely would also have quickly suppressed the fire from the enemy fire block at the saddle of Hill 1221 at the hairpin turn. They could have swept away many of the enemy positions on Hill 1221. The motor convoy could then have passed around Hill 1221 before dark. If the M19 and M16s had been supplied with ammunition and had been accompanying the motor column when it ran into the final enemy fire block at Hudong-ni, the M19 probably could have reduced that enemy fire position as well. But the M16s had long since run out of ammunition and the M19, also out of ammunition, ran out of gasoline shortly after it had pulled the last truck around the blown bridge bypass.

The failure of the rear guard, the 31st Infantry and the 57th Field Artillery, to protect the rear of the motor column at the first blown bridge was an important factor in the chaos and destruction that overtook the road column below the CCF fire block at the hairpin turn on Hill 1221. That situation reminds one of Xenophon's conversation with Cyrus on the subject of tactics in war, when the latter said: "Behind all the rest I shall station the so-called rear guard of veteran reserves. . . . a phalanx is good for nothing, unless both front and rear are composed of valiant men."[9]

A breakout effort from the inlet perimeter had been a probability for at least 24 hours before it was launched, and in that period thought should have been given to its eventuality. When the decision came, however, it was apparently entirely ad hoc, prompted by what seemed necessity. We know that Faith decided on the breakout about 10:00 A.M. on the morning of December 1 and that Majors Miller and Curtis urged it on him. They thought that the remaining force would be overrun in another night of Chinese attacks on the perimeter. When the Corsair appeared over the inlet that morning, gave Stamford a weather report indicating clearing weather about midday, and promised to lead a flight of planes in at that time, Faith made the decision to break out. The effort was projected to be one headlong dash for Hagaru-ri, covered by aircraft. It offered no options in execution to meet delays and unfavorable developments.

Not all the unit commanders, especially in the 31st Infantry, were informed of subsequent decisions. Captain Jordan, commander of M Company, for instance, did not receive notice of the breakout hour or that the breakout had started, though he had learned earlier that there would be a breakout attempt. He said that he knew that the breakout was under way only by watching the 3rd Battalion Headquarters area (he was a few hundred feet from it) and that, when he saw them going, he put his company in motion to follow.

There was a period of only two hours to get word passed around to everyone to unload trucks and vehicles of whatever they contained and load the wounded into them; cannibalize destroyed or immobilized vehicles for tires, batteries, and gasoline; form the convoy on the road—and find every possible cartridge of ammunition. There was also the task of preparing for destruction the supplies and weapons that could not be taken along. The troops had to be assigned their special roles in the breakout attempt. When the CCF saw these preparations and saw trucks pull onto the road within the perimeter, they increased their rate of fire, especially mortar fire, and a new group of wounded was added to the hundreds already present.

The question arises whether earlier in the training of the task-force units any thought was given to practice in withdrawal actions should they become necessary in combat. On this point Lieutenant May, who had been with the 1st Battalion, 32nd Infantry, since its reorganization, says, "I cannot remember one minute spent on training for a withdrawal action for anything above a squad or platoon. The lack of this knowledge was quite evident at Chosin."[10]

If the breakout had started on schedule, at noon, it would have had only about four hours of daylight. The road distance to Hagaru-ri was about 12 miles; that meant a *fast* pace of 3 miles an hour if the column was to reach Hagaru-ri before dark. Strong enemy opposition had to be assumed. No thought was given to going part way—as far as practicable, or possible, before dark and then forming a tight defense for the night with the hope of continuing the next day, when there would be a full eight hours of daylight and the prospect of continued air cover. Ammunition drops could have been arranged through Stamford's communication with the pilots overhead before night closed down.

There were few places where a night perimeter could have been improvised by the troops and the convoy en route on December 1. It would have had to make use of the reservoir shore and the railroad bed for defensive features. One site certainly would have been the area near Hudong-ni. Such a defense would have required good troop control.

The Hudong-ni area especially would have offered a good potential over-night defensive area if the 31st Tank Company and the 31st Rear had still been there, and they might have played a decisive role on the night of December 1–2 in helping the task-force column reach it and defend itself over-night. As a feature of the breakout, many junior officers and enlisted men expected a tank-infantry force from Hagaru-ri to meet them as they attacked south. But that never happened.[11]

The problems faced by a retreating force surrounded by an enemy are many, and they need to be considered carefully. Some elasticity in or devia-tion from a favored plan needs to be considered in advance. The fighting withdrawal faced by Task Force Faith on December 1 required as much plan-ning as an advance in the face of an enemy. Against expert night fighters like the Chinese, and with only one exit, certainly a continuation of an attack to the rear after dark would be most hazardous. Yet no plan was made for any options once darkness fell. During daylight hours the convoy with its uncertain and somewhat frail infantry support might keep going as long as it had strong air support, which it did have. When darkness fell and air support ended, an altogether new situation would prevail, one adverse to the task force and portending the greatest possible danger. American experi-ence in Korea demonstrated one thing beyond question: when night fell, it was time to circle the wagons and try to survive until dawn. An alternate plan should have been in mind in the event that night came before the task force neared Hagaru-ri, rather than the continuation of a blind effort to cleave through the darkness with an ever-weakening force and an ever-increasing number of wounded.

All bridges north of Hudong-ni were intact when the 31st RCT moved northward on November 25–27, and there were no physical roadblocks. It appears from the testimony of several officers that no one at the inlet pe-rimeter knew that the CCF had blown the two bridges between the inlet and Hudong-ni, making vehicular passage over them impossible. It should have occurred to the commanding officer and his staff before the day of the breakout that information on this subject was vital, and pilots should have been requested, through Stamford, to make daily reconnaissance of the road and all bridges between the inlet and the Paegamni-gang and re-port any adverse development that would hinder passage south. But no request for aerial reconnaissance of the road and bridges was made. One key officer, in response to my questioning, said that it did not occur to him or, as far as he knew, to anyone else at the inlet, before the breakout.

There was thus a lapse in obtaining intelligence that *was available* through aerial observation.[12]

The only precise contemporary documentary evidence on the time of the beginning of the breakout is found in the 1st Marine Division G-3 Journal and Message file. An air report, Message No. 19, at 12:05 P.M., December 1, stated, "Air—1/32 ready to move." This means that an aerial radio report received at Hagaru-ri reported that the 1st Battalion, 32nd Infantry, was lined up at 5 minutes past noon ready to move out. A second aerial radio message received at Hagaru-ri 45 minutes later, at 12:50, stated that the convoy, starting at 12:45, "is making some progress."[13] That left four hours of daylight. The sun would dip over the western mountain rim about 4:00 P.M., and darkness would soon follow.

There is little doubt that the napalm drop at the beginning of the breakout had a demoralizing effect on the infantry nearby and on those close enough to see its effects. Most of the survivors of the breakout felt that the task force never fully regained the momentum it had before the napalm hit the leading elements. It is not known how long this accident delayed progress of the convoy down the road, but it was not very long. Lieutenant Colonel Faith immediately set about rallying the troops at the cutting edge, and they responded. Other officers, especially Major Miller; Captain Seever, of C Company; and Lt. Henry M. Moore, the 1st Battalion P&A Platoon leader, helped Faith get the attack restored. And the fighter and bomber planes overhead were invaluable in this effort.

It was about 3:00 P.M. when the motor column began arriving at the first blown bridge. During this 2 hour interval the convoy had progressed at the rate of a mile an hour. It required another 1½ hours to get the vehicles around the blown bridge over an unimproved bypass, from 3:00 P.M. to about 4:30 P.M. Then it was beginning to get dark. After the breakout started, the remaining daylight of December 1 had been consumed in getting to the blown bridge, moving around it, and getting the trucks back on the road south of it, progress totaling about two and a half miles. At that point the prospect of getting to Hagaru-ri that night was not good. Supporting aircraft ran their last strike about half an hour later. The big enemy fire block and two physical roadblocks were just ahead on Hill 1221. Hundreds of men, virtually leaderless, were already straggling across a spur ridge of Hill 1221, only partly cleared of enemy, bypassing the CCF fire block and roadblock at the saddle of the hairpin turn, and taking off for Hagaru-ri. It was too late then, without a previous plan decided on as an option, to halt the men and form a perimeter defense for the night. When darkness came at Hill 1221, Task Force Faith had 7 more road miles between it and safety. To proceed against now-known enemy fire blocks and roadblocks ahead, in the dark with a dwindling force of men and no air cover, was a risk that should have been avoided if there had been any possible option. The breakout plan had provided for none.

Another question needs to be asked concerning the command of the 31st Infantry Task Force after Colonel MacLean disappeared at the inlet on the morning of November 29. We know that Lieutenant Colonel Faith, the commanding officer of the 1st Battalion, 32nd Infantry, assumed command in accordance with Army tradition, custom, and regulations. Because of lack of communications higher headquarters did not know of MacLean's disappearance from the inlet until General Barr's brief visit to the inlet the next day. Higher authority never appointed a new commander of the 31st RCT or officially confirmed Faith, and the latter, therefore, continued to command the 31st RCT east of Chosin to his death.

One wonders whether the situation did not require the direct action of the X Corps commander at that time. Almond learned of the loss of MacLean on the afternoon of November 30, the day after it happened. Because of the close relationship between General Barr and Lieutenant Colonel Faith, it is unlikely that Barr would have recommended a replacement for Faith. After the morning of November 30, General Smith, the Marine commander, was in command of the 31st RCT and of all other Army and Marine troops in the Chosin area north of Koto-ri. It is not likely that he would have appointed a member of the 1st Marine Division to take over direct command of the 31st RCT, and there was no Army officer senior to Faith available to him at Hagaru-ri. General Hodes, who had served since November 26 as Barr's 7th Division representative at Chosin, was not under General Smith's command. On the afternoon of November 30, General Barr had told Smith that he was withdrawing Hodes to the coast. The situation was now one in which the X Corps commander needed to act personally on the command situation at the inlet perimeter.

During the commanders' conference at Hagaru-ri on the afternoon of November 30, the plight of the 31st RCT at the inlet was much on General Almond's mind. He ordered General Smith to bring the 7th Marine regiment from Yudam-ni at once and send it to rescue the 31st RCT. But this was not a realistic order. The 7th Marines could not get from Yudam-ni to Hagaru-ri at once. They would have to fight their way through major parts of at least three Chinese divisions.

There was another course open for the top command. Brigadier General Henry I. Hodes, the assistant division commander, 7th Infantry Division, was present at Hagaru-ri and participated in the commanders' conference that afternoon. The fate of the 31st RCT was the most pressing business the 7th Division had at that moment or was to have in the succeeding weeks, and its best officer below the division commander should have been placed in charge of the 31st RCT's impending breakout. The presence of the assistant division commander would have been a positive morale factor for the troops. Hodes had been in the practice of moving about frequently among the units of the division and was rather well acquainted with most of the officers in all the battalions. Also, he had been an experienced infantry regimental commander in World War II. His rank would have secured optimum assistance. While one can assume that General Barr would not suggest to General Almond that Hodes be airlifted to the inlet perimeter to take command of the troops there, I believe that the corps commander should have grasped the nettle himself and ordered it on the spot—at Hagaru-ri on the afternoon of November 30.

The 1st Marine Division could have delivered Hodes by helicopter to the inlet the same afternoon. An arrangement should have been agreed upon by Hodes, Barr, Smith, and Almond about how they would establish radio communication between the inlet and Hagaru-ri and how needed supplies, especially ammunition and gasoline, would be delivered to the inlet perimeter so that Hodes would have a chance to withdraw the 31st RCT successfully. X Corps might also have been able to dispatch at once from Hamhung to the inlet a few hand-picked infantry officers of platoon and company rank to replace casualties and thus reinforce badly needed small-unit leadership. None of this was done. These lapses on the afternoon of November 30 are perhaps the worst command failures chargeable directly to the X Corps commander. What was required at the moment was not textbook dogma but keen common sense and recognition of what was possible.

By the time the task-force vehicular convoy passed the enemy fire block and roadblock at Hill 1221 after dark on the night of December 1, nearly all the officers and experienced noncommissioned officers had been killed or seriously wounded. Very few officers escaped to Hagaru-ri, and fewer yet who were not wounded. By dark on December 1, Task Force Faith was almost leaderless, and it had broken into fragments. Fragmentation had started soon after the convoy reached the first blown bridge and while it was moving slowly over the rough bypass around it. It was then that Chinese soldiers moved in from the north and northeast, after the rear guard failed in its mission.

In speaking to Xenophon about a similar situation, Cyrus said:

> Now first of all, I think you will do the whole army a great service if you take care at once to appoint captains and officers in the place of those who have been lost. For it is true one may say universally that without commanders nothing good or useful could ever be done; good discipline always saves, but disorder has destroyed many. . . . How could men be more easily defeated in battle than when they begin to think each of his own individual safety? And what possible success could be achieved by such as do not obey their superiors?[14]

Virtually all the officers who tried to get the rank-and-file to follow them in attacks at Hill 1221 on enemy positions commented on the reluctance, the surly unwillingness, of the men to do so, and many men who were forced to act soon deserted the effort. Jones, Bigger, Jordan, Kitz, Smith and McClymont spoke of this problem. The men were no longer normal soldiers. They were worn out; they no longer cared. All they had left was individual instinct for survival.

What did the surviving officers and men conclude upon later reflection on the 31st RCT's performance east of Chosin? Major Curtis, the 1st Battalion operations officer, wounded at the foot of Hill 1221 in the late afternoon of December 1, was with the motor convoy until its end near Hudong-ni. His experience and training had made him an especially knowledgeable infantry officer. His opinion of the adverse factors affecting the task force is worth noting. He said: "The plan did not work and the mission failed because control was lost from the outset—and, in fact—the rifle elements failed to provide flank and rear security. . . . Our main problem was maintaining control of the troops under very trying circumstances."

Curtis had thought from the beginning that Colonel MacLean should have assembled his entire 31st RCT at Hill 1221, the best defensive position on the east side of the reservoir, and that he should never have placed the 3rd Battalion, 31st Infantry, and the firing batteries of the 57th Field Artillery in the cramped area that became their perimeter at the Pungnyuri-gang inlet of the reservoir, a tactically indefensible position. He voiced his doubts at the time, but he said, "I could not even attract Faith's attention with suggestions of caution." Curtis added: "It has been a particular burden to me that I was the operations officer on an operation that failed—and failed miserably. Needless to say I have spent many hours of self-criticism and chastisement asking myself what could have been done that wasn't done." He summed up much of the underlying causes of disaster: ". . . and finally I come back to the weather—which was an over-riding factor. The cumulative effect of physical fatigue, loss of sleep, short rations, long hours of darkness, sub-zero temperature, was a numbness, dullness, lack of alertness and depression of spirit. When organization, communication, command, and control finally broke down—it was complete—and the instinct for survival took over. . . . In retrospect I have often been amazed to recall the number of seriously wounded who kept functioning—driven by this survival instinct."[15]

Captain Erwin Bigger, commanding officer of D Company (Weapons Company), 1st Battalion, 32nd Infantry, characterized the Chosin operation as follows:

Small unit leadership was as good as it could have been. Squad and platoon leaders acted professionally and bravely. Company commanders exposed themselves and were unselfish in performing their responsibilities. I am the only surviving Company Commander of 1/32 of that campaign and I was just lucky, fortunate, or what have you—even tho I was wounded. I had so many punctures in my body that I didn't even know about some of them until I reached the Marine Div. aid station.

We were frustrated however by the lack of specific instructions from senior officers. We were not sure who to look for or from what headquarters we were to receive our orders. It is obvious that although senior officers could get in by helicopter, not one came to take over elements of two different combat teams. And there was certainly a lack of coordination of the 7th Div units in the Chosin area. We never knew that there were other 7th Div units as close to us as two miles.[16]

Captain Earle H. Jordan, Jr., commander of M Company, 31st Infantry, was personally outstanding as a soldier and leader in the Chosin operation. He expressed his lasting thoughts of those days of trial in these words:

It is also my hope that regardless of the decisions and actions, or lack of such on the part of commanders at all levels, the devotion, loyalty and valor of the many enlisted soldiers and junior officers will not be denied. I mention this with particular reference to the platoon leaders, NCO's, and private soldiers of M Co. 31st Inf.

In my service in two conflicts, WWII and Korea, the period of my command of M Co. was and is the period in which I take greatest pride. Their performance in this operation was in my opinion equal to the very best as is attested to by their tenacity and toll inflicted upon the enemy.[17]

First Lieutenant Hugh R. May was probably the oldest officer in the 31st RCT, with an enviable combat record in World War II. He was knowledgeable about the troops and the organization of 31st RCT for he had been a member of one of the rifle battalions since the organization of the 32nd Infantry and the reconstitution of the 7th Infantry Division in Japan. About Chosin, May said:

> . . . the 1st Bn 32nd during the assault on Seoul did not experience enough combat of a nature to prepare them for the type of combat action we encountered at the Chosin Reservoir.
>
> In my opinion the men performed as well as could be expected under the circumstances.
>
> As long as the men had leaders they performed without question orders from their officers; once the officer ranks were decimated it was impossible to maintain control. At times some of the men performed above and beyond the expected norm for troops with as little combat experience as they had. . . .
>
> Majors Miller, Curtis, and Jones. These officers were some of the most resourceful and efficient I ever served with. They were not afraid to lay their lives on the line in order to get the job done. They were among the best I ever served with in a combat situation. They set a very fine example for junior officers and E. M. The personal bravery of Col. Faith cannot be doubted as he placed himself in jeopardy on more than one occasion, he was an inspiration to both the officers and men who served with and under him.[18]

Lieutenant Mortrude's opinion of the plight of the 31st RCT and his analysis of some of its problems are perceptive:

> Once the battle was joined with the overwhelming but unorganized Chinese forces, our withdrawals were unnecessarily precipitous and uncontrolled. Although we were lucky in the first lunge back to the 31st Regt'l perimeter, the subsequent Task Force withdrawal to Hagaru-ri was disastrous due to the lack of control. Even though the Chinese were never able to block the few infantrymen punching their way through at the head of the column, they, the Chinese, were eventually able to close in on the main body due to

lack of flank protection and the failure to hold critical terrain until passage of the entire column.

In my opinion, any retrograde movement must be at least as well planned as the conventional attack. There must, in fact, be much greater emphasis on details of command, control, and coordination. If, for example, we had been assigned successive objectives as control measures, the critical pass of the road through ground which we had seized with our spontaneous assault would not have been left uncovered. Also, there apparently was little effort on the part of the 7th Div or X Corps to coordinate or support the breakout, once they abandoned the relief effort of 28 [and 29] Nov. It was the very area from which this Division Task Force [31st Tank Company and 31st Infantry Rear CP] withdrew that became the "graveyard" of the truck column and its personnel.[19]

Captain Edward P. Stamford, USMC, had excellent credentials as an observer and good knowledge of combat practices. His report to the commandant of the Marine Corps, prepared in February, 1951, two months after the action, includes the following remarks:

Most of the Army Officers and many of the NCO's seemed to be very well trained and apparently good leaders. The weakness lay in that the 7th Inf Div lost many of its senior NCO's through transfers to units in Korea prior to its departure from Japan. The other weakness appeared to be in the training of the individual soldiers.

In my opinion the reason for the collapse of the command was due to the loss of most of the leaders in the platoons and companies in 1/32 and the timidity or lack of aggressiveness on the part of the rear guard unit (1/57) [3/31 and HQ Co. 3/31 were the designated rear guard] to move up and replace the casualties suffered in the attempt to take the road block and hill "X" [Hill 1221]. The drifting off of the troops after reaching the ridge of Hill "X" demonstrated the lack of organization and leadership when most needed.[20]

The views of one enlisted man during the breakout may be of interest, and are perhaps typical of many. Sergeant Chester L. Bair, 1st Battalion, 32nd Infantry, was present during the action. He rode on one of the trucks in the breakout effort on December 1. He escaped when the column came to its end near Hudong-ni:

In the breakout I was acting on my own as a Section Chief and a mechanic. . . . My truck was moved around somewhat in the column, but I was mostly in the middle or near the front. . . . Few people would give or take commands. There was a lot of havoc, wounded, dead, low ammunition supplies, inoperative equipment, and finally the chain of command broken, or nearly non-existent. Along with the CCF, it was extremely cold, and many men did not wish to respond to orders, many of which were wounded, once, twice, and some even more. . . .

I, too, did not make that Last Ditch Effort with a column of 20 trucks. I knew it did not stand a chance, but I thought it would make a diversion, thereby making it possible for some of us cutting out in small groups, or alone, [to stand] a better chance of escape. When many men look back they like to think of themselves as heroes or etc, but the truth of the matter when the chips are down, most try to save their hides. . . .

You must understand at the time this incident took place I was 19 years old. I was not interested in history or anything else. All I can remember is the cold, inferior clothing, worn out equipment, the noise, the wounded, and the dead. While some officers and NCO's tried to keep order and keep a chain of command as the situation worsened . . . [incomplete]. At the blown out bridge, a half-track [full-track dual-40] was pulling other vehicles across the river, while I was working on trucks, flat tires, and trying to drain gas tanks of disabled vehicles, because we needed the fuel. We took parts from the disabled vehicles, and tried to keep all the vehicles we could operative. I saw Lt. May several times, he was trying all he could to keep the vehicles operative and positioned them whereby they could be moved out at command, even though he appeared to be wounded [he was not].[21]

Major Jones is the only officer who has expressed to me his opinion that the outcome could have been no different:

In my estimation the operation East of Chosin was an example of too little to accomplish the mission assigned, rather than deficiency in quality of individuals. Time had not permitted, or planning provided, for a cohesive, organized, supplied and supported RCT, prior to the decision to attack to the north. The units were separated and could do very little to support each other. When the Chinese attacked on the night of 27–28 Nov 50 the operation was doomed to failure. The overwhelming strength of the enemy, the dispersion of the US forces, the lack of communication, the dearth of instructions from higher headquarters, the confusion and ultimately the lack of a chain of command above the RCT level, the absence of intelligence, and the lack of logistical and combat support to the RCT dictated the final outcome. And, of course, the weather played a prominent part. In my estimation, even a complete RCT, in place on the eastern side of the reservoir, would have been unable to extricate itself from that situation, and regain the relative safety of Hagaru-ri. Except for the outstanding close air support, there were no supporting fires to assist the column of wounded-laden trucks and troops breaking out from the inlet perimeter. I don't believe that any force of that size could have made a greater effort or have done better, as a group, than the ad hoc 31st RCT did from the breakout attempt on. It was just a case of not enough combat force to overcome the enemy that attacked us.[22]

Although Major Lynch, General Hodes's G-3 aide at Hudong-ni and at Hagaru-ri, did not participate in any of the actions of the 31st RCT, he knew the situation at Hudong-ni and Hagaru-ri, and he saw the remnants of Task Force Faith come into the Marine perimeter. Thereafter he was involved in the aborted effort to send a relief force to the aid of the task force. He commented: "No doubt all leaders, as well as those in my status and the men caught in this tragedy, carried away a haunting conscience, if they escaped. What was right? What was wrong? At some point in time all played Pilate in washing their hands. The Marine leaders are no exception. They had the only capability in that area and they were informed by an army major [Lynch himself] to use army tanks. Nothing came of this. By this time it was their responsibility, though belatedly."[23]

No doubt most of those who survived the ordeal east of Chosin tried later to forget as much of it as possible and did not torture their consciences about where they might have failed in one way or another and in what way they might have performed better or differently and contributed to a successful breakout. But there were some among the officer corps who have had the experience on their minds, and in at least one or two cases on their consciences, for the past thirty-five years. Colonel Wesley J. Curtis, USA, Ret., then major and the 1st Battalion S-3, is a case in point. In correspondence with Colonel Curtis, I speculated that he was probably the last officer not riding in a vehicle, though wounded, who left the task-force vehicular column at its final stop near Hudong-ni. He replied that he could not be positive that this was the case but believed it to be so. Then he wrote the following series of questions, directed to himself, and his answers:

   1. *Question:* You were aware that Faith and Miller were seriously wounded, were you not then—by law, custom, and tradition—in command?
   Answer: Yes.
   2. *Question:* Were you aware of it at the time?
   Answer: Yes.
   3. *Question:* Was it right then, for you to "cut-out"—to abandon the command?
   Answer: No.
   4. *Question:* What should you have done?

Answer: I should have remained with the truck column—regardless of the consequences.

5. *Question:* Has this bothered you—your conscience?

Answer: Yes—for the past 35 years.

6. *Question:* If you had it to do over again—would you do the same thing?

Answer: Probably, yes.

You recognize the self-indictment in the foregoing. It is made in the interest of honest history.

Now for the statement in defense of the decision I made at the time.

1. The Victorian concept (that has its roots in the days of chivalry) that a soldier's role is not to question why—but only to do or die—will not stand up to the scrutiny of a prudent and thoughtful man. A soldier's role is to fight—and live to fight another day—under conditions that favor success.

2. It is a well-established principle of tactics that success is exploited—failure is not reinforced. Also, a delaying or covering force avoids close engagement. It is obvious that tactics—as taught at Fort Benning—do not address the exact situation that existed in the Twiggae–Hudong-ni area at 2200 hours 1 Dec 1950. TF Faith had been defeated in detail. There was not an intact machine gun section, automatic rifle fire team, a skeleton rifle squad in the force. The "force" (and I use the word advisedly) was strung out along a narrow road. There was no resistance left in the column—no firing—motors in the trucks were not running—drivers were not in the cabs of the trucks. The only sound heard was the moaning of the wounded and dying. I claim that Patton in a Tiger tank—a MacArthur on a white horse could not have reversed the situation.[24]

Was it not ironic that Task Force Faith came to its final stop just short of the site of Drake's 31st Tank Company bivouac and the 31st Infantry Rear CP? Thirty hours earlier there had been 16 operable tanks and 325 soldiers in a perimeter within a stone's throw of where the convoy died—they had been there since the evening of November 27. Then, on November 30 an order came for them to withdraw to Hagaru-ri. The 7th Infantry Division Command Report, Chosin Reservoir, for the period says, "At 1100 hours 30 November this group was ordered to move to Hagaru-ri."[25]

Who ordered the withdrawal to Hagaru-ri? How was the order transmitted to Hudong-ni? And why was the order issued? A search of the 1st Marine Division G-3 Journal, November 30, 1950, fails to disclose an entry concerning an order of any kind to the 31st Rear CP and the 31st Tank Company at Hudong-ni. Yet that command would be the one authorized to issue it. The Marine G-3 Journal file does, however, record Message No. 37 at 1900 (7:00 P.M.) saying, "Serv Bn: Adv elms RCT 31 arriving Hagarri."[26] Testimony of officers in the movement says that they arrived about 5:30 P.M. We know from Captain Drake and Major Lynch that the tank company arrived at Hagaru-ri before dark and that Drake had placed his tanks in the Marine perimeter there before light failed. The service elements mentioned in the Marine G-3 Journal file may have arrived later than the tanks. The movement of these forces from Hudong-ni has been described earlier.

The question I now wish to consider is the order for the 31st Tank Company and the 31st Rear to move to Hagaru-ri on November 30. Why should such an order be issued when it was a fact, known to all the higher command, that Task Force Faith, on its only possible exit road from the inlet perimeter in any breakout attempt, would have to pass Hudong-ni? The presence there of the tank company and the 325 miscellaneous troops could be of tremendous, very possibly of indispensable, help to the task force in a breakout. This factor is magnified when one learns that the next night the end of the task force came on the level stretch of road just north of Hudong-ni. If the tanks and the other forces had been left at Hudong-ni, the part of the motor column that reached that vicinity with its hundreds of wounded might have been rescued. Withdrawing these forces from Hudong-ni had the effect of signing the death warrant for Task Force Faith and its wounded. What commander in his right mind could order such a move in the circumstances without deliberately running the risk of sacrificing the task force, and how could he be willing to take that risk?

We do not have documentary evidence that discloses who ordered the withdrawal from Hudong-ni and why it was ordered, but there is other evidence that allows one to arrive at reasonable conclusions on the subject. Under X Corps Operations Instruction No. 19 only Major General Smith, other than the X Corps commander himself, could give an order of this kind after 8:00 A.M. on November 30. We know that the X Corps commander did not issue the order. It is also known that there was no communication between Hagaru-ri and Hudong-ni at this time except over tank radios of the 31st Tank Company. Major General David Barr, of the 7th Division, was in Hagaru-ri during the morning and most of the afternoon of November 30. His assistant division commander, Brig. Gen. Henry I. Hodes, was also there and had been there since November 28. It is not known whether the order to Lt. Col. Berry K. Anderson, senior officer of the 7th Division Rear at Hudong-ni, was issued before, during, or after General Barr's visit with Lieutenant Colonel Faith that morning. It seems almost certain that Generals Barr and Hodes must have discussed the question of whether to recall the forces at Hudong-ni to Hagaru-ri. One may surmise that they —or General Barr alone—reached the conclusion that it should be done. General Barr would then have had to persuade Marine General Smith to issue such an order over his name.

But no such order is recorded in the 1st Marine Division G-3 Journal. This may be explained, however, if General Smith *verbally* approved such an order to General Barr, if the order was never committed to writing or a copy sent to the Marine G-3 duty officer, and if General Hodes transmitted the order by the one tank radio at Hagaru-ri that was netted to Drake's tanks at Hudong-ni. Both Drake and Lynch state that the tank radios were the means of transmitting and receiving the order, that no other means was available. Further, Major Lynch recalls a conversation he had with Hodes on November 30 just outside the 1st Marine Division G-3 van in Hagaru-ri: "I asked him [Hodes] about the units east of Chosin. I do not remember whether he said that these had been or would be ordered out. Gen. Hodes had apparently given orders to Anderson via the tank radio located on the NE of the perimeter near the rry [railroad] crossing earlier in the day. I did not see Anderson's headquarters and supply people arrive, but I drove General Hodes to the perimeter and watched the 31st Tank Company arrive. It was put in the defense perimeter immediately."[27] The fact that Hodes went to the Marine perimeter at the road and railroad crossing at the northeast point of the perimeter to meet Drake's tanks indicates that he knew they had been ordered out. He himself may have transmitted the order. In another place Lynch says, "He [Hodes] confirmed that he had ordered the tanks out and that they should arrive shortly."[28]

Hodes must be considered the conveyer of the order and not the initiator. We do not know who initiated it, who urged that the order be sent —whether it was Hodes, Barr, or Smith. It had to be one of the three. But we do know that the order had to be authorized by General Smith. It would seem that all three generals agreed on issuing the order, but it is likely that General Smith acceded to the 7th Division commander's desire in the matter. Yet, as commander of all the troops at Chosin, Smith cannot escape his degree of responsibility.

Lieutenant General William J. McCaffrey, USA, Ret., then lieutenant colonel and X Corps deputy chief of staff and confidant of General Almond, has stated to me that General Barr initiated the order and that General Almond was upset when he learned of the withdrawal. According to McCaffrey,

Almond asked Barr why he had had the order issued, and Barr answered in effect that he thought he should get the units out while it was still possible to do so.[29]

The withdrawal of Drake's 31st Tank Company and the 31st Rear CP from Hudong-ni on the evening of November 30 looms so large in the ultimate fate of Task Force Faith that it is important to understand the critical terrain features of the vicinity. The area west and southwest of the Hudong-ni schoolhouse CP and the tank bivouac and supply area was marsh and paddy land extending all the way to the reservoir, a little less than a mile distant. The village of Sasu-ri lay south of Hudong-ni, half a mile away, on an island-like area between divided channels of the Paegamni-gang. Sasu, the sawmill village, was on the narrow-gauge railroad at the edge of the reservoir. The tanks, as well as several machine guns, at Hudong-ni had an open field of fire in all directions except to the north and northeast, where the slope of Ko-bong gave some cover to the enemy.

Hill 1239 was the high point of a long spur ridge, west of a higher saddle, that extended westward from the higher Ko-bong mass. The spur ridge ran southwesterly down to the Hagaru-ri road a few hundred feet northwest of the tank and 31st Rear CP area. It was at the tip of this spur ridge, just above (east) of the road, that the CCF established the fire block commanding the road and railroad below and the flat paddy ground and the terrain toward the reservoir. The heavy automatic and small-arms fire from this position, together with rocket and mortar fire from the lower ground near the entrance to the Hudong-ni bivouac area, stopped Task Force Faith's motor column for the last time. There the convoy died. To withdraw the tank company and the 31st Rear at Hudong-ni while Task Force Faith was still north of them at the inlet was to abandon the men to the greatest hazard. Whatever risk for the tank company in keeping it at Hudong-ni was conjectural and needed to be taken for the greater good.

I believe that any commander who knew that Task Force Faith was to try to break out from the inlet perimeter on the morrow should not have approved the order for the tanks and troops at Hudong-ni to withdraw the day before the attempt. Any superior officer who learned of it after the order was issued and before it was executed should have rescinded it at once. The withdrawal of the forces at Hudong-ni on the afternoon of November 30 was a disastrous command decision. In the end it doomed Task Force Faith.

The Chinese had their own application of Murphy's Law. Nowhere did

the Chinese make greater errors than at Hagaru-ri. Their plan was to capture it on the first night of their general surprise attack, the night of November 27. But they did not attack Hagaru-ri that night, even though they
had divisions north, west, and south of it. They let the key to their anticipated destruction of the 1st Marine Division slip from their grasp at the
outset, and they never could regain the same favorable opportunity they
had so negligently lost. Why? The answer lies partly in the story of the
31st RCT east of Chosin.

Any thorough and critical analysis of the Chosin Campaign, in which
the 1st Marine Division played the dominant role, must consider the effect
of the action east of Chosin on the ultimately successful defense of Hagaru-
ri and the concentration there of all Marine and other troops who survived
the battles of November 27 through December 4, 1950. The successful fighting withdrawal to the coast was organized at Hagaru-ri, and it began from
there on December 6.

Just how vulnerable was Hagaru-ri from November 27 through at least
December 1, during the time the 31st RCT diverted the 80th Division from
its assigned mission and in the process consumed its major strength, thus
thwarting the intentions of the Chinese Army Group Command? To place
in proper perspective the sacrificial effort of the Army's 31st RCT east of
Chosin, the situation at Hagaru-ri at this time must be sketched briefly.

Three Chinese divisions were involved in the plan to capture Hagaru-ri
the first night of their surprise attack at the Chosin Reservoir. The 80th
Division was to come down the east side of the reservoir from the vicinity
of Kalchon-ni and attack Hagaru-ri from the north and east; the 58th Division of the 20th Army was to attack the town from the southwest—it was
already in place in its assembly areas in the hills only 5 miles away; the 60th
Division, also from the 20th Army, was to cut the road south of Hagaru-ri
at the same time the other two divisions attacked it. Only the 60th Division
carried out its mission the night of November 27–28. It cut the road in a
dozen places all the way from Hagaru-ri to Chinhung-ni at the foot of Funchilin Pass. Why the 58th Division did not attack Hagaru-ri that night remains a mystery. The 80th Division, approaching Hagaru-ri from the north
along the east side of the reservoir, ran into the Army's 31st RCT troops
and engaged them at the two infantry battalion areas along the road and
cut them off from Hagaru-ri. If the Chinese plan had been carried out as
conceived by the Chinese Army Group Command, the 80th Division would

have bypassed the 31st RCT and moved against Hagaru-ri that night. Hagaru-ri was vulnerable, and if it had been struck by a coordinated attack that night with the forces the Chinese had at hand and in position for that purpose, it could hardly have survived.

The Marine defenses of Hagaru-ri were thin and incomplete on the night of November 27. After dark on November 26 Lt. Col. Thomas L. Ridge, commander of the 3rd Battalion, 1st Marines, arrived from Majon-ni to relieve F Company, 7th Marines, at Hagaru-ri. Ridge did not have his entire battalion, however—only about three-fourths of it. He had two rifle companies, I and H, and two platoons of the Weapons Company, and there were two batteries of 105-mm howitzer artillery—Capt. Benjamin S. Read's H Battery of the 3rd Battalion, 11th Marines, and Capt. Andrew J. Strohmenger's D Battery of the 2nd Battalion, 11th Marines. Also at Hagaru-ri were miscellaneous units of X Corps and 1st Marine Division service and supply troops and some Marine and Army Engineer troops. Capt. William E. Barber's F Company, 7th Marines, left Hagaru-ri the next morning, November 27, to take up its isolated position at Toktong Pass, about midway between Hagaru-ri and Yudam-ni, on the west side of the reservoir.

Colonel Ridge and his staff made a reconnaissance of the Hagaru-ri area on the 27th, and Ridge estimated that two regiments were required to hold a suitable perimeter. Since he had less than one battalion of combat troops available, Ridge settled on a four-mile perimeter. Parts of that perimeter had no troops at all, and other parts were thinly held by service troops. During the night Ridge and his men learned of massive attacks by two Chinese divisions against the Marines at Yudam-ni, and they also knew of the heavy attacks against the Army troops north of them on the east side of the reservoir. Ridge and his staff expected an attack that night. But it never came.

I asked Colonel Ridge much later if he knew why the Chinese did not attack Hagaru-ri the night of November 27. Ridge replied:

> I can only speculate on this question. I suspect that the planned (?) attacks (CCF) at Yudam-ni and Fox Hill on the one side and delays, as you commented on, incident to actions against elements of the 7th Inf. Div. on the other side contributed to delays in whatever plans they may have had. In addition to these, you should also note the recon. and minor actions south of Hagaru-ri. In the 1950's I had a better than average knowledge of CCF tactics over the prior decade, and recall *then* thinking of the CCF tendency to be rather certain of the exact situation prior to deciding on a major at-

tack. Recall that the CCF had only patrol reporting or local civilian reports at the time. Also consider the probable confusion existent at CCF Hq at the time.[30]

General Smith at Hagaru-ri was so concerned about the enemy threat on November 28 and his slender means at hand to hold the place, that he ordered Col. Lewis B. Puller, commander of the 1st Marine Regiment at Koto-ri, to get reinforcements to him on the 29th even if they had to take heavy losses in reaching Hagaru-ri. Task Force Drysdale was the result.

From the Chinese point of view it was unfortunate—a disaster to them, eventually—that they did not attack Hagaru-ri on the night of November 27. If the CCF 80th Division had launched its planned attack that night instead of stopping to attack the separated elements of the Army's 31st RCT on its way down the east side of the reservoir, it might very well have overrun the town and the Marine defenses there, especially if its arrival had prompted the CCF 58th Division to join in the attack from the opposite side of Hagaru-ri. The capture of Hagaru-ri would have been a disaster for the 1st Marine Division.

On December 24, 1950, General Smith expressed himself on the importance of Hagaru-ri in the Chosin Reservoir Campaign to a *New York Times* reporter. On December 26, 1950, the *Times* printed the substance of Smith's remarks. "The Chinese," he said, "knew all about us all right, where we were and what we had. . . . Instead of hitting us with everything at one place, they kept hitting us at different places. Had the Chinese decided to knock out the small Marine garrison at Hagaru-ri, the task of regrouping forces would have been made immeasurably more difficult."

In their ordeal east of Chosin the men of the 31st RCT would have no difficulty accepting Lieutenant May's words as expressing the substance of their own thoughts: "This [Chosin action] was by far the worst experience of my life. There was no comparable action I was in during WW II with the ferocity and the determination displayed during the Chosin action."[31]

A noncommissioned officer, Sfc. Carrol D. Price, of Headquarters Battery, 57th Field Artillery, wounded twice at Chosin, was fortunate enough to reach Hagaru-ri, but, he said, "I lost all my friends":

> I thought and still do, that if the units had left a little earlier while we still had ammunition for our guns, if the air drops had been better, and if we had been better organized to fight as infantry, we might have gotten out. I feel strongly about it because of what happened to all my friends. We had

an enormous amount of casualties. I was through the last war and I never saw anything like that before. I was in the "Bulge" and it was nothing like this at Chosin Reservoir. This was something. It was the first time I had ever seen enemy right in the gun positions. I have been in the artillery for 12 years and I never thought I would see the day when I would have to destroy guns. We smashed sights and took it apart. The weather was so bad the trucks couldn't start, they were frozen.[32]

Another noncommissioned officer spoke in praise of the officers of the 1st Battalion, 32nd Infantry. Sergeant Stephen F. Lewis, platoon leader of the 57-mm Recoilless Rifle Section, attached to C Company, stated: "I believe if it hadn't been for our officers there wouldn't be a man alive from this unit today. Our officers carried on although some of them were wounded 2 or 3 times. I believe they did everything in this world to get everybody out. I am proud I had such officers as my superiors and I would serve under them anywhere."[33]

One must ask himself what he would have done, could have done, in similar circumstances, in that frigid wasteland after four days and five nights of constant exposure to bitter cold, almost constant enemy attack resulting in crippling casualties, little food, mental and physical exhaustion, little or no hope of help, little or no ammunition, and no communication with a higher headquarters. The Marines on the other side of Chosin were never in a completely similar situation or desperate to the same degree in all the aspects of battle. A true understanding of these factors would prompt a little humility in one's declaration of personal and unit bravery and some charity in expressing an indictment of these Army men.

In the ultimate analysis of the Chosin Reservoir action, the 7th Infantry Division troops who fought on the east side of the reservoir probably provided the narrow margin that enabled the 1st Marine Division to hold Hagaru-ri, and this in turn made possible the completion there of an airstrip from which several thousand wounded troops were evacuated to the coast, the assembling of the Marine troops at Hagaru-ri from Yudam-ni, and thereafter the fighting escape to the coast.

Credit earned and honor due is owed to those all-but-forgotten American men who for a brief period fought our nation's battles east of Chosin. Too many of our countrymen left their unmarked remains in that ancient land, poetically but mistakenly called the "Land of the Morning Calm."

Epilogue

Like the Phoenix of mythology, a new military organization rose from its own ashes to fight another day some weeks and months after Chosin.

When Maj. Robert E. Jones arrived at Hamhung at midnight, December 10, 1950, at the end of withdrawal from the Chosin Reservoir, the surviving members of the 1st Battalion, 32nd Infantry, were 3 officers, 18 enlisted men, and 4 KATUSA. Before the group moved out three days later in the great evacuation of X Corps to Pusan, in South Korea, about 30 additional survivors of the battalion joined the group. About 100 replacements were assigned to Jones on the Hungnam beach while he was waiting to load on ship. After debarking at Pusan, Jones and his men were sent north to Taegu to establish a command post in a schoolhouse on the south edge of the town. There Jones was to begin the reconstitution of the battalion. But his remnant of the 1st Battalion was still attached to the 31st Infantry Regiment. His men had only individual weapons, sleeping bags, and the clothes on their backs.

Jones's first task was to obtain stoves, vehicles, rations, clothing, and similar items for use until requisitions could be filled out and processed and a start made on obtaining prescribed equipment. During this initial period at Taegu the 31st Infantry went out of its way to assist the 1st Battalion nucleus, providing the men with shelter and with food and cooks to prepare it.

In the meantime, the 32nd Infantry Regiment levied on its other battalions for officers, noncommissioned officers, and key enlisted men to get the 1st Battalion functioning. This was a very busy and trying time for Jones, who continued to command the battalion. It meant organizing the new

units as personnel arrived, starting training programs, and establishing personnel records. An erratic personnel system, unreliable supply, the great
distance from the 32nd Infantry Regimental Headquarters, and the regrouping that had begun in Eighth Army under General Ridgway to get in readiness for a renewed UN attack added to the work and worry of men racing
against time to achieve combat readiness.

In all this turmoil of work there was also the matter of preparing the
paperwork recommending awards and decorations for those at Chosin who
had performed in a manner that merited them.[1] The first recommendation
that Jones prepared was for the Medal of Honor, Posthumously, for Lt.
Col. Don C. Faith, Jr.[2] The only other participant in the events east of Chosin who was proposed for the Medal of Honor was Capt. Edward P. Stamford, the 1st Battalion, 32nd Infantry, TACP leader. On January 23, 1951, Maj.
Gen. Field Harris, USMC, commander of the 1st Marine Air Wing, Fleet
Marine Force, wrote to Brig. Gen. Henry I. Hodes saying that Captain Stamford's performance east of Chosin "rated a top notch decoration and that
it looked to me that it was pretty close to a Medal of Honor."[3] The matter
finally found its way to the adjutant general of the Department of the Army,
who passed it on. At some point in the process the Department of the Navy
became involved, and the award became snarled in red tape. The problem
of getting action on it one way or another by two different services, the
Army and the Navy, after being proposed by an Air Wing of the Marine
Corps, apparently was too much for the mechanics of the award system.
In the end Stamford received the Silver Star from Headquarters, X Corps,
General Order No. 157, on July 22, 1951.

Upon Hugh May's return to duty with the 32nd Infantry after recovery
in the hospital, his battalion commander asked him to prepare an award
citation for Major Jones, since he was familiar with Jones's role in the action
east of Chosin. May readily complied, commenting, ". . . a job I gladly did
as he surely deserved it."

May himself did not receive an award deriving from action initiated by
the 32nd Infantry, but months later when he was being rotated from Korea
and was already in a truck at the 7th Division Headquarters waiting to go
to the port of embarkation, he was taken off the truck, and Maj. Gen.
Claude B. Ferenbaugh, commanding the 7th Division, awarded him a Silver
Star for action at Chosin.[4] The division chief of staff had apparently just
told Ferenbaugh that May deserved a decoration.

When they returned to the 32nd Infantry after recovering from their wounds in a Japanese hospital, Major Curtis and Captain Bigger were asked to write up Silver Star awards for each other. By mutual agreement they declined. These few examples of incidents attending the preparation of awards demonstrate the lack of uniformity in the procedures.

In his efforts to obtain awards and decorations for deserving members of the 1st Battalion, 32nd Infantry, Jones met with general frustration. His account of the difficulties provides a good description of the problem of securing battle awards for soldiers who merited them. His problems were especially difficult because many of the men meriting awards had been killed in action or wounded and discharged from the service, and he had almost no staff to help him with the paperwork at the time the citations should have been prepared and submitted for approval. He comments:

> When we arrived at Taegu and became busily engaged in reforming a shattered unit, there were about three dozen survivors of the Chosin campaign. I gathered them together and discussed the submission of awards to members of the unit. Much to my surprise I found a great reluctance on the part of most of the survivors to provide statements of actions they witnessed or could corroborate! In some instances, lack of education, or limited capability to express themselves in writing, might have had an influence on this reluctance. However, it seemed much deeper to me than just that, for offers of help did not elicit any greater response. Most individuals disclaimed seeing *anyone* do *anything* that warranted a decoration, and were much more inclined to discuss what they did and how they acted throughout the operation. This is only natural for survivors to so act.
>
> First of all, they knew what they did better than anyone else, and had a clear, concise picture of what happened to them throughout the entire period. In addition, under the circumstances that prevailed, heroic acts were happening continuously, concurrently, endlessly and were in fact somewhat commonplace. Many heroic acts were made by people who later became casualties, and therefore some might question the necessity of submitting a recommendation for an award for someone who would never know about it. It was also possible that some of the survivors had done some things that in their eyes surpassed any other thing they witnessed, and thus felt *they* should be written up! Also, how do you separate those acts which were indeed heroic in the classic sense, which met the criteria of having been done to accomplish the unit's mission or saving other lives, and those acts done in the pure effort of self survival? How can one determine the dividing line? Many acts were not witnessed by the survivors who could record them. Much of what occurred was later learned from first person accounts which provide much of the history of what happened. However, first person ac-

counts understandably tend to be slightly biased, then, in some cases, to over emphasize individual acts, and run the risk of being self serving. It would be so much easier to write up recommendations for awards based on those first person accounts, but the system demands, and rightly so, that events be corroborated by witnesses. In our case those witnesses were hard to find as most had become casualties and were not available to help present a full picture. As a result there were many, many individuals who were not recognized with awards as they should have been. I remember feeling very frustrated trying to remember events to support the submission of recommendations, and trying to urge others to do the same. After a while the well runs dry. I'm afraid our efforts resulted in a pitifully few awards being made. . . .

I am in general agreement with you that the citations that finally accompany decorations very often, if not mostly . . . do not resemble reality nor do they necessarily reflect accurately what actually happened. As such, the narrative descriptions have never concerned me very much. However, I do believe in the value of decorations to recognize achievement and heroic acts, and feel that they are a necessary and valued part of military, if you can overlook, or at least bear with, the verbiage that accompany them. . . .

However, there were three [awards] that I remember were simple in their submission. They were the three previously mentioned Silver Stars awards made by Gen Almond to Faith, Smalley and Stanley. I visited the Division AG Section to determine if the General Orders for these three awards had ever been published. I was informed that they had not. So, I filled out three forms on the spot, and stated simply that they had been awarded by the Corps Commander on 28 Nov 1950. No corroborating statements from witnesses were provided. These were the *only* recommendations that were not returned for rewrite or for additional information! I don't know that these recommendations actually culminated in the awards being approved, but I have always thought so.[5]

Upon reaching Pusan in the course of returning to the 32nd Infantry in March, 1951, Lieutenant Campbell thought of his South Korean KATUSA platoon sergeant, Kim Chae Ku. He remembered the address of Kim's father, who operated a store in the city. Campbell did not know what had happened to Kim in the final hours of the breakout at Chosin Reservoir, and he wanted to tell Kim's family what he knew about their son. The South Koreans, when adequately trained and led by competent Korean officers, became outstanding soldiers. General Paik Sun Yup's ROK 1st Division generally held its own alongside American divisions. Many KATUSA and regulars of the South Korean Army were brave and faithful and carried out their military duties unto death. Campbell's story illustrates this point:

I went there [to Kim's family's home in Pusan] to explain the situation to his family. Much to my surprise and pleasure, I found him there. Wounded, he had remained with the convoy until the end, attempted to fight his way out and was captured when his weapon was out of ammunition. He subsequently escaped to Hagaru-ri, was hospitalized for wounds and frostbite and because of his injuries discharged from the ROK Army, returning to his home in Pusan. When he learned that I was returning to the 32nd he insisted on coming with me. I scrounged an extra set of combat issue and a weapon from the Repo Depot in Pusan and got us both on an aircraft headed north the next day. He remained with me (almost at my side through three more combat unit assignments and two more hospitalizations) until I rotated in August 1951. I took him with me as I passed back to Pusan through rotation channels and unofficially "discharged" him there.[6]

The 7th Infantry Division remained in General Almond's X Corps as part of Eighth Army. The X Corps was rushed into combat in early January to stem a North Korean drive down the central mountain corridor toward Pusan that threatened to outflank all of Eighth Army. Only ROK troops defended that area as the New Year began. At first Wonju was the key road and railroad center that was threatened. The 7th Division started moving northward toward this new battle area at the end of December, 1950, while its 31st and 32nd regiments were being reconstituted. The Division's 17th Regiment necessarily took the lead in the advance, with the main mission of protecting the Andong–Chechon MSR in the Taeback Mountain corridor of central Korea. By the end of January, 1951, the 7th Division was concentrated in the area around Chechon, an important road center southeast of Wonju.

By this time the 31st RCT and the 1st Battalion of the 32nd Infantry had been largely reequipped and replacements taken in. Training and integration were being carried on in severe winter weather in difficult terrain—the Taeback range. General Barr left the division on January 26, 1951, rotated back to the United States, and was replaced by Maj. Gen. Claude E. Ferenbaugh.

On February 18, 1951, Operational Plan Killer called for the 7th Division to pass through the ROK 3rd and 5th divisions on the right of the US 2nd Division and the 187th Airborne RCT, to assume a major role in General Ridgway's offensive to begin on February 22 the drive back north. The units of the 31st RCT, all but destroyed east of Chosin, were back in the war.

Appendixes

It may be useful to set down some thoughts on differences between the Marines and the Army troops who fought at Chosin and their organizations. While hundreds of Marines were killed or wounded in that Siberian-type operation against the Chinese Communists in November and December, 1950, most of the Marines eventually fought their way to the coast and lived to tell the tale. A small, improvised battalion of Army troops was organized from the remnant that survived Chosin and arrived at Hagaru-ri, physically able for further service after they had rested and were reequipped. These Army troops were attached to the 7th Marine Regiment for the breakout fight between Hagaru-ri and Koto-ri, the first phase of the breakout to the coast. The comments that follow do not deal with the fighting march from Hagaru-ri to the sea at Hungnam but relate to the troops, the conditions, and the factors that surrounded them in the previous battles at the Chosin Reservoir.

There was inevitable criticism from some quarters contrasting the decimation and destruction of the Army troops east of Chosin with the successful battles of the 1st Marine Division in reaching the coast, though with very heavy casualties. The Marines, as usual, received plaudits and were canonized in the public press—the Army troops were denigrated. Why could not the Army troops do what the Marines had done at Chosin?

That there is rivalry between the Marine Corps and the US Army in their respective versions of combat operations in which they mutually participate is known to everyone who has served in one or the other of the services. I have been present in two such campaigns, one at Okinawa in World War II, and the other in Korea, and I have heard much partisan talk about both campaigns. Now, after as careful a study of the operations east of Chosin as could be made from the evidence still available, and a similar study of the Marine operations at Chosin Reservoir, I venture certain observations.

First, let us recognize some differences between the Marine troops and their organization at the reservoir and the Army troops of the 31st RCT of the 7th Infantry Division. The 1st Marine Division was overstrength, with

336

an aggregate of about 25,000 men. These men were regulars of the Marine Corps or were from the Marine Active Reserve. Nearly every one of them had had extensive training and combat experience either in World War II or previously in the Korean War. Compared with the Army forces in Korea, all of which were in a pursuit formation in November, 1950, scattered over most of North Korea, the Marine force was well concentrated. This was an extreme contrast to the quickly organized ad hoc small force of about 3,000 men of the 7th Division who were hurriedly loaded into trucks, most of them nearly 100 miles from their assigned Chosin Reservoir destination. They had no chance to plan the movement or to provide adequate supplies. The intent was to provide a regiment-size force, a decision hastily arrived at by X Corps Headquarters, to protect the right flank of the 1st Marine Division in its projected attack toward the North Korean border. The Army troops were to come from the 7th Infantry Division, but that division was already so widely scattered over northeastern North Korea that the division could not commit any one of its three regiments to the mission. The two infantry battalions that did reach the east side of Chosin Reservoir were from different regiments and had not worked together as a combat force. The officers and men of the 1st Battalion, 32nd Infantry, for instance, did not even know the officers and men of the 3rd Battalion, 31st Infantry, or those of the 57th Field Artillery Battalion, when they joined together at the inlet perimeter.

Had it been possible for the whole 32nd Infantry with its regular supporting artillery, the 48th Field Artillery Battalion, and its regular tank company to have been sent to the Chosin Reservoir, together with its usual regimental supporting units, there is little doubt that it would have given a better account of itself than did the heterogeneous force that was instead assembled there. And the same thing would probably have been true if the full 31st Infantry Regiment had been there.

Another contrast between the 1st Marine Division and the 7th Infantry Division elements east of Chosin was that the Marines did not have any South Koreans or KATUSA among its combat units; in the 7th Division units about one-fourth of the members were KATUSA. It was the almost universal opinion of the officers and noncommissioned officers of the 7th Division elements at Chosin that these recently impressed, relatively untrained KATUSA were unreliable and caused more trouble than they were worth in a combat situation. As always, there were individual exceptions to this generalization.

When the CCF struck the troops east of Chosin Reservoir in their surprise attack on the night of November 27, the 31st RCT force was scattered in seven different groups between Hagaru-ri and the forward position of the 1st Battalion, 32nd Infantry. In addition, one infantry battalion intended for the 31st RCT, the 2nd Battalion, 31st Infantry, was 40 miles away on the road leading up from the coast and never reached the reservoir. In contrast, the 1st Marine Division had two infantry regiments, the 5th and 7th Marines, and most of its artillery regiment (the 11th Marines) concentrated at Yudam-ni, on the west side of the reservoir. The other Marine infantry regiment (the 1st Marines) was in three battalion-size perimeters from the southern end of the reservoir in strong points extending southward guarding the main supply route to the coast—at Hagaru-ri, Koto-ri, and at Chinhung-ni—with supporting arms. Only one Marine tank had reached Yudam-ni. The main tank force had been unable to cross Toktong Pass because of ice on the steep road. The Marines had been able to stockpile considerable ammunition at Yudam-ni, Hagaru-ri, and the battalion strongpoints southward on the road before the CCF attack. The Army units had not been able to stockpile ammunition, gasoline, or food supplies.

And another difference must be noted. Throughout the Chosin combat the 1st Marine Division had good communications among its units and with higher headquarters. The 31st RCT, on the east side of Chosin, had poor or nonexistent communications among its units and none with higher headquarters, except for tank-radio communication between Hagaru-ri and the 31st Rear at Hudong-ni. Communication is of the highest importance in battle.

Not to be overlooked in contrasting the two forces is that the 1st Marine Division had the magnificent 1st Marine Air Wing in close air support, with its related ground TACP units with each infantry battalion. True, one Marine TACP helped the 31st RCT east of the reservoir. The Fifth Air Force TACP with the 3rd Battalion, 31st Infantry, was destroyed the first night of the battle, November 27–28, at the inlet perimeter. Many of the Army soldiers openly said that without the remaining Marine Anglico TACP led by Captain Stamford, attached to the 1st Battalion, 32nd Infantry, they could not have lasted beyond the second day. Stamford did an outstanding job in handling close air support and airdrops of supplies, but the 31st RCT did not have the continuing massive close air support that buttressed the 1st Marine Divison troops at Chosin.

The 7th Infantry Division units that fought east of Chosin were from a division with a strength of about 16,000 men, contrasted with the 1st Marine Division, with a strength of 25,000 men, and the 7th Division rifle companies had a strength at Chosin averaging about 140 to 150 men as compared with a Marine rifle company of 225 men. It must also be accepted by an objective observer that on average the Army troops at Chosin were by no means the equals of the Marines in training and combat experience. Exceptions to this were many of the Army officers and some of the noncommissioned officers. They were generally of high caliber. Most of them were either killed or wounded while carrying out their duties. Most of the combat-experienced noncommissioned officers and trained riflemen had been taken from the 7th Division during the summer months as replacements for the other Army divisions in Eighth Army fighting in Korea.

Most of the enlisted men left in the 7th Division had no combat experience, and their training was not of the highest caliber, according to many observers, though a training program was in progress in Japan in 1949 and the first part of 1950. Because of limited training areas most of the training was on company or battalion level. The replacements that were taken in at this time came from the United States and had no combat experience. Before going into Korea in September, 1950, for the Inchon Landing, the 7th Division received some officers and noncommissioned officers from the Inactive Reserve who had World War II experience. The training and battle experience of the 7th Division during the Inchon Landing and the subsequent battle for Seoul was relatively minor and in no way made of the men the kinds of veterans needed at Chosin. At the time many thought the Army should have followed the Marine Corps example and called up its trained and experienced Reserves.

It has already been mentioned that the 6,000 almost entirely untrained KATUSA in the 7th Division and spread through all its units, including the rifle companies, were a source of weakness and a handicap rather than a help in combat. The only KATUSA in the 1st Marine Division were a relatively small number who acted as interpreters and some who served as intelligence agents. In any fair analysis the facts of combat allow one to say of the 7th Division east of Chosin that most of its noncommissioned officers were dedicated soldiers, that many an enlisted man turned out to be a hero, and that many, many in all ranks died in performance of their duty. But with the depletion in combat of their leadership, the officers and the senior noncommissioned officers, the Army units east of Chosin lost cohesion and disciplined action more quickly than did the Marines, which in fact never suffered the loss of leadership in killed and wounded to the same degree as did the Army units.

I believe that the 1st Marine Division in the Chosin Reservoir Campaign was one of the most magnificent fighting organizations that ever served in the United States Armed Forces. It had to be to do what it did, to fight to a standstill the Chinese forces at every point and then to carry out a fighting retreat southward against an enemy roadblock and fire block that extended all the way from Yudam-ni to the area below Chinhung-ni, a distance of about 40 road miles. This was done in the midst of extremely adverse weather conditions. The Marines never had a brighter moment in their long history than in the Chosin Reservoir Campaign. Their officers and noncommissioned officers gave often heroic example and leadership, and the rank and file performed with disciplined professionalism. Their commanding general, Maj. Gen. Oliver P. Smith, was a model of coolness, caution, and tactical and planning abilities. All the regimental commanders were outstanding and competent, even though one of them, Lt. Col. Raymond L. Murray, was relatively young. When the Marines had to leave accumulated dead behind, they buried them at Yudam-ni and at Koto-ri. The bodies were retrieved after the armistice in 1953. Inevitably some severely wounded men were left behind when the enemy held the ground that was being fought over, but the Marines brought out most of their wounded. Chosin will deservedly remain a moment of glory in US Marines' history.

APPENDIX B *31st Regimental Combat Team Organization Chart,*
27 November 1950

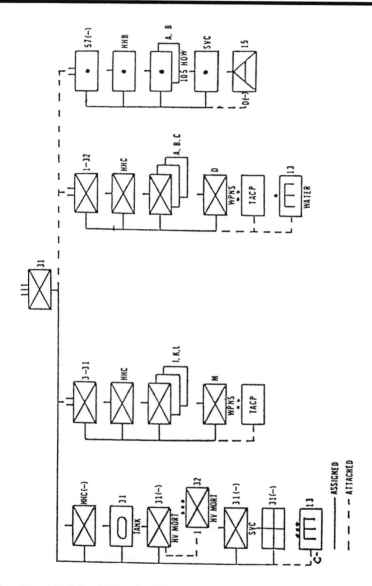

Adapted from Maj. Robert M. Coombs, "Changjin Reservoir, Korea, 1950" thesis, Command and General Staff College, 1975.

APPENDIX C 31st Regimental Combat Team, November 27, 1950 Estimated Strength

Unit	US Strength	KATUSA, Est.	Table, Organization and Equipment, Est.	Subtotal	Total
HQ and HQ Co. 31st Reg.	100 (est.)	50	–	150	
31st Tank Co.	187	–	–	187	
31st HM Co. (2 firing platoons and HQ) (est.)	106	–	–	106	
Service Co., 31st Inf. (50 included in HHC above) (est.)			–	–	
Medical Co., 31st Inf. (est.)	170	–	–	170	
1 platoon C Co., 13th Engineers	35 (est.)	–	–	35	648
1st Battalion, 32nd Infantry					
HQ and HQ Co.	101	50	–	151	
A Co.	145	50	–	195	
B Co.	139	50	–	189	
C Co.	150	50	–	200	
D Co.	137	50	–	187	
1 Platoon, HM Co., 32nd Inf.	40	–	–	40	
USMC (Anglico) TACP	5	–	–	5	967
3rd Battalion, 31st Infantry					
HQ and HQ Co.	96 (est.)	50	–	146	
I Co.	157 (est.)	50	–	207	
K Co.	141 (est.)	50	–	191	

L Co.	148 (est.)	50	—	198
M Co.	137 (est.)	50	—	187
USAF TACP	5	—	—	5
				934
57th Field Artillery Battalion (−)				
HQ and HQ Battery	141 (est.)	50	—	191
A Battery	110 (est.)	50	—	191
B Battery	107 (est.)	50	—	157
D Battery (−), 15th AAA AW Bn. (attached)	85	15	—	100
Service Battery, 57th FA Bn.	100	—	—	100
				739
				3,288

Note: The estimated strength of the 31st RCT on November 27, 1950, shown above is in some respects speculative and only roughly approximate. The figure 648 for the 31st RCT HQ and HQ Company special troops units is uncertain, but a reasonable estimate, except that for the 31st Tank Company it is rather precise. Major Lynch in a count on December 3, 1950, at Hagaru-ri gave 176 officers and men for the tank company, and its commander, Captain Drake, reported 11 casualties who had been evacuated. I know of only one platoon of C Company, 13th Engineers, that numbered 35 men. The figures for units of the 1st Battalion, 32nd Infantry, and the subtotal, 967, are considered reliable since they are based on Morning Reports for the period November 25–27, 1950 (1st Lt. Martin Blumenson notes). Blumenson (of 1st Information and Historical Team, Eighth Army) also gives an average of 50 KATUSA to a company and similar-size units, which I have adopted, though the number may have been larger in some instances. For example, Maj. James McClymont informed me that he had 100 KATUSA attached to his C Battery, 15th AAA AW, originally in Japan, but that he had only about 15 when he arrived at Chosin Reservoir on November 27. Desertions were heavy and continuous. McClymont indicated that his D Battery, 15th AAA AW Battalion, had 150 men before the 2nd Platoon was detached from the battery on a separate mission before Chosin. The figure of 85 men in his D Battery (−) was reached by deducting an estimated 65 men in the 2nd Platoon.

In his count of 31st RCT personnel at Hagaru-ri on December 3, Major Lynch counted 100 in the 57th FA Battalion Service Battery, and that figure is used here for that unit. It had suffered few if any casualties since it had been at Hudong-ni throughout the action. I can be reasonably confident of the numbers given in the table above for the 1st Battalion, 32nd Infantry; the 31st Tank Company; and the Service Battery of the 57th Field Artillery Battalion. The total for the 3rd Battalion, 31st Infantry, 934, is very close to that of the 1st Battalion, 32nd Infantry; since it would have had a number roughly comparable to that of the 1st Battalion on November 27, the 3rd Battalion figure is probably reasonably close to actuality. I believe that there were at least 3,000 troops in the 31st RCT at Chosin on November 27, and probably a somewhat larger number.

There were also some ROK troops or KATUSA attached to the 31st Heavy Mortar Company, the Medical Company, and possibly the platoon of C Company, 13th Engineers, and other small service units, but I do not know their number and have decided not to include an estimated figure for them in the table above.

APPENDIX D   *Strength of 1st Battalion, 32nd Infantry, Hagaru-ri, 4 December 1950*

Officers: Maj. Robert E. Jones
      1st Lt. Cecil G. Smith
      Lt. Barnes (48th Field Artillery, Forward Observer)

Total: 3 officers

Enlisted men:	No. Enlisted Men	No. ROKs
HQ Company	10	16
A Company	14	13
B Company	15	8
C Company	11	15
D Company	19	30
32nd Heavy Mortar (1 platoon)	3	7
Medical Company (detachment)	4	7
Total:	76	96

Source: From Maj. Robert E. Jones's report to Maj. William R. Lynch, 7th Division, G-3 Section, December 4, 1950, prepared at Hagaru-ri, Korea.

APPENDIX E   *Number of Enlisted Men of Units for Duty, 1st Battalion, 32nd Infantry, 7th Infantry Division, before and after Action against Chinese 80th Division East of Chosin Reservoir November–December, 1950*

Unit	No. Enlisted Men*	Date of Morning Report
A Company	145 16 (of original 145)	November 27, 1950 December 31, 1950
B Company	139 3 (of original 139)	November 26, 1950 December 28, 1950
C Company	150 21 (of original 150)	November 27, 1950 December 28, 1950
D Company	137 29 (of original 137)	November 25, 1950 December 28, 1950
HQ Company	101 10 (of original 101)	November 25, 1950 December 28, 1950

*Approximately 50 KATUSA were also missing from each company.
Source: 1st Lt. Martin Blumenson, notes, based on Official Morning Reports.

APPENDIX F *31st Regimental Combat Team, 7th Infantry Division, Chosin Reservoir Operation, Command and Staff List, November 27, 1950.*

31st Regiment

Commanding Officer	Col. Allan D. MacLean
Executive Officer	Lt. Col. George E. Deshon (not present at Chosin)
S-1	Maj. Hugh W. Robbins
S-2	Maj. Carl G. Witte
S-3	Lt. Col. Berry K. Anderson
S-4	
Commanding Officer, Headquarters Company	
Commanding Officer, 4.2-inch Mortar Company	Capt. George Cody
Commanding Officer, 31st Tank Company	Capt. Robert E. Drake

1st Battalion, 32nd Infantry Regiment

Commanding Officer	Lt. Col. Don C. Faith, Jr.
Executive Officer	Maj. Crosby P. Miller
S-1	Maj. Robert E. Jones
S-2	Capt. Wayne Powell
S-3	Maj. Wesley J. Curtis
S-4	Capt. Raymond Vaudreaux
Forward Air Controller	Capt. Edward P. Stamford, USMC
Commanding Officer, Headquarters Company	Captain Bauer (?)
Commanding Officer, A Company	Capt. Ed Scullion
Commanding Officer, B Company	Captain Turner
Commanding Officer, C Company	Capt. Dale Seever
Commanding Officer, D Company	Capt. Erwin B. Bigger

Note: The list of the principal staff officers is not complete as there were in the official records no roster lists of the units involved.

3rd Battalion, 31st Regiment

Commanding Officer	Lt. Col. William R. Reilly
Executive Officer	
S-1	Capt. Robert McClay
S-2	
S-3	Maj. Harvey M. Storms
S-4	Captain Adams
Forward Air Controller	First Lieutenant Johnson
Commanding Officer, Headquarters Company	
Commanding Officer, I Company	Capt. Albert Marr
Commanding Officer, K Company	Capt. Robert J. Kitz
Commanding Officer, L Company	Capt. William W. Etchemendy
Commanding Officer, M Company	Capt. Earle H. Jordan, Jr.

57th Field Artillery Battalion

Commanding Officer	Lt. Col. Ray O. Embree
Executive Officer	Maj. Max A. Morris
S-1	
S-2	
S-3 (Asst. Bn. Commander)	Lt. Col. Robert J. Tolly
S-4	
Commanding Officer, A Battery	Capt. Harold L. Hodge
Commanding Officer, B Battery	Capt. Theodore C. Goss
Headquarters & HQ Battery	Capt. Oliver G. Becker
Commanding Officer, D Battery (–)	Capt. James R. McClymont
15th Antiaircraft Battalion, Self-propelled (only 1st Platoon with Battery)	
Executive Officer	1st Lt. "Speed" Ballard

7th Infantry Division Liaison Officers at Chosin Reservoir

Brig. Gen. Henry I. Hodes, Assistant Division Commander
Maj. William Ray Lynch, Jr., G-3 Aide to General Hodes

Notes

Chapter 1

1. Lt. Col. Roy E. Appleman, *South to the Naktong, North to the Yalu (June–November, 1950): United States Army in the Korean War*, Office of the Chief of Military History, Department of the Army (Washington, D.C.: GPO, 1961), pp. 686–88, 741–45, (hereafter cited as Appleman, *South to the Naktong, North to the Yalu*); Maj. Gen. Edward M. Almond, Diary, Nov. 30, 1950, copy in author's possession (hereafter cited as Almond, Diary); Lt. Gen. William J. McCaffrey, USA, Ret., review comments on "East of Chosin" MS, Feb. 25, 1981.

2. Appleman, *South to the Naktong, North to the Yalu*, p. 764, citing author's interview with Maj. Gen. Clark L. Ruffner, Aug. 27, 1951; Lt. Col. William J. McCaffrey, X Corps deputy CS, 1950, memorandum to Gen. Almond, Dec. 1, 1954, copy provided to author by Gen. Almond; McCaffrey, review comments on "East of Chosin" MS.

3. X Corps, War Diary, Monthly Summary, Nov. 1–30, 1950, pp. 5–6 (National Archives, Federal Records Center, Record Group 407), lists the events, actions, and operational orders concerning the corps's changing mission.

4. GHQ, X Corps, Special Report on Chosin Reservoir, Nov. 27 to Dec. 10, 1950; X Corps, Plans and Orders; X Corps, War Diary, Nov. 25, 1950, Annex A to Periodic Operations Report No. 60, Operations Order No. 7.

5. Lt. Gen. William J. McCaffrey, USA, Ret., letter to author, Dec. 11, 1976.

6. Gen. Matthew B. Ridgway, USA, Ret., letter to author, Mar. 6, 1978.

Chapter 2

1. Comments based on study of 1950 map, 1916 data, scale 1:50,000, lent to author by Col. Robert E. Drake, USA, Ret. (CO, 31st Tank Co., 1950, then captain), and carried by him in the Chosin operation; study of subsequent maps, scale 1:50,000; and study of the latest-edition map, 1969–71 data, scale 1:50,000.

2. X Corps, Special Report on Chosin Reservoir Campaign; X Corps, War Diary, Nov. 26, 1950 Summary.

3. Lt. Col. Edward L. Rowny, X Corps engineer, GHQ, X Corps, Statement, May 28, 1951, copy in author's possession.

4. Capt. Nicholas A. Canzona, USMC, interview with author, 1955. Canzona was platoon leader, 1st Plat., A Co., 1st Eng. Bn., and was with A Co. at Sasu in November, 1950. The Marine Eng. Co. was recalled to Hagaru-ri on Nov. 29, 1950, to buttress the marine defenses and help defend East Hill. For withdrawal of A Co., 1st Eng., from Sasu and action at East Hill, see Lynn Montross and Nicholas A. Canzona, *The Chosin Campaign*, vol. 3 in *U.S. Marine Operations in Korea, 1950–53* (Washington, D.C.: GPO, 1962), pp. 211–20.

5. Lt. Col. Crosby P. Miller, "Chosin Reservoir, Nov–Dec 1950," October, 1953 (typescript MS, 25 pp., with marked map of east side of Chosin Reservoir; hereafter cited as Miller, MS). If Miller's reference to the battalion position" means the forward defense position, then his reference to the bridge at the Paegamni-gang as the only concrete bridge is in error, since the bridge over the Pungnyuri-gang at the inlet was also concrete. Contemporary photographs clearly show that the pillars of this bridge were concrete. But Miller is correct if he meant, as he probably did, the first position of the 1st Bn., 32nd Inf., at Twiggae and Hill 1221. See also note 8, below.

6. Appleman, *South to the Naktong, North to the Yalu*, pp. 732–38; Col. Carl G. Witte, lecture given to EOC, June 19, 1953, in which he describes some 31st Inf. action in the Fusen Reservoir area in November, 1950, copy lent to author by Col. Witte as attachment to his letter to author, Nov. 5–20, 1950; Map of Korea, Sinhung Sheet, K52T, L551, 1950, scale 1:250,000.

7. Col. Robert E. Jones, USA, Ret., letter to Maj. Robert M. Coombs, Command General Staff School, Fort Leavenworth, copy supplied to author. This is an important document, for it discusses many aspects and incidents of the action east of Chosin Reservoir not found elsewhere. Maj. Wesley J. Curtis, "Operations of the First Battalion, 32nd Infantry Regiment, 7th Infantry Division, in the Chosin Reservoir Area of Korea during the Period 24 November–2 December 1950: Personal Experience of the Battalion Operations Officer" (typescript MS, 23 pp., with map sketches, copy of 1st draft provided to author by Col. Curtis, USA, Ret.; hereafter cited as Curtis, MS). Curtis wrote this MS at the US Military Academy, West Point, N.Y., between September, 1951, and Jan. 28, 1953, using notes that he made in a hospital in Japan (he was wounded at Chosin on Dec. 1, 1950). The MS is generally accurate and a valuable primary source.

8. Miller, MS. Miller provided me with a copy of this MS in July, 1954. In his letter to me of July 7, 1954, he stated that the MS "was originally written purely as a personal record—notes jotted down before the details faded away completely."

Many of the dates and places and details have been coordinated with Major R. E. Jones who was the Bn S1 at the time." Miller was seriously wounded at Chosin and made many of these notes while in a hospital in Japan. His MS is a contemporary document of great value and includes an awesome account of his personal ordeal. It is remarkable that he survived Chosin.

9. Curtis, MS, pp. 4–5; Capt. Edward P. Stamford, USMC, "Statement on Action East of Chosin" (typescript MS), p. 1 (hereafter cited as Stamford, MS). Capt. Stamford, TACP leader and forward air controller with the 1st Bn, 32nd Inf., prepared this 19-page typescript at the request of the commandant, US Marine Corps. It was written and submitted to him in early February, 1951. Maj. Stamford provided me with a copy in 1979. This document is almost irreplaceable as a source of information on some aspects of the action east of Chosin. It is the only source known to me that gives details of the Marine Air Wing support for the 1st Bn., 32nd Inf., and later for Task Force Faith. A similar version of this MS is found on pp. 70–90 of a 97-page document reproduced by the Historical Division, HQ, USMC, dated Mar. 16, 1951, on the development of Anglico (Air Naval Gunfire Liaison Company) teams (hereafter cited as Stamford, Anglico Report). This document is based on Marine Corps extended interviews with Capt. Stamford. It has much information of value not found in his 19-page statement of early February, 1951, particularly on his own career in the Marine Corps before his attachment to 1st Bn., 32nd Inf., in Japan during the summer of 1950 and in the development of Anglico.

10. Lt. Col. Don Faith was born at Fort Sam Houston, Texas, on Aug. 26, 1918, the son of Don Carlos Faith, a career Army officer who rose to the rank of brigadier general. The younger Faith wanted to attend West Point, but was turned down as a candidate because of a dental disqualification, and afterward a draft board turned him down for the same reason when he tried to enlist at the beginning of World War II. Faith won an appeal from the latter decision and enlisted on June 25, 1941. At the time, he was attending Georgetown University in Washington, D.C., for foreign-service training. After becoming Gen. Ridgway's aide, and when the 82nd Inf. Div. was converted into an airborne division, the first in the US Army, Faith took parachute and airborne training—a short jump course—which qualified him for the 82nd Airborne Div. From February, 1942, to July, 1945, Faith served as Ridgway's trusted aide in the 82nd Inf. Div., the 82nd Airborne Div., and in the XVIII Airborne Corps when Ridgway was named its first commander. In February, 1948, Faith joined General Barr's American liaison group, which was advising Generalissimo Chiang-Kai-shek in the Chinese Civil War. During his China assignment Faith developed a strong friendship with Gen. Barr, which later continued when Barr commanded the 7th Inf. Div. in Japan and Korea. Because of Faith's extensive experience as aide to Gen. Ridgway and high-level staff assignments afterward, he was given constructive credit for the Advanced Course at the

Infantry School at Fort Benning and for the General Staff Course at Fort Leavenworth, which he had never attended. His experience and training were considered
their equivalent.

11. Col. Crosby P. Miller, USA, Ret., correspondence with author and review
comments on "East of Chosin" MS, 1976–81; author's correspondence with Curtis,
1976–81; GHQ, 7th Inf. Div., Special Order No. 195, Aug. 13, 1950, assigning both
Miller and Curtis to the 32nd Inf. Regt.

12. Author's correspondence with Curtis, 1976–81, and author's extended interviews with Curtis, 1976–81; Curtis, review comments on "East of Chosin" MS,
Feb. 16, 1981; comments to author in correspondence about Curtis from his fellow
officers in the 1st Bn.; US Military Academy, *Register of Graduates and Former Cadets,
1975* (West Point, N.Y.) p. 498, Item 13,402. Curtis was born in the Ozarks region
of Arkansas on May 9, 1918. He considered his experiences with the "Wolfhound
Regiment" (27th Inf., 25th Div.) in 1944–46 the most memorable and satisfying of
his Army career and felt that he had served under a series of fine regimental commanders, all "field soldiers," he said. When he was sent to Japan in 1950, he hoped
to be assigned to his old Wolfhound Regiment. That did not happen. He then
hoped that he might be sent to I Co., 17th Inf., in which he had served as an enlisted man at the beginning of his Army career. The 17th Inf. was now a part of
the 7th Inf. Div. He had no luck there either.

13. Curtis, MS, pp. 4–5; Stamford, MS, p. 1; Miller, MS, p. 2.

14. Curtis, MS, pp. 5–6.

15. Curtis, MS, p. 6; Stamford, MS, p. 1.

16. Lt. Col. James O. Mortrude, "Autobiographical Chronology of Chosin Reservoir Operation" (typescript MS; hereafter cited as Mortrude, MS). Mortrude sent
this document to me with his letter, Oct. 23, 1980. The document was prepared
at my request.

17. Curtis, MS, p. 6; Montross and Canzona, *The Chosin Campaign,* pp. 145–47.
Montross was a professional writer who had been associated with the Marine Corps
for many years. Canzona was a combat engineer officer, 1st Marine Eng. Bn, who
participated in the Chosin operations. Their work is based on exhaustive use of
official Marine Corps records, together with extensive interviews with Marine participants and their written affidavits of recollections and experiences. It is the official Marine Corps history of the operation and is generally a reliable one for the
Marine units involved. It is less satisfactory, however, for Army units and needs
to be extensively supplemented and enlarged to cover that topic adequately. The
most important Army units were the elements of the 7th Inf. Div. that fought on
the east side of the reservoir and those which subsequently participated in the defense of Hagaru-ri and in the Marine withdrawal to the coast. See also X Corps,
War Diary, November, 1950, pp. 27–28.

18. Mortrude, MS, pp. 1–2.

19. Lt. Col. James O. Mortrude, Retirement Form DD-214, Mar. 31, 1974, effective date; Roster, C Co., 32nd Inf., October, 1950; clipping from a Seattle newspaper, name and date missing, but apparently dating from February, 1951; statements to author by Majors Curtis and Miller and Capt. Bigger.

20. Col. James G. Campbell, USA, Ret., cassette-taped account of his experiences east of Chosin Reservoir as a platoon leader, prepared at my request (hereafter cited as Campbell, tape). Campbell taped this account on Nov. 29–30, 1980. The tape is in my possession. Résumé of Campbell's military service, 1949–50, in Campbell, letter to author, Dec. 13, 1980. Also, author's correspondence with Maj. Curtis and Capt. Bigger and author's interviews with Curtis, 1976 and 1981.

21. Curtis, MS, p. 3.

22. Ibid., p. 8.

23. Ibid.; Miller, MS, pp. 2–3. Both Curtis and Miller speak of Col. MacLean's arrival at their CP on the evening of Nov. 26. Curtis says that the 31st Inf. S-3 and S-1 and the communications officer accompanied MacLean. But Maj. Hugh Robbins, the 31st Inf. S-1, in an account he had left, indicates that he had not yet arrived at Chosin. Rather than Robbins it was Maj. Carl G. Witte, the regimental S-2, who arrived. The communications officer that Curtis mentions must have been Lt. McNally, the 31st Inf. communications officer. Lt. Col. Berry K. Anderson was the 31st regimental S-3.

24. Curtis, MS, pp. 8–9.

25. Comments about the former village of Hudong-ni are based on a study of the original black-and-white map, 1916 data, that Col. Robert E. Drake (the captain), CO, 31st Tank Co., carried in November and December, 1950, at Chosin, and on statements to the author by both Drake and Brig. Gen. William R. Lynch that, other than the schoolhouse, only house foundations were still standing at Hudong-ni in November, 1950.

26. Maj. Hugh W. Robbins, *Breakout* (n.p., n.d.), 6-page printed narrative of his experiences at Chosin Reservoir, apparently written from notes probably prepared in a hospital in Japan in December, 1950 (hereafter cited as Robbins, *Breakout*). Robbins was adjutant and S-1 of the 31st Inf. Regt. His account is an excellent source for the early movements of the 31st Inf. to Chosin Reservoir and of Col. MacLean's activities at his Advance CP. It also covers some actions at the 1st Bn., 32nd Inf., inlet perimeter on Nov. 29, 1950. Also, Col. Carl G. Witte, USA, Ret., letter to author, Dec. 15, 1978.

27. Robbins, *Breakout*; 1st Marine Div. Overlay, Special Action Report, Oct. 8–Dec. 15, 1950, vol. 2 of 3, Situation Overlay, Nov. 28–29, 1950, copy in author's possession; Maj. Ivan H. Long, AUS, Ret., letter to author, Apr. 29, 1981. Long was the 31st Inf. intelligence sergeant in November, 1950, and was with Col. MacLean at Hudong-ni and at his Advance CP. Maps of Korea, Changjin and Kalchon-ni Sheets, 1969 and 1971 data, scale 1:50,000.

28. Curtis, MS, p. 9; Drake, letter to author, Jan. 10, 1977; Witte, letters to author, Nov. 16, 1978, and May 26, 1980.

29. Lt. Gen. William J. McCaffrey, USA, Ret., review comments on "East of Chosin" MS, Feb. 27, 1981.

30. Col. Ray O. Embree, USA, Ret., letter to author, Mar. 18, 1979; 1st Lt. Thomas J. Patton, A Btry., 57th FA Bn., statement, Nov. 27–Dec. 27, 1950, n.d., but made in April, 1951, copy in author's possession.

31. Maj. James R. McClymont, letter to author, May 11, 1980 (see note 32, below); Embree, letter to author, Mar. 18, 1979.

32. McClymont, letter to author, May 11, 1980 (hereafter cited as McClymont, MS). This letter of 13 single-spaced typed pages is a narrative account of his experiences at Chosin, accompanied by a sketch map, no scale, of the 57th FA Bn., HQ Co., and his D Btry. (–), 15th AAA AW, positions on the night of Nov. 27–28, 1950. In addition McClymont provided 4 pages of answers to 27 questions I asked him. McClymont's material is a major source covering events east of Chosin, Nov. 27–Dec. 2, 1950; Patton, MS, p. 1; Roster of Officers, provided by Col. Ray O. Embree, 57th FA Bn., Oct. 15, 1950. Nearly all members of the 57th FA Bn. refer to the battery commanders Hodge and Goss after Chosin as "captain." Both were listed as first lieutenants in the October roster. They may have been promoted before the Chosin action. The same situation applies to Maj. Robert J. Tolly, S-3 of the 57th FA Bn., who is sometimes referred to as lieutenant colonel. Col. Embree says that he does not recall whether Tolly was promoted just before Chosin or subsequently. Copy of 57th FA roster for officers in author's possession.

33. Lt. Col. Earle H. Jordan Jr., letter to author, Jan. 5, 1979.

34. Ibid.

35. Col. Robert E. Drake, USA, Ret., letter to author, Nov. 17, 1977; Col. Robert E. Drake, "The Infantry Regiment's Tank Company," *Armor* 60, no. 5 (September–October, 1951): 14–17.

36. Col. Robert E. Drake, USA, Ret., letter to author, Jan. 10, 1977, with comments and answers to questions I asked him; Drake, letter to author, June 28, 1978.

37. Brig. Gen. William R. Lynch, Jr., USA, Ret., letters to author, Dec. 19, 1976, and Jan. 21, 1977.

38. 31st Inf. Command Report, November, 1950, cited in Maj. Robert M. Coombs, "Changjin Reservoir, Korea, 1950," (thesis, Command and General Staff College, 1975), p. 31, (hereafter cited as Coombs, thesis).

Chapter 3

1. Montross and Canzona, *The Chosin Campaign,* pp. 147–49, 151, 158; Curtis, MS, p. 9. Nov. 26 and 27 were hectic days for the 1st Marine Div., as well as for the 7th Inf. Div., in getting its troops in place for the X Corps attack ordered for the morning of Nov. 27. In trying to accomplish its role, the 1st Marine Div. had

to concentrate two of its regiments at Yudam-ni, the jump-off point, on the west side of the reservoir. On the 26th, the 3rd Bn., 1st Marines, less one company, arrived at Hagaru-ri and relieved the 2nd Bn., 7th Marines, which immediately moved to Yudam-ni; the 2nd Bn., 5th Marines, moved from east of the reservoir to Yudam-ni the same day and evening; and the 1st and 3rd Bns., 5th Marines, moved from east of Chosin to Yudam-ni on the 27th, the 1st Bn. not completing its move until after dark.

2. Capt. Nicholas A. Canzona, USMC, interview with author, 1952.

3. 1st Lt. Martin Blumenson, "Chosin Reservoir, 1st Battalion, 32nd Infantry, 24–30 Nov 1950," Aug. 20, 1951 (typescript MS, based on interview in Korea; mimeographed copy in files of Office of Chief of Military History, Washington, D.C.; hereafter cited as Blumenson, "Chosin Reservoir").

4. Miller, MS, p. 34. I believe that the battalion right flank of B Co. did not extend to the road but ended on the high ground of a spur ridge that ended short of the road. On the second day of action Lt. Col. Faith had to use most of HQ Co. as an improvised rifle company to extend the original right flank closer to the road to stop an enemy threat to envelop that flank.

5. Mortrude, MS, p. 2.

6. Curtis, interview with author, June 4–6, 1981, with 1:50,000-scale map of area in hand. Detailed study of map of Korea, Changjin and Kalchon-ni Sheets, 1969/1971 data, scale 1:50,000. Also, study of 1952 map of same area, 1951 data, scale 1:50,000, The 1952 map has contour intervals of 20 meters; that of 1969/1971 has 40-meter contour intervals. For the most part, the 1952 map has names similar to those the troops knew from their 1950 maps, though there are some omissions and changes from the 1950 map. The 1969/1971 data map shows villages and other place-names that are much different and in some cases are not recognizable with references in the Army's official records of the 1950 action. The locations of towns and villages are generally the same, but many of the names have been changed. Hagaru-ri, for instance, has been renamed Changjin. Terrain features are little changed.

Chapter 4

1. X Corps, War Diary, Nov. 26, 1950, Periodic Intelligence Report (PIR) No. 16, p. 3; X Corps, Special Report on Chosin Reservoir, Nov. 27–Dec. 10, 1950, p. 35; Montross and Canzona, *The Chosin Campaign*, p. 149.

2. Far East Command (FEC), Daily Intelligence Summary, No. 3207, June 21, 1951 (captured document giving CCF order of battle); X Corps, Special Report on Chosin Reservoir (Command Report), Nov. 27–Dec. 10, 1950, Maps A and B, and Maps 1, 2, and 3; FEC, Order of Battle Information, Chinese Communist Third Field Army Korean War, Mar. 1, 1951, National Archives, Federal Records Center, Record Group 407, Box 413; FEC, *Intelligence Digest* 1, no. 3 (Jan. 16–31, 1953): 30–37,

Record Group 407, Box 225; Montross and Canzona, *The Chosin Campaign*, app. G, "Enemy Order of Battle," pp. 397–98.

3. Based on the sources given in note 2 above.

4. When the 26th Army moved south to join in the Chosin battles, it apparently moved from Linchiang to Kanggje. There it turned east along the narrow-gauge railroad that crossed the mountains to the Changjin River, which it reached about 30 air miles north of the Chosin Reservoir. From there it proceeded upriver (south) to the reservoir and then up its west side to Yudam-ni.

5. The sketch of the Chinese 80th Div. is based on HQ, FEC, USAF, G-2, "Histories of CCF Army Groups Active in Korea, Part II, Ninth Army Group," *Intelligence Digest* 1, no. 3 (Jan. 16–31, 1953), esp. pp. 36–37, Record Group 407, Box 225; FEC, Daily Intelligence Summary, No. 3233, "Third CCF Field Army OB 2–6," July 17, 1951, National Archives, Record Group 407, Box 491; FEC, "Initial Commitment CCF into Korea," *Intelligence Digest*, Aug. 16–31, 1951, Record Group 407, Box 513; Montross and Canzona, *The Chosin Campaign*, pp. 397–98, app. G, "Enemy Order of Battle"; X Corps, War Diary, Nov. 1–30, 1950, pp. 23, 25.

6. GHQ, FEC, USAF, G-2, "Histories of CCF Army Groups Active in Korea, Part II, Ninth Army Group," *Intelligence Digest* 1, no. 3 (Jan. 16–31, 1953): 32–37. This source summarizes information available on the units discussed, based on hundreds of interrogations of enemy prisoners of war from the units involved, as well as study of many captured enemy documents.

7. X Corps, War Diary, November, 1950, pp. 19–21.

Chapter 5

1. Col. Robert E. Jones, letter to author, Jan. 5, 1979; Jones, letter to Maj. Robert M. Coombs, Jan. 15, 1975, copy in author's possession, courtesy of Colonel Jones, Curtis, MS, p. 10.

2. Curtis, MS, p. 10.

3. Résumé of Jones's military service, copy provided by Jones; unidentified newspaper (probably Poynor, Texas, newspaper), Nov. 24, 1950, article on Jones, quoting at length an article in the Pacific *Stars and Stripes*, copy in author's possession; author's correspondence and interviews with Col. Wesley J. Curtis, Capt. Erwin B. Bigger, Capt. Edward P. Stamford, and Maj. Crosby P. Miller, all four of whom knew Jones well at Chosin. All of them praised Jones. After Miller picked the bullet from Jones's chest, Jones put gauze and tape over the wound and took his reserve platoon up the hill. An hour later his company captured the hill. Jones did not report to a first-aid station until two days later, when the wound was already healing.

4. X Corps, War Diary, Nov. 24, 1950, Periodic Operations Report No. 59, p. 4; Blumenson, "Chosin Reservoir." Blumenson prepared this report in Korea in August, 1951. It includes information from the Morning Reports of the 1st Bn. for

the period covered. Also of use on KATUSA serving with the 1st Bn., 32nd Inf., is Jones, letter to Coombs, Jan. 15, 1975, p. 3. Appleman, *South to the Naktong, North to the Yalu,* on the first part of the Korean War, discusses the KATUSA situation relative to the 7th Inf. Div. in some detail and gives full credit to ROK units in the war.

5. Most of the information concerning Capt. Stamford's training and assignments in the USMC has been taken from Historical Division, HQ, USMC, "Interview with Captain Edward P. Stamford, Forward Air Controller (Anglico Team), attached to 1st Battalion, 32nd Infantry Regiment, 7th Infantry Division, USA, 16 March 1951," copy of this 97-page document in author's possession. Pages 1–7, 12–18, and 41–45 were especially useful. When Maj. Stamford visited me for a week in late September and early October, 1979, I learned much from him about the Anglico teams, the activities of a forward air controller working with ground troops, and specifically Stamford's work with the 1st Bn., 32nd Inf., at Chosin. Also useful have been Stamford's review comments on "East of Chosin" MS, Apr. 7, and May 7, 1981 (see also note 6 below).

6. Stamford, MS, with sketch map of east side of Chosin Reservoir, n.d., according to Stamford, prepared in January and early February, 1951 at Quantico Marine Base in Virginia at the request of the commandant, Marine Corps (see chap. 2, note 9). Stamford said that only two copies were made; one was given to him, and the other was marked "Secret" and held by the Marine Corps. Stamford's MS is one of the most valuable contemporary records relating to the action of Chosin. Stamford was in the movement of the 1st Bn. to Chosin and in the action thereafter from the beginning to the end. In comparison with all other relevant material examined, this document is of high quality and accuracy. It provides much information on some aspects not found elsewhere. In extensive interviews with Stamford I discussed the action east of Chosin in great detail. In 1979, Stamford was still a rugged, stocky man of evident physical strength and endurance. He still wore his hair crew-cut. He discussed battle with a no-nonsense, practical attitude, displayed intimate knowledge of his speciality, and took as a matter of course the need for physical and moral courage in meeting harsh battle conditions. These long discussions were supplemented when he and Mrs. Stamford visited me again on Oct. 28–29, 1980.

7. Stamford, letter to author, May 7, 1981, with three sketch maps showing the A Co. perimeter and the Chinese approach and penetrations of A Co.; Sgt. James J. Freund, Mortar Squad, Statement, attached to 7th Div., Command Report, Chosin Reservoir, National Archives, Federal Records Center, Record Group 407, Box 3172; Blumenson, "Chosin Reservoir"; Gugeler, *Combat Actions in Korea,* pp. 66–67; Stamford, Anglico Report. The Stamford, Miller, and Curtis MSS, all of which contain accounts of the beginning of the action and are substantially in agreement on the time it occurred, the main attack starting about 12:30 A.M., Nov. 28, 1950.

8. Stamford, letters to author, Apr. 7 and May 7, 1981, with sketch maps; Stamford, MS; Stamford, Anglico Report, p. 74.

9. Stamford, MS, p. 3, and Anglico Report, p. 75; Stamford, letter to author, Apr. 7, 1981, with sketch map of A Co.'s position. An article entitled "There Are Always Miracles," said to be by Capt. Edward P. Stamford (as told to Capt. Hubbard Kuokka, USMC), appeared in *Blue Book* magazine, November, 1951. It purported to tell the story of Stamford's experiences at Chosin. Stamford was incensed by the article and asked me not to use it as a source for anything about him. He said that it was inaccurate and that he did not like its tone or rhetoric. He said that the article had not been cleared with him before publication.

10. Stamford, MS, p. 5; Lt. Col. Erwin B. Bigger and Miller confirmed that Stamford commanded A Co. after Scullion was killed during the night of Nov. 27–28, 1950.

11. Bigger, letter to author, July 6, 1980; Bigger, telephone interview, May 8, 1980.

12. Bigger, letter to author, July 6, 1980; Bigger, telephone interview with author, May 8, 1980. Bigger learned after the event that the unknown soldier whose challenge sounded like "Eeeya, eeya" was asking in Chinese "Who is it?"

13. Blumenson, interview notes for "Chosin Reservoir," 1/32, July, 1951; Gugeler, *Combat Actions in Korea*, pp. 67–68; Curtis, interview with author, Curtis, May 5, 1979; Curtis, MS, p. 10; Bigger, letter to author, May 11, 1981. Blumenson says that the mess sergeant who tried to rescue Haynes was Casey. Gugeler says that Faith ordered Haynes to go up to A Co. and take command. Bigger's testimony indicates that this was not the case; Bigger, letter to author, July 6, 1980; Bigger, telephone interview with author, May 8, 1980. The spelling of the battalion S-4's name is uncertain. Everyone consulted stated that his name sounded like "Voo-dray." I have not seen a battalion roster or any other official document containing his name. Col. Miller thinks that the spelling Vaudreaux is correct.

14. Bigger, letter to author, May 11, 1981.

15. Capt. Hugh R. May, Report, Chosin Reservoir, Oct. 28, 1957 (hereafter cited as May, Report). This document is a 14-page typescript summary of May's experiences in the Chosin action. I have a copy of this document, courtesy of Col. Crosby P. Miller and subsequently courtesy of May. It is one of the valuable sources. May greatly expanded this account in two letters to the author, n.d., received in July and August, 1981, and two others to the author, Sept. 5 and Oct. 31, 1981.

16. GHQ, FEC, General Order No. 129, May 21, 1951, awarding the Distinguished Service Cross to Cpl. Godfrey; Lt. Col. Erwin B. Bigger, USA, Ret., letter to author, July 6, 1980; Stamford, MS.

17. Col. James G. Campbell, USA, Ret., letter to author, May 3, 1981.

18. Bigger, letter to author, July 6, 1980.

19. 7th Inf. Div., Command Report, Chosin Reservoir; Blumenson, "Chosin

Reservoir"; Gugeler, *Combat Actions in Korea,* pp. 67–68; Curtis, MS, pp. 10–11; Campbell, tape, Nov. 29–30, 1980.

20. Curtis, letter to author, Jan. 1, 1977, p. 4; Curtis, MS, p. 11; Maj. Robert E. Jones, Report to Maj. Lynch, G-3 Sect., 7th Div., Dec. 4, 1950; Sfc. Richard B. Luna, B Co., 32nd Inf., Statement, n.d., but made the day after he escaped to Hagaru-ri, apparently Dec. 2 or 3, 1950, attached to 7th Inf. Div. Command Report, Chosin Reservoir (hereafter cited as Luna, Statement); Robbins, *Breakout,* p. 1.

21. Stamford, interview with author, Oct. 1–3, 1979; Blumenson, "Chosin Reservoir"; Campbell, tape.

22. Capt. Robert J. Kitz, commanding officer of K Co., 3rd Bn., 31st Inf., Affidavit, presumably on Dec. 3, 1950, the day after his escape to Hagaru-ri. Kitz's affidavit is an attachment to the 7th Inf. Div. Command Report, Chosin Reservoir (hereafter cited as Kitz, Affidavit); M. Sgt. Ralph M. Payne, K Co., 31st Inf., Statement, Apr. 15, 1951; Sgt. John B. Gibbs, L Co., 31st Inf., Statement, Apr. 19, 1951.

23. Sfc. John C. Sweatman, K Co., 31st Inf., Statement, Apr. 19, 1951, copy in author's possession (hereafter cited as Sweatman, Statement).

24. 1st Lt. Thomas J. Patton, A Btry., 57th FA Bn., Statement, n.d., apparently prepared in April or May, 1951, copy in author's possession (hereafter cited as Patton, Statement).

25. Kitz, Affidavit, p. 3; Coombs, thesis, p. 35; Pfc. Lewis D. Shannon, I Co., 31st Inf., Statement.

26. GHQ, FEC, General Order No. 172, July 2, 1951, Distinguished Service Cross award to Sgt. Stanford O. Corners.

27. Mrs. Celeste B. Reilly, widow of Lt. Col. William R. Reilly, letter to author, Feb. 11, 1977, citing a long letter she said Lt. Henry Traywick had written to her in December, 1950, describing the circumstances in which he rescued her husband from his CP on the morning of Nov. 28, 1950. I have tried unsuccessfully to find Traywick to obtain his recollections. Lt. Col. Earle H. Jordan states that he met Traywick near the Communications CP just after daylight on the 28th and that Traywick told him he had driven the last of the Chinese from the area.

28. Mrs. Reilly, letter to author, n.d., received Feb. 22, 1977; newspaper clipping, Barre, Vt., n.d., carrying a news story dated Dec. 21, 1950; copy of letter addressed to "Dearest Mother and Dad," signed "Bill, Jr." (Lt. Col. William R. Reilly), Dec. 17, 1950, from Osaka Army Hospital, Japan, in which he describes the nature of his wounds at his CP on Nov. 28, 1950. In this letter Reilly mentions the great number of Chinese dead in the 3rd Bn. position: "I never saw so many dead people before—far more than the Battle of the Bulge." Lt. Col. Earle H. Jordan, in a letter to the author, Feb. 28, 1980, and in another, Feb. 5, 1979, states that Capt. Adams and the assistant S-3 (Lt. Anderson) were killed or died of wounds received in the 3rd Bn. CP and that Reilly was wounded there. How many others were injured there or escaped from the CP is unknown to me.

29. Coombs, thesis, p. 35, citing correspondence with Lt. Col. William R. Reilly.

30. Capt. Earle H. Jordan, Jr., letter to author, Jan. 5, 1979. In this letter Jordan said, "The Chinese soldiers were dressed in white." Photographs in the author's possession showing enemy dead within the perimeter confirm that their uniforms were white. In all other places of enemy action east of Chosin the Chinese uniforms were green-brown.

31. Jordan, letters to author, Feb. 5, 1979, and Feb. 28, 1980.

32. Jordan, letter to author, Jan. 5, 1979.

33. Drake, letter to author, Jan. 10, 1977; 7th Inf. Div., Command Report, Chosin Reservoir, Nov. 27–Dec. 12, 1950, p. 3; Col. Carl G. Witte, USA, Ret., correspondence with author, 1978–80; Maj. William R. Lynch, Jr., letter to author, Dec. 19, 1976, and attached list of 31st RCT strength at Hagaru-ri, Dec. 3, 1950. The 7th Inf. Div. Action Report says that the Medical Co. left Hudong-ni about 1:00 A.M. on Nov. 28. Drake thought that it was about 3:00 A.M. when the Medical Co. first sergeant arrived back at his CP and told him about the ambush. The 7th Div. Action Report states that some members of the Medical Co. fought through to the 3rd Bn., 31st Inf.

34. Lynch, letter to author, Dec. 19, 1976.

35. Hodes died at Fort Sam Houston, Texas, on Feb. 14, 1962. See also chapter 6, note 12.

36. Robbins, *Breakout.*

37. Curtis, letter to author, June 5, 1980.

38. Col. Ray O. Embree, USA, Ret., letter to author, Aug. 15, 1980. Embree, in his letter to the author, Mar. 18, 1979, discusses his reconaissance of the bivouac area during the day with Col. MacLean. Maj. James R. McClymont, USA, Ret., Statement (13 pages) and sketch map of bivouac area, on his experiences at Chosin Reservoir, n.d., prepared at the author's request and received by me on July 9, 1980 (hereafter cited as McClymont, MS). Enclosed with this narrative letter was a 4-page list of answers to specific questions I had asked in a letter to him of May 6, 1980. McClymont's statement and letter of answers to my questions are valuable sources on an important unit's actions east of Chosin Reservoir that are covered nowhere else to my knowledge, including the Army's official records, since no copy of the action of D Btry or that of the 57th FA Bn. could be found in the National Archives for the period in question—November and December, 1950.

39. McClymont, letter to author, July 7, 1980.

40. McClymont, MS, p. 4.

41. McClymont, MS, and letter to author, July 7, 1980; GHQ, X Corps, General Order No. 74, Dec. 24, 1950, award of Silver Star to Capt. James R. McClymont for action Nov. 28, 1950. McClymont in his narrative says that he found Major Tolly dead in the yard of the 1st Plat. CP. But Col. Embree assured me that

it was Maj. Max Morris, the FA executive officer, who was killed there. Maj. Tolly survived the war. Capt. McClymont was not well acquainted with the officers of the 57th FA Bn., never having met any of them until the day before he started for Chosin Reservoir. Embree, letters to author, Mar. 18, 1979, and Aug. 15, 1980. See also *Antiaircraft Journal*, March–April, 1951, p. 21, for text of Silver Star Award, Posthumously, to Roscoe M. Calcote.

42. McClymont, MS, p. 6.

Chapter 6

1. Maj. Robert E. Jones, Report to Maj. William R. Lynch, Dec. 4, 1950; Lt. Col. Ivan H. Long, AUS, Ret. (intelligence sergeant, 31st Inf., November–December, 1950), letters to author, Mar. 21, 1979, and Mar. 18, 1980; Robbins, *Breakout.*

2. Curtis, MS, p. 11; X Corps, War Diary, Nov. 28, 1950, Periodic Intelligence Report No. 65, p. 3; Robert F. Futrell, *The United States Air Force in Korea, 1950–1953* (New York: Duell, Sloan, and Pearce, 1961), p. 239 (hereafter cited as Futrell, *US Air Force in Korea*); Blumenson, "Chosin Reservoir."

3. Miller, MS, pp. 6–7; Stamford, MS, p. 6; see also Gugeler, *Combat Actions in Korea*, pp. 68–69; Stamford, review comments on "East of Chosin" MS, Apr. 7, 1981; Bigger, review comments on "East of Chosin" MS, Mar. 29, 1981.

4. Mortrude, MS, pp. 3–4, with letter to author, Oct. 23, 1980. In his tape Col. Campbell confirms the loss of this high ground at C Co.'s right flank.

5. Miller, MS, p. 7; Bigger, review comments on "East of Chosin" MS, Mar. 29, 1981.

6. Stamford, MS, p. 6. The tank was a Soviet-built T-34 that retreating North Koreans had apparently left in the possession of the CCF. Miller refers to two truckloads of Chinese soldiers in this approaching column. The Chinese were about two to three miles north of A Co. when the Corsairs and the F-51s hit them. Stamford, interview with author, Oct. 28–29, 1980.

7. Curtis, MS, p. 12; Jones, Report, to Maj. Lynch, 7th Div., G-3 Sect., Dec. 4, 1950.

8. X Corps, War Diary; Almond, Diary, Nov. 28, 1950, in GHQ, X Corps, Special Report on Chosin Reservoir, Nov. 27–Dec. 10, 1950, p. 15; Curtis, letter to author, Jan. 30, 1977; Lt. Gen. Edward M. Almond, USA, Ret., interview with author, Apr. 28–29, 1977; Blumenson, "Chosin Reservoir"; Gugeler, *Combat Actions in Korea*, pp. 69–70. In his review comments on "East of Chosin" MS, Mar. 2, 1981, Col. Jones explains how he arranged to have the three awards citations formally issued in 1951. Gugeler's account, *Combat Actions in Korea*, pp. 69–70, of the Silver Star award incident is based on Blumenson, "Chosin Reservoir," and his own correspondence with one eyewitness, but this version, as well as Blumenson's, that Smalley threw away his Silver Star, is rebutted by Col. Jones's comments. Blumenson bases his statement that Smalley threw away his Silver Star on an interview

with 1st Lt. Cecil G. Smith, who said that Smalley told him about it. There seems to be no doubt that Lt. Col. Faith threw away his Silver Star. Col. Curtis also confirms that he saw him do so.

9. Bigger, letter to author, July 6, 1980; Jones, review comments on "East of Chosin" MS, Mar. 2, 1981; Maj. Hugh R. May, letter to authors, n.d., received July 24, 1981, p. 3.

10. Lt. Gen. Edward M. Almond, USA, Ret., interview with author, Apr. 28–29, 1977; Almond, Diary, Nov. 28–29, 1950; Almond, letter to author, Dec. 21, 1976.

11. Col. Robert E. Drake, USA, Ret., letters to author, June 28, 1978, Jan. 10, 1977, Feb. 17, 1977, and Feb. 1, 1977, and review comments on "East of Chosin" MS, Feb. 22, 1978; Brig. Gen. William R. Lynch, letter to author, Jan. 21, 1977; Lynch, interview with author, June 12, 1978.

12. Both Drake and Hodes had distinguished careers in the Army after the Korean War. Hodes rose to four-star rank and was commander-in-chief of the United States Army in Europe (USAREUR), 1956.

13. The identity of the Medical Co. first sergeant is not known to me. He may have been Ernest J. Fontaine, Medical Co., 31st Inf., who is listed as killed in action in a memorandum of Feb. 24, 1951, from the Office of the 7th Div. Quartermaster to the 114th Graves Registration Sect., listing personal effects of the deceased. This document does not name the several sergeants in the list as other than simply "Sergeant." Col. Carl G. Witte, 31st S-2, 1950, provided me with a copy of this memorandum. Drake, letter to author, Jan. 10, 1977; Capt. Robert E. Drake, CO, 31st Tank Co., Memorandum, Dec. 12, 1950, to CO, 31st Inf., attachment to 7th Inf. Div. Action Report, Nov. 21–Dec. 20, 1950, National Archives, Federal Records Center, Record Group 407, Box 3172; Lynch, letter to author, Jan. 21, 1977, and interview with author, June 12, 1978; Col. Carl G. Witte, letter to author, May 26, 1980. The 7th Div. Action Report, made up after the event, indicates that about a platoon of improvised infantry from Engineers and miscellaneous service troops at the 31st Rear CP accompanied Drake's tanks on the 28th. But Drake, Lynch, and Witte, all at Hudong-ni at the time, agree that no such troops were with the tanks on that day. I have used Drake's original map, along with a 1969–72 data map, to describe the terrain approaching Hill 1221. At two places on this map blood from the Medical Co. sergeant's head wound had rotted holes in the Drake map and had discolored many other places on it—a poignant map that carried one back to the scene. Drake, letter to author, Feb. 24, 1981.

14. Lynch, letter to author, Jan. 21, 1977, and interview with author, June 12, 1978. Lynch told me that he heard Gen. Hodes give this order to Hensen and that he watched Hensen make one attempt that failed and then set out on a second one.

15. Lynch, letters to author, Dec. 19, 1976, and Jan. 21, 1977, and interview with author, June 12, 1978.

16. Drake, letters to author, Jan. 10, Feb. 1, and Feb. 17, 1977; Lynch, letters to author, Dec. 19, 1976, and Jan. 21, 1977, and interview with author, June 12, 1978.

17. Drake, letter to author, May 6, 1980; Lynch, letter to author, Jan. 21, 1977; Sgt. Jimmy P. Howle, letter to Col. Robert E. Drake, Feb. 8, 1986, copy in author's possession.

18. Witte, letters to author, May 26, 1980, and Dec. 15, 1978; 31st Inf. Command Report, November, 1950. Troop numbers at Hudong-ni are based on Lynch's memorandum of Dec. 3, 1950, and his report to X Corps (telephoned from Hagaru-ri to Maj. Gen. Clark Ruffner, chief of staff, X Corps), Dec. 3, 1950, copy of handwritten memorandum in author's possession.

19. Drake, letters to author, Feb. 1, 1977, Jan. 10, 1977, and Jan. 12, 1977.

20. Jordan, letter to author, Feb. 28, 1980; Futrell, *US Air Force in Korea*, p. 239.

21. Patton, Statement; 1st Lt. Paul C. Smithey, B Btry., 57th FA Bn., Statement, Apr. 18, 1951, copy in author's possession (hereafter cited as Smithey, Statement).

22. Smithey, Statement; 1st Lt. Edward L. Magill, with B Btry., 57th FA Bn., at Chosin, Statement, Apr. 17, 1951, copy in author's possession; Sfc. Carroll D. Price, GHQ Btry., 57th FA Bn., Statement, Apr. 18, 1951; 2nd Lt. William N. Eichorn, GHQ Btry., 57th FA Bn. (Security Plat., B Btry., at Chosin), Statement, Apr. 18, 1951; Pfc. Grover H. Powell, GHQ Btry., 57th FA Bn. (radio operator, Fire Direction Center), Statement, Apr. 18, 1951. Most of the statements and comments by artillerymen of the 57th BA Bn. quoted in the narrative and cited here were made in April, 1951. All of them refer to Goss as "captain." Harold Hodge, CO of A Btry., is also referred to as "captain." However, a roster dated Oct. 15, 1950, and provided to me by Col. Embree gives the rank of first lieutenant for both Hodge and Goss. Both officers were promoted between Oct. 15, 1950, and April, 1951, but it appears that at Chosin Reservoir both officers held the rank of captain.

23. Author's correspondence with Jordan, Mrs. Reilly, and Curtis.

24. McClymont, MS, and letter of answers to author, p. 2.

25. McClymont, letter of answers to author, p. 2. In preparing the account of events during the daytime on Nov. 28, I have consulted the 7th Inf. Div. Command Report, Chosin Reservoir, Nov. 27–Dec. 12, 1950, copy in author's possession, but it has not been cited because it contains many errors and omissions.

Chapter 7

1. Kitz, Affidavit (see chapter 5, note 22); Lt. Col. Earle H. Jordan, letter to author, Feb. 5, 1979.

2. 1st Lt. Keith E. Sickafoose, F.O., K Co., Statement, Apr. 18, 1951 (Sickafoose was assigned to C Btry., 57th FA Bn., but was on loan to K Co. at Chosin); Sfc. Robert M. Slater, section leader, D Btry., 15th AAA, Statement, Apr. 17, 1951.

3. Patton, Statement.

4. McClymont, MS, p. 7; text of Silver Star award to Sgt. Brown, *Antiaircraft Journal*, March–April, 1951, p. 13.

5. McClymont, MS, p. 7, and letter to author, July 7, 1980.

6. Sweatman, K Co., 31st Inf., Statement, Apr. 19, 1951.

7. Smithey, Statement.

8. Curtis, MS, p. 13.

9. Maj. Hugh R. May, USA, Ret., review comments on "East of Chosin" MS, n.d., received July 24, 1981; May, letters to author, n.d., received Aug. 22, 1981, and Sept. 5, 1981. Also, comments from Curtis and from Jones to author about May and his performance at Chosin.

10. May, letter to author, n.d., received Aug. 22, 1981, pp. 10–11.

11. May, Report.

12. Col. James G. Campbell, tape, and review comments on "East of Chosin" MS, Apr. 9, 1981, with sketch map of C Co. situation; Miller, MS, p. 7.

13. Mortrude, MS, p. 4, and letter to author, Oct. 23, 1980.

14. Capt. John D. Swenty, 1st Bn., 32nd Inf., Statement on Chosin, p. 1 (hereafter cited as Swenty, MS).

15. Miller, MS, pp. 7–8.

16. Robbins, *Breakout*, 2, col. 2; Stamford, MS, p. 6.

17. Robbins, *Breakout*, 2, col. 3.

18. Ibid.

19. Curtis, MS, p. 13, and letter to author, Jan. 1, 1977; Order of Battle, U.S. 7th Inf. Div., Sept. 1, 1950–Dec. 31, 1950, section f., Detached Units, p. 5 (gives dates when units such as the 1st Bn., 32nd Inf., were attached to the 1st Marine Div.); Robbins, *Breakout*, 2, col. 3; 7th Inf. Div Command Report, Chosin Reservoir, Nov. 27–Dec. 12, 1950, p. 5.

20. Sfc. Richard S. Luna, B Co., 1st Bn., 32nd Inf., Statement, ca. Dec. 3, 1950 (hereafter cited as Luna, Statement); GHQ, FEC, General Order No. 129, May 21, 1951, Distinguished Service Award to Cpl. James H. Godfrey, D Co., 1st Bn., 32nd Inf., for action Nov. 29, 1950.

21. Miller, MS, p. 8; May, Report on Chosin Reservoir, Oct. 28, 1957, p. 2.

22. Curtis, MS, p. 13.

23. Ibid.; Miller, MS; Luna, Statement; 7th Inf. Div. Command Report, Chosin Reservoir, Nov. 27–Dec. 12, 1950; Mortrude, MS, pp. 4–5. Mortrude's statement leaves no doubt that he and two platoons of C Co. covered the high ground to the left of the road during the withdrawal. Luna's statement and other sources indicate that B Co. or part of it was also part of the left (east) flank guard and that other units or parts of them also were on high ground to the left of the road in the latter part of the withdrawal. Maj. Miller's MS is explicit that A Co. was the rear guard. Maj. Curtis was the ranking officer with the left (east) flank guard.

24. May, Report, pp. 2–3.

Chapter 8

1. Robbins, *Breakout*, pp. 2–3.

2. Campbell, tape, and review comments on "East of Chosin" MS, Apr. 9, 1981; Luna, Statement; Blumenson, "Chosin Reservoir."

3. Miller, MS, pp. 8–9; May, Report, p. 3, and letter to author, n.d., received Aug. 22, 1981, p. 11.

4. Miller, MS, p. 9; Maj. Robert E. Jones, S-1, 1st Bn., 32nd Inf., Report to Maj. Lynch, G-3 Sect., 7th Div., Dec. 4, 1950 (hereafter cited as Jones, Report). This 3½-page single-spaced typewritten report is one of the important contemporary documents on the action east of Chosin. It was written only two days after the survivors reached the 1st Marine Div. lines at Hagaru-ri. It covers the entire period of action, as seen by and known to Jones from its beginning to near its end, Nov. 27–Dec. 2, 1950. Jones supplied a copy of this report to me; I did not find it among the attachments to the 7th Inf. Div. Command Report for November–December, 1950, when I searched the 7th Div. official records in the National Archives in 1974. Miller's MS is also of importance concerning the withdrawal of the 1st Bn. on Nov. 29, 1950.

5. Capt. Erwin B. Bigger, letter to author, July 6, 1980, which includes a résumé of his military service; Bigger, telephone interview with author, May 8, 1980; Col. Wesley J. Curtis, correspondence with author, 1976–81. Curtis has a high opinion of Bigger as a professional soldier. Stamford, correspondence with author, also gives Bigger a high rating.

6. Jones, letter to author, Jan. 5, 1979. Jones and Cody were old friends from World War II. Campbell, review comments on "East of Chosin" MS, Apr. 9, 1981.

7. May, Report, p. 4.

8. Miller, MS, p. 9.

9. Campbell, tape, and review comments on "East of Chosin" MS, Apr. 9, 1981; Jones, Report; Luna, Statement.

10. Luna, Statement; Kitz, Affidavit.

11. Mortrude, MS, pp. 4–5 (the words "and overshoes" were added by Mortrude in his review comments on "East of Chosin" MS, December, 1981.

12. Capt. John D. Swenty, 1st Bn., 32nd Inf., Statement, Apr. 14, 1951, p. 2 (hereafter cited as Swenty, Statement).

13. Sgt. Luna's language in his Hagaru-ri statement in early December, 1950, indicates that he was one of the six men who, with Lt. Col. Faith, removed the logs of the roadblock. Capt. Bigger, who knew Luna well from his days as commanding officer of B Co., has this to say about him: "Sgt Luna was the 1st Sgt of B/32 when I commanded that unit. He was killed shortly after the reorganization of 1/32 in Jan or Feb 51. Sgt Luna was one of the finest human beings I have ever

364 NOTES TO PAGES 141–145

known. He was soft spoken, professional, loved and was loved by his men and all men who knew him." Bigger, letter to author, July 6, 1980, p. 9.

14. Luna, Statement.

15. Mortrude, review comments on "East of Chosin" MS, May 12, 1981.

16. Robbins, *Breakout*, 3, cols. 1–2.

17. Ibid., col. 2.

18. Ibid.

19. Jones, Report; Miller, MS, p. 10; GHQ, FEC, General Order No. 201, Aug. 7, 1951, Distinguished Service Cross award for Sgt. Charles Garrigus.

20. Patton, Statement.

21. Jones, review comments on "East of Chosin" MS, Mar. 2, 1981; Bigger, letter to author and answers to questions, July 6, 1980.

22. Curtis, letter to author, Jan. 30, 1977; Kitz, Affidavit; Mortrude, review comments on "East of Chosin" MS, May 12, 1981; Campbell, review comments on "East of Chosin" MS, Apr. 9, 1981, and letter to author, May 3, 1981; Luna, Statement. References to an attack across the ice of the inlet in the early morning of Nov. 29, 1950, are found in Jones, Report; Miller, MS (Miller did not see the incident but apparently received the information from Jones, from whom he said he had received collaboration in preparing his MS); Blumenson, "Chosin Reservoir"; Gugeler, *Combat Actions in Korea*, p. 72. Gugeler used Blumenson's MS and may have based his version on it. There was no attack across the inlet into Chinese-held ground that morning as suggested in these accounts.

23. Swenty, Statement.

24. Stamford, MS, and Anglico Report, p. 81. In an interview with the author, September–October, 1979, Stamford reiterated his belief at the time that the troops he saw were enemy troops beginning their withdrawal from their night attack on the 3rd Bn. and 57th FA Bn. perimeter. Campbell saw the same troops and attempted to take them under fire from the ridge of Hill 1324. He said that it was light enough to identify them as Chinese from their clothing and actions. Campbell, review comments on "East of Chosin" MS, Apr. 9, 1981.

25. Stamford, MS, and Anglico Report, pp. 6–7, 81.

26. Curtis, letter to author, Jan. 1, 1977; Campbell, review comments on "East of Chosin" MS, Apr. 9, 1981. Events later in the day showed that the perimeter had not been reduced, but the impression that it had been is revealing.

27. Bigger, letter to author, July 6, 1980, p. 4, italics added; Bigger, telephone interview with author, May 8, 1980.

28. US Military Academy, *Register of Graduates and Former Cadets, 1975*, p. 402, Item 8998, on MacLean.

29. X Corps, General Order No. 30, Nov. 14, 1950, awarding the Silver Star to Lt. Col. William R. Reilly and to Col. Allan D. MacLean for action against Chinese forces near the Fusen Reservoir; Reilly, letter to parents at Barre, Vt.,

Nov. 20, 1950; Col. Robert E. Drake, USA, Ret., letter to author, Feb. 17, 1977; Lt. Gen. Edward M. Almond, USA, Ret., letter to author, Mar. 8, 1977; Brig. Gen. William R. Lynch, Jr., review comments on "East of Chosin" MS, May 16, 1981; Col. Robert E. Jones, review comments on "East of Chosin" MS, Mar. 2, 1981.

30. Jones, Report.

31. Bigger, telephone interview with author, Mar. 11, 1981 (in this interview I took almost verbatim notes as Bigger talked, and I typed up the notes immediately afterward); Jones, letter to author, Jan. 5, 1979, and review comments on "East of Chosin" MS, Mar. 2, 1981, p. 3. The 7th Inf. Div. Command Report, Chosin Reservoir, Nov. 27–Dec. 12, 1950, p. 5, commenting on the MacLean incident, says, "Portions of A and C Companies attacked across the ice, driving out the Chinese forces dug in there." However, no Chinese were dug in there. The command report was made up some weeks or months later from unknown sources and unknown persons; it contains many errors and extensive omissions and is not a reliable source. It is apparent, however, from internal evidence that Jones's Report, Dec. 4, 1950, was used in part. Jones has stated to me that he was not personally consulted and had no opportunity to review the 7th Div. report. Other officers of the 1st Bn., 32nd Inf., have told me the same thing.

32. Bigger, letter to author, May 11, 1981, and Bigger's sketch map of MacLean's route across the inlet enclosed with this letter.

33. Bigger, letter to author, July 6, 1980, and telephone interview with author, May 8, 1980, in which Bigger stated the same thing but added that he saw MacLean fall several times on the ice and that the Chinese were watching MacLean as he crossed. Curtis, letter to author, Jan. 1, 1977. Curtis's sketch of his route to the inlet and MacLean's crossing puts MacLean's crossing about 1,200 yards west of the bridge. Other estimates of the crossing site put it closer to the bridge. But Curtis's estimate does not differ greatly from Bigger's. Curtis probably based his estimate on the recognizable location of the spur ridge that he descended to arrive at the inlet road. Curtis apparently saw only the latter part of MacLean's crossing. Also, Maj. Gen. David G. Barr, letter written at Hungnam, Korea, to Mrs. Don C. Faith, Jr. (he addressed her as Barbara), Dec. 12, 1950, in General Matthew B. Ridgway Papers (US Army Military History Research Collections, Army War College, Carlisle Barracks, Pa.), Box 17, Folder D-1. Gen. Barr gave Gen. Ridgway a copy of this letter after the latter assumed command of Eighth Army following Gen. Walker's death. In Barr's letter to Mrs. Faith he told her all he knew about Faith's death at Chosin and also included an account of his visit with Faith on Nov. 30 at the inlet perimeter, when Faith told him about Col. MacLean.

34. Curtis, MS, p. 14, and letter to author, Jan. 1, 1977; Jones, Report, p. 2. Jones says that the 1st Bn., 32nd Inf., had closed into the 3rd Bn. perimeter by 12:30 P.M., Nov. 29, 1950, and subsequently made the search for Col. MacLean.

35. I recall reading a newspaper interview with the soldier that told of Col.

MacLean's death and burial. The soldier interviewed was probably one of the thousands turned over to American authorities during the armistice prisoner exchange in 1953. I made a clipping of the article and put it with other Korean War notes. Now, more than 30 years later, I cannot find the clipping and provide the citation. But I am so certain of the facts recounted that I have no hesitation in including them in this narrative.

36. GHQ, FEC, General Order No. 177, July 7, 1951, awarding the Distinguished Service Cross to MacLean. Unfortunately, this order is like so many other for military awards and decorations for valor, leadership, and outstanding devotion to duty in combat. Part of it is factually inaccurate when it need not have been, and some of it is overblown rhetoric. One familiar with the award-making process soon learns to distrust the accuracy of award citations.

37. Stamford, MS, p. 20, and interviews with author, Oct. 28–29, 1980; Bigger, letter to author, July 6, 1980, p. 7.

38. Stamford, Memorandum for author, Nov. 29, 1979.

39. Robbins, *Breakout*, 3, cols. 2–3.

40. Ibid., pp. 3–4.

41. Curtis, letter to author, Jan. 1, 1977.

42. Mortrude, MS, pp. 5–6, letter to author, Nov. 3, 1980, and review comments on "East of Chosin" MS, May 12, 1981.

43. Curtis, letter to author, Jan. 1, 1977; Curtis, interview with author, May 5, 1979; Stamford, interview with author, Oct. 28–29, 1980; Map of Korea, scale 1:50,000.

44. Map of Korea (Chosin Reservoir area), 1952 ed., scale 1:50,000; Map of Korea, Changjin Sheet, 1971 ed., scale 1:50,000.

45. Jones, Report; Curtis, MS, p. 14, referring to sketch of inlet perimeter for Nov. 29, 1950.

46. Lt. Col. Earle H. Jordan, Jr., letter to author, Feb. 28, 1980. In a letter to Col. Miller, undated, but probably written in October, 1953, or perhaps as late as November or December of that year, Maj. William W. Etchemendy made reference to the inlet perimeter in this vein: "L Co sector which had the north position with our left flank tied in with your C Company." Col. Miller permitted me to see this letter. Also, Miller, MS, p. 10; Jones, Report. The Curtis MS included sketches of the forward perimeter and also of the inlet perimeter. The inlet perimeter sketch showed it as reorganized by Lt. Col. Faith on the afternoon of Nov. 29, 1950, when the 1st Bn., 32nd Inf., joined the 31st Inf. troops already there. The sketches of these perimeters in Gugeler, *Combat Actions in Korea*, in the section on Chosin Reservoir, are based on the Curtis sketches, which Curtis provided to Gugeler. Curtis told me that he intended the sketches to be generalizations. The inlet perimeter that I described in the narrative and show in my own sketch is considerably smaller and of different proportions from those shown in the Cur-

tis sketches. Col. Jones, reviewing my sketch of the inlet perimeter said that he thought it "more closely resembles the actual area covered." Lt. Col. Bigger, reviewing the sketch and the narrative description, thought them "nearly correct" (Jones, review comments on "East of Chosin" MS, Mar. 2, 1981, p. 10; Bigger, telephone interview with the author, Mar. 11, 1981). Stamford's detailed discussion with me about the inlet perimeter, especially its western part, was of great help in defining its limits rather closely. I devoted a great amount of time to a detailed map study of the Changjin Sheet, Korea, scale 1:50,000 in the 1950, 1953, 1970 data eds., in arriving at my sketch of the inlet perimeter for the period from the afternoon of Nov. 29, 1950, to the early afternoon of Dec. 1. I cannot claim precise accuracy for the perimeter shape and dimensions on its southern side. I am reasonably confident about its shape and dimensions on the other sides.

47. Curtis, MS, and interview with the author, May 5, 1979; Curtis, letter to author, June 5, 1980. In this letter Curtis wrote: "I was unaware of any reorganization. Faith may well have announced one to Miller. Our method of operation did not change. Faith operated from the CP of 1/32; Miller, I, Jones, and Bigger were his 'staff'—leg men. All communication was by telephone—or on foot. It was a very small and crowded perimeter—just a short walk to the CP of the 3/31 and FA Bn.—but I must say, difficult to determine who was in charge at either place." Miller, MS, p. 10, says "I was placed in command of the 1st Bn, 32nd Inf," and said he had information from Maj. Jones that Storms and Tolly commanded the other two battalions. Author's correspondence with McClymont, Bigger, Stamford, Mortrude, and Campbell.

48. Robbins, *Breakout*, 4, col. 1; Stamford, MS, p. 8. Others also have mentioned the airdrops on the afternoon of the 29th, including Col. Ray O. Embree, letter to author, Mar. 18, 1979; X Corps, Special Report on Chosin Reservoir, Nov. 27–Dec. 10, 1950; 7th Div., Command Report, Chosin Reservoir, Nov. 27–Dec. 10, 1950; Maj. James R. McClymont, letter to author, July 7, 1980, p. 7.

49. McClymont, letter to author, July 7, 1980.

50. Col. Robert E. Drake, letter to author, Jan. 10, 1977; Stamford, interview with author, September–October, 1979. When Stamford learned from me during these interviews that 40-mm ammunition had been dropped at Hudong-ni instead of at the inlet, he exploded in wrath at the "d——d knuckleheads" who had committed the blunder. The ammunition was priceless to Task Force Faith. Stamford thought that the dual-40s might have let the task force successfully to Hagaru-ri if they had been resupplied with ammunition and fuel. Only the fact that McClymont had arrived at Chosin with two basic loads of ammunition instead of the usual one enabled the dual-40s and quad-50s to stay in the fight until the breakout and play an invaluable role in holding the inlet perimeter.

51. Curtis, MS, correspondence with author, 1976–80, and interview with the author, May 5, 1979; 7th Inf. Div., Command Report, Chosin Reservoir, Nov.

27–Dec. 10, 1950; X Corps, Special Report on Chosin Reservoir, Nov. 27–Dec. 10, 1950; Maps of Korea, 1950, 1952 and 1971 eds., Chosin Reservoir Area Sheets, scale 1:50,000.

Chapter 9

1. Col. Robert E. Drake, letter to author, Jan. 10, 1977; Drake, "A Small Unit Action," *Armor*, September–October, 1951, pp. 16–17; Col. Carl G. Witte, letter to author, May 26, 1980. The sketch map on p. 17 of *Armor* magazine cited above is inaccurate in several respects, being somewhat a composite of the two days' action, according to Drake in letter to author, Jan. 10, 1977.

2. Drake, letters to author, May 6, 1980, and Feb. 22, 1978; GHQ, X Corps, General Order No. 74, Dec. 24, 1950, awarding the Silver Star to Maj. (Chaplain) Martin C. Hoehn. The date of the action given in the order as Nov. 28, 1950, should be Nov. 29, 1950. The citation makes no mention of Hoehn using a weapon.

3. Drake, letter to author, Mar. 22, 1978.

Chapter 10

1. There is much confusion in various 7th Div. reports, statements of Lt. Col. Reidy in the 7th Div. Command Report, and in the 2nd Bn., 31st Inf. Command Report, Nov. 29–Dec. 12, 1950, on the X Corps orders and the movements of the 2nd Bn., 31st Inf., in the period Nov. 27–30, 1950. The Command Report of the 2nd Bn., 31st Inf., for the period should be the most reliable document, but it is based on interviews the division historian Maj. Jacobson, held on Dec. 15, 1950, with Lt. Col. Richard R. Reidy, the battalion adjutant, and the battalion S-2. This document is known to omit important information. The 7th Div. Command Report is also not entirely reliable. All have discrepancies in dates, and none of them includes the negative comments found in Maj. Gurfein's Statement, cited below, for obvious reasons. The version of the main events given in the narrative tries to reconcile these discrepancies with 1st Marine Div. and 1st Marine Regt. records relating to the progress of the 2nd Bn. up the road to Koto-ri, its arrival there, and the subsequent attachment to the 1st Marine Regt. Army references used are 2nd Bn., 31st Inf., Command Report, Nov. 29–Dec. 12, 1950, National Archives, Record Group 407, Box 3179; 7th Inf., Command Report, Nov. 27–Dec. 12, 1950, Record Group 407, Box 3172; 7th Inf. Div., Action Report, Nov. 21–Dec. 20, 1950, Record Group 407, Box 3172; X Corps, Special Report on Chosin Reservoir, p. 56; author's correspondence with Lt. Gen. William J. McCaffrey, USA, Ret., 1976–80; Maj. Joseph I. Gurfein, GHQ, X Corps, G-3 Air, Statement, May 26, 1951 (hereafter cited as Gurfein, Statement). For 1st Marine Div. data on the subject see Montross and Canzona, *The Chosin Campaign*, pp. 225–36.

2. Gurfein, Statement, May 26, 1951, p. 1.

3. Ibid.

4. Ibid.

5. Ibid., p. 2.

6. 7th Inf. Div., Command Report, Nov. 27–Dec. 12, 1950; 7th Div., Action Report, Nov. 21–Dec. 20, 1950; 1st Marine Div., Special Action Report, Oct. 8–Dec. 15, 1950, p. 67; 2nd Bn., 31st Inf., Command Report, Nov. 29–Dec. 12, 1950. C Btry., 57th FA Bn., was with the 2nd Bn., 31st Inf.

7. GHQ, FEC, General Order No. 177, July 7, 1951, awarding 1st Lt. Alfred J. Anderson the Distinguished Service Cross.

8. 7th Div., Command Report, Nov. 27–Dec. 12, 1950; Montross and Canzona, *The Chosin Campaign*, pp. 225–35.

9. Montross and Canzona, *The Chosin Campaign*, p. 238; Andrew Geer, *The New Breed: The Story of the U.S. Marines in Korea*, pp. 333–34.

10. Brig. Gen. William R. Lynch, letters to author, Dec. 19, 1976, and July 30, 1980, p. 4.

11. Lynch, letter to author, July 30, 1980, and review comments on "East of Chosin" MS, May 16, 1981.

12. Lt. Gen. William J. McCaffrey, USA, Ret., letter to author, Mar. 11, 1978. McCaffrey said that General Almond wanted the X Corps Advance CP at Hagaru-ri to spur the 1st Marine Div. in moving out in its scheduled attack to the west.

13. Lynch, letters to author, Jan. 21 and Dec. 19, 1976, and review comments on "East of Chosin" MS, June 12, 1978.

14. Ibid.

15. Lynch, letter to author, July 30, 1980.

Chapter 11

1. "NR: C 69953, 28 Nov 1950, From CINCFE TOKYO JAPAN SGD MACARTHUR TO: JCS WASH, DC INFO: DEPT AR WASH CD CM in 14957 28 Nov 1950," printed in full in *Pertinent Papers on Korean Situation*, 8 vols., II, 345; Gen. Matthew B. Ridgway, Memo of Record, Nov. 28, 1950, in General Matthew B. Ridgway Papers, US Army Military History Research Collections, Carlisle Barracks, Pa.

2. Eighth Army, War Diary, Nov. 29, 1950, *EUSAK* [Eighth US Army Korea] *Daily News*, Summary, gives the text of the communiqué; text of communiqué and accompanying article, *New York Times*, Nov. 29, 1950.

3. Almond, Diary, Nov. 28, 1950.

4. Maj. Gen. Courtney Whitney, *MacArthur: His Rendezvous with History* (New York: Alfred A. Knopf, 1956), pp. 423–24, lists the persons said to have been at the conference and indicates the substance of the issues discussed at the meeting. Lt. Gen. Edward M. Almond, USA, Ret., in an interview with the author, Apr. 28–29, 1977, confirmed the participants in the meeting and the comments he

and Gen. Walker made to Gen. MacArthur at the conference. Whitney errone-
ously gives the date of the conference as the night of Dec. 1, 1950.

    5. Ibid.; Lt. Col. James F. Schnabel, Ret., *Policy and Direction the First Year:
The United States Army in the Korean War* (Washington, D.C.: Office of Chief of
Military History, US Army, 1972), pp. 278–79 and n. 22; Lt. Gen. Almond, inter-
views with author, Dec. 13, 1951, Nov. 23–24, 1954, and Apr. 28–29, 1977.

    6. Almond, Diary, Nov. 29, 1950; author's correspondence and interviews with
Lt. Gen. William J. McCaffrey, USA, Ret., 1976–80.

    7. "Msg. from JCS to: CINCFE TOKYO JAPAN NR: JCS 97592 29 Nov 1950,"
Pertinent Papers on Korean Situation II, 354. In the MacArthur hearings on May 22,
1951, pp. 972ff., Sen. William Fulbright entered into a detailed examination of Gen.
Omar Bradley, chairman of the Joint Chiefs of Staff, about Gen. MacArthur's radio
message of Nov. 28, 1950, to the Joint Chiefs and their reply of the 29th.

Chapter 12

    1. Robbins, *Breakout*, 4, col. 1; Miller, MS, p. 10; Curtis, MS, p. 15; May, Re-
port, p. 4; Kitz, Affidavit; Stamford, MS, pp. 8–9.

    2. Curtis, MS, pp. 14–15; Kitz, Affidavit; Maj. James R. McClymont, letter
to author, July 7, 1980; Campbell, tape.

    3. McClymont, letter to author, July 7, 1980, and accompanying *AAA Journal*
notes, pp. 1–2.

    4. Ibid.; GHQ, Eighth Army, General Order No. 135, Mar. 12, 1951, awarding
the Distinguished Service Cross to Sgt. Harold B. Haugland, D Btry., 15th AAA
AW Bn., SP, for action Nov. 29–30, 1950; 7th Inf. Div. Command Report, Chosin
Reservoir, Nov. 27–Dec. 12, 1950, p. 6.

    5. Campbell, tape.

    6. Curtis, MS, and letter to author, Feb. 13, 1977; Mortrude, MS, p. 6; Geer,
The New Breed, pp. 333–34; 7th Inf. Div. Command Report, Chosin Reservoir, p. 6.
Majors Curtis, Miller, and Jones, the principal staff officers serving Lt. Col. Faith
at the Inlet, have told me in correspondence, in response to questions, that Lt.
Col. Faith never told them what transpired in his meeting with Gen. Barr. Lt. May's
remark, "No one seemed to know what was said to Col. Faith by Gen. Barr in
their final meeting," reflects that situation; Maj. Hugh R. May, letter to author,
Sept. 5, 1981.

    7. X Corps, War Diary, November–December, 1950; Montross and Canzona,
The Chosin Campaign, pp. 238–39; Lt. Gen. Edward M. Almond, USA, Ret., interview with author, Apr. 28–29, 1977; Almond, Diary, Nov. 30, 1950.

    8. For a brief résumé of Gen. Barr's testimony before the House Foreign Af-
fairs Committee on Apr. 6, 1949, see *Rocky Mountain News*, Dec. 13, 1976 (UPI
release, Washington, D.C.). Of course, many other newspapers in the country car-

ried the UPI release. The committee subsequently published in eight volumes the previously classified testimony (see chapter 11, note 1).

9. Stamford, MS, p. 9; Draft of Narrative of Actions of Cpl. Myron J. Smith on Nov. 30 and Dec. 1, 1950, copy in author's possession.

10. Capt. Edward P. Stamford, review comments on "East of Chosin" MS, Apr. 7, 1981.

11. Col. Wesley J. Curtis, interview with author, June 4–6, 1981.

12. Curtis, MS, pp. 15–16.

13. Miller, MS, pp. 11–12.

14. May, Report, p. 4, and letter to author, Mar. 14, 1982, supplementing original source in his report.

15. May, Report, pp. 4–5.

16. Curtis, MS, p. 16.

17. Almond, Diary, Nov. 30, 1950.

18. Geer, The New Breed, pp. 333–34.

19. X Corps, War Diary, Nov. 29, 1950, pp. 54–55; 7th Inf. Div., Action Report, Nov. 21–Dec. 20, 1950, p. 6; Lt. Gen. Edward M. Almond, USA, Ret., interview with author, Apr. 28–29, 1977; Montross and Canzona, The Chosin Campaign, pp. 238–39; Lt. Gen. Edward M. Almond, USA, Ret., letters to author, Mar. 22, 1976, and June 30, 1978. The 7th Inf. Div. Report says that the 31st RCT was informed at 8:20 A.M. on Nov. 30, 1950, that it was attached to the 1st Marine Div., but the question is: How could that have been done, and by whom? There was no communication system by which to do it. It seems reasonably certain that Faith could not have known about this until Gen. Barr's conversation with him at the inlet on the 30th. One may assume that Barr told Faith of the change in command responsibility stated in Almond's recent order, but we do not know that he did.

20. Almond, interview with author, Apr. 28–29, 1977; Almond, letter to author, June 30, 1978; Almond, Diary, Nov. 30, 1950; Brig. Gen. William R. Lynch, Jr., review comments on "East of Chosin" MS, May 16, 1981.

21. Almond, Diary, Nov. 30, 1950; Almond, interview with author, Apr. 28–29, 1977; Lt. Gen. William J. McCaffrey, interview with author, Feb. 4, 1976; McCaffrey, letter to author, Dec. 5, 1975; Montross and Canzona, The Chosin Campaign, pp. 238–39; Col. S. L. A. Marshall, interview with Col. Alpha A. Bowser, Jr., G-3, 1st Marine Div., Jan. 2, 1951, copy of transcript in author's possession.

22. Almond, Diary, Nov. 30, 1950.

23. Geer, The New Breed, pp. 333–34; Curtis, MS, and author's extended correspondence and interviews with Curtis, 1976–80; Brig. Gen. William R. Lynch, Jr., interview with author, June 12, 1978, makes it clear that Lt. Col. Faith did not receive any message from Gen. Smith on Nov. 30 or Dec. 1, 1950, while he was still in the inlet perimeter. Faith made the move out of the perimeter on his own

judgment and decision. The 1st Marine Div. situation at the Chosin Reservoir on Nov. 30, and its inability to send a relief column from Hagaru-ri to assist Task Force Faith on Nov. 30 or Dec. 1 is well summarized in 1st Marine Div., Special Action Report, Oct. 8–Dec. 15, 1950, vol. 2, Annex Charlie, Nov. 29, 1950, Periodic Operations Report No. 64, pp. 2–3.

Chapter 13

1. Montross and Canzona, *The Chosin Campaign*, p. 219; Nicholas A. Canzona, interview with author, July, 1952; Brig. Gen. William R. Lynch, interview with author, June 12, 1978.

2. Lynch's tabulation of 31st Inf. was reported from Hagaru-ri to the X Corps CP at Hamhung on Dec. 3, 1950. This report was given by radio telephone to X Corps Chief of Staff Maj. Gen. Clark Ruffner; copy supplied to author by Gen. Lynch.

3. Lynch, letters to author, Dec. 19, 1976 and July 30, 1980; Col. Robert E. Drake, letters to author, Feb. 1 and Dec. 23, 1977. Drake's letter to author of Feb. 19, 1978, included a sketch of the 31st Rear and 31st Tank Co. area with the locations of the schoolhouse and other features.

4. 7th Inf. Div. Command Report, Chosin Reservoir, p. 7; Capt. Robert E. Drake, Memorandum to CO, 31st Inf., Dec. 12, 1950 (attached to 7th Div. Action Report, Nov. 21–Dec. 20, 1950); extract from letter from Capt. George S. Rasula, Feb. 4, 1951, sent with letter from Ivan H. Long to Col. Carl G. Witte, Mar. 4, 1952 (Col. Witte provided the author with a copy of the Long-Rasula correspondence); Witte, letter to author, Dec. 15, 1978; Drake, letter to author, Jan. 10, 1977; Lynch, interview with author, June 12, 1978.

5. Lynch, letter to author, July 30, 1980, p. 5.

6. Lt. Gen. William J. McCaffrey, USA, Ret., interview with author, Feb. 4, 1976.

7. Lynch, interview with author, June 12, 1978, and extensive correspondence with Gen. Lynch.

8. Statement of Col. Alpha A. Bowser, G-3, 1st Marine Div., to Col. S. L. A. Marshall in Marshall's interview with Bowser, Jan. 2, 1951, p. 5 of interview typescript; copy in author's possession.

9. Drake, Memorandum to CO, 31st Inf., Dec. 12, 1950; Maps of Korea, Changjin Sheet, scale 1:50,000.

10. Witte, letter to author, Dec. 15, 1978; Drake, letter to author, Jan. 10, 1977, says "We had no trouble on the road to Hagaru-ri." Lynch, interview with author, June 12, 1978. Witte, in his letter of Dec. 15, 1978, wrote, "I don't recall anything out of the ordinary about the move except it was not easy to gather the perimeter forces."

11. Drake, letter to author, May 8, 1978; 1st Marine Div., G-3 Journal, Nov. 30,

1950, Msg. 37; 1st Marine Div., Special Action Report, Oct. 8–Dec. 15, 1950, vol. 2, Annex Charlie, Nov. 30, 1950, p. 68. An entry in the 1st Marine Div., G-3 Journal, Dec. 30, 1950, at 1900 (7:00 P.M.) states: "Serv Bn: Adv elems RCT 31 arrived Hagaru-ri." The 1st Marine Div. Action Report says, "At 1900 Headquarters elements of RCT-31 and the 7th Infantry Division ADC Group closed the Hagaru-ri area." These sources indicate that the Hudong-ni group from the 31st RCT arrived just before dark, somewhat later than the statements of participants indicated. The Marine citations indicate that it was after dark. Perhaps the Marine citations were entered a bit late in the G-3 Journal. In any event, the evidence is clear that Drake's tanks arrived just before dark and were in the Marine perimeter by dark.

Chapter 14

1. Robbins, *Breakout*, 4, cols. 2–3; Stamford, MS, p. 9; Miller, MS, p. 12.

2. Mortrude, MS, pp. 6–7; Lt. Col. James O. Mortrude, in review comments on "East of Chosin" MS, May 12, 1981, changed slightly his original wording.

3. Maj. James R. McClymont, letter to author, July 7, 1980, p. 10; *Antiaircraft Journal*, July–August, 1951, p. 19; May, Report, p. 5; Stamford, MS, p. 9; Curtis, MS, p. 16.

4. Curtis, MS, p. 16; Capt. Earle H. Jordan, Jr., review comments on "East of Chosin" MS, Jan. 5, 1979.

5. May, Report, p. 5.

6. Miller, MS, p. 12.

7. Curtis, MS, pp. 16–17.

8. GHQ, X Corps, General Order No. 74, Dec. 24, 1950, awarding the Silver Star to Pfc. Stanley E. Anderson, gunner of a 3.5-inch rocket launcher, L Co., 3rd Bn., 31st Inf.

9. Curtis, MS, pp. 16–17; Kitz, Affidavit. It appears that at the point of penetration, L Co. men, in the composite K Co. commanded by Capt. Kitz, joined the boundary of Capt. Seever's C Co. at that company's eastern extremity. There, Hill 1200 constituted a rounded crest at the northern end of a long ridge that sloped down from the south. From the crest of Hill 1200 there was a sudden drop of 100 feet northward to the Pungnyuri-gang, east of the point where the bridge crossed it at the head of the inlet. This was also a battalion boundary between the 1st Bn., 32nd Inf., and the remnants of the 3rd Bn., 31st Inf. Maj. William W. Etchemendy, in a letter to Col. Crosby P. Miller, n.d., but written after October, 1953, referred to an earlier episode at this spot, saying, "L Co sector which had the north position with a left flank tied in with your C Company." In November–December, 1950, at the inlet perimeter, Etchemendy, then captain, commanded L Co., 31st Inf. I have based my description of the point of enemy penetration on a study of Map of Korea (1970 data), scale 1:50,000, and comments by Campbell.

10. Campbell, tape, and letter to author, Dec. 13, 1980, and attached two sketches

of Lt. Wilson's route of movement to the point of enemy penetration, based on his observation of the event.

11. Curtis, MS, p. 17; Gugeler, *Combat Actions in Korea*, pp. 75–76, has the most detailed description of Wilson's fight to regain the knob, based on statements of participants or observers of it; see Gugeler's n. 28. Gugeler has told me about his correspondence with Col. Wilson on the subject. Lt. Col. Erwin Bigger states that Lt. Wilson's father, Col. Robert Wilson, Sr., was deputy commander of the Pusan Area Command at the time of his son's death. Bigger stayed overnight with Col. Wilson at Pusan when he returned from the hospital in Japan on his way to rejoin the 32nd Inf. in Korea in early 1951. He learned then that Col. Wilson had interviewed many survivors of the Chosin battles and had acquired from them a detailed knowledge of the inlet fighting and of his son's death; Bigger, letter to author, July 6, 1980. Lt. James G. Campbell, platoon leader of Bigger's Machine Gun Platoon, also visited Col. Wilson at Pusan in early March, 1951, when he was returning to duty with the 32nd Inf. from a Kyoto hospital and confirms Bigger's remarks about Col. Wilson's accumulation of information about the inlet battles. Campbell, tape, and letter to author, Dec. 13, 1980.

12. Kitz, Affidavit; Bigger, letter to author, July 6, 1980; Miller, MS, p. 12; Curtis, MS, p. 18.

13. Gugeler, *Combat Actions in Korea*, p. 76, citing interview with Campbell.

14. Miller, MS, p. 12.

15. Curtis, MS, p. 17–18.

16. Col. Edward P. Stamford, interview with author, Oct. 28–29, 1980.

Chapter 15

1. Blumenson, "Chosin Reservoir"; Gugeler, *Combat Actions in Korea*, p. 77.

2. Curtis, MS, p. 19; Stamford, interviews with author, September–October, 1979; Stamford, review comments on "East of Chosin" MS, Apr. 7, 1981. In Stamford's MS for the commandant, USMC, written in February, 1951, p. 9, Stamford said of his action on Dec. 1, 1950, asking for air support, "At daylight Col. Faith made preparations to fight south to Hagaru-ri and had me send a message requesting aircraft and to notify CG, 7th Inf. Div of his contemplated action." This statement, read literally, could be misleading about the time Faith decided and made preparations to fight out of the perimeter and the time Stamford sent the radio message for air support and to notify Gen. Barr, 7th Div. The account given in the narrative is believed to be correct and was approved by Stamford.

3. Author's correspondence with Curtis, Miller, Jones, and McClymont and interviews with Curtis and Stamford; Curtis, Miller, and Stamford, MSS; May, Report.

4. McClymont, letter to author, July 7, 1980; May, Report, p. 6; Miller, MS, p. 13; Curtis, MS, pp. 18–19.

5. May, Report, p. 6, says that he was to destroy the vehicles left behind, but in his letter to author, n.d., received Aug. 22, 1981, p. 7, he gives his statement as quoted.

6. Miller, MS, p. 14. Capt. Bauer, not previously identified, was CO of HQ Co., 1st Bn., 32nd Inf. Capt. Jack Thompson was an assistant to Capt. Bauer.

7. Capt. Earle H. Jordan, Jr., letters to author, Jan. 5, 1977, and Oct. 30, 1978.

8. Cpl. Helmuth Bertram, M Co., 31st Inf., Statement, Apr. 19, 1951, copy in author's possession. In World War II, Bertram fought in the German army at Stalingrad and Moscow.

9. Mortrude, MS, pp. 7–8.

10. Swenty, Statement, p. 2.

11. 7th Inf. Div. Command Reports, Chosin Reservoir; Curtis, MS, and correspondence with author; McClymont, letter to author and attachments, July 7, 1980; Capt. Hugh R. May, letter to author, n.d., received Aug. 22, 1981, p. 7.

12. Stamford, MS, p. 10.

13. Kitz, Affidavit; Luna, Statement.

14. Jordan, letter to author, Oct. 30, 1978.

15. May, Report, p. 6, and letter to author, Sept. 5, 1981; Capt. Erwin B. Bigger, letter to author, July 6, 1980, and telephone interview with author, May 8, 1980; Campbell, tape, and review comments on "East of Chosin" MS, Apr. 9, 1981. At first Bigger did not know what had happened to his eye and remembered only that a medic did something to it. Later, some of those present told him that it was out of its socket and that the medic replaced it. In author's telephone interview with Bigger, Mar. 13, 1982, Bigger said that both of Capt. Jack Thomspon's legs were broken in this mortar-shell explosion.

16. Curtis, MS, pp. 18–19.

17. Campbell, review comments on "East of Chosin" MS, Apr. 9, 1981.

18. Curtis, letter to author, Feb. 18, 1981.

19. 31st Regt. Sgt. Maj. John A. Lynch, Jr., Statement quoted in press release issued by EUSAK, n.d., apparently in March or April, 1951, copy in author's possession.

20. Blumenson, notes for "Chosin Reservoir"; Curtis, MS, p. 19; Curtis, interview with author June 4–6, 1981; Stamford, MS, p. 10, and interview with author Oct. 2, 1979.

21. Statement of Lt. Col. J. L. Winecoff, assistant G-3, 1st Marine Div., to Col. S. L. A. Marshall in Marshall's interview with Winecoff, Jan. 2, 1951, copy of transcript in author's possession.

22. Jones, letter to Maj. Robert M. Coombs, Jan. 15, 1975, pp. 12–13, copy in author's possession, courtesy of Col. Jones.

23. Kitz, Statement; Sfc. John C. Sweatman, K Co. 31st Inf., was another of those who broke through the ice and fell into the water but escaped. In his state-

ment, Apr. 19, 1951 (copy in author's possession), he says that he walked three miles after the mishap before he reached the truck column. There an officer told him to get out of his clothes and into a sleeping bag.

24. Miller, MS, p. 14.

25. 1st Marine Div., Special Action Report, Oct. 8–Dec. 15, 1950, p. 26.

26. Campbell, tape; Robbins, *Breakout.*

27. 1st Marine Div., G-3 Journal, Message no. 19, at 12:05 P.M., and no. 21, at 12:50 P.M.

28. Jones, Report, p. 2; Curtis, MS, pp. 19–20; Robbins, *Breakout,* 5, col. 1.

29. Mortrude, MS, pp. 8–9, and letter to author, Nov. 3, 1980.

30. Maj. Edwin S. Anderson, USA, Ret., telephone interview with author, Nov. 3, 1980.

31. Curtis, letter to author, Feb. 18, 1981; US Military Academy, *Register of Graduates and Former Cadets, 1975,* Item 17337, p. 577, on Marshburn, and Item 7446, p. 581, on Foster. This source gives Dec. 3, 1950, as the date of Marshburn's death and Dec. 2, 1950, as the date of Foster's death. I believe that both men died on Dec. 1, 1950.

32. Stamford, Memorandum, Oct. 3, 1979, prepared for author at latter's request, giving details he remembered of the breakout start. He also prepared a sketch, no scale, showing features he discussed.

33. Ibid. The ramp Stamford mentioned in his account was a slide built over the road to skid logs from the high ground down to the inlet and from there into the reservoir at high water in the spring to raft them down to the sawmill at Sasu.

34. Robbins, *Breakout,* 5, cols. 4–5.

35. 1st Lt. Cecil G. Smith, A Co., 32nd Inf., Dec. 3, 1950, at Hagaru-ri, National Archives, Record Group 407, Box 3172 (hereafter cited as Smith, Statement); Luna, Statement; Dr. Lee Yong Kak, Statement to 1st Marine Div., n.d., but presumably made early in December, 1950, copy in author's possession (hereafter cited as Kak, Statement).

36. May, letter to author, n.d., received Aug. 22, 1981, pp. 4–5. In the same letter May said: "I did not see Lt. Moore KIA. HQ Co. trooper told me Lt. Moore was killed on Hill 1221 during the air strike that hit our troops." Chinese and American troops were intermingled in close combat at the time of this strike, which is discussed later in the narrative.

37. Ibid.

38. Miller, MS, p. 15; Stamford, interview with author, September, 1979. Lt. Mortrude agreed with Stamford that only one napalm tank was dropped.

39. Miller, letter to Maj. Gen. Field Harris, Fleet Marine Force–Atlantic, May 23, 1952, copy in author's possession.

40. Swenty, Statement, pp. 3–4.

41. Memorandum for Col. Dyer, unsigned, n.d. (copy in author's possession,

courtesy USMC), reports on a series of the division's records from 1950 into 1952 on the use of napalm.

42. Stamford, MS, p. 18.

43. Stamford, letter to author, Nov. 30, 1980.

44. Bigger, letter to author, July 6, 1980.

45. Miller, review comments on "East of Chosin" MS, Mar. 26, 1981.

46. Mortrude, MS, p. 15.

47. Miller, MS, p. 15.

48. Robbins, *Breakout*, 5, col. 2.

49. Luna, Statement.

50. Miller, MS, pp. 15–16; Col. Crosby P. Miller, USA, Ret., telephone interview with author, Oct. 9, 1979.

51. Curtis, MS, p. 20.

52. Patton, Statement.

53. Pvt. Edward E. Bilyou, L Co., 31st Inf., Statement, April 19, 1951.

54. May, Report, p. 6; May, letter to author, Sept. 5, 1981, and letter to author, n.d., received Aug. 22, 1981, pp. 6–7.

55. Jordan, letter to author, Jan. 5, 1979.

56. McClymont, letter to author, July 7, 1980, p. 10.

57. Kitz, statement.

58. Sfc. John C. Sweatman, K Co., 31st Inf., Statement, Apr. 19, 1951.

59. Curtis, MS, p. 20.

60. Curtis, letters to author May 9, 1976, and Jan. 30, 1977; Col. Alpha A. Bowser, 1st Marine Div. G-3, told S. L. A. Marshall in an interview, Jan. 2, 1951, that Gen. Hodes had prepared the order and Gen. Smith had signed it. Transcript of Marshall's interview with Col. Bowser in author's possession.

61. Mortrude, MS, p. 10; Mortrude, letters to author, Oct. 23, 1980, and Nov. 3, 1980; Mortrude, in review comments on "East of Chosin" MS, May 12, 1981, changed a few words in the quotation.

62. Swenty, Statement, p. 4.

63. Curtis, MS, p. 20; Miller, MS, p. 16; May, Report, p. 6; Mortrude, MS, p. 10, and letter to author Oct. 23, 1980; and telephone interview with author, April 11, 1980; Mortrude, interview with author, Apr. 21, 1982.

Chapter 16

1. Curtis, interview with author, June 6, 1981.

2. Miller, MS, pp. 16–17.

3. Swenty, Statement, p. 4.

4. Curtis, MS, pp. 20–21; Curtis, review comments on "East of Chosin" MS, Feb. 20, 1978.

5. Capt. Hugh R. May, letter to author, n.d., received Aug. 22, 1981, p. 8. Lt.

Col. James O. Mortrude (then 2nd lt.), platoon leader of 3rd Plat. in Seever's C Co., told the author that his information from others in the company was that Seever was killed in action early in the breakout; Curtis, MS, also states this.

6. May, Report, p. 7.

7. May, letter to author, n.d., received Aug. 22, 1981, pp. 5, 7–8.

8. GHQ, FEC, General Order No. 201, Aug. 7, 1951, awarding Sgt. Charles Garrigus the Distinguished Service Cross for action at Chosin Reservoir, Nov. 27–Dec. 1, 1950.

9. Jones, Report, p. 2.

10. Robbins, *Breakout*, 5, cols. 2–3.

11. Stamford, MS, p. 11, and Anglico Report, p. 85.

12. Miller, MS, p. 17.

13. May, Reports, p. 7.

14. Maj. James R. McClymont, letter to author, July 7, 1980, p. 11. Other officers and enlisted men were under the impression that the M19 and the M16s were out of ammunition by the time they reached the blown bridge. 7th Inf. Div., Command Report, Chosin Reservoir, p. 8, says that the M19 and M16s were out of ammunition by that time.

15. Col. Crosby P. Miller, USA, Ret., telephone interview with author, Oct. 9, 1979; May, letter to author, n.d., received Aug. 22, 1981.

16. Stamford, interview with author, Oct. 28–29, 1979; Stamford, Anglico Report, p. 85.

17. Miller, MS, p. 18.

18. Curtis, review comments on "East of Chosin" MS, Feb. 14, 1981, and interview with author, June 6, 1981.

Chapter 17

1. Patton, Statement, April 18, 1951, pp. 2–3.

2. Swenty, Statement, Apr. 14, 1951, p. 4.

3. Pfc. James R. Owens, L Co., 31st Inf., Statement, Apr. 19, 1951.

4. Lt. Col. Ivan H. Long, letters to author, Mar. 21, 1979, and July 10, 1979. Long estimated that he was a prisoner for about eight hours, but apparently the time was shorter. Long subsequently attended Officer Candidate School, was commissioned, and eventually rose to the rank of lieutenant colonel in the Army Reserve, retiring in May, 1977.

5. Robbins, *Breakout*, pp. 5–6.

6. Miller, MS, pp. 17–18. Capt. Earle H. Jordan, Jr., M Co., 31st Inf., was informed that Maj. Storms had been wounded and placed in one of the trucks at Hill 1221. Capt. Stamford called in the air strike.

7. Col. Crosby P. Miller, telephone interview with author, Oct. 9, 1979.

8. Capt. Edward P. Stamford, interview with author, Oct. 28–29, 1980.

9. Stamford, MS, pp. 12–13; Miller, MS, p. 18.

10. Stamford, MS, p. 13.

11. Dr. Lee Yong Kak, assistant surgeon, 1st Bn., 32nd Inf., a Korean doctor from Seoul, wrote about the incident that took place at Hill 1221: "Some of the men refused to attack so Colonel Faith shot and killed one soldier with a .45 pistol." Kak, Statement. Capt. Stamford wrote: "About this time Col. Faith shot a ROK soldier who was trying to tie himself to the underside of a truck and who was apparently unhurt. The ROK when told to get out by Col. Faith kept saying 'Eti' (Japanese for 'hurt')." Stamford, MS, p. 12. Capt. Erwin Bigger, in letter to author, July 6, 1980, p. 8, wrote: "At the road block near 1221 Rok soldiers were tying themselves up to the undercarriages of the trucks in order to ensure that if the truck made it, they would. I saw Col. Faith order two of them to rejoin the fight and they refused. He shot both of them." Lt. Col. Edwin S. Anderson (WOJG and assistant personnel officer, 1st Bn., 32nd Inf., in December, 1950) said that in interviews of 76 members of the 1st Bn., 32nd Inf., several of them mentioned this incident. Anderson, telephone interview with author, Nov. 3, 1980.

12. Stamford, interview with author, Oct. 28–29, 1980; Stamford, letter to author, May 7, 1981, describes how the 1st Marine Air Wing had improvised a drop container similar to the heavy canvas packets used for airdrops from cargo aircraft. He said that this Corsair was loaded for the drop at the Marine airfield at Wonsan.

13. Smith, Statement.

14. Capt. Erwin B. Bigger, letter to author, July 6, 1980, pp. 2, 7. The term "Blue Boys," meaning Korean civilians dressed in blue, was in common use among troops at Chosin to refer to the Koreans used in the G-2 intelligence sections who crossed into enemy territory at night to gather information from native inhabitants about enemy movements and numbers in the neighborhood. Sometimes they even mixed with Chinese forces. Capt. Patton's and Capt. Bigger's groups must have been the first to enter Marine lines. While he was on Hill 1221, Bigger saw enemy flares go up from the high ground eastward. He believed them to be signals to CCF farther south along the road that Americans were moving in their direction. Bigger, telephone interview with author, May 8, 1980.

15. Vincent T. Navarre, letter to Capt. Edward P. Stamford, Oct. 15, 1951, copy in author's possession.

16. Bigger, review comments on "East of Chosin" MS, Mar. 29, 1981; Bigger, letter to author, July 6, 1980, 2. Curtis also has commented on the complete breakdown of radio communications between elements of the task force once it left the inlet perimeter.

17. Mortrude, MS, pp. 11–13.

18. Luna, Statement.

19. Kak, Statement, p. 3.

20. Robbins, *Breakout*, 6, cols. 1–2. Robbins's account of the party's arrival at

Hagaru-ri in the night is also covered somewhat differently in Maj. Jones's account in Report, Dec. 4, 1950.

21. Maj. James R. McClymont, letter to author, July 7, 1980, pp. 11–12.

22. Ibid., p. 12. Information given to McClymont about the M19, as stated in his letter and attachments of July 7, 1980, was incorrect. Stamford says that he ordered the M19 to the side of the road at Hill 1221, where he was loading wounded into trucks at the rear of the column, because the M19 driver told him that it was out of fuel—Stamford did not want the M19 to stop suddenly and block the road ahead. Stamford, interview with author, Oct. 28–29, 1980.

23. Kitz, Statement.

24. Ibid. Kitz's narrative is not clear on whether he and the others with him attacked up the road toward the roadblock at the hairpin turn or whether he went up the slope toward the crest of Hill 1221, as others had done. He uses the phrase "Hill top," but he also says that his group knocked out three roadblock positions on the way. Then he refers to his men taking off "across country." He also speaks of large numbers of Chinese at the bottom of the hill, apparently meaning in the valley north of Hill 1221.

25. Swenty, Statement, p. 5.

26. Ibid., pp. 5–6.

27. Jones, letter to author, Mar. 2, 1981; Jones, review comments on "East of Chosin" MS, Mar. 2, 1981; Jones, letter to author, Feb. [Mar.] 14, 1981.

28. Jones, letter to author, Feb. 8, 1979.

29. Jones, Report to Maj. Lynch, G-3 Sect., 7th Inf. Div., Dec. 4, 1950, p. 3.

30. Jordan, letter to author, Jan. 5, 1979. In a subsequent letter to author, Feb. 28, 1980, Jordan enclosed a sketch of the Hill 1221 area, the hairpin turn, the location of the log roadblock, and the spot where a Chinese-thrown grenade hit Lt. Col. Faith. A sketch drawn by Col. Jones for the author locates the features in a manner similar to Jordan's sketch. Jones's location of the place where Faith was wounded had to depend on information received from others subsequent to the event, for he did not know of it at the time it happened.

31. GHQ, FEC, General Order No. 186, July 18, 1951, awarding the Distinguished Service Cross to Jordan; GHQ, FEC, General Order No. 166, June 28, 1951, awarding the Distinguished Service Cross to Gray. In each instance the award superseded a previous Silver Star award. Maj. Robert E. Jones received the Distinguished Service Cross for action on Dec. 1, 1950, at Chosin in GHQ, FEC, General Order No. 128, May 21, 1951.

32. Jordan, letter to author, Feb. 5, 1979.

33. Jones, letter to Coombs, Jan. 15, 1975; copy in author's possession, courtesy of Col. Jones.

34. Jones, Report, p. 3.

35. 11th Marine Div., S-3 Journal File, Dec. 2, 1950, copy of message in author's

possession. The author had tried unsuccessfully to establish communication with Col. Fields Early Shelton, USA, Ret.

36. Col. James G. Campbell, USA, Ret., letter to author, Dec. 13, 1980.

37. May, Report, p. 8.

38. May, letter to author, Oct. 31, 1981, pp. 5-6.

Chapter 18

1. Stamford, MS, p. 13. Stamford told me that the logs were small and that there were only a few of them. This log block was easily removed. The burned-out tank was the main obstacle; it squarely blocked the road.

2. Stamford, interview with author, Sept. 26-Oct. 3, 1979.

3. Stamford, MS, pp. 13-14. Lt. Barnes was the 1st Bn., 32nd Inf., artillery liaison officer.

4. Vincent J. Navarre, surgeon, 1st Bn., 32nd Inf., letter to Capt. Edward P. Stamford, Oct. 15, 1951, copy in author's possession.

5. Navarre, letter to Maj. Gen. Field Harris, USMC, Fleet Marine Force-Atlantic, US Naval Base, Norfolk, Va., May 4, 1952, copy in author's possession.

6. Jones, Report, Dec. 4, 1950, p. 3. Italics supplied by author. In this report Jones frequently refers to himself in the third person.

7. Col. Robert E. Jones, letter to author, Jan. 5, 1979. Jones made much the same comment in a letter to Maj. Robert M. Coombs, Jan. 15, 1975, in which he wrote: "I was able to get enough people together to unload the first three vehicles of the convoy which had been knocked out and get the convoy moving around the hairpin turn to the road block made up of immobilized tanks and trucks. It was at that point that I decided to take all the able bodied and walking wounded, other than the guards left for the wounded, and attempt to fight our way back to the Marine lines for help."

8. Sgt. Jessie R. Dorsey, D. Btry., 15th AAA, Statement, Apr. 17, 1951.

9. Stamford, MS, p. 14.

10. Capt. Hugh R. May, letter to author, n.d., received Aug. 22, 1981, p. 6.

11. Col. James G. Campbell, letter to author, Dec. 13, 1980. Campbell had earlier stated the same thing in his tape.

12. Stamford, interviews with author, Sept. 26-Oct. 3, 1979, and Oct. 28-29, 1980.

13. May, Report, pp. 8-9; Jones, Report, corroborates May.

14. May, Report, pp. 9-12.

15. Robbins, *Breakout*, 6, cols. 2-3.

16. Stamford, MS, pp. 14-15; Stamford, interview with author, Sept. 26-Oct. 3, 1979. Stamford prepared for the author a detailed sketch map (in the possession of the author) of his movements from the vicinity of Twiggae to Hill 1167, south of the Paegamni-gang and Sasu-ri.

17. Col. Wesley J. Curtis, review comments on "East of Chosin" MS, Feb. 16, 1981, p. 6.

18. Curtis, interview with author, June, 1981, pp. 4-6.

19. Campbell, review comments on "East of Chosin" MS, Apr. 7, 1981.

20. Stamford, MS, pp. 15-16; Stamford, review comments on "East of Chosin" MS.

21. Stamford, letter to author, Jan. 30, 1979.

22. Stamford prepared for the author a detailed sketch map of his movements after his escape at the foot of Hill 1239, adjacent to Hudong-ni.

23. Curtis, interview with author, June 6, 1981.

24. Curtis, review comments on "East of Chosin" MS, Feb. 16, 1981, p. 7; letter to author Feb. 20, 1978; and interview with author, June 6, 1981.

25. Curtis, letter to author, and review comments on "East of Chosin" MS, Feb. 20, 1978; Curtis, letter to author, Sept. 10, 1978.

26. Maj. William W. Etchemendy, letter to Col. Crosby P. Miller, n.d., in response to a document (cited here as Miller, MS) that Miller sent to him in October, 1953 (I was unable in two tries to establish communication with Col. Etchemendy, USA, Ret.); Col. George S. Rasula, USA, Ret., letter to author, Aug. 12, 1981; Capt. Rasula, letter, to Lt. Col. Lester K. Olson, Feb. 4, 1951, copy in possession of author, courtesy of Rasula.

27. Miller, MS, pp. 19-22.

28. GHQ, FEC, General Order No. 201, Aug. 7, 1951, awarding the Distinguished Service Cross, Posthumously, to Sgt. Charles Garrigus, 1st Bn., 32nd Inf., for action Nov. 27-Dec. 1950.

29. Sfc. Carroll D. Price, HQ Btry., 57th FA Bn., Statement, Apr. 18, 1951.

30. Cpl. Ambrose J. Feist, I Co., 31st Inf., Statement, Apr. 19, 1951; M.Sgt. James W. Coartney, 31st heavy Mortar Co., Statement, April, 1951.

31. Lt. Col. Ivan H. Long, letters to author, Mar. 21, 1979, and July 10, 1979.

32. Campbell, letter to author, Dec. 13, 1950, amplifying his earlier tape recording; Campbell, review comments on "East of Chosin" MS, Apr. 9, 1981.

33. Campbell, tape.

34. Campbell, letter to author, Dec. 13, 1980.

35. Stamford, interview with author, Sept. 27-Oct. 3, 1979; Stamford, letter to secretary of the Navy, Sept. 19, 1952, copy in author's possession.

36. Miller, MS, pp. 19-20.

37. M.Sgt. Carl A. Truett, M Co., 31st Inf., Statement, Apr. 19, 1951.

38. Smithey, Statement.

39. Sgt. Victorio R. Nonog, I Co., 31st Inf., Statement, April, 1951.

40. Cpl. Ambrose J. Feist, I Co., 31st Inf., Statement, Apr. 19, 1951.

41. Sfc. William C. Tillery, B Btry., 57th FA Bn., chief of section, 105-mm howitzers, Statement, Apr. 18, 1951.

42. Sfc. William Mahon, K Co., 31st Inf. Statement, Apr. 19, 1951.

43. This journal message is initialed in pencil that is so obscured as to be unreadable; it might be "GSS." Whatever the correct initials, they represent someone in the 1st Marine Div., G-3 Sect. "Hecklers" in the message refers to any type of aircraft equipped to fly at night and to harass enemy positions and troops. 7th Inf. Div. Command Report, Chosin Reservoir, p. 8, says that Faith was wounded by a hand grenade, a statement probably based on Jones, Report.

44. Maj. Robert E. Jones, Memorandum to Major William R. Lynch, Jr., G-3 Sect. 7th Div. APO 7, Dec. 4, 1950, p. 3. Jones's report to Lynch indentified the Lt. Shelton mentioned in the 11th Marine S-3 message as Fields Early Shelton, a lieutenant in the 31st Heavy Mortar Co., a unit of Task Force Faith. US Military Academy, *Register of Graduates and Former Cadets of the United States Military Academy, 1975*, p. 550, has the following reference to Shelton: "16012 Fields Early Shelton: B-OH 11 Jul 24; A-Ky: Inf: 31st Inf 7 Div KW 50–51 CR-CI-PH): CGSC 58: Ret 74 Col."

45. Col. Robert E. Jones, USA, Ret., review comments on "East of Chosin" MS, Mar. 2, 1981.

46. Letter from Maj. Gen. David G. Barr, Dec. 12, 1950, Hungnam, Korea, to Mrs. Don C. Faith, Jr., Alexandria, La., copy in General Matthew B. Ridgway Papers, US Army Military History Research Collections, Carlisle Barracks, Pa., Box 17, Folder D-L. Mrs. Faith was in Japan with her 3½-year-old daughter, Barbara Ann, when her husband was reported killed in Korea. She returned to the United States in December.

47. Ridgway Papers, Box 17, Folder D-L, copy of Memorandum to CG, 7th Inf. Div., from WOJG Edwin S. Anderson on status of Lt. Col. Don C. Faith, Jr., Jan. 9, 1951. This is a copy that Gen. Barr provided Gen. Ridgway in Korea because he knew that Ridgway would want all possible details about the death of his former aide in the 82nd Airborne Div. and the XVIII Airborne Corps in Europe in World War II; Maj. Edwin S. Anderson, USA, Ret., interview with author, Nov. 3, 1980; Anderson, letter to author, n.d., postmarked Oct. 31, 1980.

48. Ridgway Papers, Box 17, Folder D-L, WOJG Anderson, Memorandum to CG, 7th Inf. Div.; Map of Korea, 1971 Topo Information, Changjin Sheet, scale 1:50,000; Lt. Gen. Ridgway, letter to Mrs. Don C. Faith, Jan. 26, 1951, Ridgway Papers, Folder D-L; May, letter to author, Oct. 31, 1981, p. 6; Mrs. Annie Randolph Wilbur, letter to author, Mar. 30, 1980. Mrs. Wilbur said that Don and Barbara had one child, a daughter named Barbara Ann, about four years old at the time of her father's death. Don was survived also by two brothers and his father and mother. Barbara, who remarried, died in 1960, and is buried in Alexandria, La. At the time Mrs. Wilbur wrote to me, Col. Faith's daughter was named Mrs. Stephen Broyles.

49. Gen. Barr, in the MacArthur hearings on June 22, 1951 ("Military Situation

in the Far East: Hearings before the Committee on Armed Services and the Committee on Foreign Relations," US Senate, 82nd Cong., 1st sess. [Washington, D.C.: GPO, 1951], pp. 2948ff.), said that Lt. Col. Faith's widow had received the Congressional Medal of Honor, Posthumously, for her husband the preceding day. For an account of the ceremony as planned, see the *Washington Post* and *Washington Star*, June 20, 1951. The citation for the Medal of Honor was not well prepared and departs in some particulars from a factual record of Faith's known actions in the period Nov. 27–Dec. 2, 1950. He deserved a better statement. Lt. Col. Faith received a special kind of honor when a Fort Benning, Ga. Dependent School was dedicated on Sept. 15, 1952, as the Don C. Faith School. A special Bicentennial issue of the school newspaper, *New Faith* 4, no. 4 (May, 1976), devotes almost its entire space to the memory of Lt. Col. Faith, including many articles relating to his school years in the Columbus, Ga., public high school, his time in Officer Candidate School at Fort Benning, and his subsequent army career. It includes photographs of his own family and of his father and mother. In a ceremony at Fort Benning in 1976, Lt. Col. Faith's name was placed in the Fort Benning Officer Candidate School Hall of Fame. Gen. Ridgway was asked to send a letter that could be read at the ceremony. He gladly consented, writing in part: "I know of no one who more richly deserves that honor, and every honor awarded him during his devoted service in peace and in war, than does Don Faith. He was my Aide for three and one half years. I could have asked for no more devoted assistant, or finer Aide, associate, and companion—conspicuous for high principled integrity, selfless devotion to duty, fearlessness in combat, compassionate consideration for others, cheerfulness and sense of humor." Ridgway, letter to Jerome C. Cox, principal, Fort Benning Dependent Schools, Don C. Faith School, Nov. 5, 1976.

Chapter 19

1. William J. Hingston, letter to author, n.d. (ca. June 27, 1980).

2. Miller, MS, pp. 22–25. After many operations Miller's left hand had finger stumps too short to hold a pen. Each of the fingers of his right hand had two joints left. Having been left-handed, he had to learn to write with what remained of his right hand. His leg wounds healed so that his knee gave him no problem as long as he exercised it properly. Miller remained in the Army in a useful role; as of this writing he is retired and living in Virginia.

3. Kak, Statement, p. 4.

4. Lt. Col. Ivan H. Long, AUS, Ret., letter to author, July 10, 1979.

5. Col. James G. Campbell, USA, Ret., review comments on "East of Chosin" MS, Apr. 9, 1981; Campbell, tape, Nov. 28–29, 1980.

6. Vincent J. Navarre, letter to Capt. Edward P. Stamford, Oct. 15, 1951, copy in author's possession, courtesy of Capt. Stamford.

7. Allied Translation and Interrogation Service (ATIS) Interrogation Reports

(Enemy Forces), Issue 22, No. 2706, Dec. 14, 1950, p. 17, National Archives; ATIS Interrogation Reports (Enemy Forces), Issue 22, No. 2736, Dec. 21, 1950, p. 123, National Archives.

8. GHQ, FEC, Daily Intelligence Summary, No. 3028, Dec. 24, 1950, National Archives, Federal Records Center, Record Group 407, Box 99.

9. The comments about Finfrock and the group of wounded Americans at the truck on the morning of Dec. 2, 1950, are based on Gugeler, *Combat Actions in Korea*, p. 87, who gives his source in his n. 37 as a statement or affidavit by Sfc. Willard Donovan, attached to 7th Inf. Div., Command Report, Chosin Reservoir. I did not find the Donovan statement in several attachments to the 7th Div. records of the Chosin Reservoir Campaign in the National Archives, Federal Records Center, Record Group 407, when I examined the 7th Inf. Div. records there in 1974. Often such attachments are lost or misfiled after they have been used. Also, different sets of official Army records do not always have complete sets of attachments.

10. Lt. Col. Ray Embree, letter to author, Mar. 18, 1979; Patton, Statement; Maj. (Chaplain) Martin C. Hoehn, HQ, 31st Inf., Statement, Apr. 19, 1951; 2nd Lt. William N. Eichorn, HQ Btry., 57th FA Bn., Statement, Apr. 18, 1951.

11. For arrangements made for the exchange of these prisoners, see Walter G. Hermes, *Truce Tent and Fighting Front: The United States Army in the Korean War* (Washington, D.C.: GPO, 1966), pp. 414–19.

12. *New York Times*, Apr. 30, 1953; *Washington Post*, May 7, 1953. In 1953 some returning American prisoners of war told lurid stories of Chinese atrocities on the battlefield that must be viewed with some skepticism since they do not conform to the general Chinese behavior, which is well documented. The Chinese soldiers did not usually torture their prisoners. The record of the North Koreans' treatment of prisoners is worse than that of the Chinese.

13. Map of the Hagaru-ri Defense Perimeter, Nov. 28–29, 1950, in Montross and Canzona, *The Chosin Campaign*, p. 199. The northwestern arc of the Hagaru-ri perimeter was essentially unchanged in the period Dec. 1–4.

14. 1st Motor Transport Bn., 1st Marine Div., Jan. 14, 1951, Annex Item to 1st Marine Div. Special Action Report, Oct. 8–Dec. 15, 1950, p. 10; Lt. Col. Olin L. Beall, USMC, CO, HQ, 1st Motor Transport Bn., 1st Marine Div., Statement, n.d., apparently written in 1951, pp. 3–4 (hereafter cited as Beall, Statement); copies of both in author's possession. Geer, *The New Breed*, pp. 343 ff., has a generally good account of Beall's rescue efforts. All the above sources, however, appear to err on the dates on which the events occurred. They place the events as occurring Dec. 2–5, 1950; they actually occurred Dec. 1–3, 1950. These errors may have been caused by erroneous dates in 1st Motor Transport Bn., Special Action Report, Oct. 8–Dec. 15, 1950, which was prepared more than a month after the events and is dated Jan. 14, 1951, and which both Beall and Geer, writing at a later time, used to date the events.

15. USMC, résumé of Olin L. Beall's service to 1935; Beall's statement. Beall was born Aug. 15, 1898, at Beltsville, Md. He was promoted from gunner with rank of warrant officer to first lieutenant in 1942 and served in the Pacific Theater in World War II. He was commissioned lieutenant colonel in July, 1948. He was a hard-bitten, no-nonsense officer of the "old breed," but, as his performance at Chosin showed, he had a big heart and much humanity.

16. Beall, Statement, pp. 4–5.

17. Sgt. Joe A. Medina, Statement, quoted in Public Information Office (PIO) EUSAK (press release), for delivery to the United States, n.d., apparently March or April, 1951.

18. Geer, *The New Breed*, pp. 344–45; Montross and Canzona, *The Chosin Campaign*, p. 245; 1st Motor Transport Bn., Annex Item, 1st Marine Div., Special Action Report, Oct. 8–Dec. 15, 1950, pp. 10–12.

19. Beall, Statement, p. 7. Beall's statement was submitted to the 1st Marine Div. apparently in 1951 but possibly later.

20. Ibid., pp. 4, 7.

21. 1st Motor Transport Bn., Report, Annex Item, 1st Marine Div., Special Action Report, Oct. 8–Dec. 15, 1950, p. 12, report dated Jan. 14, 1951.

22. For the sources used in this description of Beall's rescue work, see notes 13–21 above and Lt. Col. George G. Boram, inspector general, Report on 7th Div., Chosin Action, p. 9. A word should be added about Geer, who interviewed persons involved in Beall's rescue work and gave many details not included in either Beall's Statement or in the 1st Motor Transport Bn.'s official report (see note 21).

23. Almond, Diary, Dec. 5, 1950.

Chapter 20

1. 7th Inf. Div., Action Report Dec. [2], 1950, National Archives, Federal Records Center, Record Group 407, Box 3172; Montross and Canzona, *The Chosin Campaign*, p. 245, n. 30. In the note Montross and Canzona cite as their source "1st Mar Div tel to S-3, 11–12 Mar, 1150 2 Dec 1950." The latter entry, "11–12 Mar," is not clear. My examination of 1st Marine Div., G-3 Journal, Dec. 2, shows that Serial Entry 12, sent out at 11:50 A.M. to the 11th Marines concerned a 1st Marine force in the Yudam-ni area or elsewhere. A search in the G-3 Journal and Message File did not disclose such a message to a Task Force Faith relief force, and a telephone message could not have been sent to such a force in any event.

2. Statement of Col. Alpha A. Bowser, 1st Marine Div. G-3, to Col. S. L. A. Marshall in an interview beginning at 7:00 P.M. on Jan. 2, 1951, p. 6 of typescript. Typescript of Marshall's interview with Col. Bowser and Lt. Col. J. L. Winecoff, assistant G-3, in author's possession; Col. Robert E. Jones, review comments on "East of Chosin" MS, Mar. 2, 1981, p. 8.

3. Marshall's interview with Bowser (see note 2 above), p. 6. There was no 7th Div. CP at Hagaru-ri.

4. Machine copy of handwritten order, Serial Entry 18 in 1st Marine Div., G-3 Message File, Dec. 1, in author's possession, courtesy of USMC.

5. Machine copy of this handwritten memorandum in author's possession, courtesy of USMC. In Item No. 1 the two groups from the 7th Div. were then under 1st Marine Div. command, not under 7th Div. command as the wording implies. In my interview with him on June 12, 1978, Brig. Gen. William R. Lynch, USA, Ret., identified the person in the 1st Marine Div. G-3 Sect. to whom he handed this memorandum as the assistant G-3—Lt. Col. J. L. Winecoff. In the same interview Lynch confirmed that Gen. Hodes was in the office of the chief of staff, X Corps, at Hamhung when the telephone conversation took place with him at Hagaru-ri, and Lynch identified the handwriting as his.

6. 1st Marine Div., G-3 Journal, Nov. 29–Dec. 3, 1950, machine copy in author's possession, courtesy of USMC.

7. GHQ, FEC, Daily Intelligence Summary No. 3028, Dec. 24, 1950, National Archives, Federal Records Center, Record Group 407, Box 99.

8. Col. Thomas L. Ridge, USMC, Ret., letter to author, Mar. 27, 1977.

9. Lynch, letter to author, July 30, 1980, p. 2.

10. Lynch, letter to author, May 18, 1981, and review comments on "East of Chosin" MS, June 3, 1981.

11. Author's interview with Brig. Gen. William R. Lynch, USA, Ret., June 12, 1978.

12. Capt. Robert E. Drake, letter to author, Jan. 10, 1977. Drake's reference to a Marine regimental CP must be to Lt. Col. Ridge's 3rd Bn., 1st Marine CP, which was also the Hagaru-ri Defense Command CP. There was no Marine regimental CP in Hagaru-ri at that time. In his memorandum to the CO, 31st Inf., Dec. 12, 1950, Drake refers to assisting in the evacuation of survivors of Task Force Faith, saying that his unit recovered about 20 men who had been wounded in action. He is referring to men who came through the Marine perimeter where a few of his tanks took position on Dec. 2. I have prepared in MS form a history of the X Corps in northeast Korea, including its evacuation from Hungnam and the battles on the Hagaru-ri perimeter. I also have in MS form a history of the CCF 2nd Phase Offensive against Eighth Army in the west, which drove that army out of North Korea and back to Seoul.

13. Col. Wesley J. Curtis, letter to author, June 5, 1980, p. 6; Capt. Erwin B. Bigger, letter to author and review comments on "East of Chosin" MS, Mar. 29, 1981, and telephone conversation with author, Mar. 11, 1981; Lynch, review comments on "East of Chosin" MS, June 3, 1981.

14. Col. Berry K. Anderson died on Aug. 9, 1974. Brig. Gen. Hodes rose to

commander in chief, USAREUR, in 1956 and retired as a four-star general in 1959. He died at Fort Sam Houston, Texas on Feb. 14, 1962. Lt. Gen. Oliver P. Smith, CG, Fleet Marine Force, Atlantic, retired on Sept. 1, 1955, having been advanced to four-star rank. He died on Dec. 25, 1977 in Los Altos, Calif.

Chapter 21

1. Montross and Canzona, *The Chosin Campaign*, p. 245; Curtis, MS, p. 17; Coombs, Thesis; "31st Regimental Combat Team 27 Nov 1950, Estimated Strength," pp. 83–85 (see Appendix C of this book); author's correspondence and interview with Brig. Gen. William R. Lynch, Jr. See Appendix C for estimated breakdown of personnel count in the 31st RCT, Nov. 27, 1950.

2. Montross and Canzona, *The Chosin Campaign*, pp. 245–46; Geer, *The New Breed*, pp. 342–43.

3. Montross and Canzona, *The Chosin Campaign*, pp. 287–88, and app. H, "Air Evacuation Statistics," p. 399; 7th Inf. Div., Command Report, Chosin Reservoir, Nov. 27–Dec. 12, 1950; Stamford, MS, p. 16; Col. Wesley J. Curtis, letters to author.

4. Geer, *The New Breed*, p. 343, discusses Hering's evacuation problems and procedures.

5. Maj. William R. Lynch's count of 31st RCT troops at Hagaru-ri, Dec. 3, 1950, reported to X Corps, night of Dec. 3, 1950, copy in author's possession, courtesy of Gen. Lynch. See Appendix C for unit breakdown of Lynch's count. There is one error in unit identification in his handwritten tabulation—the 15th AAA AW is mistakenly listed as the 50th AAA AW.

6. Lynch, letter to author, Dec. 19, 1976.

7. The comments about the CCF 80th Div. are based on GHQ, FEC, USAF, G-2, "Histories of CCF Army Groups Active in Korea, Part II, Ninth Army Group," *Intelligence Digest* 1, no. 3 (Jan. 16–31, 1953), esp. pp. 36–37, National Archives, Federal Records Center, Record Group 407, Box 225; GHQ, FEC, Daily Intelligence Summary, "Third CCF Field Army, OB 2–6," No. 3233, July 17, 1951, Record Group 407, Box 491; GHQ, FEC, "Initial Commitment CCF into Korea," *Intelligence Digest*, no. 6 (Aug. 16–31, 1951), Record Group 407, Box 513; Montross and Canzona, *The Chosin Campaign*, pp. 397–98, app. G, "Enemy Order of Battle"; X Corps, War Diary, Nov. 1–30, 1950, pp. 23, 25.

Chapter 22

1. Brig. Gen. William Lynch, Jr., USA, Ret., letter to author, July 30, 1980, pp. 3–4; Lynch, letter to author, Mar. 14, 1978; Lynch, interview with author, June 12, 1978.

2. Lynch, letter to author, July 30, 1980.

3. Maj. Edward P. Stamford, interviews with author; Stamford, Anglico Report, pp. 93–97; Stamford, letter to author, Apr. 7, 1981.

4. Col. Wesley J. Curtis, letter to author, Feb. 16, 1979, p. 4.

5. Col. Ray O. Embree, USA, Ret., letter to author, Mar. 31, 1981.

6. Capt. Hugh R. May, letter to author, Sept. 5, 1981, p. 4.

7. Maj. James R. McClymont, letter to author, Aug. 12, 1980.

8. Capt. Erwin B. Bigger, letter to author, July 6, 1980, p. 9.

9. Xenophon, *Cyropaedia*, 2.187, Loeb Classical Library (Cambridge, Mass.: Harvard University Press, 1943).

10. May, letter to author, Sept. 5, 1981, p. 6.

11. Lt. Col. James O. Mortrude, interview with author, May 30, 1983.

12. Curtis, MS, p. 19, states that Faith decided to break out of the perimeter and "reach Hagaru-ri in a single dash rather than risk another night in the perimeter." Most of Faith's staff agreed with that decision.

13. 1st Marine Div., G-3 Journal, Dec. 1, 1950, Message No. 19 at 12:05 P.M. and No. 21 at 12:50 P.M. Earlier, at 10:30 A.M., Message No. 9 indicates that the Marine air officer reported that the "31st and 32nd Inf Units east side of Reservoir requesting air drop." It is not known whether such an airdrop was delivered at the inlet perimeter before the breakout began, but I have seen no evidence that it was.

14. Xenophon, *Cyropaedia*, 2.73, 305.

15. Curtis, letters to author, Jan. 1, 1977, Sept. 10, 1978, and Feb. 20, 1978.

16. Lt. Col. Erwin B. Bigger, USA, Ret., letter to author, July 6, 1980, p. 8.

17. Capt. Earle H. Jordan, Jr., letter to author, Feb. 1, 1980.

18. May, letter to author, n.d., received July 24, 1981, pp. 1, 4.

19. Mortrude, MS, pp. 14–15, enclosed with letter to author, Oct. 23, 1980.

20. Stamford, MS, pp. 16–19, and Anglico Report, pp. 89–91.

21. M. Sgt. Chester L. Bair, Ret., letter to author, Sept. 3, 1981.

22. Col. Robert E. Jones, USA, Ret., review comments on "East of Chosin" MS, Mar. 2, 1981, pp. 9–10.

23. Lynch, review comments on "East of Chosin" MS, May 16, 1981.

24. Curtis, letter to author, Mar. 1, 1981, pp. 4–5.

25. 7th Inf. Div. Command Report, Chosin Reservoir, Nov. 27–Dec. 12, 1950, p. 7.

26. 1st Marine Div., G-3 Journal, Nov. 30, 1950, Message No. 37, 1900 hours.

27. Lynch, letter to author, July 30, 1980, p. 5.

28. Lynch, letters to author, Dec. 19, 1976, and Mar. 14, 1978.

29. Gen. William J. McCaffrey, interview with author, Feb. 4, 1976. McCaffrey said, "Barr ordered the withdrawal." Technically, Barr could not order the withdrawal, but he could have asked Gen. Oliver Smith to do so.

30. Col. Thomas L. Ridge, USMC, Ret., letter to author, Mar. 27, 1977.

31. May, letter to author, n.d., received Aug. 22, 1981.

32. Sfc. Carroll D. Price, HQ Btry., 57th FA Bn., Statement, Apr. 18, 1951.

33. Sgt. Stephen F. Lewis, C Co., 1st Bn., 32nd Inf., Statement, Apr. 15, 1951.

Chapter 23

1. These paragraphs are based largely on Col. Robert E. Jones, USA, Ret., review comments on "East of Chosin" MS, Mar. 2, 1981, pp. 5-6.

2. Ibid., p. 7.

3. Maj. Gen. Field Harris, USMC, CG, 1st Marine Air Wing, Fleet Marine Force, letter to Brig. Gen. Henry I. Hodes, Jan. 23, 1951, copy in author's possession.

4. May, letters to author, n.d., received Aug. 22, 1981, pp. 9-10, and letter to author, n.d., received July 24, 1981, p. 2.

5. Jones, review comments on "East of Chosin" MS, Mar. 2, 1981, pp. 5-8.

6. Col. James G. Campbell, USA, Ret., review comments on "East of Chosin" MS, Apr. 9, 1981, p. 2.

Bibliographical Note

Aside from official records, little exists in print on the subject of Chosin. The unit command reports and other records of the US Army units that participated in the action east of Chosin are contained in Record Group 407, in the National Archives, Federal Records Center, Federal Building No. 1, 4205 Suitland Road, Suitland, Maryland 20409. This record group includes all the unit records of the Army pertaining to the Korean War.

For the units that fought east of Chosin, the circumstances that led to the tragedy are not documented in records or command reports. There are no records on deposit in the National Archives for the 1st Battalion, 32nd Infantry; the 3rd Battalion, 31st Infantry; or the 57th Field Artillery Battalion, for the Chosin Reservoir action in November, 1950. I found none when I worked in the records there in 1974–75. Several years later a request to the National Archives for a search of these records yielded the reply that the search had turned up no such records. Probably none were ever prepared. All the units involved were part of the 7th Infantry Division.

The 7th Division record files had two documents relating to Chosin. One was a "Special Report on Chosin Reservoir," undated, but signed by Maj. Gen. Claude B. Ferenbaugh, who assumed command of the division on January 26, 1951. This report had been prepared by unknown persons some months after the events related and was fragmentary and unreliable. The second document in the division files was a 7th Division Action Report for the month, but nearly barren of information concerning those of its units that were east of Chosin. Included and attached to this document, however, were a number of statements or affidavits written by participants in the Chosin operation a few days after their escape to the Marine perimeter at Hagaru-ri. The most important of these was a four-page, single-spaced typed report by Maj. Robert E. Jones, the S-1 of the 1st Battalion, 32nd Infantry, addressed to Maj. William R. Lynch, Jr., G-3 Section, 7th Infantry Division, who was at Hagaru-ri at that time. It is a general outline of the action at Chosin Reservoir as known by Major Jones. Another item attached to the 7th Division report was a one-page report by Capt. Robert E. Drake of the 31st Tank Company in the action; other documents were brief affidavits by Capt. Robert J. Kitz, commander of K Company, 3rd Battalion, 31st Infantry, and by Sgt. Richard S. Luna of the 1st Battalion, 32nd Infantry, telling of their experiences and knowledge of the Chosin action.

There are in the records no rosters of personnel in the units involved at Chosin, and for that reason it has been impossible to provide the full name of many individuals mentioned in the narrative, or to provide a complete table of the personnel making up the regimental and battalion staffs. When an individual's full name was available from other sources, I used it when the individual was mentioned in the text.

The records of the X Corps are complete and do provide a catalog of orders and instructions issued affecting the deployment of the forces at Chosin Reservoir but had few details of events there. Of special value concerning Maj. Gen. Edward M. Almond, the X Corps Commander, is his daily diary, maintained by one or the other of his aides who was with him each day. This diary was made a part of the X Corps Command Report, but the entire diary kept by General Almond throughout his participation in the Korean War is on file in his personal papers deposited in the US Army Historical Research Center at Carlisle Barracks, Pennsylvania. A copy is deposited with the 1st Marine Division records, and by permission of General Almond, I have a copy of his typed diary.

The records of the 1st Marine Division are complete, and the G-3 Journal and Message file has important information concerning some aspects of the Army action east of the reservoir, of the arrival of survivors at its Hagaru-ri perimeter, and of Lt. Col. Olin Beall's role in rescuing more than 300 Army survivors from the reservoir and its shore in the vicinity of Hudong-ni. This material has been made available to me through the Historical Branch of the US Marine Corps.

Lt. Col. George G. Borum, inspector general of the Army's X Corps, "Report of Investigation of Chaplain (C) Lt. Commander Otto Sporrer's Charges against the 31st Infantry," consisting of statements made and testimony taken in Korea in April–May, 1951, became available to me and provided considerable material concerning the action east of Chosin. Most of it came from survivors of the 3rd Battalion, 31st Infantry and the 57th Field Artillery Battalion, who were on active duty with those units at the time of the investigation.

Another body of material that must be considered primary, contemporary sources were the manuscripts written by four prominent participants of the action. Majors Crosby P. Miller, Wesley J. Curtis, Hugh W. Robbins, and Capt. Edward P. Stamford describe in these manuscripts their experiences in the Chosin action. In nearly all cases these manuscripts were based on notes written while the wounded men were hospitalized in Japan in the weeks immediately following the action in Korea.

Nine months after the operation, 1st Lt. Martin Blumenson of the 3rd Historical Detachment in Korea conducted a series of interviews with some surviving members of the 1st Battalion, 32nd Infantry. He prepared a report entitled, "Chosin Reservoir, 1st Battalion, 32nd Infantry, 24-30 November 1950," dated August 20, 1951. A copy of that report is on file with the US Army History Center, Washington, D.C. It contains much that is factual, but it also has some hearsay evidence that is not factual and must be used with discretion.

Published works that contain information and partial treatment of the action east of Chosin are the following few:

Geer, Andrew. *The New Breed: The Story of the U.S. Marines in Korea*, New York: Harper and Brothers, 1954.
Gugeler, Capt. Russell A. *Combat Actions in Korea*, Washington, D.C.: The Association of the U.S. Army, 1954. Chapter 7, "Chosin Reservoir," pp. 62–87, is a partial account of the action east of Chosin, based on Martin Blumenson's MS, and supplemented by his own limited interviews. It contains some errors but is the only account previously in print. It centers primarily on the 1st Battalion, 32nd Infantry's part in the operation.
Military Situation in the Far East: Hearings before the Committee on Armed Services and the Committee on Foreign Relations, United States Senate, Eighty-Second Congress, First Session, to Conduct an Inquiry into the Military Situation in the Far East and the Facts Surrounding the Relief of General of the Army Douglas MacArthur from His Assignments in that Area (in 5 vols.). Washington, D.C.: U.S. Government Printing Office, 1951.
Montross, Lynn, and Nicholas A. Canzona, *The Chosin Campaign,* vol. 3 in *The U.S. Marine Operations in Korea, 1950-1953* (4 vols.). Washington, D.C.: U.S. Government Printing Office, 1957. This volume is the official Marine Corps history of the Chosin Reservoir campaign. It is an excellent account of the Marines in the campaign but leaves much to be desired concerning the Army's participation in the same campaign. One recognizes that it was never intended to be an account of the Army participation in any detail.

It is not feasible to list all the hundreds of letters and the several lengthy interviews with Army participants of the Chosin Reservoir campaign that make up the main body of source material used in this book. They are all listed in the notes documenting this work. It was a tedious and major task to locate the majority of these participants, who over a period of years contributed in varying degrees to the writing of this book. Without their help it would not have been possible to put the story together. Collectively they constitute the main source for the book. I used only the recollections of their personal experiences and direct knowledge of events; I avoided the use of any hearsay evidence. I compared all evidence with that of other bearing on the same point and evaluated it as objectively as possible. I am aware that the story is not entirely complete but believe that the main events have been salvaged for a credible account.

Index

East of Chosin was composed into type on a Compugraphic phototypesetter in eleven point Janson with two points of spacing between the lines. Janson was also selected for display. The book was designed by Larry Hirst, composed by Metricomp, Inc., and bound by John H. Dekker & Sons. The paper on which this book is printed bears acid-free characteristics for an effective life of at least three hundred years.

TEXAS A&M UNIVERSITY PRESS : COLLEGE STATION